A Biblical Theology of the Book of Isaiah

A Biblical Theology
of the Book of Isaiah

DOUGLAS W. KENNARD

WIPF & STOCK · Eugene, Oregon

A BIBLICAL THEOLOGY OF THE BOOK OF ISAIAH

Copyright © 2020 Douglas W. Kennard. All rights reserved. Except for brief quotations in critical publications or reviews, no part of this book may be reproduced in any manner without prior written permission from the publisher. Write: Permissions, Wipf and Stock Publishers, 199 W. 8th Ave., Suite 3, Eugene, OR 97401.

Wipf & Stock
An Imprint of Wipf and Stock Publishers
199 W. 8th Ave., Suite 3
Eugene, OR 97401

www.wipfandstock.com

PAPERBACK ISBN: 978-1-7252-5478-7
HARDCOVER ISBN: 978-1-7252-5479-4
EBOOK ISBN: 978-1-7252-5480-0

Manufactured in the U.S.A. 04/14/20

This book is dedicated to Kenneth Barker who first led me through Hebrew exegesis of Isaiah and for whom a first draft of this manuscript was prepared decades ago as a doctoral student.

This substantially modified manuscript reflects my passion and continuing study and exposition for my students studying Isaiah in Hebrew and English.

Contents

Abbreviations	ix
CHAPTER 1: Introduction	1
CHAPTER 2: Sovereign Yahweh	11
CHAPTER 3: Sovereign's Attributes	34
CHAPTER 4: Humanity under God	62
CHAPTER 5: Israel in Covenant Relationship with Yahweh	78
CHAPTER 6: Sin and Judgment	113
CHAPTER 7: Motifs of Judgment	129
CHAPTER 8: The Nations in Judgment	140
CHAPTER 9: Redemption and Salvation	152
CHAPTER 10: Prophecies of the Sign-Child	176
CHAPTER 11: Davidic Branch	186
CHAPTER 12: Servant of Yahweh	194
CHAPTER 13: Exodus unto Kingdom	213
CHAPTER 14: Kingdom	222
Select Bibliography	233
Author Index	257
Subject Index	263
Scripture Index	265

Abbreviations

AfO	*Archiv für Orientforschung*
AfOB	*Archiv für Orientforschung: Beiheft*
Ag. Ap.	Josephus, *Against Apion*
AnBib	*Analecta biblica* series
ANEP	*Ancient Near Eastern Pictures Relating to the Old Testament.* Edited by James Pritchard.
ANET	*Ancient Near Eastern Texts Relating to the Old Testament.* Edited by James Pritchard.
Ant.	Josephus, *Jewish Antiquities*
ARW	*Archiv für Religionswissenschaft*
Ascen. Isa.	*Ascension of Isaiah*
As. Mos.	*Assumption of Moses*
ASTI	*Annual of the Swedish Theological Institute*
B. or *b.*	*Babylonian Talmud*
BA	*Biblical Archaeologist*
BASOR	*Bulletin of the American Schools of Oriental Research*
Bat.	Rabbinic *Baba Batra*
BBR	*Bulletin for Biblical Research*
BDB	Francis Brown, S. D. Driver, and Charles Briggs, eds. *A Hebrew and English Lexicon of the Old Testament.* Oxford: Clarendon, 1907.
Bib	*Biblica*
BJRL	*Bulletin of the John Rylands University Library of Manchester*
BN	*Biblische Notizen*

BR	*Biblical Research*
BSac	*Bibliotheca sacra*
BV	*Biblical Viewpoint*
BZ	*Biblische Zeitschrift*
BZAW	*Beihefte zur Zeitschrift für die alttestamentliche Wissenschaft*
CBQ	*Catholic Biblical Quarterly*
Cherubim	Philo, *On the Cherubim*
CTM	*Concordia Theological Monthly*
DBS	*Dictionnaire de la Bible: Supplement*. Edited by L. Pirot and A. Robert.
DSD	*Dead Sea Discoveries*
1 En.	*First Enoch*
ʿEd.	Rabbinic *ʿEduyyot*
Esar	*Esarhaddon Treaty*
ExpTim	*Expository Times*
EvQ	*Evangelical Quarterly*
EvT	*Evangelische Theologie*
Good Person	Philo, *That Every Good Person is Free*
Ḥag.	Rabbinic *Ḥagigah*
HTR	*Harvard Theological Review*
HUCA	*Hebrew Union College Annual*
Int	*Interpretation*
JAOS	*Journal of the American Oriental Society*
JBL	*Journal of Biblical Literature*
JBTh	*Jahrbuch für biblische Theologie* (Neukirchener)
JETS	*Journal of the Evangelical Theological Society*
JNES	*Journal of Near Eastern Studies*
JJS	*Journal of Jewish Studies*
JNES	*Journal of Near Eastern Studies*
JTS	*Journal of Theological Studies*

JSJ	*Journal for the Study of Judaism in the Persian, Hellenistic, and Roman Periods*
JSOT	*Journal for the Study of the Old Testament*
JSOTSup	Journal for the Study of the Old Testament: Supplement Series
JSP	*Journal for the Study of the Pseudepigrapha*
Jub.	*Jubilees*
Kel.	Rabbinic *Kelim*
KTU	*Keilalphabetische Texte aus Ugarit.* Edited by Manfried Dietrich et al.
LQ	*Lutheran Quarterly*
m.	*Mishnah*
Meg.	Rabbinic *Megillah*
Mek.	Rabbinic *Mekilta*
Mes.	Rabbinic *Metzi'a*
Nid.	Rabbinic *Niddah*
NIDOTT & E	*New International Dictionary of Old Testament Theology & Exegesis.* Edited by Willem VanGemeren.
NIDNTT	*The New International Dictionary of New Testament Theology.* Edited by Colin Brown.
'Ohal.	Rabbinic *'Ohalot*
Ps. Sol.	*Psalms of Solomon*
Q within numbers	Qumran manuscript (e.g., 11Q13 2.2 is read as cave#Qdocument #chapter.#verse)
Qidd.	Rabbinic *Qiddušin*
Rab.	*Rabbah* often with a biblical book, such as Leviticus (*Lev.*)
RB	*Revue biblique*
RevExp	*Review and Expositor*
RQ	*Römische Quartalschrift für christliche Altertumskunde und Kirchengeschichte*
Sanh.	Rabbinic document *Sanhedrin*
SBLMS	Society of Biblical Literature Monograph Series
SCS	Society of Christian Scholars series (Scholars Press)

Šebu	Rabbinic *Šebuʿot*
SBL	Society of Biblical Literature
Sem.	Rabbinic *Semaḥot*
Šabb.	Rabbinic document *Šabbat*
SNTSMS	Society for New Testament Monograph Series
SwJT	Southwestern Journal of Theology
Tan.	Rabbinic *Tanḥuma*
Ṭehar.	Rabbinic *Ṭeharot*
Tg. Ps.-Jon.	Targum Pseudo-Jonathan
TB	*Theologische Bücherei: Neudrucke und Berichte aus dem 20. Jahrhundert.*
TDNT	*Theological Dictionary of the New Testament.* Edited by Gerhard Kittel and Gerhard Friedrich.
TDOT	*Theological Dictionary of the Old Testament.* Edited by G. Johannes Botterweck and Helmer Ringgren.
Tg. Isa.	Targum Isaiah as an Early Jewish commentary on Isaiah
T. Hez.	Testament of Hezekiah
TQ	*Theologische Quartalschrift*
TRu	*Theologische Rundschau*
TrinJ	Trinity Journal
TS	Theological Studies
Ṭ. Yom	Rabbinic *Ṭul Yom*
TWOT	*Theological Wordbook of the Old Testament.* Edited by R. Laird Harris et al.
TynBul	Tyndale Bulletin
Vis. Isa.	Ascension of Isaiah
VT	*Vetus Testamentum*
VTE	*Succession Treaty of Esarhaddon*
VTSup	Supplements to Vetus Testamentum
WAC	Michael Wise, Martin Abegg, and Edward Cook. *The Dead Sea Scrolls: A New Translation.* San Francisco: HarperSanFrancisco, 2005.

War	Josephus, *Jewish War*
Worse	Philo, *That the Worse Attacks the Better*
WTJ	*Westminster Theological Journal*
Y.	*Jerusalem Talmud*
ZA	*Zeitschrift für Assyriologie*
ZAW	*Zeitschrift für die alttestamentliche Wissenschaft*
ZTK	*Zeitschrift für Theologie und Kirche*

CHAPTER 1

Introduction

As a book, Isaiah has impacted the theology of Judaism and Christianity more than any other biblical book except perhaps Deuteronomy. Additionally, Isaiah joins with Deuteronomy and the Psalms as the most frequently quoted and interpreted books of the Bible within early Judaism, NT literature, and Christian patristic literature. Walter Brueggemann announced that "the book of Isaiah is like a mighty oratorio whereby Israel sings its story of faith."[1] Carol Dempsey wrote that the book of Isaiah is "one of the richest and most complex books of all prophetic literature in the Bible. Grand in style, lush in imagery, and unparalleled in a theological agenda and message."[2]

A biblical theology tries to surface and describe God and his relations presented in the biblical text.[3] Obviously, these textual understandings are filtered through the subjective perspectives of the interpreter who can reasonably describe what the text says in its trajectory.[4] However, this is not an attempt to get behind the text into the mind of an author, for all that is known from the author is what the text actually says in its trajectory. So, this is not a theology of human author(s) for likely Isaiah (or other authors) believes additional things not composed within the book. Furthermore,

1. Brueggemann, *Isaiah 40–66*, 1.
2. Carol Dempsey, *Isaiah*, 1.
3. The descriptive textual methodology employed reflects Kennard, "The Reef of the O.T."
4. Douglas Kennard presents a subjective epistemology and hermeneutic that can arrive at reasonably accurate biblical theology (*A Critical Realist's Theological Method*, 1–276). Ulrich Simon concurs and presents "Calvin's sober and reasonable approach" as an example of a similar method arriving at what the text says (*A Theology of Salvation*, 7).

this approach embraces the ancient Near Eastern context, which may have sources that inform the text, even though the present emphasis is describing the Isaiah text.[5] Likewise, this contextual approach is sensitive to development within textual and confessional traditions, within which the book of Isaiah contributes. However, the emphasis of this study is the contributions from the text of Isaiah. Therefore, this is a theology of the manuscript of Isaiah. John Oswalt identified that "the book of Isaiah is the most holistic of the biblical books. In its present form it encompasses the sweep of biblical theology better than any other single book in the canon."[6]

In *A Biblical Theology of the Book of Isaiah*, the author will treat the book, without conjecturing whether it had been produced by various authors. Even if one critically divides the book of Isaiah into parts, a case could be made for presenting a theology of the whole book of Isaiah because major themes can be found in all portions of the book.[7] There is actually very little in the book identifying how the composite book came together. For example, the book of Isaiah identified several times that a vision, or word of God, came to or from Isaiah the prophet (1:1; 2:1; 7:3; 13:1; 20:2–3; 37:2, 5–6, 21; 38:1, 4, 21; 39:3, 5, 8). This is a significant list identifying that a prophet named Isaiah is actively involved with the first half of the book. Noticing this fact and that the topics change emphasis from judgment to salvation with chapters 40–66, Ibn Ezra proposed that the second half of the book is likely written by someone other than Isaiah.[8] The emphasis

---

5. Jacob Stromberg separates sources from discourse too forcefully in *An Introduction to the Study of Isaiah*, 95–106.

6. Oswalt, *The Book of Isaiah: Chapters 1–39*, 52.

7. Unified Isaiah theology is developed by several who critically divide the book into three parts, including: Vriezen, "Essentials of the Theology of Isaiah"; Roberts, "Isaiah in Old Testament Theology"; Beuken, "Isa. 56:9–57:13—An Example of the Isaianic Legacy of Trito-Isaiah"; Sweeney, "Reconceptualization of the Davidic Covenant," 41; Goldingay, *The Theology of the Book of Isaiah*, "The Theology of Isaiah"; Ma, *Until the Spirit Comes*, 168–200. Likewise, a number of critical scholars argue that theological themes organically continue through the whole book sufficient to argue for interpreting the book holistically (Childs, *Introduction to the Old Testament as Scripture*, 325–27; Ringgren, "Some Observations"; Ackroyd, "Isaiah I–XII," "Isaiah 36–39"; Clements, "The Unity of the Book of Isaiah," "Beyond Tradition History"; Brueggemann, "Unity and Dynamic in the Isaiah Tradition," 89–107, esp. 96; Rendtorff, "Zur Komposition des Buches Jesaja," 295–320, esp. 320, "The Composition of the Book of Isaiah," "Isaiah 6 in the Framework," "Isaiah 56.1 as a Key," *The Old Testament: An Introduction*, 190–92, and "The Book of Isaiah: A Complex Unity"; Oswalt, *The Book of Isaiah: Chapters 40–66*, 4; Williamson, *The Book Called Isaiah*, 86, 116–244; Sommer, "Allusions and Illusion," 156).

8. Ezra, *The Commentary of Ibn Ezra on Isaiah*, especially when he comments on passages 40:1; 42:10; 45:4–5; and 49:4; but this view was developed into Deutero-Isaiah by Eichhorn, *Einleitung in das Alte Testament*, 3:76–97 and Döderlein, *Esaias*, xii–xv;

of the incomparable Yahweh and the servant bringing in kingdom shifts to another emphasis of kingdom itself, prompting Duhm to divide Isaiah 56–66 from the rest of the book as Trito-Isaiah.[9]

In contrast to these thematic and verbal divisions of the book of Isaiah, archeological copies of the book of Isaiah always present a whole book with no copies that evidence manuscript endings or beginning around these thematic divisions: Isa 39 to 40, nor 55 to 56. For example, the Isaiah scroll 1QIsa^a from Qumran and its copy on display in Jerusalem's shrine of the book evidence a fully intact Isaiah scroll with frayed edge rarely encroaching into text that is circulating around 125 BC and placed in Qumran's cave one by 68 AD.[10] The only break in this 1QIsa^a is a three-line space at the bottom of a column at the end of chapter 33 where there was a change of scribe, as evident by a change of paleography.[11] Additionally, there are fragmentary copies of Isaiah (1QIsa^b, 4QIsa^b, 4QIsa^c, 4QIsa^e, 5Q3; Mur3) which in their same jars contain fragments sampling across the whole of the book of Isaiah.[12] Furthermore, as early as 190 BC, the book of Sirach 48:24 refers to the writings of Isaiah comforting Zion in a manner that combines Isa 40:1 and 61:1–2 as from the prophet Isaiah.[13] Also, Josephus refers to Isa 45:1–6 concerning Cyrus as having been composed "two hundred and ten years earlier" during the ministry of Isaiah as indicated by Isa 1:1.[14] Major forms of Hebrew codex as unified manuscripts contain essentially the whole of Isaiah even though they identify paragraph and section breaks but none of them break between first, second, and Trito-Isaiah.[15] Similarly, LXX manuscripts contain unified whole Isaiah manuscripts, which do provide paragraph and section breaks, but none of those breaks occur between first, second, and

---

Watts, *Isaiah 1–33* (rev. ed.), lxvii; Dillard and Longman, *Introduction to the Old Testament*, 268–69; Smith, *Isaiah 1–39*, 57.

9. Bernard Duhm (*Das Buch Jesaiah*, xv, xx, 389) presents ch 56–66 as III Isaiah; also in the 1922 ed., vii identified Isaiah 40–66 as attached to Jeremiah; also in *Die Theologie der Propheten*, 277–79; Watts, *Isaiah 1–33* (rev. ed.), lxiii–lxx; Goldingay and Payne, *Isaiah 40–55*, 1:2.

10. Ulrich, "Isaiah, Book of," 384.

11. Goldingay and Payne, *Isaiah 40–55*, 1:4.

12. Ulrich, "Index to the Contents."

13. Oswalt, *The Book of Isaiah: Chapters 1–39*, 29.

14. Josephus, *Ant.* 11.1.2–3, also 10.2; Young, *The Book of Isaiah*, 3:198.

15. Comparisons are made with Leningrad Codex, Bombrgiana Codex, Aleppo Codex, and Codex Babylonicus Petropolitanus. For example, the tenth-century Aleppo Codex breaks between chapters 33 and 34 at the bottom of column 27 when a second scribe replaced the previous scribe, as is evident in the change of orthography, but that does not provide an argument for beginning Deutero-Isaiah with Isa 34, contrary to Brownlee, *The Meaning of the Qumran Scrolls for the Bible*, 247–59, and Torrey, *Isaiah 40–55*, 44–46.

Trito-Isaiah.[16] The *Babylonian Talmud* identified the Isaiah manuscript as a whole document, expressing descriptions of "destruction" and that "Isaiah is full of consolation."[17] Based on early Jewish authors, Qumran evidence, MT, Old Greek, and LXX evidence, Eugene Ulrich affirms that there is a unified edition of Isaiah circulating within early Judaism.[18]

Additionally, Jesus, Matthew, Luke, and Paul all identify that the book should be identified as a whole document from the prophet Isaiah. That is, they specifically claim that portions from all three divisions are to be recognized as from the prophet Isaiah. For example, Jesus identified that Isaiah 29:13 (Matt 15:7; Mark 7:6) and Isa 61:1 (Luke 4:17) are appropriately referred to as from Isaiah. Furthermore, Matthew identified that Isa 6:9 (Matt 13:14), Isa 9:1 (Matt 4:14), Isa 29:13 (Matt 15:7), Isa 40:3 (Matt 3:3), Isa 42:1 (Matt 12:17–18, 21), and Isa 53:8 (Matt 8:17) are all quotes across the book of Isaiah and identified as from the prophet Isaiah. There are more quotes from Isaiah across these books of the NT, but they are not necessarily identified as from the prophet Isaiah. Likewise, Luke identified that Isa 6:9 (Acts 6:9), Isa 53:7 (Acts 8:28–30), and Isa 61:1 (Luke 4:17) were all from the prophet Isaiah. Furthermore, Paul identified Isa 1:9 (Rom 10:16), Isa 10:22 (Rom 9:27, 29), Isa 52:15 (Rom 15:12), Isa 53:1 (Rom 10:16), and Isa 65:1 (Rom 10:20) are all identified to come from the prophet Isaiah. Therefore, in this book, the author will treat the book of Isaiah as a whole document and refer to the book of Isaiah and any portion of it as simply "Isaiah."

The book begins identifying itself as a vision (hzn) of Isaiah the son of Amoz, probably born in Jerusalem and ministering primarily to Judah (Isa 1:1). The word "vision" (hzn) is most relevant to specific visions (Isa 29:7; Hos 12:10; Hab 2:2; 1 Chr 17:15), such as the vision Isaiah saw ($'r'h$) of the throne room of God (Isa 6:1). However, the word can also be used as a collective indicating a number of visions or revelations over a period as in Isa 1:1 (1 Sam 3:1; Ezek 7:26; 12:22–23; Prov 29:18).[19] Many of these visions are not specifically described as something seen by Isaiah because the role of such a prophet is not primarily to explain how he got his information, it is to declare the information with the authoritative "thus says Yahweh." Young clarifies the supernatural origin for this revelation.

> The word does not refer to inward sight or perception, nor is it a metaphorical name for the prophet's own insight, intuition

---

16. Comparisons are made between Siniaticus, Alexandrinus, and Vaticannus.
17. *B. Bat.* 14b.
18. Ulrich, "Isaiah, Book of," 386.
19. Young, *The Book of Isaiah*, 1:30; in this light, Josephus, *Ant.* 3.7.7; 10.11.7 calls Moses and Isaiah the "divine prophet."

or mental perception. It signifies rather the "sight" of what God had placed in the prophet's mind or had revealed to him. It here denotes all that is given in writing in the book before us, and thus clearly attests the supernatural origin of the entire prophecy. It is not human opinion or reasonings or cogitations of Isaiah's own mind which are here presented, but a special revelation of God to Isaiah which in some sense inexplicable to us was "seen" by him.[20]

Such an indication of vision established the divine source for the revelation of covenant lawsuit of Isa 1 and the others to follow. Isaiah becomes Yahweh's messenger, speaking the word of Yahweh.[21] The communication of this vision by Isaiah orally and then in written form is a downward divine act of revelation and divine self-revelation.[22] Responding to this revelation, there is a strong contrast between the author Isaiah receiving vision insight (Isa 1:1; 29:7) and God blinding the people in their rebellion (Isa 6:9–12).[23] In fact, the concept of "prophet" (*nby'*) reflects the erring blinded prophets making Israel's rebellion worse (Isa 3:2; 9:15; 28:7; 29:10) and Isaiah's faithfulness to the role of truthfully communicating God's word, especially in the Hezekiah pericope (Isa 37:2; 38:1; 39:3).[24]

Other superscriptions identify that the vision content was the "word" (*dbr*) or an oracle, which Isaiah saw (*ḥzh*), further conveying that these come through vision as well (Isa 2:1; 13:1). However, the description of "word" places the emphasis on the message conveyed rather than developing the means utilized by Isaiah to obtain the message in the first place. If the reception is identified, usually this prophetic word is communicated to the ruling king through the prophet's ministry (Isa 7:1–25; 37:21–35; 38:4–8, 21–22; 39:3–8).[25] However, most of the passages in Isaiah do not identify a specific recipient for Isaiah's prophecy. It is clear in the context that these visions seen by the prophet Isaiah were not seen by others in their rebellion. However, the regular use of parallel lines in poetry identify that the author(s) tried to reach the king and the people with more than content

---

20. Young, *The Book of Isaiah*, 1:30.
21. Ross, "The Prophet as Yahweh's Messenger."
22. Mary Healy, "Knowledge of the Mystery," in Healy and Parry, *The Bible and Epistemology*, 137; Kennard, *Epistemology and Logic*, 133.
23. Carroll, "Blindsight and the Vision Thing."
24. The *Tg. Isa.* broadens the declaration of Isaiah as "prophet" rightly declaring God's word throughout the first half of the book (5.1, 3; 8.17; 9.5; 22.14; 24.16; Chilton, *The Glory of Israel*, 52–54).
25. Guenter, "The Word of the Lord."

by disarming them with a style that haunts one to one's bones and leaves the audience longing for Yahweh's resolution in kingdom.

With the emphasis on the message that Isaiah communicates in the text, the person of Isaiah enters the narrative only briefly to 1) see the throne room vision and repent of his uncleanness (Isa 6:1, 5–8) and 2) occasionally to confront a king with a message (Isa 1:1; 2:1; 7:3—8:4; 37:2–7; 38:1–8; 39:5). Rarely does the text develop Isaiah's presence except to introduce the message the text describes, so the emphasis of the book of Isaiah is on the message contained therein, not a person named Isaiah. In those rare moments that Isaiah has more presence, then he becomes part of the message, such as the name "Isaiah" meaning "Yahweh saves," or the radical drama of walking naked for three years as a sign to indicate Assyria's impending conquest of Egypt and Cush, and a nude dispersion dishonoring them unto slavery (Isa 20:2–4).

Occasionally the message contained signs accompanying supernatural prophecy of a future conquest in a dramatized empirical form, but the text does not discuss whether there were various interpretations of the signs, so the text of Isaiah including signs could function on an epistemic level of common sense realism (Isa 20:3; 7:11, 14; 8:18; 19:20; 37:30; 55:13; 66:19).[26] The most developed of all these signs is the sign-child, which still can function epistemically as common sense realism because the text simply declares the supernaturally informed timing of events without discussing various interpretations; but that will be developed in a chapter of its own due to the detail given in the text (Isa 7:11, 14; 8:18; also 37:30). In that later development, supernaturalism will be explained primarily concerning timing of the prophecy until the LXX translation and early Christianity identified a "virgin." However, there is one sign that Isaiah includes prophetic promise and supernatural empirical fulfillment that in the text of Isaiah probably graduates to a form of Lockean confirmation for Hezekiah's healing by moving a shadow back ten steps on a set of stairs (Isa 38:7, 22).[27] Isaiah does not develop how this sign was accomplished, just that it was declared in advance, that it did occur, and that it was reassuring for Hezekiah to indicate that he would be healed before the healing was completed. These are the

---

26. Reid, *Inquiry into the Human Mind*; William Abraham, "The Epistemology of Jesus: An Initial Investigation," in Moser, *Jesus and Philosophy*, 158–59; Brueggemann, *Pathway of Interpretation*, 115.

27. Locke, Essay *Concerning Human Understanding*, 1.1.15; 2.11.8–9; 2.32.6; 3.3.6–8, "A Discourse of Miracles," "The Reasonableness of Christianity." Pre-modern empiricism is apparent in Lactantius, "Workmanship of God," in *Divine Institutes*, 9–10; Keener, *Miracles*, 1:35–208, "Miracle Reports."

few empirical evidences that the Isaiah text provides, for most of the text is simply announcing the message from the authority that Yahweh declared it.

Isaiah's ministry as enumerated by the introductory superscription spans from late in the reign of Uzziah (Isa 1:1; perhaps 740 BC) with Uzziah dying in 736 BC (Isa 6:1) until at least a few years after Sennacherib's invasion around 701 BC to include the Babylonian contingent visiting Hezekiah (Isa 39), so maybe 740–697 BC. Isaiah had unusual access to the royal court (Isa 7:3–17; 37:6–35), perhaps because he may have been a cousin to Uzziah.[28] Isaiah might have ministered longer than this, but this time frame is based upon the limited chronographic textual evidence available. There is no mention of how long the author(s) survive beyond Hezekiah's reign. Tradition describes a single author, Isaiah, fleeing from King Manasseh and hiding in a hollow tree, only to be sawn in two and dying (Heb 11:37).[29] If this tradition is true, then Isaiah might have been alive as late as Manasseh's reign, which occurred about 687–642 BC.

There is broad agreement that the book of Isaiah contains a variety of genres including covenant lawsuit, taunt, vision, salvation oracle, and narrative accounts in which all characters, even God, are active participants. This mashup of genres creates a composite document that plays off the accounts in the near context.

The overall message for the book is that *sovereign Yahweh judges all the earth and Israel for the purpose of recreating them into his ideal kingdom centered in Jerusalem under the messianic Davidic servant-king.* The following is a brief summary of the sections of the book to show how they contribute to the overall message.[30]

Isaiah 1–39 develops judgment on Judah and the nations contrasted with a leitmotiv of Davidic king and kingdom. Isaiah 1–12 focused on Judah's sin and the impending invasion of Assyria. Isaiah 1; 2:6—4:1; and 5:8–30 develop covenant lawsuits against Judah by Yahweh with the possibility of them repenting and being redeemed. The leitmotiv of an eschatological kingdom for Judah is developed in Isaiah 2:1–5; 4; 9:2–7; and 11–12 as a time of intimacy with Yahweh, brought about by a Davidic king reigning empowered by Yahweh's spirit and peace. This emphasis fits well within the meaning of the title of the book: "Isaiah" meaning "Yahweh saves." Amid these themes, Isaiah 6 provides a vision of Yahweh as the sovereign holy

---

28. *Meg.* 10.2; *b. Soṭah* 10b.

29. *Ascen. Isa.* 1.1–3.12; 5.1–4, 11–14; *Vis. Isa.* 6–11; *T. Hez.* 3.13–4.22; Justin, *Dial.* 120.5; Tertullian, *Pat.* 14; Origen, *Ep. Afr.* 9; Hippolytus, *Antichr.* 30.

30. Most of Goldingay, *Theology of the Book of Isaiah*, 20–87 is a lite commentary rather than a summary; also as a nice summary is Ma, *Until the Spirit Comes*, 179–200 following a theology of the book of Isaiah, 168–178.

king who will generously forgive his prophet, but Judah has gone too far into rebellion so that Isaiah is to prepare Judah for captivity and dispersion. So, chapter 6 is not an initial call for Isaiah but one that changes the focus of his ministry from repentance and hope to destruction, captivity with hope to follow eschatologically. However, such destruction of Judah will not happen under Assyria if they believe the sign-child provides them guidance through the impending difficult time.

Isaiah 13–35 develops Yahweh as sovereign in bringing judgment upon the nations because their destiny is in his hands (Isa 13–23), Yahweh sovereignly acts in history, in which the nations are impotent to act, especially in a universal section (Isa 24–27).[31] Five prophecies beginning with attention-getting "Woe" or "Hey"[32] prompt why Israel should trust King Yahweh, rather than foolishly trusting these other nations (Isa 28–33). Trusting the nations brings about a desert, whereas trusting Yahweh brings Israel into a kingdom garden (Isa 34–35).

The nations are condemned for their pride (Isa 13:11, 19; 14:11; 16:6; 23:9; 24:21; 25:11; 28:1), which shows them as creating idols instead of submitting to Yahweh (Isa 2:6-22; 17:7-11). Additionally, in their pride, the nations are condemned for their violation of Israel's covenant relationship with Yahweh (but Jerusalem was also culpable for its destruction, Isa 22). The nations are also condemned for abuse of Israel (Isa 25:4; 26:21) or because Israel depended upon them as a greater security than Yahweh himself (Isa 18:2; 19:18-22; 20:6). The center of the section (Isa 17:12-14) and the conclusion (Isa 24–27) develop that the judgment comes upon the nations from Yahweh. The specific judgments come upon specific nations with an emphasis on the most troubling, namely: Babylon (Isa 13:1—14:23; 21:1-10), Assyria (Isa 14:24-27; 19:23-25), and Egypt (Isa 19:1—20:6). Other nations judged include Philistia (Isa 14:28-32), Moab (Isa 15:1—16:14), Damascus (Isa 17:1-11), Sudan (Isa 18:1-7), Edom (Isa 21:11-12), Arabia (Isa 21:13-17), and Tyre (Isa 23:1-17). At the climax of this judgment a worldwide judgment occurs, utilizing cosmic disturbances (Isa 24). In these last days death will be abolished, and the dead will be raised into kingdom (Isa 25:8; 26:19). As before, a leitmotiv of Yahweh ruling in kingdom with his Davidic king provides a fruitful salvation banquet and harvest for Judah amid the nations (Isa 9:6-7; 11:4, 10, 14-15; 15:5; 25:6—27:13). In response, the nations bring tribute to Jerusalem (Isa 14:1-2; 18:7; 23:15-18; 45:14 MT; 60:5-7, 11, 13, 16;

---

31. This paragraph reflects summaries from Oswalt, *The Book of Isaiah: Chapters 1–39*, 297.

32. Goldingay, *Theology of the Book of Isaiah*, 53.

61:6; 66:12) and worship Yahweh in Israel's salvation (Isa 2:1-4; 19:18-25; 25:6-10a; 42:1-4; 45:22-25; 49:6; 51:4-6; 55:3-5; 56:3-8; 66:18-24).[33]

Isaiah 36-39 expresses Deuteronomic history bridging Israel's situation from the Assyrian threat to the rise of the Babylonian threat. If Israel remains faithful in obedience to the terms of the everlasting Mosaic covenant, then they will have everlasting blessing as Yahweh's faithful servants (Isa 56:4-6). However, when Israel rebels, they break this covenant and Yahweh as great king will bring covenant curse upon them (Isa 24:5; 33:8). Sennacherib subdued the coast and the city of Lachish, and then sieged Jerusalem, describing that he had captured Hezekiah "like a bird in a cage" (Isa 36:1-20).[34] Sennacherib's emissary ultimately claims that Assyria is challenging Yahweh's strength (Isa 36:18-20) and that Egypt can't help Judah. When Hezekiah hears the boastful Assyrian taunt, he repents, tears his clothes in mourning, and prays for the remnant to be protected by Yahweh (Isa 37:1-4, 14-20). Isaiah responds that Hezekiah need not fear this blasphemy, for Sennacherib will return and be killed by sword in his own land because he arrogantly challenged Yahweh (Isa 37:6-7, 21-29). A sign provided to Hezekiah indicates that in the third spring Judah can plant and eat their crops because the Assyrian threat will be past (Isa 37:30-35). Isaiah describes that the angel of Yahweh killed 185,000 of Sennacherib's troops (Isa 37:36), and Sennacherib returned to Nineveh and was killed by his sons, as Isaiah had predicted (Isa 37:7, 36-38; 2 Kgs 19:36-37; 2 Chr 32:21).[35]

In the same era, before Sennacherib left, Hezekiah became mortally ill and was expected to die, but through his tears he prayed to Yahweh, "Remember I have walked before you in truth with my whole heart and have done good in your sight" (Isa 38:1-3, 6). Isaiah was sent with a confirming sign to Hezekiah indicating a promise of covenant blessing of fifteen more years of life and deliverance from the Assyrian siege (Isa 38:4-8, 22; 2 Kgs 20:8-10). Hezekiah's lament transforms into a confession of trust for salvation from death because only in this life is praise to Yahweh available, which is cause for worshiping Yahweh in the temple with instruments (Isa 38:10-20).

In the wake of Hezekiah's healing, emissaries from Merodachbaladan come and Hezekiah foolishly shows them the wealth of the temple and his house (Isa 39:1-4). Such an attitude demonstrates some degree of self-sufficiency such that Isaiah responds from Yahweh that all they have seen, Babylon will take away into captivity (Isa 39:5-7). Hezekiah callously

---

33. There is a helpful summary in Davies, "Destiny of the Nations," 104-5, whereas in the rest of the article (93-120) he argues for the unity of the book of Isaiah.

34. *Esar* 582-84; *Annals of Assyrian Kings* in *AfOB* 9, p. 58 lines 12-18.

35. Tob 1:21.

responds to this covenant curse by expressing that this was good because he selfishly thought at least there will be peace and truth in his own days (Isa 39:8).

Isaiah 40-48 presents Yahweh electing the remnant of Judah through a new exodus because he is the incomparable one beyond all others. This section develops the clearest presentation of monotheism in the OT: "apart from me there is no god" (Isa 44:6). Yahweh is living when idols rot and topple. Yahweh is the creator of everything, including the trees and rocks carved into idols, and also Yahweh is creator of the humans who worship them. Yahweh knows and predicts events before they happen, such as Cyrus being raised up to grant Judah's return to the land of promise. Yahweh has raised up Isaiah and will raise his prophetic servant to cultivate remnant Israel. Yahweh is active in history to bring about the new exodus returning the remnant into the new kingdom. Yahweh is Judah's savior to recover them in new covenant transformation in kingdom.

Isaiah 49-55 portrays incomparable Yahweh as raising his servant prophet to accomplish atonement. A prophetic servant has been selected by Yahweh to provide a clear call back to fear and trust of Yahweh their savior (Isa 42:1-4; 49:1-7; 50:1-11). Yahweh's righteous servant will atone for the world's sin and be blessed so that he can continue to intercede for the transgressors (Isa 52:13—53:12). Shout for joy and be invited into the salvation provided by Yahweh and his servant.

In Isaiah 56-66, Yahweh raises his ideal kingdom as the high point of all eras, contrasted with a leitmotiv of the judgment destroying all rebels. Goldingay develops this section as framed by a chiasm.[36] Yahweh includes foreigners in the service of Yahweh (Isa 56:1-8; 66:18-24). Yahweh challenges Jerusalem concerning community life (Isa 56:9—59:8; 65:1—66:17). Israel responds with prayer to Yahweh's forgiveness and restoration (Isa 59:9-15a; 63:7—64:12 [MT: 64:11]). Visions of Yahweh present him acting in judgment (Isa 59:15b-21; 63:1-6) and restoring Jerusalem (Isa 60:1-22; 61:10—62:12). Within a chiasm the center emphasis developing the prophet's commission establishing the character of kingdom as a spirit endowed Jubilee under an everlasting covenant of blessing (Isa 61:1-9).

---

36. Goldingay, *Theology of the Book of Isaiah*, 75; Beuken, "Main Theme of Trito-Isaiah."

CHAPTER 2

Sovereign Yahweh

THE BOOK OF ISAIAH develops God as the sovereign king. This expresses the basic proposition of OT theology, "the conception of Yahweh as the *ruling* Master or Lord."[1] God's sovereignty is evident in his traditionally described royal roles. Through this divine expression, Jack Miles develops Yahweh's regal eloquence.

> It is Isaiah, not Jeremiah, who brings out the eloquence in the Lord God. It is when the Lord is speaking to Isaiah that he goes most deeply and recklessly into himself, providing the most searching inventory of his own responses to the agony occasioned in his own life by the agony he has inflicted on his chosen people. To read these responses is to pass through the crises in the life of God in the company of the God who is suffering it.[2]

YAHWEH, THE DIVINE NAME

Isaiah utilized the concept of "name" as representing the person and character of Yahweh. "The name" (*sem*) was "the active essence or revealed character by which God made himself known"[3] (Isa 42:8). The concept of "name" implies reputation as an extension of the character as known by others. In Isaiah 30:27 it is "the name of Yahweh" that comes aggressively in judging

---

1. Wright, "Terminology of Old Testament Religion," 404.
2. Miles, *God: A Biography*, 202.
3. Barker, "Toward a Theology of Isaiah," 4; Alexander, *Prophecies of Isaiah*, 1:484; Parke-Taylor, *Yahweh: The Divine Name*, 16.

wrath. Also, in Isaiah 29:11, Yahweh declares that redeemed Israel "will keep my name holy." Again, in Isaiah 24:15; 25:1; and 50:10 the parallelism shows the person and name of God to be the same referent. Christopher North agrees that "the name" and "Yahweh" in Isaiah are almost synonyms for Yahweh himself.[4]

In Isaiah and during the Exodus, "Yahweh" means he is the one defined by relationship to be there for his people Israel. In Exodus 3:14 and the new exodus in Isaiah 42:8 the name "Yahweh" develops from the "to be" verb (*'hyh*) "I AM WHO I AM," and "I AM has sent me." This verbal name is either a *Qal* imperfect emphasizing God's presence as the unchanging one who can be counted on as present aid (as in the rescue of Israel from Egypt and the recovery back from Babylon),[5] or a *Hiphil* imperfect emphasizing that "God will always be there to create and provide what is needed!"[6] The possibility that the name "Yahweh" is a *Hiphil* means that Yahweh's name promises continual presence and future aid for Israel whenever they will need it. This memorial name then emphasizes God's presence in very practical ways to meet Moses' and Israel's needs. Grammatically, the verb could be either option (*Qal* or *Hiphil*). However, with either option there is no development of divine aseity (a Greek philosophical concept of eternal existence of God in these verses); rather a much more practical idea is being presented to provide any needed aid, which reflects God's election commitment to Israel and the divine plan to carry out the new exodus from Babylon. Therefore, God's name is as he reveals it to be in personal self-disclosure.[7] Some also conjecture that this naming of God to Moses is the first instance in which the name "Yahweh" is used, but this is unlikely with Moses' mother Jochebed having the name of Yahweh imbedded within her own name (Exod 6:20). The name Yahweh occurs 421 times in Isaiah alone.

Extending Yahweh's commitment to revelational presence and election providence, Yahweh identifies that "I Yahweh am with you" (Isa 43:2, 5). Goldingay develops the meaning of "Yahweh" and this affirmation of divine presence as a continuing relational commitment with the nation Israel to facilitate a new exodus unto kingdom.

> Like the name Yhwh with its explanation in terms of God being there, present and active, the declaration "I am with you" suggests a reality that is dynamic, occasional, extraordinary,

---

4. North, *The Second Isaiah*, 205.

5. Barker, "Lord"; Kaiser, *Toward an Old Testament Theology*, 107; Snaith, *Distinctive Ideas of the Old Testament*, 59.

6. Albright, *Stone Age to Christianity*, 15–16, 259–61.

7. Childs, *The Book of Exodus*, 76; Goldingay, *The Message of Isaiah 40–55*, 91–92.

visible and unexpected rather than static, regular, orderly and permanent. It implies taking someone's side in a way that brings protection, support, deliverance and success, and engenders the response of confidence and courage rather than fear, and obedience rather than resistance. It encourages people to live in history and to live with apparent uncertainty. It is a declaration normally made not to groups but to special individuals, so that here once again a commitment to an individual is "democratized" in its application to the exiles. God says "I am with you" not only to people such as Jacob, Joseph, Moses, Joshua, David and Jeremiah, but to the community as a whole. Yet this application to the community does reaffirm a significance of the motif going back to the exodus. When Yhwh says to Moses, "I will be with you," this is for Israel's sake, and Israel is thus to be assured that "I will be" is also their God acting on their behalf (Exod 3:12, 14; Deut 20:3-4; 31:8).[8]

The new exodus is grounded upon the revelation of Yahweh and the promise "I will be with you" (Isa 43:2, 5).

ELOHIM/EL, THE DIVINE APPELLATIVE

The appellative of "Elohim" is seen in Isaiah much less than the name Yahweh. The term "El" suggests "power, greatness, vastness, height, according as they are represented by the conceptions of the day."[9] The earlier meaning of "El" may have been "to be strong" or "powerful leader," extending the sphere of control, or to possess a binding force.[10] Cassuto identifies Elohim as "a Transcendental Being who existed completely outside and above the physical universe."[11] He is the creator of the physical universe (Isa 40:28; 45:18; 49:5). He is the living God as opposed to the impotent false gods (Isa 37:4, 17). However, the plural word also refers to pagan "gods" (Isa 43:10)[12]

8. Goldingay, *The Message of Isaiah 40-55*, 105.
9. John P. Lange, "Genesis," In Lange, *Commentary on the Holy Scriptures*, 1:109.
10. H. B. Kuhn, "God, Names of," 2:762; Preuss, *Old Testament Theology*, 1:149.
11. Cassuto and Abrahams, *The Documentary Hypothesis*, 31; Isa 8:21; 25:1; 28:26; 44:6; 45:5, 14, 21; 46:9; 54:5; 55:5; 58:2; 59:2, 13; 61:6, 10; 62:3, 5; 64:4.
12. Pagan texts also describe their deities as visible objects, such as Sumerian *Inanna* described as the evening star (Chiera, *Sumerian Religious Texts*, no. 1; Reisman, *Two Neo-Sumerian Hymns*, 147–211) and Babylonian *Shamash* with the sun (Meissner, "Ein altbabylonisches Fragment," 1.10–11, 13) but all creation references in Isaiah remove the possibility of deities as heavenly objects (Isa 13:10; 38:8; 41:25; 45:6; 49:10; 59:19; 60:19–20).

and "idols of these gods"[13] (Isa 44:10, 15, 17; 45:20; 46:6). In contrast, Yahweh is the powerful God who controls all history and nations (Isa 7:11–13; 13:19; 37:16; 52:7; 66:9), judging them (Isa 51:15, 20; 58:4; 61:2), saving a remnant (Isa 17:10; 25:9; 35:4, 20; 40:1–9; 41:10; 45:15; 52:10, 12; 60:19), and standing firm as the source of power (Isa 30:18; 41:10; 49:5). From this basis Elohim is the source of law, wisdom, and prophetic communication (Isa 1:10; 8:19; 21:10, 17; 26:13; 46:9; 54:6; 57:21; 65:16).

IMPLICIT INDICATIONS OF DIVINE RULE

The prophet Isaiah develops God as king. Yahweh is explicitly demonstrated to be king through the words *'adon* and *melek*. The word *'adon* is built from the onomatopoetic words for father and mother (*'adhan* and *'adhath*).[14] The word is mainly used of earthly lords in the OT, but at times it is used of God "to emphasize Yahweh's rule over all the world."[15] One of the most distinctive features of the use of the word in Isaiah is that of preceding it with an article (as in Isa 3:1), but the word without the article is used interchangeably and in the same contexts (as in Isa 3:15).[16] No clear pattern emerges and the meaning is the same, so it probably is simply a matter of style.[17] When the suffix *i* is used in *'adoni* there is an honorific or intensive plural of rank, which strengthens the root meaning unto a distinctive title for God, meaning "Lord over all."[18]

Parallel to this usage is the epithet *melek* or "king," which was used frequently of Yahweh as the One who reigns.[19] The term is often used of Yahweh's reign over Israel reflective of their covenant relationship (Isa 6:5; 8:21; 32:17, 22; 33:22; 41:21–22; 43:15; 44:6). The verb is employed in an

---

13. Pagan texts join Isaiah in referencing idols as gods (Jacobsen, "The Graven Image," 16–17 containing: King Agum kakrime of Babylon inscription VR 1.44–2.17; Nebuchadnezzar 1 inscription IV R pl. 20, no. 1.9–18; Nabonidus inscription Nabonid Nr. 8.1.14–25).

14. Otto Eissfeldt, "אֲדֹנָי," in *TDOT* 1:59; Ugaritic texts CTA, 23 (SS) and 24 (NK).

15. Otto Eissfeldt, "אֲדֹנָי," in *TDOT* 1:61–62; Brettler, *God is King*, 42–44.

16. Lust, "The Divine Titles הָאָדוֹן and אָדוֹן, 148.

17. Marvin Sweeney considers that the word without the article is an indication of a late addition (*Isaiah 1–39*, 106–11). However, in Isaiah the word is found interchangeably with or without the article.

18. Otto Eissfeldt, In *TDOT* 1:63, 72; Vriezen, "Essentials of the Theology of Isaiah," 132; Barker, "Lord."

19. Brettler, *God is King*, 30–33; Smith, "The Concept of God."

eschatological sense when God rules during the kingdom age (Isa 24:23; 52:7). In this context it can identify "Your God reigns" (Isa 52:7).[20]

In contrast to earthly kings who die in their temporality, 'adoni continues as the everlasting king over all (Isa 6:1, 5). In fact, the concept of God's holiness in Isaiah has to do with his being set apart in this distinct category of everlasting transcendent king. Unlike Rudolf Otto's concept of "Wholly Other" as a negative idea of what a human is not, holiness is better understood as a positive concept, that of whatever is being emphasized in the context, such as the everlasting transcendent divine kingship.[21] In the vision, Isaiah spends few words to describe God except to focus on his distinctive regal glory, which at this moment fills the creation and will be strongly revealed in the exodus unto kingdom (Isa 6:3; 40:5).[22] When Isaiah sees this vision and hears the "glowing ones" (*seraphim*) call out God's holiness, Isaiah recoils in terror of his sin. Such fear and reverence is the proper response when confronted with the transcendence of Yahweh (Isa 6:2–3, 5; 8:13). Yahweh's holiness is then communicated through the glowing one who carried it to Isaiah to touch his lips and make Isaiah appropriate to carry the message of judgment.

The ancient Near Eastern concept of king included six major functions, all of which Yahweh fulfills. In the ancient Near East, the king was a mediator representing the gods to the people and a priest representing the people before the gods.[23] The people viewed the king as the "deputy of the supreme god," and for the Hittites and Egyptians the king upon death became a god.[24]

The king in the ancient Near East was also often a priest in contact with the spiritual realm. As king, Yahweh has a unique role with this spiritual realm. Yahweh is essentially spiritual as seen by *ruah* as a synonym for God evident in the parallelism in Isaiah 30:1 and 34:16. A person within the godhead is also the spirit in a unique and complete manner extending from God (Isa 11:2). The spiritual realm is more a reality for Yahweh than the physical (Isa 31:3).

---

20. Stuhlmueller, "Yahweh-King and Deutero-Isaiah," 34–36.

21. Contra Otto, *The Idea of the Holy*, 6, 25, whose idea is too Kantian; Kennard, *Biblical Covenantalism*, 1:259–67.

22. Mihelic, "The Concept of God in Deutero-Isaiah," 33–34, where he thinks Yahweh's returning glory is the greatest vision of Deutero-Isaiah.

23. Barker, "Office and Functions of Ancient Kingship."

24. Guterbock, "Authority and Law in the Hittite Kingdom," 17:23; Goetze, *Kleinasien*, 3:95.

In Isaiah 6, Yahweh is flanked by "glowing ones" (*seraphim*) that are usually identified with guarding courtiers (*cherubim*)[25] of the spiritual realm which are found in palaces and temples throughout the ancient Near East. Their presence surrounding Yahweh further identifies Yahweh is the divine king. Otto Kaiser explains their role in highlighting the separateness or holiness of God.

> The heavenly King does not appear alone to the prophet. Yahweh is surrounded by the seraphim (6:2), ministering spirits, in considerable numbers, just as an earthly ruler is surrounded by his followers and courtiers. They shut him off from the gaze of man . . . The seraphim reverently conceal their faces and private parts with their wings. Even the heavenly beings who day and night surround their God and serve him, are similar to men in that they cannot and may not look upon the face of God. The sight of him would be fatal for them as well . . . The attitude of the angelic beings emphasizes the infinite distance between God and every creature, and recalls the holiness of God to Isaiah.[26]

The presence of *seraphim* indicates that Yahweh is the king on the throne to rule the universe.

SUZERAINTY TREATY CONTEXT

Yahweh presents himself as a great king and judge utilizing covenant lawsuit in Isaiah that echoes a suzerainty treaty in Exodus 19–24, Deuteronomy, and Joshua 24. "Yahweh takes his place in court; he rises to judge the people. Yahweh enters into judgment against the elders and leaders of his people" (Isa 3:13–14). "For Yahweh is our judge; Yahweh is our lawgiver; Yahweh is our king; it is he who will save us" (Isa 33:22).

The inclusion of covenant lawsuits in Isaiah (Isa 1–5; 41–42; 48; 57–58; 66) identified that Yahweh is a great king and judge and that Israel is functioning under a suzerainty treaty. The greatness of the suzerain is indicated by the context of application of the covenant. These covenant lawsuits also range over the nations around Israel and eventually eschatologically over the whole earth (Isa 13–34), indicating that Yahweh is great over the whole earth, including the ancient Near East and Israel. Ernst Wright concludes that the presence of covenant lawsuits indicates that God presents himself as king and judge.

---

25. Possibly the same as "living creatures," *seraphim*, and *cherubim* (Isa 37:16; Ezek 1:5, 13–22; 3:13; 10:1–22; 11:22; Rev 4:6–9; 5:6; 6:1, 6; 7:11; 14:3; 15:7; 19:4).

26. Kaiser, *Isaiah 1–12*, 76; Leupold, *Exposition of Isaiah*, 1:136.

The heavenly lawsuit implies a Suzerain, one who claims authority over all powers on earth, and who is presiding over the highest tribunal in the universe. Furthermore, it implies a covenant which the Suzerain has granted a vassal, a covenant which the vassal has broken.[27]

With covenants and lawsuits, Isaiah indicates that Yahweh is king and judge by pressing a covenant lawsuit Yahweh has against Judah and Israel on the basis of their rebellion against Yahweh as king in violating the Mosaic covenant.[28] The Mosaic covenant is a suzerainty treaty which Yahweh bound upon Israel when he brought them out of Egypt (Isa 10:26; 11:16). Under this arrangement the Jews are already in the Mosaic covenant, which means that they need to obey the covenant to be blessed, for if they disobey they will be cursed. The Mosaic covenant continued to bind[29] generations of Jews in Isaiah's day under this same Mosaic covenant curse. Unfortunately, Judah and Israel stubbornly did evil in breaking God's covenant commands, so King Yahweh brought disaster upon them with no preventative option (Isa 1:7–10).

Such a prophetic exhortation responds to the suzerainty treaty stipulations as did Hittite diplomatic correspondence which followed any vassal's disobedience to suzerainty treaty stipulations, threatening devastation for the vassal from the great king if the vassal does not quickly comply with what the suzerainty treaty demanded in the stipulations section. For example, the "Letter from Hattusili III of Hatti to Kadashman-Enlil II of Babylon" threatens Babylon with a severe military campaign if they do not swiftly submit to the terms of the Hittite suzerainty treaty governing them.[30] The analog for such diplomatic correspondence in the OT is the prophets, calling Israel back to faithfully serving Yahweh. To the extent that the great king is powerful, the vassal should fear and comply with the terms of the suzerainty treaty. To the extent that the vassal's disobedience is answered by diplomatic correspondence (or prophets), the vassal should immediately and fully submit to the stipulations of the suzerainty treaty. To not comply would bring covenant curse from the great king.

A suzerainty treaty was made between two parties who did not have equal rights, so it is a treaty imposed by a great king upon his vassal (usually

---

27. Wright, "Terminology of Old Testament Religion," 404.

28. Nielsen, *Yahweh as Prosecutor and Judge*.

29. The binding or prescriptive nature of covenant stipulations will be discussed in the chapter "Israel in Covenant Relationship with Yahweh" in this book.

30. An example is the "Letter from Hattusili III of Hatti to Kadashman-Enlil II of Babylon," see #23 in Beckman, *Hittite Diplomatic Texts*, esp. 138–39; Thompson, *The Book of Jeremiah*, 169.

the king of the subjected nation). The form of this treaty is the most helpful covenant form for understanding certain texts of the Bible since this form can be found in Exodus 20:1—Leviticus 26:46; Deuteronomy as a whole; Joshua 24; and in fragmentary ways in the following: 1 Samuel 12; 2 Chronicles 29:6—31:21; 34:13—35:19 (parallel 2 Kgs 22:9-22); Ezra 9:2—10:44; Nehemiah 9:5—10:34; and the Asaph covenant renewal liturgies of Psalm 50 and 81.[31] The fact that this covenant form is utilized strongly indicates that Yahweh presents himself as the divine king in these texts.

The suzerain made a decree as a great king and imposed it upon his vassal, the king of the subjugated nation. The interests were overwhelmingly those of the great king. The vassal king is obligated to obey and consent to the terms of the oath. The curses are primarily directed toward whoever violates the great king's rights. This kind of treaty is primarily an inducement of the vassal's future loyalty. Through the treaty the vassal king obtained a promise of protection for his country and dynasty, but he could not affect the terms of the treaty.[32] Mendenhall describes it this way:

> The primary purpose of the suzerainty treaty was to establish a firm relationship of mutual support between the two parties (especially military support), in which the interests of the Hittite sovereign were of primary and ultimate concern. It established a relationship between the two, but in its form, it is unilateral. The stipulations of the treaty are binding only upon the vassal, and only the vassal took an oath of obedience. Though the treaties frequently contain promises of help and support to the vassal, there is no legal formality by which the Hittite king binds himself to any specific obligation. Rather it is the Hittite king by his very position as sovereign is [sic] concerned to protect his subjects from claims or attacks of other foreign states. Consequently, for him to bind himself to specific obligations with regard to his vassal would be an infringement upon his sole right of self-determination and sovereignty. A most important

---

31. These texts support especially the Pentateuch sources as suzerainty treaty: Mendenhall, "Covenant Forms in Israelite Tradition"; Muilenberg, "Form and Structure of Covenant Formulations"; Baltzer, *Das Bundesformular*; Lohfink, "Der Bundesschluss im Land Moab," *Das Hauptgebot*; McCarthy, *Treaty and Covenant*, "Covenant and Law"; Kline, *Treaty of the Great King*; Buis, "Les formulaires d'alliance"; Mayes, *Deuteronomy*; Knutson, "Literary Genres in PRU IV," 153; Finch, "Theology of Deuteronomy"; Rendtorff, *The Covenant Formula*; Kennard, *Biblical Covenantalism*, 1:115–243, 2:14–17; Duggan, *Covenant Renewal in Ezra-Nehemiah*; Taggar-Cohen, "Biblical *Covenant* and Hittite *išhiul* reexamined"; *Mek.* to Exod 20:17; *Midrash Tan.* to Deut 5:21.

32. Weinfeld, *Deuteronomy and the Deuteronomic School*, 74–75.

corollary of this fact is the emphasis upon the vassal's obligation to *trust* in the benevolence of the sovereign.[33]

While Isaiah as a manuscript is not itself a suzerainty treaty, it is helpful to enter into the mindset of such a treaty as a background since Isaiah has Yahweh respond to this framework with covenant lawsuit, implying treaty violation. Foundationally, a suzerainty treaty has the following formal elements: preamble, historical prologue, stipulation, treaty validation, list of witnesses, and curses and blessings.

In the *preamble* there is the name, titles, and genealogy of the great king Yahweh (Exod 20:1; Deut 1:1–5; Josh 24:2; Neh 9:5–6; Ps 50:1). The emphasis is upon the majesty and power of the great king, who confers a relationship upon the vassal, who is not even mentioned at this point.

The *historical prologue* describes in detail the previous relationship between the two, particularly the benevolence and continuity of great king Yahweh toward vassal Israel (Exod 20:2; Deut 1:6—4:43; Josh 24:2–13; 2 Chr 29:6–9; Neh 9:7–37; Ps 81:5–12). Here a rationale is provided to demonstrate why the vassal should be loyal to the great king, either because he as a vassal has been favored with sustenance or military assistance (as in the exodus) or because he has been spared from the severe punishment which he deserves. Significant themes develop like: the suzerain king is great; he is the initiator in the relationship; he is sovereign; he is irresistible in battle; he is the refuge for the vassal seeking aid and protection; and he is gracious in spite of the vassal's unfaithfulness.

> What the description amounts to is this, that the vassal is obligated to perpetual gratitude toward the great king because of the benevolence, consideration and favor which he has already received . . . the vassal is exchanging *future* obedience to specific commands for *past* benefits which he received without any real right.[34]

One of the stylistic features, utilizing "I-Thou," emphasizes the personal relationship of obligation and gratitude. This may be in first or third person, but "the covenant form is still thought of as a personal relationship, rather than as an objective, impersonal statement of law."[35] In this, historical and didactive content is used with a rhetorical emphasis to move the will of the vassal to loyalty.

---

33. Mendenhall, *Law and Covenant*, 30; Polak, "Covenant at Mount Sinai."
34. Mendenhall, *Law and Covenant*, 32.
35. Mendenhall, *Law and Covenant*, 33.

The *stipulation* section states in detailed obligations imposed upon and accepted by vassal Israel (Exod 20:2—Lev 25; Deut 4:44—26:19; Josh 24:14-15; 2 Kgs 22:9, 11; 2 Chr 29:5; 30:1-5; 31:2-19; 35:1-19; Ezra 9:2; Neh 10:29-34; Pss 50:16; 81:8-10, 13). The focus of the stipulations section is underscoring how vassal Israel is to be loyal to suzerain Yahweh. The primary duties imposed on the vassal are to: be loyal and trust the great king; be prohibited from enmity of anything within the sovereignty of the great king; pay tribute; provide military assistance; renounce foreign diplomatic contacts; report plots against the great king; extradite fugitives; and indicate succession to the Hittite throne.[36] Because the stipulations are prescriptive for the vassals, all controversies between vassals are to be unconditionally submitted to great king Yahweh for judgment.

Treaty validation provides for: 1) vassal Israel pledging by oath, 2) the treaty being stored in the temple of the vassal's deity (Yahweh), and for 3) the treaty to be read aloud at set intervals before the subordinate (Exod 24; 25:16; Lev 27; Deut 27-30; 31:9-13, 26; Josh 24:16-18; 2 Kgs 22:15-22; 2 Chr 29:10; 30:6—31:1; 34:13-33; Ezra 9:2; 10:44; Neh 8; Ps 50:5).[37] The initial ceremony would often involve the vassal pledging obedience by an oath as occurred in Exodus 24. The treaty is kept in the temple out of the reach of the vassal, for tampering with the treaty was prohibited. The periodic public reading familiarized the entire population with the obligations of the great king and increased the respect for the vassal king by describing the warm relationship which he enjoyed with the great king.

In a usual suzerainty treaty there is an invocation of the gods of the great king and the vassal to act as *witnesses* to the covenant because these gods are the ones who will enforce the treaty. However, with Yahweh as the monotheistic God guaranteeing the covenant, the witnesses include: the people themselves; heaven and earth; notable trees; and stones set up (Exod 19; 24:4-13; Deut 4:26; 27:1-8; 30:19; 31:19-28; 32; Josh 21-27; Neh 9:38—10:29; Ps 50:1-6).

The *Curses and blessings* section helps to ensure loyalty (Exod 19:5-6; Lev 26; Deut 28-30; Josh 24:19-20; 2 Kgs 22:13-20; 2 Chr 31:20-21; 34:21-25; Ezra 9:7-15; Neh 10:29; Pss 50:7-23; 81:11-16). If the vassal

---

36. Mendenhall, *Law and Covenant*, 33-34; Beckman, *Hittite Diplomatic Texts*, 3, and the corroborative reading of sixty documents contained therein; Kennard, *Biblical Covenantalism*, 1:104-243, makes a prolonged case from Exodus and Deuteronomy for prescriptive stipulations to the covenant vassal Israel in the contextual relationship with Yahweh. Engagement of more recent arguments on this issue will occur in the chapter concerning "Israel in Covenant Relationship with Yahweh" in this book.

37. Mendenhall, *Law and Covenant*, 34; Beckman, *Hittite Diplomatic Texts*, 3, and the corroborative reading of sixty documents contained therein.

obeys, blessings are promised. The threat of divine retribution as a response to disobedience is the glue that held the Hittite empire together. Nonetheless, some of the Hittite vassals were willing to risk the wrath of the gods and the power of the Hittite armies to achieve independence, as shown by the revolts that frequently broke out upon the death of the great king. However, letters written to the offending vassal threatening them to submit show that the stipulations were not merely suggestions and the curses were a real threat responding to vassal disobedience.[38] Additionally, the fact that the Hittite empire was able to quash these rebellions shows that the covenant stipulations really do bind the vassal into a covenant relationship that the great king insists on enforcing to the vassal's demise if necessary. A vassal's rebellion does not render the covenant null and void. Rather, even in the midst of rebellion, the vassal remains obligated within the terms of the covenant, and thus rebellion begets curse from the suzerain.

These treaties were enforced in other ways as well by the Hittite empire. One of the most expedient was to establish a personal bond with a more prominent vassal through a diplomatic marriage. For example, Hittite princesses were sent to establish diplomatic relationships with Mittanni, Hayasa, Amurru, and Ugarit in the Hittite documents that Beckman published.[39] Such imagery of Yahweh wedding Israel is apparent in Hosea in the giving of the Mosaic covenant during the exodus and Isaiah in initiating a new exodus.

> I betroth you to me forever.
> I betroth you to me in righteousness, with justice, with lovingkindness and mercy.
> I betroth you to me with faithfulness and you shall love the Lord.
> (Hos 2:19–20 [MT: 2:21–22])

> You will be a crown of beauty in the hand of Yahweh,
> And a royal diadem in the hand of your God.
> It will no longer be said to you, "Forsaken,"
> Nor to your land will it any longer be said, "Desolate;"
> But you will be called, "My delight is in her,"
> And your land, "Married"; for Yahweh delights in you in you,
> And your land will be married.
> For as a young man marries a virgin, so your sons will marry you;
> And as the bridegroom rejoices over the bride, so God will rejoice over you. (Isa 62:3–5)

38. For example, "Letter from Hattusili III of Hatti to Kadashman-Enlil II of Babylon," see #23 in Beckman, *Hittite Diplomatic Texts*, 138–39, introduction and section 4.

39. Gary Beckman identifies which documents and place in the documents addresses this (*Hittite Diplomatic Texts*, 4).

Additionally, there is the possibility of a Hittite garrison being established in a vassal's land to protect the vassal from external threat, but also to keep an eye on the vassal and help ensure that these vassals will comply with the terms of the treaty.[40] The fact that ambassadors were sent from the Hittite great king with written letters demanding compliance (analogous to the book of Isaiah) shows that the suzerainty treaty form was not for mere court guidance; the vassal must comply or suffer the wrath of the great king and his gods.[41] Likewise, the book of Isaiah demands compliance of Israel to Yahweh.

With such threats of war and divine wrath, the stipulations show themselves to be binding. So, the vassal is bound by the terms and stipulations of the treaty, and the use of a suzerainty treaty as a covenant method conveys this obligatory relation from great king Yahweh to vassal Israel. When vassal Israel disobeyed, great king Yahweh would respond with covenant lawsuit, echoing the framework that this suzerainty treaty instituted.

HOLY SPIRIT

The word "spirit" (*ruaḥ*) is an onomatopoetic word meaning "to breathe out through the mouth with violence."[42] It is used of words which are of empty breath or wind (Isa 26:18; 41:29). The concept of "breath" includes the sense of power in violent judgment (Isa 4:4; 11:4; 30:28; 33:11), similar to the hot scorching sirocco wind that blows from the desert (Isa 4:4; 7:2; 40:7). The idea is that one cannot see wind or spirit, but one can see the effect in the trees and in its destruction or re-creation of new circumstances.[43] The effect of Yahweh's activity is clear among Israel and the nations, in the same manner as wind (*ruaḥ*) accomplishes a significant effect in blast and hurricane as well (Isa 4:4; 7:2; 11:4, 15; 17:13; 26:9, 18; 27:8; 32:2; 33:11; 37:7; 41:16, 29; 42:5; 57:13; 64:6 [MT: 64:5]).

When this word is used of the spirit of God, a fuller concept is in view. Yahweh's primary realm is essentially spiritual and thereby permanent and reliable (Isa 31:3) for he himself is spirit (Isa 30:1; 34:16; Ps 139:7). In Isaiah 34:16, "spirit" is identified as Yahweh's presence, as evident by the parallelism

---

40. One example of this is mentioned in the treaty with Targasnalli of Hapalla, in Beckman, *Hittite Diplomatic Texts*, 70.

41. Beckman provides examples of court correspondence of this nature in *Hittite Diplomatic Texts*, #23 on 138–39 and 142–43; and #30 on 169–73. Louis Cohn-Haft also translates a prayer of Mursilis to placate the Hittite storm god to release his curse from violating such a treaty (*Ancient Near East and Greece*, 177–79).

42. Snaith, *Distinctive Ideas of the Old Testament*, 183.

43. Dreytza, *Der theologische Gebrauch von RUAḤ*.

in the verse.[44] The word "spirit" becomes a substitute for "God" (Isa 34:16; 63:10, 14). So, the spirit of Yahweh could be considered, as Aubrey Johnson develops, an "extension of God's personality."[45] As such, the spirit of Yahweh has all the attributes of Yahweh, like holiness, since they are two different ways of referring to the same divine being (Isa 63:10, 14).

No development of a Trinity is present in Isaiah contrary to Leon Wood's development of spirit in the OT. Also, Eichrodt is too close to the concept of the Trinity with his view that the spirit of God is one of three cosmic powers.[46] However, there is an agent referred to apart from Yahweh who fulfills the role of a sent one from Yahweh (Isa 48:16).[47] In this sense, the spirit is the "medium through which God exerts his controlling power."[48] This controlling power is demonstrated in Yahweh using a wind for judgment (Isa 27:8; 28:6). The link between the strong, overwhelming wind of the desert and the all-powerful spirit of God is seen in the fury, speed, and violent destruction which they cause (Isa 30:28; 40:7; 59:19).

God's spirit provides the covenant to Israel so that they might have his guidance (Isa 63:11). For example, Yahweh's spirit brought about the exodus and clear passage through the Red Sea (Isa 63:10–11).

The spirit of Yahweh also provides a role of wisdom from his divine character to facilitate divine counsel (Isa 11:2; 30:1; 40:13–14).[49] Such divine ability is provided for the mediatorial leadership whom God uses.

The spirit of God has a significant ministry empowering and anointing the Davidic king.[50] Such an anointing of this messianic figure by the spirit fits within the empowerment of prophetic filling.

> The ruach Yahweh fills those who receive it with an immense energy, physical, moral and spiritual, so that they have the strength to resist anybody and everybody and to accomplish the task imposed on them by God. It makes those who are called

---

44. Ma, *Until the Spirit Comes*, 31–32. There is no evidence in Isaiah that the concept of "spirit" emerges from Mesopotamian demons, contra Volz, *Der Geist Gottes und die Verwandten Erscheinungen*.

45. Johnson, *The One and the Many*, 6–7, 19–20, 36–37; Ma, *Until the Spirit Comes*, 29, 31–32, 155.

46. Eichrodt, *Theology of the Old Testament*, 2:46; Leon Wood wrongly views the OT though NT Trinitarian development (*The Holy Spirit in the Old Testament*).

47. This independent agency is developed by Ma, *Until the Spirit Comes*, 31.

48. North, *The Second Isaiah*, 182.

49. Ma, *Until the Spirit Comes*, 70, 72.

50. Koch, *Geist und Messias*.

into perfect instruments in the hands of Yahweh, one might say, into an extension of God in this world.[51]

The spirit of Yahweh rests on the messiah and bestows upon him unusual abilities in wisdom, character development, and power to accomplish Yahweh's task (Isa 11:1–3). Yahweh's spirit empowers the leadership for Israel to facilitate the benefits of kingdom (Isa 11:1–3; 59:19, 21; 61:1–3). The messiah anointed by the spirit performs the roles of proclaiming the good news, freeing captives, bringing about the favorable year of the Yahweh, and the day of Yahweh's wrath (Isa 61:1–2). The spirit also enables the binding up of the brokenhearted and comforting those who mourn. Additionally, through the spirit's ministry the messiah will bring about the proper order for the nations (Isa 42:1).

The holy spirit maintains a ministry directly with Israel and will facilitate the eschatological kingdom.[52] The holy spirit was among Israel in the days of Moses and the exodus, giving them rest (Isa 63:11, 14). Yet the people grieved the holy spirit so that he turned and fought against them as an enemy (Isa 63:10). This enmity will not last forever because there shall be a time in which the spirit is poured out upon Israel in indication of kingdom blessings (Isa 32:15; 44:3; Joel 2:28–32). The kingdom is characterized by and facilitated by Yahweh's spirit being poured forth upon Yahweh's people (Isa 32:15–20; 44:3–5). In this eschatological kingdom day, Yahweh will make a covenant to never remove his spirit from Israel, which will foster in them continuous speaking and living the words of Yahweh (Isa 59:21).

The spirit is intimately related to the concept of power and judgment. He is also involved throughout the messiah's ministry and the plan for Israel's salvation.

DIVINE JUDGE

The role of holding Israel and the nations to account for their response within a covenantal relationship identified that Yahweh is the judge (*špṭ*).[53] Isaiah 33:22 says, "Yahweh is our judge, Yahweh is our lawgiver, Yahweh is our king; he will save us." Yahweh engaged Israel in a judging role (*Niphal* of *špṭ*) but there was no one in Israel who could intercede (*Niphal* of *špṭ*) for Israel, so Yahweh acted as judge for righteousness (*špṭ*, Isa 51:5; 59:15).

---

51. Vriezen, "Ruach Yahweh (Elohim)," 51.

52. Special emphasis of Koch, *Der Geist Gottes im Alten Testament* and *Geist und Messias*.

53. Brettler, *God is King*, 44–45; Nielsen, *Yahweh as Prosecutor and Judge*.

Nielsen explains that Yahweh serves as both prosecutor and judge in pursuing Israel in covenant lawsuit.

> It is characteristic of the prophetic lawsuit that Yahweh enjoys the dual role of prosecutor and judge. That Yahweh appears as prosecutor can be explained by the fact that it is he who has been wronged. The wrong is understood by the prophets as a breach of the covenant which was originally established between Yahweh and his people. At Sinai, Yahweh promised to be Israel's god, while the people contracted to be his holy, and thus obedient people. It is apparent in the lawsuit that Israel has abandoned the Covenant, which justifies Yahweh's prosecution of his people.
>
> The fact that Yahweh also plays the role of judge must be understood in the same context. Heaven and earth were witnesses when the Covenant was made, but according to the OT, no other gods were able to function as guarantors of the compact. Thus only Yahweh himself is empowered to ensure the keeping of the Covenant, and to keep the people up to the standard of its demands.[54]

The Mosaic covenant demands require righteousness of others or Yahweh will judge them (Isa 51:5; 59:15).

Israel should have judged the vulnerable by protecting them (such as the orphan and widow) but Israel did not protect them, so Yahweh's judgment will come on Israel (Isa 1:17, 23). When Yahweh's judgment comes it destroys all opposition because he has the right over his vineyard (Isa 5:3; 40:23). Part of this judgment is that Yahweh removes unrighteous judges (Isa 3:2). Eventually, Yahweh will remake Israel so that they will defend the vulnerable (Isa 1:26). Part of his method to establish Israel in righteousness is to establish a Davidic king (empowered by the spirit of Yahweh) who will judge deeper than what is seen so that the vulnerable will be protected (Isa 11:3; 16:5).

THE DIVINE WARRIOR

The concept of the divine warrior spread across the book of Isaiah indicates the divine king militant arranging armies to execute his judgment on Israel or the nations who abused Israel.[55] Yahweh of "hosts" (*Sabaoth*) is the "name"

---

54. Nielsen, *Yahweh as Prosecutor and Judge*, 74.

55. Watts, *Isaiah 1–33* (rev. ed.), cxi; Cross, "The Divine Warrior," 28–30; Neufeld, *God and Saints at War*, 11–32; similar expression of Marduk in *Enuma Elish*, in *ANET*, 66.

(*sem*) of the God of Israel, especially in the second half of Isaiah (Isa 47:4; 48:2; 51:15; 54:5). Though the word "sabaoth" is mostly used in the first half of Isaiah where God is defeating nations in judgment. "Sabaoth" is from the form meaning "soldier" or "army," and thus would indicate Yahweh as "general" or as "captain of the guard" or as "Yahweh militant." The title is taken various ways including: Yahweh militant; the creator or sustainer or overthrower of armies (Isa 34:2); head of the armies of Israel, angels, or stars (Isa 40:26); or of head over the whole of creation (Isa 45:12).[56] Israel's army is included within the concept of "hosts" (1 Sam 17:45), but the hosts are broader than Israel because Israel was defeated at times when Yahweh of hosts was not. Furthermore, the stars are included among the "host of heaven" (Deut 4:19; 17:3; 2 Kgs 17:16; 21:3, 5; Isa 40:26; 45:12). LXX Isaiah usually just transliterates Hebrew *sabaoth* as κύριος σαβαωθ (Isa 1:9), but sometimes in contextual use the word "sabaoth" is replaced by "Lord" (Isa 8:13; 9:13, 19 [MT: 9:18]; 19:17–20; 24:23) or "God" (Isa 10:23, 26; 14:27; 24:21; 44:6). To make matters more complex, the LXX psalms often translate "*sabaoth*" as the "Lord of powers" and a number of other prophets often translate it in the LXX as "Lord almighty" (Jer, Hos, Amos, Nah, Hag, Zech, Mal).

Yahweh Sabaoth is the excellent warrior. He takes the outfit of a warrior, including the breastplate of righteousness that sustains him (Isa 59:16–17).[57] His helmet is of salvation, which is his goal (Isa 59:17).[58] His garments are of vengeance[59] because he executes his judgments. His cloak is of zeal because he does everything effectively, whole-heartedly, and completely. With this preparation, "Yahweh will march out like a mighty man, like a warrior he will stir up zeal; with a shout he will raise the battle cry and will triumph over his enemies" (Isa 42:13). Through his arm of power, he conquered over Rahab and the primordial forces of chaos (drying up the waters of Teham), showing in a polemical form that Yahweh is the sovereign warrior who conquers all opposition even from the earliest times (Isa 51:9–10) and continues to bring retribution to his enemies (Isa 59:18). Likewise, through his arm of power, he brings salvation for Israel (Isa 52:10; 59:16; 63:5, 12).

---

56. Ross, "Jahweh Sebaʾot in Samuel and Psalms," 76.

57. This imagery is retained in Wis 5:18; though 1 Thess 5:8 and Eph 6:14 shift the armor to be the Christians' armor; Neufeld, *"Put on the Armour of God,"* 132–33.

58. This imagery is retained in Wis 5:18 preventing harm rather than providing salvation; 1 Thess 5:8 adds that salvation is hope within the Christians' armor; Eph 6:17.

59. This imagery is retained in Wis 5:17 but altered in Eph 6:14–17 to more spiritual weaponry, perhaps altering "wind" of Isa 59:19 for "spirit" (πνεύματος; Eph 4:17); Neufeld, *"Put on the Armour of God,"* 143.

It is Yahweh as divine king and not Baal who rides swiftly into war on the clouds as his chariot[60] (Isa 19:1; Deut 33:26; Pss 18:10 [MT: 18:11]; 68:33 [MT: 68:34]; 104:3). He comes and the nations fear. They melt before him as he brings their plans to nothing, defeating Egypt (Isa 19:1–4). A banner is set up for Yahweh as he gathers a mighty army together (Isa 13:1). These warriors are gathered to carry out the wrath of Yahweh against Babylon and Assyria (Isa 13:2–5). They are gripped with fear and become impotent before him (Isa 13:6–8). He uses supernatural means coupled with his human army to destroy them utterly. This finds its fulfillment progressively and ultimately in the defeat of Babylon the great (Rev 17–18). Yahweh as the divine warrior avenges ultimately through the messiah as the warrior-king concluding conflict with Babylon.

> Who is this coming from Edom from Bozrah, with his garments stained crimson? Who is this, robed in splendor, striding forward in the greatness of his strength? "It is I, speaking in righteousness, mighty to save." Why are your garments red, like those of one treading the winepress? "I have trodden the winepress alone; from the nations no one was with me. I trampled them in my anger and trod them down in my wrath; their blood spattered my garments, and I stained all my clothing for the day of vengeance was in my heart, and the year of my redemption has come. I looked but there was no one to help, I was appalled that no one gave support; So, my own arm worked salvation for me, and my own wrath sustained me. I trampled the nations in my anger; in my wrath I made them drunk and poured their blood on the ground." (Isa 63:1–6)

Yahweh's role of warrior is in essence his omnipotence and irresistibility since Yahweh is lord over all powers in heaven and earth.[61] The role of warrior was a facet of the role of king (2 Sam 11:1). Yahweh is the supreme warrior bringing salvation and judgment because he is supreme king.[62]

YAHWEH'S ARM

A metaphor to communicate Yahweh in these roles is that of his "arm" (*zra*), which as a warrior is his weapon-wielding arm to destroy his enemies or reap

---

60. Baal demonstrates he is the *high god* by riding the clouds (*UT* 51.11, 18; 68.8, 29, in *ANET*, 130–32).

61. Parke-Taylor, *Yahweh: The Divine Name in the Bible*, 64–65.

62. Oehler, *Theology of the Old Testament*, 443; Ross, "Jahweh Seba'ot in Samuel and Psalms," 86; Miller, *The Divine Warrior*, 173–75.

the crop of his enemies (17:5; 30:30; 48:14). Yahweh's arm rules in a compassionate manner (Isa 40:10), so it also acts as judge and protector for the vulnerable (Isa 33:2; 51:5). Yahweh's arm has led Moses during the exodus (Isa 63:12). The arm of Yahweh redeems and saves Israel (Isa 59:16; 62:8; 63:5). Yahweh's arm also carries the vulnerable sheep, as Yahweh shepherds Israel (Isa 40:11; and also *ḥṣn* "arm" or "bosom" for "shepherd carrying" Isa 49:22).

YAHWEH AS SHEPHERD

Yahweh is revealed in this kingly shepherd role throughout the OT (Gen 48:15; 49:24; Exod 15:13; Pss 31:4; 44:12; 48:15; 74:1; 77:21; Isa 40:11; 49:9–10; 63:11; Jer 31:10; Ezek 34:12–13; 37:24; Hos 4:16; Mic 2:12; 4:6–8; Zeph 3:19). Within this context, Israel is alluded to as "the people of Yahweh and the sheep of his pasture" (Pss 79:13; 95:7; 100:3). Eichrodt develops that Yahweh was the shepherd as the Babylonian and Egyptian kings were shepherds of their own people.

> The imagery of the shepherd also describes the lovingkindness of Yahweh as the fulfillment of that association with Israel which he established in the beginning. The office of a shepherd as an image of kingship is of course found throughout the Near East, and is ascribed to gods as well as to kings, often in stereotyped forms. This element of the courtly style always has something of an official stamp, as a result of which the characteristics of love and providential care appear simply to be taken for granted as involved in faithfulness to the kingly calling.[63]

This imagery of the shepherd reaches a high point in the book of Isaiah. Yahweh as the great shepherd has brought forth his flock from Egypt, described in the exodus motif (Isa 63:11). The imagery has compassion and love with provision for all needs: "He tends his flock like a shepherd; he gathers the lambs in his arms and carries them close to his heart; he gently leads those that have young" (Isa 40:11).[64] Goldingay describes this compassionate shepherding role.

---

63. Eichrodt, *Theology of the Old Testament*, 1:236–37; Stuhlmueller, "Yahweh-King and Deutero-Isaiah," 32–33; Brettler, *God is King*, 65.

64. With this text, sometimes there is a common illustration of a shepherd breaking the leg of a straying sheep, probably first mentioned by Robert Munger as a surprising practice of a contemporary Syrian shepherd (*What Jesus Says: The Master Teacher and Life's Problems*), but there is no ancient evidence of this practice and there is no biblical reason to mention such a practice. The biblical emphasis is on compassion, not discipline. Jewish shepherding practice would carry a lamb as a means of bringing it back to the flock without harming it even if it had strayed (*Sem. Rab.* 2.2; Luke 15:4–6; Matt

> Pasturing the flock and leading the mothering ewes to watering places together (to pasture or feed would not normally imply giving food to the animals, but taking them to where they can find it), as do gathering lambs and carrying them. In each case the second expression heightens the first: the prophet moves from pasturing sheep in general to the ewes' particular need for water and rest, and with respect to the lambs moves from gathering/arm to carrying/bosom. The verse as a whole suggests the personal caring of Yhwh for Israel as a flock. While it is always the people as a whole that Yhwh is concerned for (the prophet is not individualistic), the caring is one that recognizes and meets the distinctive needs of its many members.[65]

Isaiah applies this shepherding compassion to the new exodus.

> They will feed beside the roads and find pasture on every hill.
> They will neither hunger nor thirst nor will the desert heat or the sun beat upon them.
> He who has compassion on them will guide them
> And lead them beside springs of water. (Isa 49:9-10)

Yahweh is the great shepherd over Israel (Isa 40:11; Ps 80:1) and the nations (Isa 14:30; 34:6; Ps 100:3; Ezek 39:18).[66] God is the shepherd enabling his people to pasture safely and even lie down relaxed, knowing that they are protected from any wild beast.

OUR FATHER

As an expression of corporate prayer, Yahweh is addressed as "our Father" (*'bynŭ*, Isa 63:16 twice; 64:8 [MT and LXX: 64:7]; perhaps even 9:5 [MT and LXX: 9:6]; Deut 1:31; 8:5; Pss 27:10; 68:5[6]; 103:13).[67] The concept of "father" indicates a relation with another group (Isa 3:6; 8:4; 22:21), which means that Yahweh has a relationship with the corporate nation of Judah. In light of this relationship, Isaiah refers to Judah as Yahweh's children (*bnym*, Isa 1:2; 30:1) and Yahweh's people (*'m*, Isa 65:2). Within the concept of "father" in relation to a nation, the declaration "Yahweh as Father" indicates that he is king, in a similar manner as David is father to Judah (Isa 22:24;

18:12–14). There is much risk with a lamb having a broken leg, and most shepherds have enough sheep in their care to avoid intentionally increasing personal care needlessly.

65. Goldingay, *The Message of Isaiah 40–55*, 31.

66. This is contrary to Friedrich Keil's view that lambs, rams, and goats are emblems of all the classes of people (*Prophecies of Jeremiah*, 8:309).

67. Watts, *Isaiah 1–33*, 24.

38:5). The situation of Yahweh as father who redeems Judah is made more acute because they are orphaned from Abraham and Israel by their sin (Isa 63:16).[68] In contrast to this vulnerability, God is their father showing compassion to initiate a new exodus on their behalf (Isa 63:16; Hos 11:1). As father, Yahweh creates a salvation that protects Judah (Isa 64:7).

OUR MOTHER

In the same manner as "father" describes sovereign Yahweh over a family and kingdom, in Isaiah, "our mother" is also used to describe Yahweh, especially with regard to the exodus birthing of Yahweh's people (Isa 63:8; Deut 32:18; Hos 11:1).[69] This female presentation of Yahweh is an advance over previous OT revelation in crafting a metaphor of female generosity, nursing, and pain to describe Yahweh's involvement with Israel. From the vantage point of the eighth century BC, mother Yahweh cries out in pain, "I have reared children . . . and they rebelled against me" (Isa 1:2–4). After demonstrating Yahweh is the sovereign potter, Isaiah further illustrates this creation role by parenting: "Woe to anyone who says to a father, 'What are you begetting?' Or to a woman, 'To what are your labor pains for birth?'" (Isa 45:10). Again, after keeping silent until Judah's Babylonian captivity is nearly over, Yahweh says, "Like a woman in labor I will groan, I will gasp and pant" as Yahweh prepares to birth and lead Judah on the new exodus (Isa 42:14–16).[70] Sovereign Yahweh comforts Judah by not forgetting them so that they are included in the new exodus: "Can a woman forget her nursing child, and have no compassion on the son of her womb? Even these may forget, but I will not forget you" (Isa 49:15).[71] Yahweh reminds the remnant of Israel that as a mother, he will carry them because "you have been borne by me from my belly, and have been carried from my womb" (Isa 46:3–4).[72] Thus, the divine parental role includes the maternal labor, birthing, and care of Judah.[73]

---

68. Gruber, "Motherhood of God"; Schmitt, "Motherhood of God"; Niskanen, "Yhwh as Father, Redeemer, and Potter," 397–407, esp. 399–400.

69. Niskanen, "Yhwh as Father, Redeemer, and Potter," 402; Goldingay, *Old Testament Theology*, 2:112.

70. Mollenkott, *The Divine Feminine*, 15; Goldingay and Payne, *Isaiah 40–55*, 1:48; Brettler, "Incompatible Metaphors," 117; Darr, "Like Warrior, like Woman."

71. Similar to 2 Esd 1:28–29; Mollenkott, *The Divine Feminine*, 20–21; Goldingay and Payne, *Isaiah 40–55*, 1:48; Brettler, "Incompatible Metaphors," 116.

72. Mollenkott, *The Divine Feminine*, 27–28; Brettler, "Incompatible Metaphors," 116.

73. Niskanen, "Yhwh as Father, Redeemer, and Potter," 405 n. 26.

Israel's and Jerusalem's re-creation into kingdom is also developed through mother Yahweh's future birthing, weening, and nourishing comfort (Isa 66:7–13). In the passage, the imagery shifts from mother Israel birthing and weening its post captivity population to Yahweh birthing and weening all Israel as a comforting imagery for kingdom.

> Before she travailed, she brought forth,
> before her pain came, she gave birth to a boy.
> Who has heard such a thing? Who has seen such things?
> Can a land be born in one day?
> Can a nation be brought forth all at once?
> As soon as Zion travailed, she also brought forth her sons.
> "Shall I bring to the point of birth, and not give delivery?" Says Yahweh.
> "Or shall I who gives delivery shut womb?" Says your God.
> Be joyful with Jerusalem and rejoice for her, all you who love her;
> Be exceedingly glad with her, all you who mourn over her;
> That you may nurse and be satisfied with her comforting breasts;
> That you may suck and be delighted with her bountiful bosom.
> For thus says Yahweh, "Behold I extend peace to her like a river,
> And the glory of the nations like an overflowing stream;
> And you shall be nursed, you shall be carried on the hip and fondled on the knees.
> As one whom his mother comforts, so I will comfort you;
> And you shall be comforted in Jerusalem." (Isa 66:7–13)

In extending peace to Israel, Yahweh owns the breasts and postures to ween Israel in the comfort of kingdom.

Perhaps this feminine-gendered language facilitates relating to God in merciful generosity, so that God is not merely conceived of as a patriarchal father. Some passages could be understood as an ambiguous parent where the gender of father or mother is not the point, rather the parental compassion which redeems Judah is developed (Isa 63:8). Perhaps this multigendered language helps to balance the patriarchal emphasis of the OT to show that as a spirit-being God is actually beyond gender but comforts as a mother. However, most of these passages boldly develop Yahweh as mother to Israel in female gendered ways, and that should not be diminished by patriarchy, nor trans-gendered patterns. Yahweh presents self as mother and there is an important place for believing God's words.

REDEEMER

The idea of "redemption" (*g'l*) originates in family law—in recovery from indentured service or repurchase of property by the nearest kinsman so that the redeemed might live and work their land again (Lev 25:25-26, 47-55; Ruth 2:20; 3:9-12; 4:1-12).[74] Goldingay defines this familial concept of redeemer.

> A restorer (*gō'ēl*) is a member of the family who has the resources and capacity to come to the aid of another member of the family in need and is under moral obligation to do so. Yhwh agrees to be defined by that family relationship with Israel and the obligations it brings. Punishment cannot be the last word in this relationship.[75]

The second half of Isaiah strongly calls Yahweh "the Redeemer," while only one other prophet used this title, only once (Isa 41:14; 43:14; 44:6, 24; 47:4; 48:17; 49:7, 26; 54:5, 8; 59:20; 60:16; 63:16; Jer 50:34). Eichrodt developed Isaiah's concept of Yahweh Redeemer.

> Yahweh is the "*go'el*," the Redeemer, who is obligated to ransom his near of kin (Isa 43:3; 49:26; 60:16); the wife who has been visited with double the appropriate punishment needs to be appeased and encouraged to enable her to forget her misery (Isa 40:2; 54:6ff); Yahweh's love is the bestowing of a privilege which is bound to work out in the form of Israel's supremacy over other nations (Isa 43:4; 49:22ff; 52:4f; 60).[76]

Such a relationship is not one of equals, but it certainly is a personal one with intimacy.[77] This intimacy is sourced in the covenant which expresses divine election (Isa 14:1; 43:20; 49:7). Page Kelley explains, "To refer to the Lord as Israel's Redeemer means two things. First, it means that the covenant bonds that bind Israel to God and God to Israel are strong and intimate as family ties. Second, it means that no price is too great for God to pay for the redemption of His people (Isa 43:3-4; 54:5-8)."[78]

Israel was initially rescued by exodus from Egypt by Yahweh redeeming them (Isa 43:1; 63:9; Exod 15:13; Pss 77:16; 106:10). Such redemption (*g'l*) appears in parallel with the standard Deuteronomic exodus synonym

---

74. Blenkinsopp, *Isaiah 40–55*, 110–11.
75. Goldingay and Payne, *Isaiah 40–55*, 1:51.
76. Eichrodt, *Theology of the Old Testament*, 1:255.
77. Snaith, *Distinctive Ideas of the Old Testament*, 107.
78. Kelley, *Judgment and Redemption in Isaiah*, 59.

"ransom" (*pdh*; Deut 7:8; 9:26; 13:6; 15:15; 21:8; 24:18; Isa 35:9-10; 51:10-11; Jer 31:11; Hos 13:14). As redeemer, Yahweh formed Israel from the womb through exodus from Egypt and will redeem them from captivity in Babylon (Isa 44:24; 60:16). While there is some development in the first half of Isaiah (Isa 35:9-10 [*pdh*]), the emphasis in Isaiah for Yahweh redeeming (*g'l*; Isa 44:22-23; 48:20; 52:9) Israel has to do with Yahweh orchestrating the new exodus from Babylon in the second half of Isaiah (Isa 41:14; 43:14; 47:4; 48:17; 62:12; 63:4). Yahweh, the general, prophesied his redemption of Israel (Isa 44:6; 59:20). Yahweh called Israel as a forsaken wife in rebellion to redeem her back with his loyal love (Isa 54:5, 8; 63:4, 9). This makes Israel the redeemed of God (Isa 35:9; 51:10; 62:12; 63:4). Such a concept of holy redemption includes separating out a people, land, or whatever Yahweh touches as a distinct group experiencing the benefits of redemption. The responsibility of the redeemer was to see that the redeemed received full rights and privileges of their redemption. Yahweh has a legal relationship with Israel where he expressed his loyal love and pity (Isa 63:9). Such redemption provides Yahweh the opportunity to declare and demonstrate that he is the king (Isa 44:6). Yahweh redeems Israel by choosing Israel and demonstrating this redemption for all to see by bringing them back in a new exodus (Isa 49:7, 26; 60:16).

A frequent parallel statement with *g'l* is that of Yahweh as "savior" (*mwšy'*; Isa 60:16).[79] Yahweh is Israel's savior (Isa 43:3, 11; 44:26; 45:15, 21; 60:16). Isaiah speaks often of God's salvation (Isa 45:8; 46:13; 49:6, 8; 51:5-8; 52:7, 10). This is no surprise, for his very name "Isaiah" means "salvation of Yahweh," or as a verb "Yahweh saves." Yahweh promised to send a savior to deliver Israel (Isa 19:20). Though Yahweh is himself the savior, he gives Egypt and Cush over to Assyria-Babylon in the place of Israel to facilitate them in a new exodus (Isa 43:3; 45:15; 49:26; 63:8). In fact, there is no savior except Yahweh (Isa 43:11; 47:15). All will see Yahweh is the savior bringing about redemption for Israel (Isa 60:16). Ultimately, "Israel is saved by Yahweh with an everlasting salvation" (Isa 45:17). As savior, Yahweh demonstrates that he is incomparable (Isa 43:3, 11; 45:15, 21).

---

79. Blenkinsopp, *Isaiah 40–55*, 112.

CHAPTER 3

Sovereign's Attributes

YAHWEH IS DESCRIBED IN Isaiah as having superior attributes facilitating his reign. Unlike most modern theology texts that present attributes from mediaeval Greek or Latin topical lists, Isaiah operates within ancient Near Eastern categories that connect Yahweh with the context of: impending threat of captivity; a narrative for making sense of loss during this captivity; and renewal of Israel through a new exodus unto kingdom. Yahweh manifests himself as having the following characteristics: sovereign, holy, incomparable, living, righteous, jealous, wrathful, and loving This chapter will explore these attributes, which enable God to rule supremely. The character of a kingdom takes on the character of the king. So, these attributes not only praise God for his greatness but also reflect the character of his great kingdom over which he rules.

SOVEREIGN

Yahweh's sovereignty is an expression of his ability to rule in an ancient Near Eastern sense. Isaiah develops the fullest and most diverse statement of the sovereignty of God anywhere in the OT. Within the concept of sovereignty there are three foci of omniscience, omnipotence, and sovereignty will that are always together. These traits are particularly evident in the manner in which the sovereign knows, purposes, speaks, acts powerfully, and acts with respect to evil.

Yahweh is the only true God (Isa 45:14, 21). In this role he is the only source of truth (Isa 45:19), for he is the possessor of all wisdom and bestows it in a rich supply to those who fear him (Isa 28:29; 31:2; 33:6). Eichrodt affirms that Isaiah used "outstandingly powerful expressions for the divine knowledge that embraces everything without exception."[1] This knowledge extends to future events and to mundane affairs of his creature's lives. God hears and knows the situation before a person prays (Isa 37:4). He alone proclaims prophecy such that his understanding excels beyond what any other person can fathom (Isa 40:28). God is also the source for counsel and wisdom in farming (Isa 28:26, 29).[2] With such an exhaustive resource of wisdom within himself, no one can advise God (Isa 41:28).

The word *y's* is used in several of these instances, extending the concept of knowledge to purposing. One example of this word referring to Yahweh's purpose is found in Isaiah 14:24-27, which summarizes the theology for chapters 13-23.

> Yahweh almighty has sworn,
> "Surely, as I have planned, so it will be,
> And as I have purposed, so it will stand.
> I will crush the Assyrian in my hand;
> On my mountains I will trample him down.
> His yoke will be taken from my people,
> And his burden removed from their shoulders."
> This is the plan determined for the whole world;
> This is the hand stretched out over all nations.
> For Yahweh almighty has purposed,
> And who can thwart him?
> His hand is stretched out, and who can turn it back? (Isa 28:28)

In contrast with world powers, Yahweh is the only one to carry out these plans. However, his messianic ruler extends Yahweh's rule by joining him in these same abilities: as wonderful counselor he is able to establish wise plans, and as mighty God he is able to realize these plans (Isa 9:6).

Yahweh's sovereignty expressed itself in speaking "the word of God" as God's revelation to humans. The concept of God's self-disclosure to humans is an anthropomorphism which attempts to express the immeasurable God in a meaningful manner.[3] An exposé of Hebrew *dbr*, meaning "word" or "message," serves as the basis for the following remarks. Divine speech is

---

1. Eichrodt, *Theology of the Old Testament*, 2:184 describing Isa 41:22-24; 43:10-13; 44:6-8; Zech 4:10; and Job 28:24.

2. Yahweh's advice concerning farming includes: 1) leveling and breaking up the soil (Isa 28:24-25), 2) sowing seed in their respective separate places (Isa 28:25), 3) threshing of caraway and cumin with a rod (Isa 28:27), 4) threshing grain, done by driving wheels of a cart over it (Isa 28:28), and 5) after threshing the grain, grinding it to make bread (Isa 28:28).

3. Roehrs, "Theology of the Word of God," 262-63.

represented as an expression of the thinking and planning of Yahweh (Isa 19:17; 23:9; Jer 51:29; Amos 3:7). Yahweh is described as having a mouth which speaks his word (Isa 58:14). God's speaking is a real act providing his word (Isa 5:9; 8:11; 14:24; Jer 25:30; Amos 3:7–8). Yahweh's speaking occurs in a definite space and time (Isa 5:9; 16:13–14; 22:14; Jer 1:13; Ezek 3:12). Yahweh's speech serves as a polemic because, unlike with Yahweh, there is no speaking that comes from the gods (Isa 41:22–26; 43:9; Jer 10:5). However, for Israel to hear the word of Yahweh, they need to first open their eyes and ears to receive its message (Isa 50:4). Once they are made ready to perceive the message, the spirit of Yahweh can provide the message (Isa 61:1; 2 Sam 23:2; 1 Kgs 22:24; Joel 2:28; Zech 7:12; Neh 9:30; 1 Pet 1:11). Yahweh's thoughts and ways are infinitely higher than human expression, so they are not totally comprehended by the people (Isa 55:8–9). Yahweh's word is not spoken in secret (Isa 45:19). Yahweh speaks truth and it stands fulfilled (Isa 45:19, 23).

Yahweh's sovereignty is expressed in omnipotence. Yahweh is the mighty God (Isa 10:21), the mighty one of Israel (Isa 1:24; 10:34; 33:21; Gen 49:24; Ps 132:2, 5). Yahweh is able to do anything consistent with his nature. Yahweh is *šddy*, the "almighty" (MT emphasis) or "overpowerer crushing opposition" (LXX emphasis: συντριβὴ, Isa 13:6). As such, the Babylonian Talmud understood this reference to indicate the "self-sufficient one."[4] Yahweh's omnipotence is evident throughout his actions described in the book (Isa 40:26, 28). It is also stated in a simple manner as a merism Isaiah offered as a sign to Ahaz, "Ask Yahweh your God for a sign whether in the deepest depths or in the highest heights." That is, Ahaz could have any sign he wants because God is able to deliver it (Isa 7:11). The power of Yahweh stems from the fact that the whole world belongs to him.[5] Yahweh created everything (Isa 37:16). So, by contrast, Isaiah 40:22 describes Yahweh as omnipotently sovereign; humans are as grasshoppers in the presence of he who sits upon the circle of the earth.[6] Yahweh raised up nations to destroy other nations (Isa 13:3–4, 17). Yahweh whistled, and the Assyrians came as a rod in Yahweh's hand (Isa 5:26; 7:18; 10:5–11). Yahweh is swift and controls the timing concerning what is to be done (Isa 13:22). Yahweh is to be feared, for in one

---

4. B. Ḥag. 12a.
5. Vriezen, "Essentials of the Theology of Isaiah," 132–33.
6. The description of the earth in the Bible is not specific enough to identify it's shape definitely. In Isaiah 40:22 and Job 22:14 "circle of the earth" could mean an earthen disk, a sphere, or ellipsoid if it is taken to be synthetic parallelism, whereas if these verses are synonymous parallelism they describe a vault of the firmament. Both possibilities permit God to view the earth as small in comparison.

night he can save some and remove others (Isa 17:10, 12–14). Yahweh is the strong one who scatters his enemies (Isa 33:3).

Another description of Yahweh is that he is the rock. In the role as the rock he is a fortress of protection (Isa 17:10) continuing everlastingly and is thus worthy of human trust (Isa 26:4; 30:29). Yahweh is the sure foundation and thus the rich store for salvation, wisdom, and knowledge. As such, he is the only rock for these outcomes (Isa 44:8). The human response that permits an individual to receive what Yahweh provides is the fear of Yahweh (Isa 33:6). However, for the unbeliever Yahweh is a stone to stumble over as their destruction (Isa 8:14). Perhaps by extension, Yahweh lays in Zion a tested foundational cornerstone (MT: *mwsd*, "foundational cornerstone" or LXX: ἀκρογωνιαῖον, "capstone" or the crowning point) that is other than himself (Isa 28:16).[7] In the MT the word describes a stone for the foundation to support the walls and roof of a large structure, and thus the stone is costly, select, valued, and honored. The LXX shifts to "capstone" or the crowning point. Both metaphors are valued stones for the construction of the building by Yahweh. If people believe in this tested-stone, then their lives can be built without being disturbed by the earthquakes of life.

Yahweh's sovereign power is also seen in the anthropomorphisms "arm" and "hand." Yahweh's hand turns against the nations in judgment (Isa 1:25; 9:12, 17, 21; 10:4; 40:2). Yahweh's hand creates Israel and guarantees that they shall be redeemed (Isa 41:20; 60:21), for "you are my witnesses declares Yahweh, that I am God. Yes and from ancient days I am he. No one can deliver out of my hand. When I act, who can reverse it?" (Isa 43:12–13). The mighty King Yahweh comes to deliver and restore his people with power and his arm ruling for him (Isa 40:10). His military weapon-wielding arm stands for his strength and power (Isa 51:9; 63:12). Yahweh's arm delivers judgment upon the nations and salvation for Israel (Isa 51:5; 59:16; 63:5). Yahweh's arm is long enough and strong enough to save Israel. Such effectiveness in deliverance was demonstrated in the plague of darkness initiating the exodus and in the Red Sea crossing (Isa 50:2–3; Exod 10:21–29; 14:21–31). "Yahweh will lay bare his holy arm in the sight of all the nations and all the ends of the earth will see the salvation of our God" (Isa 52:10).

The potter-clay motif develops the same sovereignty theme with intimate involvement by Yahweh. Brueggemann develops, "Yahweh as potter does a 'hands-on' crafting of the object. It has often been noted that the verb *form* (*yṣr*) as it pertains to creation is not by dictum, but by actual

---

7. The ambiguity of the referent in this passage has fostered views of the cornerstone being: Jerusalem, Hezekiah, a remnant, confidence in the land, and Christ (Young, *The Book of Isaiah*, 2:301–3). First Pet 2:6–8 identified Isa 28:16 as referring to Christ in parallel to Isa 8:14 and Ps 118:12.

engagement with the raw stuff (clay) out of which the object is formed (Gen 2:7, 19; Jer 18:3–6; Isa 45:9)."[8] With intimate creating, the potter has the absolute right to do as he pleases with the pottery he makes (Isa 29:16; 45:9; 64:8; Rom 9:19–24). There is no place for Yahweh's creation to question their creator as to why he has made them the way that they are. Yahweh is sovereign.

Yahweh has power for evil or destruction (Isa 19:14; 29:10). Yahweh's "spirit" or "wind" or "breath" (*ruaḥ*) is like the hot, dry sirocco wind from the desert that in one afternoon dries out and destroys fragile vegetation, thus called "evil" or "destruction" (*rʿ*, Isa 40:7; 45:7).[9] Parallel to Yahweh's destroying with wind or covenant curse is Yahweh sovereignly creating blessing. Eichrodt states that this view of evil spirit "is distinguished from that of paganism by the fact that the evil spiritual power is subordinated to the punishing God, and does not appear as an unpredictable demonic being, operating independently."[10] There is no rival to God nor dualism because Yahweh creates evil (*rʿ*) particularly in the form of disaster or calamity due to judgment (Isa 45:7). This evil fostered by spirit expressed itself in Isaiah by hardening Israel with spiritual drunkenness and deep comatose sleep (Isa 19:14; 29:10). As God told Isaiah, "Make the heart of this people calloused; make their ears dull and close their eyes" (Isa 6:10). As such, every word the prophet uttered made Israel wiser in their own eyes and more determined not to repent, thus hastening judgment.[11] While Yahweh hardens hearts, he is nowhere guilty of sin. The individuals who are hardened are responsible for their sin; they are universally condemned in judgment throughout the book. Reflecting this culpability, Isaiah 63:17 says Yahweh hardens Israel's heart and thus permits[12] them to wander from his ways until they shall be redeemed. Furthermore, Yahweh who inflicts the wounds is also the healer who brings them back (Isa 30:26).

However, especially in non-creation narrative accounts, Yahweh reacts to human choices of rebellion. So, the divine response is reactive to the human initiation in the context. In such relational settings, Yahweh presents himself in a self-restrained relationship, as Goldingay develops.

---

8. Brueggemann, *Theology of the Old Testament*, 277.

9. Similar to *Enuma Elish* table 1, lines 105–10, in Hays, *Hidden Riches*, 50–51; Eichrodt, *Theology of the Old Testament*, 2:55; 1 Sam 16:14; 18:10: 19:9; Judg 9:23.

10. Eichrodt, *Theology of the Old Testament*, 2:55.

11. Kaiser, *Isaiah 1–12*, 83; Eichrodt, *Theology of the Old Testament*, 2:178.

12. Permissive *Hiphil*: Waltke and O'Connor, *Introduction to Biblical Hebrew Syntax*, 445–46, Item 27.5; Williams, *Hebrew Syntax*, 31, Item 170.

It has been the story of a wrestling match with one of the partners having absolute power to overwhelm the other, but fighting with one arm tied behind his back, refraining from exercising that absolute power. It has taken up the wrestling match God fought with the original Israel, with whom God also fought in that self-restraining way.[13]

HOLY

Oswalt elevates these themes of sovereignty and holiness together in the holy divine king.

> In no other biblical book are the wonder and grandeur of the biblical God so ably displayed. This should not be surprising when we think of the vision which was vouchsafed to Isaiah at the opening of his ministry. Certainly throughout this book which bears his name God is "high and lifted up" (6:1). He is the "Holy One," and "the whole earth is full of his glory" (6:3). This awareness of divine majesty shapes every presentation of God.[14]

"Holy" (*qds*) is an ontological metaphysical category that means "separate."[15] This system of holy develops categories always applicable to the cult and the divine.[16] In Akkadian, *qadasu* and *qadistu* are synonyms to "clean" or "pure," while *qadsutu* means "holy as set apart to god."[17] In Ugaritic, *qds* means holy ontologically within the categories pertaining to god, such as shrine, priest, and cult prostitute.[18] Even the biblical concept retains *qds* as including Canaanite temple prostitutes as holy or set apart for their pagan worship (Gen 38:21–22; Deut 23:17). So, *qds* is not about

---

13. Goldingay, *Old Testament Theology*, 1:648.

14. Oswalt, *The Book of Isaiah: Chapters 1–39*, 1:32; Goldingay, *Isaiah*, 8 charts Yahweh as holy at the center of the book.

15. Neusner and Chilton, "Sanders's Misunderstanding of Purity," 205, 208, 211; Jackie Naudé, "קָדֹשׁ," in *NIDOTT & E* 3:877; Thomas McComiskey, "קָדַשׁ," in *TWOT* 2:786; W. Kornfeld, "קָדֹשׁ," in *TDOT* 12:522; Gammie, *Holiness in Israel*, 9–11; Jan Wilson, "*Holiness*" and "*Purity*," in *Mesopotamia*; *Sifra Qedošim Pereq* 11.21; *Šemini Pereq* 12.3.

16. Vriezen, "Essentials of the Theology of Isaiah," 132; Neusner, *History of the Mishnaic Law of Holy Things*, esp. 1:17.

17. Jackie Naudé, "קָדֹשׁ," in *NIDOTT & E* 3:878; Thomas McComiskey, "קָדַשׁ," in *TWOT* 2:787; W. Kornfeld, "קָדֹשׁ," in *TDOT* 12:523–24.

18. Jackie Naudé, "קָדֹשׁ," in *NIDOTT & E* 3:878; Thomas McComiskey, "קָדַשׁ," in *TWOT* 2:787; W. Kornfeld, "קָדֹשׁ," in *TDOT* 12:524–25.

morality but is an ontological category of being identified in relationship to God as separate or sacred.

The antonym to holy is "common" (ḥl, Lev 10:10; 1 Sam 21:4-5; Ezek 22:26; 44:23).[19] At times common can be identified with unclean as a synonym (Lev 10:10; Ezek 22:26; 44:23). However, ḥl does not mean unclean because at times only clean objects are contemplated, and the holy clean object is designated as distinct from the common clean object. The term *common* (ḥl) usually occurs in comparisons designating what is not holy as set apart as that which is holy (qds). For example, in Ezekiel's temple there will be a five-foot wall built around the temple court marking off that holy area around the temple from the common area farther out (Ezek 42:20). Likewise, within the clean land a special area is ultimately set apart for the priests to dwell in as holy for their dwellings, and a smaller portion is for common use near their dwellings (Ezek 48:11–12, 14–15). These are all the instances where ḥl is used in the biblical text, which illustrates that qds does not really mean separate from a lesser level (as Rudolf Otto's *numinous* developed[20] probably more reflective of a Kantian *noumena* metaphysical idea and followed by Mircea Eliade's sociological dualism informed by broad international religious practice[21]). Instead, qds means separate to its ontological level of being. These levels of being are separated to God as a part of a chain of being in their appropriate closeness to God.

Holy (qds) means "separate as in a level of being."[22] The supreme example of holiness of being is that Yahweh is himself holy and thus defines the standard of what holiness means, separate to his category of being (Isa 5:16; 6:3; 57:15; Lev 11:44; 19:2; Num 20:12–13; 27:14).[23] "Holy" (qds) is even used as a synonym for the divine name (Isa 40:25). As "Holy One of Israel," God demonstrates himself as holy in judgment (Isa 1:4; 5:16, 24; 30:11; 31:1; 37:23; 47:4) and salvation (Isa 10:20; 12:6; 17:7; 29:19; 30:15; 40:25; 41:14, 16, 20; 43:3, 14–15; 45:11; 48:17; 49:7; 54:5; 57:15; 60:9, 14). All that is Yahweh is holy. He has: a holy arm (Isa 52:10; Ps 98:1), a holy word (Ps 105:42), and a holy spirit (Isa 63:10–11; Ps 51:11). All that holy Yahweh touches is holy: the holy city (Isa 52:1), the holy mountain (Isa 57:13; Exod

---

19. Donald J. Wiseman, "חָלַל," in *TWOT* 1:289–90; D. F. O'Kennedy, "חָלַל," in *NIDOTT & E* 2:146–47; W. Dommershausen, "חָלַל," in *TDOT* 4:410–17.
20. Otto, *The Idea of the Holy*.
21. Eliade, *The Sacred and the Profane*.
22. Kennard, *Biblical Covenantalism*, 1:259–67.
23. Olyan, *Rites and Rank*, 17.

19:33), holy day (Isa 58:13), holy people Israel (Isa 11:9; 62:12; Ezek 28:22, 25), holy house (Isa 63:15; 64:11)[24] with holy courts (Isa 62:9; Ezek 42:20).

The central passage to illustrate Yahweh as holy is Isaiah chapter 6. Here Yahweh's holiness is in close connection to his kingship. In contrast to the temporality and frailties of human rulers dying, Yahweh transcends far above them in his continuing reign on the heavenly throne (Isa 6:1-2). The vision is so lofty that Isaiah does not describe Yahweh himself but rather focuses on his regal glory with his holiness. Such regal glory is the "weighty majesty" (MT) and "splendor" (LXX) attendant upon the manifestation of God. The *seraphim*[25] (literally, "glowing ones") accentuate Yahweh's separateness by calling out in triplet "holy" which should be understood as a Hebraic metaphor for the supremacy of holiness: "Holy, holy, holy is Yahweh of hosts" (Isa 6:2-3).[26] This later term for Yahweh, "*Sabaoth*," indicates that he is the "General of his armies." The *seraphim* are part of the courtiers and guards within these armies of Yahweh Sabaoth. In such a reign and as executor of his warfare, Yahweh is supremely holy. Furthermore, the *seraphim* picture Yahweh's holiness by covering their feet and faces with their wings. Covering the feet probably includes a euphemism for covering private parts,[27] especially since no *cherubim* in the ancient Near East has been presented as wearing any clothing. After seeing the vision, Isaiah's first utterance emphatically declares Yahweh to be the king (Isa 6:5) as Isaiah recoils in terror, confessing his uncleanness and sin. Such fear and reverence are the proper human response when confronted with the holiness of Yahweh (Isa 6:2-3, 5; 8:13). Yet it shows that while holiness is not essentially purity or morality, it can raise ritually appropriate issues like uncleanness, and the related issue of Isaiah's sin. Isaiah's confession raised the issues within the relationship among holy, clean, and righteousness. Isaiah is intimately aware of his own sin and the sin of Israel, and the gulf of their uncleanness which these cause between them and Yahweh's holiness. Yahweh's holiness graciously extends to Isaiah a glowing coal carried by a glowing one (*seraph*)

---

24. Temple Scroll (11Q19-21, 4Q524, 4Q365a) 35.8-9; 46.9-12; 52.19.

25. Possibly the same as "living creatures" and *cherubim* (Isa 37:16; Ezek 1:5, 13-22; 3:13; 10:1-22; 11:22; Rev 4:6-9; 5:6; 6:1, 6; 7:11; 14:3; 15:7; 19:4). There is no evidence for Trinity in Isaiah based on comparisons with: *Ascen. Isa.* 1 "Beloved" or angel of Holy Spirit, nor Origen, *Fr. Prin.* 3.4 allegorical interpretation of *seraphim* fused with the statement of "holy, holy, holy"; contra Hannah, "Isaiah's Vision in the Ascension of Isaiah."

26. Second Temple Judaism continues to see God's holy dwelling in heaven (1QH 3.34; 1QM 12.1-2; 1QS 10.3; 1QSb 4.25).

27. Kaiser, *Isaiah 1-12*, 76; Leupold, *Exposition of Isaiah*, 1:136.

for the purpose of cleansing and forgiveness, much like the Akkadian lip purification ritual purported to accomplish.[28]

With such cleansing and forgiveness obtained through an alternative to sacrifice, Isaiah no longer has terror before Yahweh. What is left is the fear of Yahweh that results in obedience without a fear of others (Isa 6:7–8; 8:12–13; 29:23). When Yahweh called for his messenger, Isaiah quickly responded.

The message he was to declare as the messenger of the king was to harden Israel's heart, drawing the contrast further between Yahweh and his people. There is a strong contrast between the author Isaiah receiving vision insight and forgiveness (Isa 1:1; 6:7; 29:7) and God blinding the people in their rebellion to prepare them for judgment (Isa 6:9–12).[29] The end result of this activity would speed Yahweh's judging holiness to destroy rebellious Israel.

When holy Yahweh established a relationship with Israel, this relationship and Yahweh's personal holy presence demand Israel to be holy as well: "You shall be holy for I Yahweh your God am holy" (Lev 19:2; 11:44–45). Yahweh's holiness separates Israel to be metaphysically separate: "Thus you are to be holy to me, for I Yahweh am holy; and have set you apart from the peoples to be mine" (Lev 20:26). To enter into Yahweh's presence and to continue in Yahweh's presence as a relationship involving his benefits requires Israel to be holy (Exod 19:10, 14; Lev 11:44–45; 19:2; 20:7; Num 11:18; Josh 3:5; 1 Sam 16:5; Joel 2:16; Isa 6:5). While holiness essentially is occupying a separate metaphysical level, it shows itself by doing distinctive deeds reflecting holiness, because each metaphysical level is separate for a purpose which reflects its level. To Israel, Yahweh commands, "You shall consecrate yourselves therefore and be holy for I am Yahweh your God and you shall keep my statutes and practice them; I am Yahweh who sanctifies you" (Lev 20:7–8). Obedience to a morality does not render Israel holy, but because they are separated by God to a relationship with him, the implication for Israel is that they should obey his standards. The context develops in which specifics identify Israel as set apart to Yahweh, such as faith (Deut 32:51), or not profaning Yahweh's name (Lev 22:32), or being ready to be involved in Yahweh's sacrifices (1 Sam 16:5). Israel's obedience in the Mosaic

---

28. Hurowitz, "Isaiah's Impure Lips," esp. the sources mentioned on 49 n. 26.

29. Carroll, "Blindsight and the Vision Thing." Unfortunately, generations later during Jesus' ministry, Israel was still filling out this pattern of blindness so that Jesus' parabolic ministry also prepared them to be swept into judgment under the Romans, and such Jewish blindness becomes a justification for Paul's gentile ministry (Matt 13:13–17; Mark 4:11–13; Luke 8:10; John 12:39–41; Acts 28:24–28; Evans, "Isaiah 6:9–13 in the Context of Isaiah's Theology").

covenant is with regard to holiness, and the whole of the Mosaic covenant command system (such as the Decalogue) is dependent upon and contained within holiness (Lev 19:2–37).[30] Furthermore, each respective group in relationship with Yahweh reflects appropriate standards which Yahweh tailors for them. For example, the Levites set themselves apart for their duties (1 Chr 15:12; 2 Chr 30:17; 31:18).

Holiness does not mean moral purity. For example, the garments that Aaron wore set him apart as the high priest, and yet garments have no intrinsic moral value—thus, amoral holiness (Exod 28:3). Yahweh is the one who set Israel apart by his choice—not their works or lifestyle, but holiness beneath morality (Exod 31:13). An Israelite's separation could be defiled by a man dying close to him, evidencing no immorality on his part, though he must start his separation again—amoral reduction of holiness to common (Num 6:11). The concept of morality is easily read into a passage like 2 Samuel 11:4, but it should be understood to say Bathsheba had to wait for a time to be legally pure from the "uncleanness" of the sex act. The issue was not her recovery from the sin of adultery, for which the punishment was death. In this context, the word had not yet come concerning David's forgiveness. Therefore, Bathsheba is immoral and becoming holy through the cleansing process. Additionally, idolatry is immoral, yet the people are set apart for a sacred assembly for Baal—immoral holiness (2 Kgs 10:20). As an adjective, *qdš* refers to temple prostitutes separated to their pagan shrines for licentious Canaanite worship—immoral holiness (Gen 38:21–22; Deut 23:17).[31] Furthermore, the enemies of Judah were set apart by God for destruction and captivity—holy common immoral nations (Jer 6:4; 22:7; 51:27–28). Objects and times in themselves have no moral state, which further helps to clarify that holy (*qdš*) does not mean morality. For example, Exodus 28:38 says that the holy things separated by Israel have iniquity transferred to them by the sin of Israel but that a small gold plate on the priest's turban takes the iniquity away (Exod 28:36). Thus, the idea of "holy" (*qdš*) does not include moral purity because these amoral objects cannot be in iniquity and morally pure at the same time and in the same manner.

Likewise, time can be set apart as holy—amoral holiness. In the creation God set the Sabbath apart as holy in that he stopped his creative work for that day (Isa 58:13; Gen 2:3; Exod 20:11; 31:17) and then called Israel to likewise consider and treat the Sabbath as holy by stopping from their work (Exod 20:8–11; 31:13–17). Childs connects Sabbath with the tabernacle in

30. *Seder Eliyah Rab.* 145; *Sipra Qodashim* par. 1.1; *Lev. Rab.* 24.5; Milgrom, *Leviticus 17–22*, 1602–3.

31. Jackie Naudé, "קדש," in *NIDOTT & E* 3:878; Thomas McComiskey, "קדש," in *TWOT* 2:787; W. Kornfeld, "קדש," in *TDOT* 12:524–25.

the book of Exodus: "The first account of the tabernacle closes with the Sabbath command (31:12ff.); the second account of its building begins with the Sabbath command (35:1ff.) . . . The connection between the Sabbath and the tabernacle is therefore an important one."[32] This relationship is reflected within the holiness code, "You shall keep my Sabbaths and revere my sanctuary; I am Yahweh" (Lev 19:30).

INCOMPARABLE

Compared to Yahweh, the other kings in Isaiah are impotent and fleeting, for the only successful kings in Isaiah are Yahweh and his anointed. C. J. Labuschagne develops the idea of sovereign superiority as the incomparability of Yahweh.[33] Incomparability explores those qualities that distinguish Yahweh from other god concepts. Incomparability is a theme of polemic and an affirmation of loyalty in ancient Near Eastern documents, but no section has so prolonged a development and depth of polemic as does incomparable Yahweh in Isaiah 40–48.

Yahweh is the living and true God (Isa 37:4, 17; 57:15). Yahweh repeatedly said through the prophet, "I am Yahweh, there is none else, there is no God beside me" (Isa 45:5-6, 14, 18, 21; 44:6-8; 46:9). This stress on monotheism contributes to the incomparability theme in that there are no other existing gods, nor does Yahweh have an equal. For example, idols cannot be favorably compared to Yahweh for they are the work of men's hands and thus totally dependent upon humans for their existence and form (Isa 40:18-20; 44:9-20).

> Yahweh cannot be portrayed by an idol or by any likeness in the creation which he has made (Isa 40:18ff). Yahweh is Lord over the gods who are being represented in various forms (Isa 40:19-20). For this reason, he is incomparable. The worthlessness of the Babylonian gods is shown by the fact that they can be reproduced in various forms (Isa 40:25).[34]

Many of the ancient Near Eastern idols come from common trees which serve as a source for firewood, so the fact that part of the wood is burned and another part is worshiped is completely absurd (Isa 44:14-20).[35]

---

32. Childs, *The Book of Exodus*, 541; Gammie, *Holiness in Israel*, 20, agrees.
33. Labuschagne, *Incomparability of Yahweh*.
34. Mihelic, "Concept of God," 36.
35. Holter, *Second Isaiah's Idol Fabrication*.

These idols are of no significance. Vos recognized that Isaiah identified such idols as "godlets" or "good-for-nothing-ones."

> Isaiah has a sarcastic term for naming the idols, *'elihim*; this, though not of the same terminology as *el*, yet reminds of it, but by making out of the word a diminutive, represents the pagan gods as "godlets," or (etymologically taken) as "good-for-nothing-ones." The false god fails to measure up to the conception of full deity (Isa 2:8, 18, 20; 10:10ff; 19:1, 3; 31:7; [40:18–20; 41:6–7, 28–29; 44:9–20; 45:16–20; 46:1–2, 5–7]).[36]

In this same vein, Yahweh calls the idol worshipers before him in judgment (Isa 41:21–24). In his accusation he demonstrates they are unable to do that which is characteristic of deity. Then, Yahweh further demonstrates that the idols are unable to do anything at all: "Do something, whether good or bad" (Isa 41:23). Yahweh concludes concerning these false gods that they are nothings; they do not exist. In fact, Isaiah identifies that the false gods are "empty winds" or "farts" (Isa 41:29; 26:18). Which means that these false gods cannot accomplish anything. "You are less than nothing and your works are utterly worthless. He who chooses you is detestable" (Isa 41:24). From this basis the idol worshipers should be ashamed. Those who make idols are nothing (Isa 44:9). They are ignorant, with blinded eyes and a deluded heart (Isa 44:18–20).

Isaiah utilized graphic language in Isaiah 46:1 for "Bell bent down; Nebo is stooping." The polemic is against the Babylonian god Bell, which is equivalent to Marduk, and Nebu or as LXX reads Dagon, Marduk's son (Isa 46:1 LXX; Jer 50:2). The verb *krʿ* means "bend the knee," as in military conquest (Isa 45:23; 65:12) or religious prostration (1 Kgs 8:54; 19:18; Ps 95:6) or collapsing in death (Isa 10:4; 65:12; Judg 5:27).[37] The LXX interprets it to mean "was shattered" (συνετρίβη). Such collapse had occurred historically before when the idol Dagon fell and was shattered before the ark of the covenant (1 Sam 5:2–7). Rashi and the Talmud understood this reference in Isaiah 46:1 to be that the Babylonian gods defecated upon themselves, not able to reach the toilet as they were utterly conquered by Yahweh.[38]

Yahweh is incomparable over time-bound idols in that Yahweh reaches beyond time and is everlasting with time. The "lasting God" Yahweh is the first and the last, before whom no being was formed and after whom nothing

---

36. Quote is from Vos, *Biblical Theology*, 236; with Oswalt, *The Book of Isaiah*, 1:123 adding the texts in brackets; also "worthless ones" (Zech 11:17; Job 13:4).

37. Goldingay, *The Message of Isaiah 40–55*, 302; Goldingay and Payne, *Critical and Exegetical Commentary*, 2:70.

38. *B. Meg.* 25b; Goldingay and Payne, *Critical and Exegetical Commentary*, 2:70.

will exist (Isa 40:28; 41:4; 43:10–16; 44:6; 48:12). As the "first," Yahweh is identified as the creator.[39] In Isaiah, the description of Yahweh as "creator" does not stand alone as a separate attribute or creation act, for creation in Isaiah is always connected to re-creation unto kingdom, thus the "last."[40] When first extends to the last, there is a bounding of time coupled with his consistent sovereign intervention in history leading to a concept of immutability in his nature.[41] Westermann clarifies that "what is expressed here is not the permanence of an always existent divine being, but the contrast between god and history in its totality ('and with the last I am still he')."[42] This contrast includes a strong polemic against all other gods who eventually cease to exist. The merism (first and last) declares that Yahweh is the only God who is from everlasting to everlasting, thus permeating beyond the whole of time (Isa 43:10). In contrast, in Mesopotamia, Egypt, and Canaan, the gods grew old, and younger ones came along and replaced them. There is no hint in Isaiah of Yahweh aging and becoming irrelevant. The declarations of Yahweh's transcendence over the world and time provided a basis for comfort within Judah's captivity.

> Men only learned to value Yahweh as the eternal, immortal God, when they had brought home to them in the most painful manner the transience of the nation, an experience which caused many to question even the living power of the national God. During the Exile, therefore, there are frequent references to the eternal God, whom the stars obey, and before whom this fleeting world cannot tremble (Isa 40:28; 60:19); to the everlasting King, who puts the false gods to shame; to the eternal Governor, exalted over the world and time (Isa 26:4). With this intense emphasis on the transcendence of God eternity was also naturally included within his attributes.[43]

A further question underscores that Yahweh has no rival: "What counselor has informed him?" (Isa 40:13). Whybray argued that likely an assembly of heavenly beings, perhaps *seraphim*, could provide such counsel for Yahweh.[44] Oswalt and Oosting answer him that in this context there is more likely a consistent polemic that Yahweh does not utilize any counsel

---

39. Stuhlmueller, "'First and Last' and 'Yahweh-Creator.'"

40. von Rad, "Theological Problem," 131–43, esp. 134; Goldingay, *Old Testament Theology*, 1:79.

41. Eichrodt, *Theology of the Old Testament*, 1:192.

42. Westermann, *Isaiah 40–66*, 65.

43. Eichrodt, *Theology of the Old Testament*, 1:183.

44. Whybray, *The Heavenly Counsellor*, 80–81.

as a further metaphor of incomparability.⁴⁵ Yahweh later answers his own question that he does not utilize counsel: "I Yahweh have planned it and I will bring it to pass" (Isa 46:11).

Christopher North even defends that Yahweh is contemporary with all history.⁴⁶ What is being considered is not theological aseity (a Greek concept of eternity in which a simple divine existence is mystically beyond the heavenly forms). In Hebrew concepts, history had a beginning in a creation and it would have a consummation in judgment and kingdom. Yahweh stands apart from this linear time in a different dimension, which allows him to extend beyond the bounds of time and exist during time. This would not be an Einsteinian dimension such as space-time, for such space-time would still be in real history.⁴⁷ Rather, Isaiah utilized a new spiritual dimension in a conceptual manner of thinking.⁴⁸ That is, Yahweh's involvement with time is not the same as the concept of time which humans possess. Isaiah used mixed tenses, which seem to imply that the present and future are all present to Yahweh. North explores this concept with passages such as Isaiah 48:4–5 which says, "I *knew* how stubborn you *are*" and "therefore I told you long ago," before the nation existed.⁴⁹ No eternity of Yahweh is worked out in detail, but there are a few hints that advance beyond the continuity of everlasting time for Yahweh. Yahweh is contemporary with all history. "Ever since anything came to pass, there am I" (Isa 41:4; 48:16).

Yahweh is creator of everything.⁵⁰ One expression of his creator role is that he is the only one that "stretches out the heavens" as a tent (Isa 42:5; 44:24; 45:12; 51:13, 16; Ps 104:2).⁵¹ Isaiah 40:22 identifies that God then sits in this heavenly tent. Goldingay develops this sacred tent as God's dwelling to look down on humanity as insects and to sovereignly act in the world.⁵²

---

45. Oswalt, *The Book of Isaiah: Chapters 40–66*, 2:59–60; Oosting, "The Counselor of the Lord," though he considers the counselor might be Yahweh's own spirit (362–64) and perhaps a literary analogy following Job 28:27 (370).

46. North, *The Second Isaiah*, 180–81.

47. Kennard, *Classical Christian God*, 43–62; Cullmann, *Christ and Time* demonstrates that 'wlm and αἰώνιος mean temporally "everlasting."

48. A new dimension such as is discussed by Wittgenstein, *Philosophical Investigations*; Abbott, *Flatland*; Kuhn, *Structure of Scientific Revolutions*.

49. North, *The Second Isaiah*, 180–81.

50. Stuhlmueller, "Theology of Creation in Second Isaias"; Norman Häbel, "Yahweh, Maker of Heaven and Earth."

51. *Ex. Rab.* 29.6 identifies that no one pitches the heavenly tent on God's behalf, for only he is able to do so.

52. Goldingay, *The Message of Isaiah 40–55*, 56.

Brueggemann identifies that in creating, sovereign Yahweh brings order, blessing, and peace to his creation.

> The God who creates (*br'*, *'sh*, *qnh*, *dbr*, *yṣr*) is the one who can transform any circumstance of chaos into an ordered context where fruitfulness, blessing, prosperity, and well-being are obtainable. The verbs of creation refuse to accept as a given any situation of death and disorder.[53]

Yahweh is also the creator in ways that show his incomparable superiority. For example, Babylon had gods associated with sun (*Shamash*), moon (*Sin*), and all planets and stars were identified with named deities who purportedly governed different aspects of life, be it national, royal, natural, or daily life. In this polemical challenge Yahweh alone creates all the heavenly objects which had been taken to symbolize Babylon's pantheon (Isa 42:5; 44:24; 48:12–13; Ps 89:11–13). Then Isaiah develops Yahweh's sovereignty over them in leading them forth, naming them, and bestowing on them his vigor and strength, which leaves no star lacking (Isa 40:25–26; Ps 147:4). Blenkinsopp developed that Isaiah is bold in affirming that the God of the captive people "created the heavens (Isa 42:5; 45:18), sun, moon, stars, and constellations (Isa 40:26; 45:12)"[54] whom the captors worshiped as gods. Yahweh spread out the sky by his handbreadth (*tpḥ*; Isa 40:22; 42:5; 44:24; 45:12; 51:13, 16) or span (*zrt*; Isa 40:12), meaning the Babylonian astronomical calculations ultimately depend upon Yahweh.[55] Likewise, the huge creator Yahweh measures out all the seas in the hollow of his hand, polemicizing other deities in the Babylonian new year's festival (Isa 40:12).[56] While in this *Akitu* festival *Shamash* demonstrated lordship by weighing the earth and heavens in a balance,[57] Isaiah describes Yahweh demonstrating his incomparability by utilizing the same balance scales, but now the earth, hills, and humans are but "dust on scales" or as small as grasshoppers (Isa 40:12, 15, 22; 29:5). So, the creation doesn't count against God's presence at all. Yahweh alone is creator of light and darkness (Isa 45:7), the earth (Isa 40:28; 45:18), and humans (Isa 27:11; 40:28; 44:24; 45:12). This means that

---

53. Brueggemann, *Theology of the Old Testament*, 207.

54. Blenkinsopp, *Isaiah 40–55*, 193.

55. Blenkinsopp, *Isaiah 40–55*, 293.

56. Babylonian Akitu festival describes Bel-Marduk measuring the waters in rearrangement, not initial creation (*ANET*, 309, 2.333 and 332, 2.240–41; Hanspeter Schaudig, "Bēl Bows, Nabu Stoops!"; Baltzer, *Deutero-Isaiah*, 67).

57. *Hymn to Shamash*, line 22; *ANET*, 387b; Lambert, *Babylonian Wisdom Literature*, 126–27, 319; Goldingay, *The Message of Isaiah 40–55*, 36; and maybe some parallels with Egyptian and Persian traditions (Smith, "II Isaiah and the Persians").

Yahweh is sovereign as the potter is for the potsherd and as parents are for their baby (Isa 45:9-10).

Thus, Yahweh is in absolute control of all things (Isa 45:5-13); there is no other god. John Oswalt develops that through creation Yahweh identifies himself as more ultimate than any pagan deity whose claim for control is only in rearranging things.

> For Isaiah, the doctrine of creation is fundamental. As Maker of the world, God has the right to determine its direction, and moreover, he does have a direction in mind for it. This is not so for the pagan gods. Although those religions can speak of beginnings, their polytheism and their heavy involvements with the social and natural status quo prevent them from speaking of noncontingent, purposive creation. It is this which Isaiah has in mind in the numerous attacks on the idols in chs. 40-48 (41:21-24; 42:8-9; 43:8-9; 44:7-8; [45:12, 18; 46:9-11; 48:6-7, 12-13] etc.). The gods do not know the origin of things and they do not know the end. For the pagan mind, beginnings are theoretical and endings are all but unthinkable. The continuance of the present is all it knows. Nor is the emphasis upon creation limited to chs. 40-48. It appears here in ch. 29[:17] and also in 17:7, 8 (contrast between Maker and gods made with hands) and 37:16 (God, unlike the gods, made the earth; 6:3 [filling all the earth with his glory]).[58]

Yahweh as creator serves to identify that Yahweh is the one who intervenes in history (Isa 40:20, 25-31; 43:1, 7, 15; 45:7-25; 48:7, 12-13). This sentiment is expressed by Psalm 135:5-6, "Yahweh is great, and that our Lord is above all gods. Whatever Yahweh pleases he does, in heaven and earth." Only one with supreme creative power could comprehensibly direct the events of history and overcome all obstacles placed in the way of his people's salvation. More than any other prophet, Isaiah has a comprehensive conception of God's activity in the whole history of Israel. Yahweh's incomparable greatness over the rulers of the earth is evident in his transcendent throne being above the heavens in contrast to the temporary reign of earthly rulers (Isa 40:21-24). He uses these earthly rulers, such as Cyrus, to accomplish his purpose because he is the creator of all and none can oppose him (Isa 45:11-13; 51:12-16; 52:1-6). Yahweh is the only God and thus creates light and darkness, prosperity and disaster (Isa 45:5-7). In fact, the covenant curse calamity that sovereign Yahweh creates is experiential evil (r^c) for all who undergo it. There is no room for dualism or a

---

58. Oswalt, *The Book of Isaiah*, 1:536-37; Kennard added verses within brackets.

supposed rivalry, for Yahweh is sovereign over the whole range of options. John Mauchline emphasizes that Yahweh's victory over the nations demonstrates his supremacy in history: "If the impotence and untrustworthiness of Egypt had been demonstrated in this crises and the might of Assyria had been humiliated before the power of Yahweh, then there was no other god who could vie with him or pretend to share his supremacy."[59] Yahweh is he who intervenes in history, showing himself as the only supreme being; all other gods are impotent. Labuschagne pressed the impotence of idols even further in discussing Isaiah 46.

> It is interesting to note that the prophet regarded as the primary difference between Yahweh and the idols, the fact that Yahweh actively carries and saves (verse 4), while the idols have to be carried "as burdens on weary beasts" (verses 1 and 7), unable to save (verse 7; cf. 45:20), unable to move from their place (verse 7).[60]

In fact, Babylon's idols cannot save themselves from captivity (Isa 46:1–2). Yahweh the sustainer of Israel shall rescue Israel in the end (Isa 46:3–4). The idols cannot act, but Yahweh does what he pleases (Isa 46:5–11).

Yahweh not only controls history as it happens; he fulfills it before it occurs through his prophetic pronouncements. In Judaism, a prophet had to have complete accuracy in his prophetic pronouncements or he could be considered presumptuous, to which Israel was to respond with stoning the false prophet (Deut 18:17–22). This ability and requirement of complete accuracy leaves Yahweh as the only one who can predict the future accurately, even with details. Yahweh is thus supreme such that no one and nothing can be favorably compared with him. Labuschagne developed the extent of Yahweh's incomparability from Isaiah 49:9.

> Yahweh proclaims his incomparability: "I am God, and there is none like me, declaring the end from the beginning and from ancient times not yet done." For Deutero-Isaiah this quality of Yahweh affords clear proof that he is utterly distinct from the gods and that he is the only true God (cf. also 44:6 and 41:23). Yahweh's ability to declare the future, which Deutero-Isaiah associates with his incomparability (cf. also Jer 10:7), is consequent upon the fact that he has revealed himself as the all-wise Controller of history. Yahweh not only regulates human history, but also determines what is yet to be. Here we meet the idea of Yahweh's intervention in history carried to its ultimate

---

59. Mauchline, *Isaiah 1–39*, 39.
60. Labuschagne, *Incomparability of Yahweh*, 112.

conclusions, the most outstanding attribute of the incomparable God spanning past, present and future.[61]

Yahweh is the vocal God in contrast to dumb idols. Yahweh makes prophecy that is fulfilled both in the book and now in the historical record (Isa 46:9-10). Kenneth Barker explained that Yahweh's sovereignty is the dynamic reason why Yahweh can declare his incomparability, "since Yahweh's rule extends into the future—indeed, he reigns forever—he can predict what will happen (41:4; 43:10; 44:6-8; 45:21-22; 46:9-10)."[62] Yahweh puts the idols on trial and challenges them to produce fulfilled prophecy. The conclusion is that they are silent, unable to speak, let alone predict. Those idols are false gods (Isa 41:26, 28-29). Yahweh next takes up his own challenge.

> I am Yahweh; that is my name!
> I will not give my glory to another or my praise to idols.
> See, the former things have taken place, and new things I declare;
> Before they spring into being I announce them to you. (Isa 41:8-9)

The background for Yahweh's boldness is the fulfillment of the intricate prophecy throughout the book.

For example, Yahweh demonstrates his incomparability and supremacy by declaring that he will raise an anointed (messiah) king from the East named Cyrus, who will liberate his people Israel from the Babylonians (Isa 41:2-4; 45:1-7). This prediction does not claim Cyrus will be the new Davidic king because the concept of "messiah" or "anointed" does not require a one and only specific Davidic messiah but also can include priests (Lev 4:3; Dan 9:25), prophets, and other heavenly eschatological figures.[63] In this unique setting Yahweh anointed a king for a Gentile empire. Anointed Persian Cyrus succeeded his father as king in 559 BC, conquering Babylon in 539 BC and setting out an edict facilitating the return of a remnant of Jews to the land of Israel under Ezra's leadership during the 530s to rebuild the Jerusalem temple (Ezra 1:1-4; 2 Chr 36:22-23).[64] Josephus claims that

---

61. Labuschagne, *Incomparability of Yahweh*, 114.

62. Barker, "Toward a Theology of Satan," 8.

63. Anointed historical and eschatological priests (CD 7.18-20; 12.23-13.1; 14.19; 19.10-11; 20.1; 1QS 9.10-11; 1QSa 2.11-15; 4QFlor 1 11-12; 4Q175; 4Q541; *T. Levi* 18.2-5); anointed prophets (4Q521; Josephus, *Ant.* 20.97, 169-70); other eschatological figures (Pss. Sol. 17:32; 1QS 9.10-11; *1 En.* 48.10); contrary to Baltzer, *Deutero-Isaiah 40-55*, 225, and Fried, "Cyrus the Messiah?" 373, 390-93.

64. Cyrus Cylinder; *Nabonidus Chronicle*; Behistun Inscription; Herodotus, *Histories* 1.46-216; Xenophon, *Cyropaedia*; Josephus, *Ant.* 10.231-32, 247-48; 11.1-20; with dates provided by Steven Schweitzer, "Cyrus the Great," in Collins and Harlow, *Eerdmans Dictionary of Early Judaism*, 504-6.

Cyrus initiated this Jewish return in response to reading Isaiah's prophecies concerning him.[65] No other person could foretell the coming of Cyrus; only Yahweh was able to foretell his coming and make his victorious conquest of the nations possible.

The prophet's role is as the "seer" (*nb'*) called by Yahweh to be his "messenger" (*mlk*) and to speak for him. Isaiah and other human prophets are officers of the heavenly court sent out to Yahweh to tell his people the message in the same manner as an ancient Near Eastern royal messenger would.[66] Since Isaiah received the message from God, it was expounded with divine authority. Usually the message was quite clear and was communicated to the audience who needed to repent. At times reliable witnesses signed documents to increase the confidence that the prophecy was unforgeable and should be received in faith (Isa 7–8). When these statements are put in written form, they remain as diplomatic correspondence providing guidance or threatening devastation for a rebellious vassal if the vassal does not quickly comply with the suzerainty treaty stipulations. For example, the "Letter from Hattusili III of Hatti to Kadashman-Enlil II of Babylon" threatens Babylon with severe military campaign from the Hittites if they do not swiftly submit to the terms of the binding suzerainty treaty that they are violating.[67] The Isaiah text functions similarly to these diplomatic correspondences.

When the prophecy did not go to the group described within the prophecy (such as Isaiah's prophecy against Assyria or Babylon), then the prophecy is as good as accomplished within the textual terms when its time will come. In such conditions, judgment is certain. However, if the word of Yahweh is given directly to the person to be judged, then it contains an implied condition within the prophecy to be responded to with the outcome dependent upon the recipient's response. For example, Isaiah tells sick Hezekiah, "Thus says Yahweh, set your house in order for you shall die and not live" (Isa 38:1). Yet when Hezekiah turned his face to the wall and prayed to Yahweh, reminding Yahweh of his faithfulness and weeping bitterly, Isaiah was sent back to inform Hezekiah, "Thus says Yahweh, I have heard your prayer, I have seen your tears; behold I will add fifteen years to your life" (Isa 38:4–5). That is, what seemed unconditional as a prophecy was in fact conditional upon the response of the recipient's repentance. Furthermore, even within the dominant sovereignty of Yahweh, human engagement with Yahweh in fervent prayer can change what look to be certain future events.

---

65. Josephus, *Ant.* 11.5–7.

66. Holladay, "Assyrian Statecraft," 31.

67. An example is the "Letter from Hattusili III of Hatti to Kadashman-Enlil II of Babylon"; see #23 in Beckman, *Hittite Diplomatic Texts*, 138–39; Thompson, *The Book of Jeremiah*, 169.

A similar conditionality was implied when Jonah announced that Nineveh would be destroyed in forty days and, with Jonah acknowledging Nineveh's repentance, God's judgment did not come upon them (Jonah 3:4–10). However, much of the prophecy in Isaiah comes with the proviso that Israel will not be turned back from warnings of judgment (Isa 6:9–13). That is, though Isaiah had earlier offered redemption for his people without conquest and exile, what follows Isaiah 6 clarified that Israel was unresponsive, resulting in the certainty of impending captivity. The prophecy that came to Israel thereafter came with certain judgment, thus without any condition. The prophecy proclaimed against other nations, such as Babylon, gives no evidence of the other nations having received these messages either from a prophet directly or in written form, so they stand as unconditional prophecies from Yahweh.

Many would see that the concept of the divine word has empowerment inherent in the word. One of the author's professors, Isaac Rabinowitz, explained this view from Isaiah 55:10–11.

> The author of these verses obviously believed that the "word of the Lord"—a phenomenon, be it noted, comparable in palpability to rain or snow—was such that, once introduced ("sent") into the world, it had the capacity of acting to fulfill itself at some subsequent time, to make its communicative or expressive signification "come true" as accomplished fact.[68]

In this view, the word of God is power laden, which irresistibly achieves its end. Such a view of an empowered word is common among Israel's neighbors. For example, Marduk proves his kingship in heaven by speaking a word of power which annihilates a robe and then recreates it.[69] Additionally, in a hymn to the moon-god *Sin*, it is said, "When thy word settles down on the earth, green vegetation is produced . . . The word makes fat the sheepfold . . . The word causes truth and justice to be."[70] Likewise, an

---

68. Isaac Rabinowitz, *Toward a Valid Theory*, 319; Mowinckel, *The Spirit and the Word*, 90; Stuhlmueller, *Creative Redemption in Deutero-Isaiah*, 169–208; McKenzie, "Word of God in the Old Testament"; Fuerst, "Word of God in the Old Testament," 316; Grether, *Name und Wort Gottes*, 103–7, describes the word of God as a missile with a time fuse; Eichrodt, *Theology of the Old Testament*, 2:69, insists that the words, once spoken, remain effective or even dangerous "for a long time, like a long-forgotten mine in the sea, or a grenade buried in a ploughed field"; Jacob, *Theology of the Old Testament*, 127, speaks of God's word as a "projectile shot into the enemy camp whose explosion must sometimes be awaited but which is always inevitable"; O. Procksch, "The Word of God in the Old Testament," in *TDNT* 4:93; Roehrs, "Theology of the Word of God," 264; Thiselton, "Supposed Power of Words," 283.

69. *Enuma Elish* 4.22–26, in Hays, *Hidden Riches*, 49.

70. "Hymn to the Moon-god," in *ANET*, 386.

Egyptian hymn speaks of *Amon Re-Atum-Har-Ashti* speaking into existence all humans, gods, and animals.[71] Isaiah has similar speech concerning the power of Yahweh's word as a polemic against the silence of the idols and false gods (Isa 41:17–29; 42:9; 44:6–8; 45:4). Yahweh pronounces weighty declarations of judgment against nations (Isa 13:1; 14:28; 15:1; 17:1; 19:1; 21:1, 11, 13; 22:1; 23:1). These words of judgment overtake the group Yahweh addressed (Deut 28:15; Isa 9:8; Zech 1:5–6). This is similar to Yahweh striking the earth, setting it ablaze, and slaying the wicked with his breath or spirit (Isa 11:4; 30:33). What Yahweh says will be fulfilled because his purpose for destruction or deliverance is revealed through his speech (Isa 1:19–20; 21:16–17; 24:3; 25:8; 40:5; 44:24–28; 58:14) and he does not take back his word (Isa 31:2). Likewise, the sure word of divine promise (particularly about Yahweh's coming to deliver and restore his beleaguered people) will endure forever to be fulfilled (Isa 40:6–8). However, in Isaiah, the word is not an actual essence in itself but finds its effectiveness in the powerful will of God for which it is the audible expression, and thus together they change the course of history. The effectiveness of Yahweh's word rests upon God who stands behind his word and accomplishes it. This pattern is evident in Isaiah 48:3 where Yahweh speaks, "I foretold the former things long ago, my mouth announced them, and I made them known; then suddenly I acted, and they came to pass."

However, Yahweh announcing and informing in a context of deliverance also fits within a pattern that guarantees Israel's exodus (Isa 43:12 parallel to Exod 14:5, 30; 15:14).[72] Thus, this is a further polemic of the real God speaking in contrast to the Babylonian so-called gods.

Yahweh Sabaoth is the warrior par excellence. He takes the outfit of a warrior with the breastplate of righteousness, helmet of salvation, and garments of vengeance, and the cloak of zeal (Isa 59:16–17). With this preparation, incomparable Yahweh will be victorious over his enemies (Isa 42:13). Yahweh is the supreme sovereign warrior who conquers all opposition from the earliest beginning (Isa 51:9–10). He continues to bring judgment upon his enemies (Isa 59:18). Likewise, no opposition will be able to prevent Yahweh from bringing about salvation for Israel (Isa 52:10; 59:16; 63:5, 12).

It is Yahweh, as cloud rider and thus *the supreme incomparable divine king*,[73] who rides into war on his cloud chariot (Isa 19:1; Deut 33:26; Pss 18:10 [MT: 18:11]; 68:33 [MT: 68:34]; 104:3). He comes; the nations melt as

---

71. "Hymns to the Gods as a Single God," in *ANET*, 371, col. 2.

72. *Ex. Rab.* 29.5; Goldingay, *The Message of Isaiah 40–55*, 204.

73. Baal demonstrates he is the *high god* by riding the clouds (*UT* 51.11, 18; 68.8, 29, in *ANET*, 130–32).

he defeats Egypt, Assyria, and Babylon (Isa 13:2–5; 19:1–4). Ultimately with the victory won, Yahweh brings in his kingdom (Isa 63:1–6).

Isaiah's creation theology means that Yahweh is also the only one who can re-create the heaven and earth to salvifically make kingdom (Isa 40:28–31). As Carroll Stuhlmueller identified, this new creation is grounded in creation as "an *historical* act of God, accomplished upon the earth over the powers of *nature*," which extends to exodus, "a *personal* God who acts by the power of His word and so creates a new land of paradise for the *poor and lowly* who have been purified of their guilt (Isa 40:2; 42:18–22; 43:2–7)."[74] Stuhlmueller concluded, "To call creation a salvation-event at once imparts an eschatological quality to the first act of God; at the same time eschatology becomes the completion, the fulfillment or the goal of creation!"[75] Thus, incomparable Yahweh re-creates the universe into kingdom.

Yahweh is incomparable as the God who exists, predicts, acts, creates, intervenes in history, feels emotions deeply, judges the rebellious, and redeems his people into a re-created kingdom. Yahweh has no equal! No one even comes close!

LIVING

Probably a subcategory under incomparability is that God is the living God (*hyh*, Isa 37:4, 17; 49:18), which is synonymous to identifying that God is a soul (*nps*, Isa 1:14; 42:1). Both words (*hyh* and *nps*) combine to communicate that God is vibrant, active, and acts in the midst of human situations. God is the source of life originally (Gen 1:20–30; 2:7). Furthermore, special emphasis on the living (*hyh*) quality of God is developed within the former prophets of Samuel and Kings and the latter prophets of Jeremiah and Ezekiel, but Isaiah mentions that God is living to support his incomparability. Perhaps the precarious situations in Isaiah (and the obvious need to trust God) highlight God as alive to show that he can redeem Israel from any risk.

RIGHTEOUS

The Hebrew OT primarily expresses *ṣdk* as "righteousness," meaning "faithfulness to an acceptable order."[76] The acceptable order is usually a covenant

---

74. Stuhlmueller, "Theology of Creation in Second Isaias," 449, 453. Emphasis original.

75. Stuhlmueller, "Theology of Creation in Second Isaias," 464.

76. Kennard, *Biblical Covenantalism*, 1:285–89; not an allusion to a West Semitic deity (contra Whitley, "Deutero-Isaiah's Interpretation of *sedeq*") but Yahweh has these

order which God or a king established. Righteousness is thus very practical in habituating acts of doing right action in the right way (Isa 40:14). The word "righteousness" is in synonymous parallelism with terms such as salvation, light, glory, and peace (Isa 46:12; 51:5–8; 56:1; 59:9, 11; 61:3, 10; 62:1–2).[77] Antonyms to "righteousness" include a range of words for sin and rebellion.

Justice was to be the concern of righteous kings as attested with the ancient Near Eastern law codes such as Hammurabi's. Righteousness of the king was especially evident in protecting the poor and vulnerable from the rich and powerful who might be inclined to oppress them (Isa 10:1–4). Attributes which establish a king's throne included: loyal love, faithfulness, justice, and speeding the cause for righteousness (Isa 16:5). Laurence Toombs develops how these attributes overlap.

> Justice and love are paired as if they were virtually the same thing. How can this be? The ancient Near East considered the problem of justice as an aspect of power. The strong in society can be counted on to protect themselves, but at least some of the powerful exploit those who are in an inferior or less advantageous position. The function of law, quite simply stated, is to protect the weak, and justice is the spirit and apparatus by which this is done . . . Justice, therefore, localizes love and charts its course of action. It places love on the side of the oppressed, the weak.[78]

Consistent with this understanding, Jože Kraovec identified that in Isaiah 5:16, Yahweh's holiness and righteousness depicts the divine reign in kingdom, not punitive justice to establish his kingdom.[79] Wildeberger underscores this claim because "the Holy God shows himself holy through his righteousness."[80]

Yahweh is the righteous one (Isa 24:16; 26:7). He does righteous acts (Isa 30:18). God loves righteousness (Isa 61:8) and requires humans to be righteous (Isa 1:17; 56:1). Yahweh's righteousness is a factor in demonstrating his incomparability (Isa 45:21). God's righteous acts exalt himself and show himself to be holy (Isa 5:16). When Yahweh's holiness is manifest, his

---

covenantal traits as the section develops. Coste, *Righteousness in the Septuagint of Isaiah*.

77. Vos, *Biblical Theology*, 254.

78. Toombs, "Love and Justice in Deuteronomy," 406.

79. Kraovec, *La Justice (SDQ) de Dieu*, 79; Wildberger, *Isaiah 1–12*, 206; Watts, *Isaiah 1–33*, 61–62; von Rad, *Old Testament Theology*, 1:377; contrary to how Moberly ("Whose Justice? Which Righteousness?") over-pressed Rolf Rendtorff's generalization of the use of the word in parts of Isaiah ("Composition of the Book of Isaiah," 162).

80. Wildberger, *Isaiah 28–39*, 619.

righteousness is also present. Such a glimpse of righteousness confronts individuals and Israel with their sin (Isa 6:3-7). Knowledge of God prompts right action, for their ethic was grounded in their religion.

Yahweh's righteousness is the author of both judgment and salvation. Because he is righteous, he is the judge and accuser of sinful Israel (Isa 3:13-14). This divine righteousness brings judgment on sin (Isa 5:16; 10:22). He also hides his presence from sinful Israel (Isa 8:17; 30:18).

Yahweh's righteousness vindicates his people and the judges of other nations (Isa 41:10-11; 50:8; 51:5; 54:1, 14, 17; 59:16-17). Yahweh's righteousness results in salvation for his people (Isa 45:8). Saving righteousness can appear as an attitude or intension of God (Isa 46:4, 13), but it is objectified in acts outside of his person. The word "righteousness" occasionally is said in the plural, probably intensifying its reality or demonstrating that righteousness works out in many acts (Isa 45:24; Mic 6:5). Because Yahweh is supremely righteous, he makes the path of righteous humans smooth (Isa 26:7). Isaiah admits that righteousness from Yahweh will be provided to the one who serves him, as evident by the example of his servant (Isa 49:4). Eichrodt identifies that Isaiah develops that Yahweh will fill with justice and righteousness both Zion and the gentiles who align with them.

> He taught men to see the operation of Yahweh's righteousness in the redemption acts by which he proposed to restore the covenant people, and to this end he coupled the concept of righteousness with those of God's covenant, lovingkindness, loyalty and succor (42:6, 21; 45:8, 13; 46:13; 51:6). This righteousness might also take the form of judgment on the heathen (41:2, 10ff; 58:2; 59:16f; 63:1) . . . But the decisive element was that of God's gift of salvation, both to Israel and to the Gentile World (51:5; 45:24), through the setting up of the covenant.[81]

Yahweh is reigning now in righteousness, but there will be a day in which his kingdom will manifest his righteousness abundantly under the reign of the righteous Messiah (Isa 9:6; 11:3-5).

JEALOUS

Yahweh is a jealous God. The main word for jealousy (qn') can in some circumstances refer to zeal. The root is probably related to the Arabic word meaning to become intensely red (or black) with dye, and thus drawing

---

81. Eichrodt, *Theology of the Old Testament*, 1:246.

attention to the color produced in the face by deep emotion.[82] Such a jealousy "results in an intense hatred but it is concerned for others, it becomes a power capable of accomplishing the most noble deeds."[83] Half of the biblical uses of the word refer to God's jealousy, especially in Isaiah and Ezekiel. Eichrodt connects these instances of Yahweh's jealousy with his holiness using Johannes Hänel's coined term *"eiferheiligkeit"* (jealousy-holiness).[84] In this concept the separateness of Yahweh finds an intense expression in Yahweh's personality of a strong desire for the separateness of what is his (Isa 42:13; 59:17; Josh 24:19; Nah 1:2). The concept comes out of the covenant code (Exod 20:5; 34:14; Deut 5:9) in the establishing of a special relationship between Yahweh and his people, Israel.

Joyce Baldwin develops that Yahweh's jealousy also stems from his loyal love (Isa 63:15; 37:30–32); "God's jealousy is a measure of the intensity of his love towards those with whom He has entered into covenant. So great is His love that He cannot be indifferent if they spurn Him by disobedience or sheer carelessness."[85]

Yahweh, the king, warns against forgetfulness of allegiance to Yahweh, "for Yahweh your God is a consuming fire, a jealous God" (Deut 4:24; 6:15; 29:18–19; 32:16, 21). The fire of God's jealousy will be experienced in all kinds of calamities, culminating in the destruction of Israel at the hands of enemy armies (Deut 29:20–28). Worse than such forgetfulness is outright presumption and flagrant violation (Deut 29:19; Heb 6:10). Israel engaged in such flagrant rebellion and Yahweh divorced her into the Babylonian captivity (Deut 24:1, 3; Isa 50:1; Jer 3:8). Israel's alignment and public worship of pagan deities caused[86] Yahweh's jealousy (Isa 41:21–29; 43:10–12; 44:9–20).

In Isaiah, Yahweh's jealousy empowers his role as warrior as he avenges and saves (Isa 42:13; 59:17; 63:15). As warrior Yahweh delivers, Yahweh fulfills a related role of kinsman-redeemer (Isa 63:15–16). The results of Yahweh's jealousy include the destruction of his enemies (Isa 26:11; 42:13) and the salvation of a remnant from among Israel (Isa 37:32). Yahweh's jealousy and might is placed alongside his compassion in a prayer for Israel to their Father petitioning him to return to his needy people (Isa 63:15–16; Joel 2:18).

---

82. E. Reiter, "*qnʾ*," in *TDOT* 13:48; Baldwin, *Haggai, Zechariah, Malachi*, 101–2.

83. Baldwin, *Haggai, Zechariah, Malachi*, 102.

84. Eichrodt, *Theology of the Old Testament*, 1:210; Hänel, *Die Religion der Heiligkeit*, 49–50, 196–98.

85. Baldwin, *Haggai, Zechariah, Malachi*, 102.

86. Using the *Hiphil* of causation, E. Reiter, "*qnʾ*," in *TDOT* 13:55–56.

WRATHFUL

Yahweh's wrath grows out of his jealousy. This anger is the spontaneous feeling suddenly flooding through the life of a soul. Such wrath is the "normal manifestation of a conscious personality defending itself against the attacks of its environment, it signifies when applied to God, the emphatic personal character of the Deity."[87]

There is a multiplicity of expressions used for Yahweh's wrath. *Zā 'ap* describes the storming or raging of his anger (Isa 30:30).[88] *Ḥēma* builds off the verb *yāḥam* (to be hot), meaning anger or rage as a fire burning within.[89] *Ḥāron* expresses Yahweh's fierce anger occurring on the judgment day of Yahweh (Isa 13:9, 13).[90] *'ebra* is used in parallel with the previous word and generally means an overflow of anger or wrath.[91] *Qāṣap* is used of the general wrath which Yahweh presents against Israel because of their sin (Isa 47:6; 57:17; 64:5 [MT 64:4]).[92]

Some might view Yahweh in wrath as a vicious despot,[93] but there is a legitimate reason for his wrath. As king he needs to judge the sin of his creation. Such judgment is an expression of his righteous wrath. Yahweh is angry against his rebellious people, resulting in judgment and death (Isa 5:24-25). He grieves over their unrepentant revelry and non-trusting self-sufficiency, pronouncing judgment with no available recovering atonement (Isa 22:4, 11-14). Yahweh's wrath against rebellious Israel will not be appeased until they are swept into captivity and fully judged (Isa 5:25-30; 9:12, 17, 21; 10:4; 12:2). When this is accomplished, his wrath is redirected against Assyria and others who opposed his people Judah (Isa 13:3, 5; 30:31-32). The concept of the day of Yahweh has historical roots in these judgments but finds ultimate fulfillment in an eschatological tribulation (Isa 13:9-13; 24; 25:2-7; 26:20-21; 34:2).

The cup of God's wrath is one of the most graphic figures used to express God's wrath. Psalm 74:8 [MT: 74:9] describes it as "a cup in Yahweh's hand, with foaming wine, well mixed (with toxic ingredients), which Yahweh pours out its contents upon all the wicked of the world to drink from

---

87. Eichrodt, *Theology of the Old Testament*, 1:258.
88. BDB 277.
89. BDB 404-5.
90. BDB 354.
91. BDB 720.
92. BDB 893.
93. Eichrodt, *Theology of the Old Testament*, 1:265.

the cup until it is emptied to the dregs causing them to become demented."[94] The cup is full of calamities, including: rain, destruction, famine, and sword (Isa 51:19). Those to whom Yahweh gives his cup of wrath are powerless to refuse it.[95] Those who receive Yahweh's cup will stagger in a senseless stupor under Yahweh's judgment (Isa 51:17, 21-22). It is prepared for Israel because of their sin (Isa 51:17-22). Often the explicit realization is through the Babylonian exile: "Babylon is a gold cup in Yahweh's hand, making the whole earth drunk; the nations drank of her wine and so became mad" (Jer 51:7; 25:15-28; Isa 51:17-23; Lam 4:21; Ezek 23:31-33; Hab 2:16). Eventually, Yahweh's cup of wrath will be removed from Israel and be aimed at her tormentors (Isa 51:23).

LOVING

In sharp contrast to his wrath, Yahweh also expresses love. *'hb* is broadly love of all kinds.[96] The objects of divine love are many, including: individuals (Deut 4:37; 2 Sam 12:24; Isa 48:14; Ps 146:8; Prov 3:12; 15:9), groups such as Israel (Deut 7:8, 13; 23:6; Isa 43:4; 48:14), places such as Jerusalem (Ps 78:68; 87:2), and traits such as righteousness (Isa 61:8; Pss 11:7; 33:5; 37:28; 45:8; 99:4). This love underlies election as an unconditional love.[97]

Very often such love is expressed within covenant through a multiplicity of words. *Ḥesed* is "goodness" and "kindness" and "loyal love" primarily within a covenant relationship.[98] The word has a sense of "loyalty" within it, which becomes apparent when it is in parallel relationship with *šmʿ* (Isa 55:3; Gen 32:11; Deut 7:9; Pss 25:10; 26:3; 31:24; Prov 3:3; 14:22). In these concepts both parties reciprocate with loyal love. It originates in Yahweh's goodness and expresses itself in various ways which Yahweh obligates himself to demonstrate.[99] Yahweh's loyal love includes faithfulness, justice, peace, and speeding righteousness.[100] In Isaiah 54:6-10, "Yahweh promises Israel, his bride, who had been chastened by expulsion, to take her back into his favor and forever to show her the *ḥesed* that is entailed in the marriage union."[101]

---

94. Douglas Kennard's translation with close parallels to North, *The Second Isaiah*, 216.

95. North, *The Second Isaiah*, 216.

96. BDB 12-13; Snaith, *Distinctive Ideas of the Old Testament*, 167; Glueck, *Hesed in the Bible*, 1.

97. Snaith, *Distinctive Ideas of the OT*, 172.

98. Glueck, *Hesed in the Bible*, 77; Eichrodt, *Theology of the Old Testament*, 1:232.

99. Glueck, *Hesed in the Bible*, 81.

100. Glueck, *Hesed in the Bible*, 58, 80, 87, 89.

101. Glueck, *Hesed in the Bible*, 84; Eichrodt, *Theology of the Old Testament*, 1:68, 254.

> In a surge of anger I hid my face from you for a moment,
> but with everlasting kindness I will have compassion on you,
> says Yahweh your redeemer.
> Though the mountains be shaken, and the hills removed,
> Yet my unfailing love for you will not be shaken,
> Nor my covenant of peace be removed,
> says Yahweh, who has compassion on you. (Isa 54:8, 10)

Yahweh's love provides compassion desiring good for Judah (Isa 8:6). Yahweh compassionately comforts his afflicted Judah to bring them back through a new exodus (Isa 40:1-2). The thought of his people is always before Yahweh (Isa 49:13-16). This acknowledgement fosters in Yahweh a compassion initiated toward sinful Israel (Isa 65:2). The new covenant is an expression of Yahweh's faithfulness to Israel and his servant (Isa 49:7; 61:8). Yahweh delights in restored Israel as a bridegroom over his bride (Isa 62:5). Yahweh guarantees comfort for the righteous remnant on the basis of his past action with Abraham and Israel (Isa 51:1-3). Such compassion is shown through deeds of salvation as the Father of a people—his sons (Isa 63:7-9, 15-19; 64:8). This loyal love is so compassionate that Isaiah breaks out into praise of Yahweh's greatness.

> I will tell of the kindness of Yahweh,
> The deeds for which he is to be praised
> According to all Yahweh has done for us—
> Yes, the many good things he has done for the house of Israel,
> According to his compassion and many kindnesses. (Isa 63:7)

CONCLUSION

Yahweh is sovereign. All other attributes develop the character of this king, thereby showing the nobility of his reign. He cannot be compared with any other; he is far their superior. He is separate (holy), in a class of his own. Morally he is righteous, jealous, wrathful, and loving in a pure, undefiled sense.

CHAPTER 4

Humanity under God

PSALM 8:4 ASKS GOD the question in prayer, "What is man, that thou dost take thought of him?" and then answers this question in praise to the majestic God who made humans for majesty and rule (Ps 8:5–6, 9; Isa 45:12).

> God made him a little lower than God,
> and dost crown him with glory and majesty!
> Thou hast made him to rule over the works of thy hands;
> Thou hast put all things under his feet. (Ps 8:5–6, 9)

This psalm orients the reader and prayer to focus on understanding humans in light of God's creation design and the revelational framework that describes us. Painting on this canvas invites a descriptive biblical theology's assessment of humans, to which this text is itself contributing.

Following this approach results in a *functionalism* (because of the redundant descriptions of holistic humanity in the model), which I call a *multi-faceted unity* (of: image of God, soul, spirit, body, heart, mind, will, and conscience [only in NT]). However, the concreteness of especially Hebrew descriptive words could also be appealed to in claiming this model as an ontological model because it is describing the way we are from a biblical perspective. Since that is the case, we should think about ourselves in this manner.[1]

For example, within Christendom there are many views of the nature of the human being. Among the most prominent are two views rooted in Platonism that have had long-standing traditions in Christianity. Dichotomists,

---

1. A broader engagement of anthropology in biblical theology can be found in Kennard, *A Critical Realist's Theological Method*, 367–408; Wolff, *Anthropology of the Old Testament*; and Bratcher, "Biblical Words Describing Man."

following the *Epistle to Diognetus*, make a distinction between the material and immaterial parts of a human, indebted to Plato's soul and body concepts.[2] Theologians adhering to this view argue that soul and spirit are used interchangeably, whereas trichotomists, following Justin Martyr, point out that soul and spirit are distinct.[3] This trichotomy view expresses the Neoplatonic trichotomy view of spirit, soul, and body.

In the twentieth century, additional views of humanity emerged, including advocates of a holistic model. For example, one holistic model in the wake of Gestalt psychology maintains that the person is greater than the sum of his parts.

In the second half of the twentieth century within the descriptive biblical theology movement, a model of the human being as a multifaceted unity gained dominance in the discipline. The near unanimity among biblical theologians embracing this model can be seen by its treatment in the theological wordbooks[4] and by the scholarly descriptions of humanity from specialized biblical theologies,[5] which corroborate the word studies of this chapter.

IMAGE OF GOD

A range of traditional options identify how several theologies understand humans to be made *in* the image of God. For example, Irenaeus proposed "image of God" to describe reason and free will, while "likeness" he identified as the supernatural endowment through the Spirit.[6] Aquinas follows Irenaeus's view identifying the *imago dei* as retained at the fall, but the likeness as lost at the Fall.[7] In contrast, Martin Luther and John Calvin identified "image of God" as identical to "likeness" in that both affirm original righteousness and the ability to reason.[8] Both Reformers saw these qualities as significantly marred in the fall. Emil Brunner took "image of

---

2. *Epistle to Diognetus*.

3. Martyr, *1 Apol.* 1.29, in *Saint Justin Martyr*, 57; van Kooten, *Paul's Anthropology in Context*, which presents a tripartite model especially philosophically; however, on pp. 376–7 the Pauline model is presented as more complex, akin to the development in this chapter.

4. Such as *TDNT*; *TDOT*; *NIDNT*; *TWOT*; and *NIDOTT & E*.

5. Dunn, *Theology of Paul the Apostle*, 51–78; Wolff, *Anthropology of the Old Testament*; Bratcher, "Biblical Words Describing Man"; Kennard, *A Critical Realist's Theological Method*, 367–408.

6. Irenaeus, *Against Heresies* 3.23.5 and 5.6.1.

7. Aquinas, *Summa Theologica* 1.93.4.

8. Luther, *Genesis*, 1:60–62; Calvin, *Institutes of the Christian Religion*, 1:1.

God" as a symbol for "moral uprightness or righteousness of God."[9] In contrast, Karl Barth identified "image of God" as essentially the relationality of humans that permits relationship with God and fellow humans after the pattern of the divine relationships within the Trinity.[10] Additionally, Thomas Torrance and G. C. Berkouwer identify "image of God" as "the focal point in the interrelationships between God and the universe."[11] None of these traditional views are how the Bible or the descriptive biblical theology movement uses the term of "image of God."

The concept of humankind as the "image of God" is first introduced in the creation account in Genesis. As God creates humans, he formulates an image of himself (Gen 1:26–28). The words for "image" (ṣlm, εἰκόνα) and "likeness" (dmt, ὁμοίωσιν) imply that characteristics attributed to God in this passage are reflected in humanity. There is no distinction between the two words; they are totally interchangeable.[12] In this Genesis 1 instance, Eugene Merrill clarifies that the *b* ("in") is best understood as the "*beth of identity*" and parallel to the *k* ("according to") in indicating functionality.[13] That is, "image and likeness of God" means that humans function in the role as *representation* and *representative* of God.

This account introduces humans as a *representation of God* on earth. In the ancient Near East, kings would erect images of themselves indicating regions that were appropriately within their domain. For example, Ramesses II had his image hewn out of rock at the mouth of the *nahr el-kelb* on the Mediterranean north of Beirut, indicating he ruled this area.[14] Therefore, as God's image, humans indicate by their very presence that God rules the earth. This emphasis of the greatness of God's creative and sovereign power reflects the emphasis of the first literary unit (Gen 1:1—2:3) as it polemicizes other ancient Near East cosmologies. "Image of God" contributes to this polemic because we are living images that can accomplish something, in contrast to

---

9. Brunner, *Man in Revolt*, 388.

10. Barth, *Church Dogmatics*, 3/2:196.

11. Torrance, *Divine and Contingent Order*, 129; Berkouwer, *Man: The Image of God*, 87–89, 179, 197–98.

12. Victor Hamilton, "דָּמָה," in *TWOT* 1:192; *Lev. Rab.* 34.3; R. Hillel emphasized wholeness of "image" and "likeness" as synonyms; Rubin, "Body and Soul," 153–54.

13. Merrill, "Image of God," 443–44.

14. Wolff, *Anthropology of the Old Testament*, 160–61; additional support comes from other inscriptions of statuary, like the *Tell Fekheriye Inscription* 1, 12, 15–16, which also use image and likeness words, translated in Millard and Bordreuil, "Statue from Syria," 137; 4Q504 frag. 8, lines 4–6; A. H. Konkel, "דָּמָה," in *NIDOTT & E* 1:969–70.

the lifeless idols prohibited throughout the biblical text (Isa 41:29; 44:12–17; Num 33:52; 2 Kgs 11:18; 2 Chr 23:17; Ezek 7:20; Dan 3:1–15).[15]

As God's representative on earth, humans picture God as both sovereign ruler and creator.[16] Thus, human images of God are designed by God to rule the creation (Gen 1:26). To help facilitate this ruling, human images of God are blessed to both reproduce themselves and thereby facilitate this ruling of the created order (Gen 1:28). "Filling the earth" connects these two themes, showing the extent of human procreative power and making it possible for humans to rule. Creation and rule require a male and a female in the human realm. Persons are individually God's image, and as a married pair the couple is also God's image—not that relationality is meant by image, but that individually we humans contribute toward ruling and that married pairs also contribute toward ruling (being fruitful, multiplying to fill the earth so subduing and ruling can occur). God's image as one, yet plural, hints at the majestic creator character of *Elohim*.[17] From the chaotic images of formlessness that begin the passage, God shows his goodness through purposefully designing creation and then man in his image. Humans are to bring this creation under our control, which would include remaking it purposefully for the ends we think are best under our stewardship to God.

Genesis goes on to develop the idea that God's image included being his son, fitted by a loving Father with an appropriate situation, work, life, and marriage (Gen 2:23–24; 5:1–3; Luke 3:38).[18] The few additional references to humans as God's image indicate that this image continues beyond the fall (Gen 5:1, 3; 9:6; Jas 3:9), though dragged through futility and death as a result of sin.

Isaiah does not use *ṣlm* with regard to humans, but it does use *dmt* with reference to a plural group of Babylonian humans (Isa 13:4). Furthermore, in contrast to Yahweh's incomparability, *dmt* is used to indicate that no object, and especially no idol, is comparable to God (Isa 40:18). The lifeless idols do not represent a god nearly as well as living humans represent Yahweh, with our ability to act, procreate, and rule in God's creation.

---

15. Vawter, *On Genesis*, 55.

16. Merrill, "Image of God," 442, 444–45; *Gen. Rab.* 8.10; *b. Sanh.* 38b; Wis 2.23; Sir 17.3–4; *m 'Abot* 3.14; *b. Meg.* 9a; 28a; von Rad, *Old Testament Theology*, 1:146; also "εἰκών," in *TDNT* 2:392; O. Flender, "Image, Idol, Imprint, Example," in *NIDNTT* 2:287; A. H. Kookel, "דְּמוּת," in *NIDOTT* 1:969; Wolff, *Anthropology of the Old Testament*, 159–65; John Hartley, "צֶלֶם," in *TWOT* 2:768.

17. Kennard, *Classical Christian God*, 87–89.

18. Also, the Egyptian sense of "Image of God" in *Instruction of Merikare* 1.106; Merrill, "Image of God," 442.

SOUL

The concept of "soul" (*npš*) connects a human with God and the rest of the living creation. That is, the language of "soul" is used to refer to the living God who delights (Isa 42:1). Animals join humans as being "living souls" (Isa 1:14; 19:10; 55:3; 56:11; Gen 1:20, 24, 30; 2:7; 9:4–5, 10).[19] The animals pre-modernly described as souls are non-microbial animals (fish, foul, insects, reptiles, amphibians, and mammals). "Soul" has a holistic connotation in that it signifies a *complete living being*.[20] The emphasis on "life" means that the term is sometimes a synonym for "life" (Isa 15:4; 38:17; 43:4; 53:12). The words for "soul," *nephesh* (*npš*) in the Hebrew and *psyche* (ψυχὴν) in the Greek, have developed from the idea of breath to mean the whole person who both breathes and desires, lives and moves (Isa 26:8–9; 42:1; 61:10; 66:3; Exod 23:12; Deut 12:12).[21] Very few biblical references develop "soul" as a part of a human,[22] and in those cases it refers to the throat or neck, the organ of breathing (Isa 51:23; Jer 15:9; Luke 2:35).[23] In other places, "soul" stands in the place of a pronoun, indicating living persons (Isa 3:9; 43:4; 44:20; 46:2; 47:14; 51:23) and even personified *sheol* (Isa 5:14). At times, "soul" in Hebrew has a pronominal suffix "his soul" or "my soul," which in these instances is not a part of a person but akin to "my life" (Pss 3:2; 6:3; Isa 3:9; 15:4; 26:9). Body and soul combine together to express the totality of Assyria which will be destroyed (Isa 10:18).

This biblical concept of soul is very different from the philosophical and traditional theological alternatives. For example, Tertullian followed the Stoics in conceiving of the human soul as corporeal, generated with the

---

19. H. Seebass, "נֶפֶשׁ," in *TDOT* 9:510–16; Edmund Jacob, "ψυχὴ," in *TDNT* 9:620, 639–40, 648–49, 653; D. C. Fredericks, "נֶפֶשׁ," in *NIDOTT & E* 3:133; Bruce Waltke, "נֶפֶשׁ," in *TWOT* 2:589–91.

20. Wolff, *Anthropology of the Old Testament*, 24–25; H. Seebass, in *TDOT* 9:510–16; Edmund Jacob, in *TDNT* 9:620, 639–40, 648–49, 653; D. C. Fredericks, in *NIDOTT & E* 3:133; Bruce Waltke, in *TWOT* 2:589–91; Dunn, *The Theology of Paul the Apostle*, 76–78; McKenzie, *Dictionary of the Bible*, 839; Rahner and Vorgrimler, *Theological Dictionary*, 442–43; Cooper, *Body, Soul & Life Everlasting*, 42–43; Nancy Murphy, "Human Nature," and Ray Anderson, "On Being Human," in Brown et al., *Whatever Happened to the Soul?*, 22, 178, 186; 11QTemple 51.19; 54.20; 61.12; 1QS 11.13; CD 12.11–12; 1QH 2.2, 24; 3.6; 5.17–18; 9.18; 15.16.

21. Colin Brown, "ψυχὴ," in *NIDNTT* 3:676, 679.

22. Wolff, *Anthropology of the Old Testament*, 24–25; Edmund Jacob, "ψυχὴ," in *TDNT* 9:620, 639–40, 648–49, 653; D. C. Fredericks, "נֶפֶשׁ," in *NIDOTT & E* 3:133; Bruce Waltke, "נֶפֶשׁ," in *TWOT* 2:589–91; Dunn, *The Theology of Paul the Apostle*, 76–78; Pannenberg, *Anthropology in Theological Perspective*, 523.

23. Albert Dihle and Edmund Jacob, "ψυχὴ," in *TDNT* 9:609, 618. An unusual use of *npš* means "perfume boxes" (Isa 3:20).

body, but departs from them in considering the soul to be depraved by sin and renewed by regeneration.[24] Plato reasons that the soul is an eternal form for each human, which as eternal continues from a pre-incarnate existence to a post-incarnate afterlife, while our shadowy bodies are birthed and then decay.[25] While Origen followed Plato's view of soul,[26] Augustine modified the concept in the direction of Neoplatonism, denying eternal preexistence and affirming a created tripartite quality of each human soul to reflect the Trinity.[27] In contrast, Aristotle and Aquinas proposed a hylomorphic view in which the material human is formed as soul.[28] René Descartes proposed a radical form of substance dualism in which the soul is akin to a thinking substance that is the real person within the extended substance of body.[29] Karl Barth identifies that body and soul are a "concrete monism," both terms describing the unique and singular experience of the person.[30] None of these philosophical or traditional theological views captures the sense of the biblical text and the biblical theology movement on the holistic human concept of soul as life or person.

Biblically, soul can be likened to the self or person. This concept refers to the most basic or elemental aspect of the person. Thus, soul is the relationship of the person to himself and others on an ontological level. We should not define "person" in a Cartesian or Lockean manner as *a self-aware individual* or in an Aristotelian manner as *having the capacity of self-assertion and self-manipulation*. Furthermore, the unborn are even called by God before birth (Isa 49:1, 5; Gen 25:22–23; Judg 13:2–7; Jer 1:4–5; Gal 1:15).

Furthermore, a person as soul (*npš*) wills and feels hate, love, grief, joy, patience, fear, despair, bitterness, and sympathy (Isa 1:14; 26:8–9; 29:8; 32:6; 38:15, 17; 42:1; 53:2; 58:3, 5, 10–11; 61:10; 66:3; Jer 12:7; 13:17; Job 6:4; 30:25; Pss 6:3; 35:9; 42:5; Prov 31:6). The continuing legacy of the living self is the soul.

Within a person there is the cultivation of his awareness of himself as the agent of his own thought and behavior.[31] In other words, the self

---

24. Tertullian, *An.* 4–5, 10–11, 24, 27, 38, 41, 51, in Ante-Nicene Fathers, 3:183–229.

25. Plato, *Cratylus*, 93; *Phaedrus*, 124; *Phaedo*, 244–46; *Laws*, 763–64.

26. Origen, *Princ.* 2.9.6, in *On First Principles*.

27. Augustine, *Civ.* 7.23, 11.23, 13.2, 19.3, 21.3, 22.4.

28. Aristotle, *Top.* 4.6; *Metaph.* 5.8; 7.10; 8.3; 12.5; 13.2; and *Soul* 2.1–3; Aquinas, *Summa Theologica* 1.3.1; 1.18.3 ans and rep 1; 1.51.1 rep. 3; 1.70.3 ans and rep 2; 1.72.1, rep 1; 1.75–76; 1.97.3 ans.

29. Descartes, Meditations. 135–36, 208–9.

30. Barth, *Church Dogmatics*, 3/2:393.

31. Kierkegaard, *Sickness unto Death*.

relates to the person's experience of himself, without the trappings of social façade or presentation, the individual as he stands before himself, as it were, psychologically naked. Thus, self as context or perspective is the primary personal experience.

Implicit in the biblical discussion of the soul or self is the suggestion that the person can only have a self-reflective relationship to himself in context. For example, when attempting to empathize with another person, an individual will experience increasing levels of understanding as he gains more information about the context in which the other lives. Thus, the self is understood in relationship to one's awareness of one's thoughts, feelings, and behaviors in response to one's environment, both physical and spiritual. This has significant implications for the person in terms of purpose, meaning, and definition.

SPIRIT

In contrast to image of God and soul, "spirit" does not refer to the person as a whole but rather indicates a facet of her being (Isa 19:3; Dan 7:15; Zech 12:1). It is that aspect of the person relationally oriented to God and other spirit beings.[32] For example, Isaiah 19:3 indicates that the Lord in his judgment "demoralizes the spirit" of the Egyptians "within them."

Several philosophers and theologians conceive of the traditional concept of spirit to be identical to that of soul, often in a dichotomy of spirit or soul and body. For example, Tertullian followed the Stoics in conceiving of the human spirit as corporeal, generated with the body.[33] Plato reasons that the spirit is an eternal form for each human, which as eternal continues from a pre-incarnate existence to a post-incarnate afterlife, while our shadowy bodies are birthed and then decay.[34] While Origen followed Plato's view of spirit,[35] Augustine modified the concept in the direction of Neoplatonism, denying eternal preexistence and affirming a created tripartite quality of each human spirit or mind to reflect the Trinity.[36] In contrast, Aquinas

---

32. Wolff, *Anthropology of the Old Testament*, 36; Friedrich Baumgärtel, Werner Bieder, Erik Sjöberg, and Edward Schweizer, "πνεῦμα, πνευματικος," in *TDNT* 6:362–63, 367, 370, 375–76, 396–401; M. V. VanPelt, W. C. Kaiser, and D. Block, "רוּחַ," in *NIDOT & E* 3:1075–77; Barton Payne, "רוּחַ," in *TWOT* 2:837; Dunn, *Theology of Paul the Apostle*, 77; Colin Brown, "Spirit, Holy Spirit," in *NIDNTT*, 3:693–94.

33. Tertullian, *De an.* 9, in *Against Praxeas*.

34. Plato, *Cratylus*, 93; *Phaedrus*, 124–26; *Meno*, 179–80; *Phaedo*, 250; *Timaeus*, 452–54.

35. Origen, *Princ.* 2.9.6, in *On First Principles*.

36. Augustine, *Civ.* 8.16; 19.

proposed a hylomorphic view in which the material human is formed as soul which constitutes a spiritual and immortal aspect of life.[37] René Descartes proposed a radical form of substance dualism in which the spirit is akin to a thinking substance that is the real person within the extended substance of body.[38] Paul Tillich conceives of human spirit as an existential dimension extending an Einsteinian relativistic metaphysic, within which human existence participates along with God.[39] Wolfhart Pannenberg metaphorically illustrates the relationship of spirit in God and in humanity through Michael Faraday's universal force field which relates the effect of electricity on another dimension, that of magnetism.[40] Many of these views are foreign to the biblical text, though Tillich's and Pannenberg's metaphors may have some relevance if corralled back in ontological and functional directions to reflect the biblical ideas (though complex scientific metaphors may put most people off rather than be an aid to relate significance).

The Hebrew and Greek words for "spirit" (*ruḥ* and πνεῦμα) refer to air in motion (Exod 14.21).[41] By extension, "spirit" can refer to the breath of humans or animals (Gen 7:15; Eccl 3:21; 12:7) and to God's life-giving breath (Gen 45:27; Job 17:1; 27:3).[42] However, well over two-thirds of the uses of *ruḥ* and πνεῦμα apply to God and his angels (Isa 31:3; 30:1; 34:16; John 4:24; Zech 1:9). This preponderance of uses emphasizes *a dimension of existence that is not normally taken into account*, for clearly God and the angels act within the visible world (Isa 27:8; 28:6; 2 Kgs 6:16-17; Dan 10:20-21).[43] At times, this spiritual ontological dimension appears in the

---

37. Aquinas, *Summa Theologica* 1.29.1, rep 5; 1.75.4; 1.76.1, ans.; 1.118.3 ans.; 3. suppl.79.1 ans and rep 4.

38. Descartes, Meditations, 51-52; 60; 77-81; 98; 119-20; 130; 135-36; 152; 155-56; 207-8.

39. Tillich, *Systematic Theology*, 3:15-30, 111-61, 297-423.

40. Pannenberg, *Systematic Theology*, 1:382-84; I think the universal ambiguity of Faraday permits Pannenberg's metaphor rather than extending it to the specificity of Maxwell's equations.

41. Wolff, *Anthropology of the Old Testament*, 32-33; Hermann Kleinknecht, Friedrich Baumgärtel, and Werner Bieder, "πνεῦμα, πνευματικος," in *TDNT* 6:334-35, 360, 368; Barton Payne, "רוּחַ," in *TWOT* 2:831; E. Kamlah, "Spirit, Holy Spirit," in *NIDNT* 3:690-91.

42. Wolff, *Anthropology of the Old Testament*, 33-35; Hermann Kleinknecht, Friedrich Baumgärtel, and Werner Bieder, "πνεῦμα, πνευματικος," in *TDNT* 6:360-61, 368; E. Kamlah, "Spirit, Holy Spirit," in *NIDNTT* 3:690-91; M. V. VanPelt, W. C. Kaiser, and D. Block, "רוּחַ," in *NIDOTT & E* 3:1073-74; Barton Payne, "רוּחַ," in *TWOT* 2:836; Dunn, *Theology of Paul the Apostle*, 77.

43. Wolff, *Anthropology of the Old Testament*, 36; Friedrich Baumgärtel, Werner Bieder, Erik Sjöberg, and Edward Schweizer, "πνεῦμα, πνευματικος," in *TDNT* 6:362-63, 367, 370, 375-76, 396-401; M. V. VanPelt, W. C. Kaiser, and D. Block, "רוּחַ," in

visible world somewhat like a three-dimensional sphere penetrating a two-dimensional flatland.[44] This actual dimension of spirit goes deeper than the existential dimension in which Tillich described the realm of the spirit. The uninitiated may not be sensitive to spirit presence or be able to explain spirit nature, while those who lift their eyes from the four-dimensional world of space and time will find a whole realm racing with activity that affects human existence at every turn. No one can grasp the spirit with his hands, just as no one is able to catch the wind, but the effects of the spirit are evident in our environment (Isa 7:2; 17:13; John 3:8). Therefore, since God is spirit, an individual must be spiritually alive to relate to him. Thus, *spirit is that avenue through which God encounters the person* (Isa 32:15; 44:3; Joel 2:28–32; Rom 8:16; Gal 6:18; Phil 4:23; 2 Tim 4:22; Phlm 25).

While the human spirit includes intellect (1 Cor 2:14), emotions (Exod 7:8; Num 5:14; 1 Kgs 10:5; 21:5; Isa 25:4), and will (Num 14:24; Ezra 1:15; Pss 32:2; 51:10, 12), it extends beyond these human facets to include an orientation to the spiritual dimension.

With reference to death, animals are also said to have spirit (*ruḥ*), and thus it is beyond our awareness whether their spirits ascend or descend in the experience of death and the decay to dust that animals have in common with humans (Eccl 3:19–21). However, some animals get into the everlasting kingdom, for Isaiah 11:6–8 presents their presence as part of the undoing of the fall and divine oracle of judgment. In kingdom animals will live in peace with their predators, including peace between the seed of women (children) and serpents.

BODY

The body describes a human in the *physical dimension and in relationship to others*. Plato considers that humans are pure spirit utilizing a body for their existence in world of shadows.[45] Origen and Augustine followed Plato's view of spirit, but they modified the concept of body and physical things in the direction of affirming creation of bodies as a good, accomplished by the

---

NIDOTT & E 3:1075–77; Barton Payne, "רוּחַ," in *TWOT* 2:837; Dunn, *Theology of Paul the Apostle*, 77; Colin Brown, "Spirit, Holy Spirit," *NIDNTT*, 3:693–94. Daniel Lys affirms the wind, divine, and human roles of "spirit" but neglects to include angelic uses ('*Ruach*,' *le souffle dans l' Ancient Testament*).

44. Abbot, *Flatland*, v, 68–78, 93–94, 97–100; Tillich, *Systematic Theology*, 3:15–30, 111–161, 297–423.

45. Plato, *Cratylus*, 124–26; *Phaedrus*, 179–80; *Meno*, 231; *Phaedo*, 250; *Timaeus*, 452–54.

creative act of God.⁴⁶ Reflective of his Aristotelianism, Aquinas proposed a hylomorphic view in which the material human is formed as soul, utilizing a body for the person's connectiveness to the world.⁴⁷ René Descartes proposed a radical form of substance dualism in which the spirit is akin to a thinking substance that is the real person within the extended substance of body.⁴⁸ In contrast, Nancey Murphy, Warren Brown, and Elving Anderson advocate a nonreductive physicalism that considers humans as a "whole complex function, both in society and in relation to God, which gives rise to 'higher' human capacities such as morality and spirituality."⁴⁹ Their concept supports a full conceptuality of embodiment that may be helpful here. However, biblical literature presents a balance between the extreme views which see body as either "the totality of man from every aspect,"⁵⁰ or reduce it to solely the material.⁵¹

The biblical words for body used in the MT and LXX reflect that "body" describes a human in the *physical dimension and in relationship to others*. For example, Rudolf Bultmann and the descriptive biblical theology movement emphasize that the concept of "body" is holistic of the human person: "man does not have a *sōma*; he is *sōma*."⁵² The words for "body," *bśr* in the Hebrew and σῶμα and σάρκα in the Greek, are typically defined as corpse, flesh, or meat (Isa 31:3; 65:4; 66:17; Lev 4:11; Deut 21:23). These words also indicate that the body contacts its environment and others through various members (i.e., reaching with the hand, walking with the feet, speaking with the mouth and tongue, seeing with the eye, and hearing with the ears). In other contexts, the words emphasize ownership of servants and possessions (Num 8:7; Job 4:15; Mark 5:29; John 2:16; Eph. 2:15; Rev. 18:13). However, the words *bśr*, σῶμα, and σάρκα also refer to the whole body. In this sense, for example, *bśr* is used as a personal pronoun indicating the individual as

---

46. Origen, *Princ.* 2.9.6, in *On First Principles*; Augustine, *Civ.* 8.16; 19.

47. Aquinas, *Summa Theologica*, 1.29.1, rep 5; 1.75.4; 1.76.1, ans.; 1.118.3 ans.; 3. suppl.79.1 ans and rep 4.

48. Descartes, *Meditations*, 60; 77–81; 98; 119–20; 130; 135–36; 152; 155–56; 207–8.

49. Brown et al., *Whatever Happened to the Soul?*, 2, 25, 49–72, 99–148; Murphy, *Bodies and Souls*.

50. Dahl, *Resurrection of the Body*, 121–26.

51. Gundry, *Soma in Biblical Theology*, 156.

52. Bultmann, *Theology of the New Testament*, 1:194; Wolff, *Anthropology of the Old Testament*, 28–29; N. P. Bratsiotis, "בָּשָׂר," in *TDOT* 2:318, 323–31, esp. 325–28; Friedrich Baumgärtel, Edward Schweizer, and Rudolf Meyer, "σῶμα," in *TDNT* 7:1056, 1058, 1111; John Oswalt, "בָּשָׂר," in *TWOT* 1:136; R. Chisholm, "בָּשָׂר," in *NIDOTT & E* 1:777–78; Dunn, *Theology of Paul the Apostle*, 56–61; J. A. Motyer, "Body, Member, Limb," in *NIDNTT* 1:233–38; Hans Conzelmann, "Der Brief an die Kolosser," 137; Robinson, *The Body*.

a whole (Ps 119:120). Further, body is not merely something a human *has* but something he *is*.

Isaiah describes body as a shadowy and weakened continuing existence beyond death in *sheol*. The word *sheol* refers to the grave in several passages and thus contains the body. As the shadowy and weakened intermediate state, *sheol* contains relational and physical body imagery such as spirits of dead kings sitting on thrones and rising to meet the king of Babylon in his death (Isa. 14:9). Additionally, upon conjuring up Samuel, both the medium and Saul become terrified at the real bodily presence of the prophet (1 Sam 28:12–21).

Body extends beyond the physical in relational ways as well.[53] Clearly some relational uses are more physically dependent like the body in the sexual relationship and the resulting offspring (Gen 2:24; Matt 19:5–6). Such singleness of body in marriage argues for lifelong monogamous marriage as the design, and therefore identifies that divorce is less than the best that God has for us. Furthermore, the physical relationship a person has to blood relatives, all human, and all life involves this physical component (Isa 40:5–6; 49:26; Gen 6:12, 17; 29:14; Ps 145:21; Rom 1:3; 13:20). Such relationality should be encouraged by the ethical choices we make.

The words used for "body" also describe a mindset or way of being. In the OT, a fleshy (*bśr*) heart, one that is responsive and obedient, contrasts with a heart of stone, describing a rebellious and unrepentant attitude. For example, in Ezekiel 11:19 and 36:26, God tells the prophet that he promises to take the heart of stone from the people of Israel and give them a heart of flesh. This transformation makes them responsive and obedient to God—the new covenant way of being.

HEART

The most emphasized concept of biblical anthropology is "heart" (*lb* and καρδία), which stands *wholistically for a person thinking and feeling* (Isa 15:5; 32:6; 33:18; 40:2; 41:22; 42:25; 44:19; 47:7).[54] Rarely do philosophers and

---

53. Wolff, *Anthropology of the Old Testament*, 29; N. P. Bratsiotis, "בָּשָׂר," in *TDOT* 2:319; Friedrich Baumgärtel, Edward Schweizer, and Rudolf Meyer, "σῶμα," in *TDNT* 7:1066–80, 1111; R. Chisholm, "בָּשָׂר," in *NIDOTT* 1:778; Dunn, *Theology of Paul the Apostle*, 56–57, 59–61; Cooper, *Body, Soul & Life Everlasting*, 44–45.

54. Wolff, *Anthropology of the Old Testament*, 40, 44–55; Friedrich Baumgärtel, Johannes Behm, and Edmund Jacob, "καρδία," in *TDNT* 3:607, 611–13; "ψυχή," in *TDNT* 9:626–27; Andrew Bowling, "לֵב," in *TWOT* 1:466–67; Alex Lac, "לֵב," in *NIDOTT & E* 2:749; T. Song, "Heart," in *NIDNTT* 2:181–82; McDonald, *Christian View of Man*, 24–25.

theologians develop a meaningful description of humanity with the concept of heart, though John Calvin does.[55] This is only a slight surprise, since the biblical orientation of the Reformation can be understood to lead toward the descriptive biblical theology movement which expounds the concept here. Within this biblical perspective, only rarely does the biblical term for heart identify the biological pumping organ in the chest, enabling life and movement (Exod 28:29; 1 Sam 25:37; Luke 21:34).

In the Bible the concept is usually *holistic for a person thinking and feeling*. For example, T. Song identifies "*Leb* means less an isolated function than the man with all his urges, in short, the person in its totality (Ps 22:26; 73:26; 84:2)."[56] Walter Eichrodt echoes this sentiment that the heart is "a comprehensive term for the personality, its inner life, its character. It is the conscious and deliberate spiritual activity of the self-contained human ego."[57] Thus, the exhausted traveler needs to eat, strengthening his heart so that the whole person may be revived (Gen 18:5; Judg 19:5, 8; 1 Kgs 21:7). However, these words also provide a metaphor for the person with all her abilities. In the OT, *lb* conveys the idea of *a person in his totality* (Pss 22:26; 73:26; 84:2). It also suggests that action done to someone's heart is action done to a person (Exod 9:4; 28:29).

At times *lb* refers to the "mind" (Isa 33:18; 46:8; 47:10; 51:7) or even the act of considering something (Isa 57:1, 11; 65:17). Usually the wholistic emphasis develops the character of the person (Isa 29:13; 59:13). Often the character is developed by adding a modifier to the heart, such as: hard, merry, fearful, deceived, stubborn, sinful, contrite, and broken (Isa 6:10; 24:7; 35:4; 45:20; 46:12; 57:15, 17; 61:1; 63:17). A complete heart is the character of walking before God in truth, thus having the proper character (Isa 38:3). Even God refers to his own character by the word heart (Isa 63:4).

From a different perspective, heart encompasses the emotional disposition of the person.[58] The status of the heart dominates all the manifestations of life: "A joyful heart makes a good face, but when the heart is sad, the spirit is broken" (Prov 15:13; Isa 66:14). In many passages the heart is depicted as suffering, constricted, evil, grieved, broken, and sad (Neh 2:2; Deut 15:10; Ps 34:18; 1 Sam 1:8; John 16:6). Comforting words enlarge the heart of a suffering person (Isa 40:2; Gen 34:3; Ps 119:32). On the other

---

55. I am aware that "heart" did not make it into *The Institutes* as a subsection, like in bk. 1, ch. 15, but it is a concern there, and Calvin is faithful to exposit it in the commentaries and sermons. Calvin, *Commentaries*, Deut 29:4; Isa 51:7; Matt 14:24; John 12:40; Rom 2:15; Eph 1:16; 1 Thess 3:13; and Sermon No. 45 on Deut 4:22.

56. T. Song, "Heart," in *NIDNTT* 2:181.

57. Eichrodt, *Theology of the Old Testament*, 2:143.

58. Dunn, *Theology of Paul, the Apostle*, 74–75.

hand, traumatic events can stun or numb the heart (Gen 45:26), while fear can cause it to sink (Gen 42:28; 1 Sam 17:32; Ps 40:12). The heart experiences positive emotions such as love, joy, peace, generosity, faith, and courage (Judg 16:15; 2 Sam 15:6; 2 Cor 7:3; 1 Sam 2:1, 8; Acts 2:26; Deut 28:47; Exod 35:5; Pss 78:8; 27:14). Likewise, it can experience negative emotions including pride, envy, anger, contempt, worry, and fear (Isa 7:2; 1 Sam 4:13; 2 Chr 26:16; Prov 10:3; 23:17; John 14:1, 27; 16:6). Heart also represents human mentality as a process involving the whole person in contrast to concepts such as mind, conscience and will, which are faculties of heart.

Also, parallel to "heart" the word "bowels" (*m'yym*) presents inner feelings perhaps such as stirrings of an inner harp (Isa 16:11; 63:15). Other references to *m'yym* in Isaiah refer to the "womb" or perhaps "inner self where seed" comes from (Isa 48:19 perhaps either gender depending on synonymous or synthetic parallelism; Isa 49:1 "womb" birthing servant of Yahweh). Edward Young described such inward parts as deep stirring of emotions, "The shaking which moved Isaiah was one that agitated him to the very inmost depths of his being . . . it was a profound, soul stirring emotion resulting from a deep affection for those to whom he was to preach."[59]

MIND

The philosophical and theological discussions about mind primarily discuss two concerns: 1) the relationship of mind to body, and 2) the effect of sin on the mind.

A survey of the mind-body relationship between the extremes of Hobbes's materialism[60] and Berkeley's idealism[61] would include those who try to relate mind and body. Plato advocates a noninteractive parallelism between mind and body[62] that is modified by some others, such as Augustine, into a divine illuminational occasionalism.[63] Descartes considers that the mind and body interact with each other.[64] In contemporary Christianity, Nancey Murphy, Warren Brown, Elving Anderson, and Robert Van Gulick

---

59. Young, *The Book of Isaiah*, 1:466.
60. Hobbes, *Leviathan*, 49, 52, 162.
61. Berkeley, *Human Knowledge*, sect. 18–20, 50.
62. Plato, Timaeus, 452–53, 474–76.
63. Augustine, *Enarrat. Ps.* 118; *De peccatorum meritis*, 1.25.38; *Civ.* 10.2. The medieval church tends to appreciate platonic illuminationism following Augustine until Aristotelian sensibility wins out in the wake of Aquinas.
64. Descartes, *Discourse* 5 and 6 (p. 60–61); *Meditations* 6 (p. 99), and *Objections and Replies* (p. 207–9).

advocate a nonreductive physicalism that considers humans as a "whole complex function, both in society and in relation to God, which gives rise to 'higher' human capacities such as morality and spirituality."[65] Other forms of materialism propose different mechanisms. In contrast, this book aligns with Tillich in identifying that the mind can follow the spirit into being conceived of as a different dimension that overlappingly interacts with the body.[66] Additionally, there are a wide variety of functionalisms (and this chapter is one form) where different kinds of constructs yield the same mental event.

Biblically, "mind" more than any other concept is referred to by a number of words which carry approximately the same meaning, including the MT: *yd'* (with *nkr* just used as "acknowledgment," Isa 61:9; 63:16), and the LXX: νοῦς.[67] They are usually used as descriptions of how people *think* or commands about how they should think. The scope includes thought, understanding, assessment, intent, and purpose (Isa 1:3; 9:9 [MT and LXX: 9:8]; 10:7 [LXX]; 29:24; 40:28; 42:25; 44:18; 48:6-8; 56:10-11; 63:16). The concept of "know" expresses a selective meaning of "literacy" when texts are developed in the context (Isa 29:12). The concept of "mind" overlaps in synonymous parallelism with "soul" (Isa 56:10-11), "spirit" (Isa 29:24), and "heart" (Isa 29:13; 42:15; 10:12 [LXX]). There is even an instance in which "steadfast mind" (*yṣr*) is emphasized because it comes from the concept of "to form," as Oswalt develops in Isa 26:3, "Thus as a noun it frequently refers to that which is formed (Isa 29:16; Ps 103:14; Hab 2:18), often thoughts, purposes, or intentions (Gen 6:5; 8:21; Deut 31:21; 1 Chr 28:9; 29:18)."[68] Elsewhere in the OT references to liver, kidneys, and bowels convey that an individual's mental, spiritual, and ethical impulses proceed from the center of his being (1 Sam 25:37; Job 19:27; Ps 16:7; Prov 13:25; 14:33; 23:16; Lam 2:11) but in Isaiah only "bowels" (*m'yym*) is included as a parallel to "heart" (Isa 16:11; 63:15). God's mind knows omnisciently about people he transcends and himself (Isa 37:28; 44:8). The mind knowing primarily emphasizes a practical knowledge of allegiance and the morality that reflects

---

65. Brown et al., *Whatever Happened to the Soul?*, 2, 25, 49-72, 99-148; Murphy, *Bodies and Souls*; Nancey Murphy "Reductionism: How Did We Fall Into It and Can We Emerge From It?" and Robert Van Gulick "Reduction, Emergence, and the Mind/Body Problem," in Murphy and Stoeger, *Evolution and Emergence: Systems, Organisms, Persons*, 19-73.

66. Tillich, *Systematic Theology*, 3:15-30, 111-61, 297-423.

67. Paul Gilchrist and Marvin Wilson, "יָדַע," in *TWOT* 1:366, 2:580; Dunn, *Theology of Paul the Apostle*, 73-74; J. Goetzmann, "Mind," in *NIDNTT* 2:616-20; McDonald, *Christian View of Man*, 24-25.

68. Oswalt, *The Book of Isaiah*, 1:468.

such allegiance (Isa 29:13; 42:16; 45:4–5, 20; 59:8, 12; 10:12 [LXX]). Such a knowledge of allegiance is reflected as a personal knowledge of God himself and the blessings he provides (Isa 19:21; 46:28; 49:23; 60:16). Such personal knowledge and blessing are empirically evident to others as God demonstrates he is Israel's savior (Isa 49:26).

Mind as described in biblical literature is self-involved in logical, sequential analysis of information perceived via the person's senses and spirit. It is self-engaged in processes such as perceiving, attending, analyzing, and remembering. The process of comprehension and development of a response to incoming information is influenced by numerous factors, including neurological impairment, acute psychological states, and affectively laden memories.

Biblical literature depicts the mind as an active organizer of experience. Rather than being a blank slate that passively registers external experience, mind actively organizes it in *a priori* meaningful ways. Self as mind is capable of abstracting from thought; that is, it can imagine that which it has not been exposed to through experience. It can automatically assume not-A when A is presented. In other words, while capable of demonstrative (linear) thinking, mind processes dialectically. Rather than unipolar thought, the human being tends to engage in multipolar thinking. For example, having no experience with a piece of information, an individual may experience doubt or skepticism that may lead to other possible ways of considering it—an indication of dialectical thought.

The ability for dialectical reasoning has significant implications for the nature of man, including the possibility of free will as a form of determinism and the capacity to love. Further, suspension of this type of reasoning may contribute to problems related to ineffective living or pathology.

WILL

One of the subcategories of mind is will. The human will is a mental capacity involved in *choice*.[69] Several words in MT and LXX literature including the Hebrew (*'bh*, and *m'n*) and the Greek (θέλω) suggest *desire, purpose, and choice* (Isa 28:12; 30:9, 15; 42:24; 1:20). In other books, often these words are used in the context of God's choosing, but this is not Isaiah's use. This suggests that choices made by God or man are authentic in nature and cause events to occur (Acts 2:23).

---

69. Colin Brown, "Will, Purpose," in *NIDNTT* 3:1015; Gottlob Schrenk, "θέλω," in *TDNT* 3:44–47; Leonard Coppes, "אָבָה," in *TWOT* 1:4.

Lived out in daily activity, will is the self's awareness of his responsibility for actions. Self as will plans and initiates responses to her environment. As a faculty of mind, "will" can choose to respond for reasons that may appear contrary to external contingencies, hence, Victor Frankel's statement that an individual always has the freedom to choose how he will react even when all other freedoms have been denied.[70]

CONCLUSION

Isaiah's view of a human is a *multifaceted unity* (of: image of God, soul, spirit, body, heart, mind, and will). The concreteness of especially the Hebrew descriptive words make a claim that this view is an ontological, functional model.

---

70. Victor Frankel, *Man's Search for Meaning*.

CHAPTER 5

Israel in Covenant Relationship with Yahweh

WILLIAM DUMBREL STATES THAT the major theme in the book of Isaiah is Yahweh's covenantal commitment to Judah and the city of Jerusalem.[1] This divine commitment was substantially channeled through the Mosaic covenant. In many instances in Isaiah, *twrh* could be translated as "instruction" (such as the future instruction of God's ways in Isa 2:3), but it is best to understand *twrh* as "laws" contained within the everlasting Mosaic covenant in Isa 24:5, due to the parallelism in the verse. So at least in this case, Isaiah 24:5 is a clear reference to covenant nomism or Deuteronomism, which is a live possibility if Deuteronomy is patterned after a second millennial BC Hittite suzerainty treaty.[2] In such a view, Yahweh imposed an everlasting covenant relationship upon Israel that elects them into a lasting relationship with Yahweh (Isa 24:5; 28:9–10; 40:14; 59:20).[3] This means that Isaiah's prophecy identifies that the Law

---

1. Dumbrell, "Purpose of the Book of Isaiah," 111–28, esp. 112; *The Faith of Israel*, where he develops the essence of Isaiah's theology on 97–111, esp. 99. Also emphasizing the Jewish essence of Isaianic theology is Chisholm, "A Theology of Isaiah," 305; House, *Old Testament Theology*, 272–73.

2. Douglas Kennard argues for this suzerainty treaty covenant renewal pattern in *Biblical Covenantalism*, 1:161–243; Van Goudoever describes Isaiah giving the Law in a parallel to the exodus context in "The Celebration of the Torah in the Second Isaiah"; contrary to Jensen, who positions Isaiah's use of *twrh* within wisdom terminology because he dates Deuteronomy to a later date (*The Use of Tora by Isaiah*).

3. *Tg. Isa.* 28:9–10; Chilton, *The Glory of Israel*, 15; Polaski, "Reflections on a Mosaic Covenant."

is prescriptive to the vassals under suzerain Yahweh to the extent that they are in covenant relationship.

Some propose *torah* to be judicial wisdom and thus not prescriptive, recognizing the ancient Near Eastern context of broadly shared legal stipulations and that there are no ancient court documents available in the modern world describing ancient Near Eastern court decisions which show appeals to specific legal texts or stipulations as specifically prescriptive.[4] For example, John Walton admits that it "is possible" that there is evidence in Persia where Darius decreed the codification of Egyptian laws but concludes that such evidence is not clear enough to conclude for prescription because the court text does not reference a specific law violated.[5] Furthermore, John Collins claims this judicial wisdom genre through the later lens of Sir 24.23-24 and 4Q525 fragments 2-3, column 2, verse 4, which texts identify that *torah* is God's wisdom and that walking in the way of *torah* is the wise way to live. Both points by Walton and Collins are substantially less than what is needed to exclude the prescriptive value of the Law stipulations. The fact that wisdom is present in legal genres does not exclude prescriptive legal texts, in the same manner as narrative genre is not excluded by including some wisdom statements within it. There is broad recognition that ancient Near Eastern law codes and biblical covenant stipulations share considerable overlap in expression and content.[6] For example, most ancient Near Eastern law codes are casuistic or case law, which describes a scenario as if it emerged from a court decision with "model verdicts" including legal consequences or covenant curse being provided within case law (Exod 21-23).[7] As such, no court rationale need be provided later in a trial record, since such rationale is already provided as prescriptive within the casuistic stipulation of the covenant. The fact that casuistic legal texts describe a case is assumed not to be prescriptive by some,[8] but that is an

---

4. Kraus, "Ein zentrales Problem"; Jensen, *Use of Tora by Isaiah*; Roth, "The Law Collection of King Hammurabi," 9-31; Bottéro, *Religion in Ancient Mesopotamia*, 169-70; Westbrook, *History of Ancient Near Eastern Law*, summarized and adapted by Collins, *Invention of Judaism*, 25, 66-67, 88-90, 96, 184; LeFebvre, *Collections, Codes and Torah*; Jackson, *Wisdom Laws*; Hayes, *What's Divine About Divine Law?*; van de Mieroop, *Philosophy Before the Greeks*; Berman, *Inconsistency in the Torah*, 108-15; McConville, "Wisdom and Torah in Deuteronomy"; Walton and Walton, *Lost World of the Israelite Conquest*, 89-93; *Lost World of Torah*, 18-39; this book is critiqued at this point by Erickson, Review of *The Lost World*, 614; Walton, "Understanding Torah."

5. Walton, "Understanding Torah," 5; Walton and Walton, *Lost World of the Torah*, 30.

6. Roth, *Law Collections*; Jackson, *Comparison*; Wright, *Inventing God's Law*; Barmash, "Ancient Near Eastern Law," 1:17; Kennard, *Biblical Covenantalism*, 1:161-243.

7. Walton and Walton, *Lost World of the Torah*, 20.

8. Walton and Walton, *Lost World of the Torah*, 29.

arbitrary assumption when consequences are developed for a legal scenario with consequences shows that the texts are prescriptive. Additionally, there are instances in which concentrated apodictic laws are also present in ancient Near Eastern law codes, especially linked to curse formula (similar to Exod 20:5, 7 and reverse of Exod 20:11-12). With curse consequences embedded within stipulation, there is no need to provide a later trial rationale to indicate that they are prescriptively binding.[9] However, there are also some Old Babylonian trial records which show that the court decisions reflect ancient Near Eastern law codes, but these court decisions may not reference specific texts of the law codes, so some conclude that the decisions are not based upon the available law codes, such as Hammurabi[10] and thus should not be considered as prescriptive legislation.[11] However, the expectation of specific references to legal texts is insisting on modern citation practices rather than noting the issues and practices that ancient court decisions do reference. This sentiment funds the claims for biblical scholarship that Exodus and Deuteronomy are paraenetic exhortation instead of law.[12]

Instead, I have argued elsewhere that Exodus contains a suzerainty treaty and Deuteronomy is a covenant renewal document in the form of a suzerainty treaty, and thus both contain prescriptive stipulations.[13] For example, biblical Law presents itself as providing the theoretical background from which to make decisions (Exod 18:13-26, esp. verse 20; Num 11:16-17), so that one should not be surprised if not many court decisions are found in later narrative texts. Furthermore, there are court decisions that show clear court dependence upon the authoritative biblical Law code issues, even though a specific citation might not be referenced.[14] For example, a Sabbath law breaker was judged by the court and found guilty and thus stoned as Yahweh declared (Num 15:32-36 reflecting Exod 20:8-11; 31:13-17; 34:21). So, in this instance the specific violation of the Sabbath

---

9. Gevirtz, "West Semitic Curses"; Stamm, "Dreissig Jahre Dekalogforscung," 189-239, 282-305; Kilian, "Apodiktisches und kasuistisches Recht"; Gerstenberger, *Wesen und Herkunft*, 23-88; Gese, "Der Dekalog als Ganzheit betrachtet"; Nielsen, *The Ten Commandments in New Perspective*; Schulz, *Das Todesrecht im Alten Testament*; Pettinato, *Archives of Ebla*, 103-5.

10. Landsberger, "Die babylonischen Termini," 2:219-34, esp. 226-27; Walton and Walton, *Lost World of the Torah*, 30.

11. Kraus, "Ein zentrales Problem"; Roth, "Law Collection of King Hammurabi."

12. Jackson, *Wisdom Laws*, 3-23; Wells, "What is Biblical Law?," 224-25.

13. Douglas Kennard argues for this suzerainty treaty covenant renewal pattern in *Biblical Covenantalism*, 1:115-88.

14. Several scholars agree that biblical Law is authoritative and applicable (Chirichigno, *Debt-Slavery in Israel*, 136-37; Falk, *Hebrew Law in Biblical Times*, 11; Greenberg, "Some Postulates of Biblical Criminal law."

law is mentioned showing the stipulation to be prescriptive. This case is significant, for the legal issue appears again in Isaiah as a covenantal prosecutable offense and as one small measure indicating faithfulness within covenant nomism (Isa 56:2–6; 58:13; 66:23).[15] Likewise, a series of court decisions upheld Yahweh's initial assessment (Num 27:4, 7) that the daughters of Zelophehad should inherit land in the wake of the conquest since their father died without any sons (Num 36:2 court decision confirmed; Josh 17:4–6 court decision confirmed and the land was divided). While the text does not reference a textual precursor, the narrative does reference the previous court decisions as the basis for the subsequent action (Num 36:2 and Josh 17:4, 6 include the decision of Num 27:7 within them). Furthermore, a court decision began as a land redemption case and legally expanded to a Levirate marriage reflective of the biblical laws (Ruth 4:2–15 depending on Lev 25:24–28 and Deut 25:7–10).[16] However, if the stipulation section is viewed through the lens of covenant stipulation of a suzerainty treaty, there is also evidential grounds for viewing the stipulations as prescriptively binding by taking into account ancient Near Eastern diplomatic correspondence which follows a disobedience to suzerainty treaty stipulations.[17] Thus, the volume of prophetic accounts in the OT show the engagement in life analogous to this diplomatic correspondence. If Israel does not comply, then suzerain Yahweh will bring covenant curse upon them. Marvin Sweeny argued that this Isaiah use of *twrh* is consistent with the covenant nomist reforms of Ezra.[18] Furthermore, in early Judaism, the *Isaiah Targum* presents that the Law is binding with consequences if Israel does not comply with its terms.[19]

In Isaiah, this everlasting covenant relationship is one identified by Law, which Israel violates (Isa 24:5; 33:8). Such use of *twrh* defines the framework and standards for righteousness (Isa 42:4, 21; 51:4, 7)[20] and is the opposite of rebellion (Isa 1:10; 5:24; 8:16, 20; 24:5; 30:9; 42:24). Eventually, in such a righteous life, the people will internalize Yahweh's Law as a new covenant pattern (*twrh*, Isa 51:7; Jer 31:33).

---

15. Wells, "'Isaiah' as an Exponent of Torah," 140–55, esp. 141.

16. Timothy Willis argues that the authoritative Law is not rigid in absolutes but provides guidance for the elders to flexibly apply in their situation (*The Elders of the City*, 306).

17. An example is the "Letter from Hattusili III of Hatti to Kadashman-Enlil II of Babylon," see #23 in Beckman, *Hittite Diplomatic Texts*, 138–39.

18. Sweeney, "The Book of Isaiah as Prophetic Torah," 56–58, 65.

19. *Tg. Isa.* 5.20c; 28.9–10; covenant nomism is discussed by Chilton, *The Glory of Israel*, 13–18, 66.

20. Sweeney, "The Book of Isaiah as Prophetic Torah," 63.

Such a suzerainty treaty was made between two parties who did not have equal rights, so it is a treaty imposed by a great king (or suzerain) upon his vassal (usually the king of the subjected nation). The form of this treaty is the most helpful covenant form for understanding certain texts of the Bible since this form can be found in Exodus 20:1—Leviticus 26:46; Deuteronomy as a whole; Joshua 24; and in fragmentary ways in the following: 1 Samuel 12; 2 Chronicles 29:6—31:21; 34:13—35:19 (parallel 2 Kgs 22:9–22); Ezra 9:2—10:44; Nehemiah 9:5—10:34; and the Asaph covenant renewal liturgies of Psalm 50 and 81.[21]

The suzerain made a decree as a great king and imposed it upon his vassal, the king of the subjugated nation. The interests were overwhelmingly those of the great king. The vassal king is obligated to obey and consent to the terms of the oath. The curses are primarily directed toward whoever violates the great king's rights. This kind of treaty is primarily an inducement of the vassal's future loyalty. Through the treaty the vassal king obtained a promise of protection of his country and dynasty but he could not affect the terms of the treaty.[22] Mendenhall describes a suzerainty treaty as establishing a relationship for mutual support.

> The primary purpose of the suzerainty treaty was to establish a firm relationship of mutual support between the two parties (especially military support), in which the interests of the Hittite sovereign were of primary and ultimate concern. It established a relationship between the two, but in its form it is unilateral. The stipulations of the treaty are binding only upon the vassal, and only the vassal took an oath of obedience. Though the treaties frequently contain promises of help and support to the vassal, there is no legal formality by which the Hittite king binds himself to any specific obligation. Rather it is the Hittite king by his very position as sovereign is concerned to protect his subjects from claims or attacks of other foreign states. Consequently for him to bind himself to specific obligations with regard to his vassal would be an infringement upon his sole right of

---

21. These texts support especially the Pentateuch sources as suzerainty treaty: Mendenhall, "Covenant Forms in Israelite Tradition"; Muilenberg, "Form and Structure of Covenant Formulations"; Baltzer, *Das Bundesformular*; Lohfink, "Der Bundesschluss im Land Moab," *Das Hauptgebot*; McCarthy, *Treaty and Covenant*, "Covenant and Law"; Kline, *Treaty of the Great King*; Buis, "Les formulaires d'alliance"; Mayes, *Deuteronomy*; Knutson, "Literary Genres in PRU IV," 153; Finch, "Theology of Deuteronomy"; Rendtorff, *The Covenant Formula*; Kennard, *Biblical Covenantalism*, 1:115–243, 2:14–17; Duggan, *Covenant Renewal in Ezra-Nehemiah*; Taggar-Cohen, "Biblical *Covenant* and Hittite *išhiul* reexamined"; *Mek.* to Exod 20:17; *Midrash Tan.* to Deut 5:21.

22. Weinfeld, *Deuteronomy*, 74–75.

self-determination and sovereignty. A most important corollary of this fact is the emphasis upon the vassal's obligation to *trust* in the benevolence of the sovereign.[23]

A suzerainty treaty has the following formal elements: preamble, historical prologue, stipulation, treaty validation, list of witnesses, curses and blessings. The first three parts are in a set order, while there is some flexibility of the order of the final three components of the treaty. These items are not specifically in Isaiah but are presumed for Isaiah to reflect diplomatic correspondence in response to a treaty containing these elements (in Exodus, Deuteronomy, and Joshua 24). The fact, Hezekiah's reforms with suzerainty forms before Sennacherib invades show that these suzerainty treaty patterns are in the context of Isaiah's ministry to kings such as Ahaz and Hezekiah (2 Kgs 18:3–6; 2 Chr 29:3–21; 30:1—31:21).[24] Also, occasionally in Isaiah these elements will be answered specifically.

In the *preamble* there are the name, titles, and genealogy of the great king. The emphasis is upon the majesty and power of the great king, who confers a relationship upon the vassal, who is not even mentioned at this point. Isaiah answers this grandeur of suzerain Yahweh with Yahweh's incomparability (Isa 40–48).

The *historical prologue* describes in detail the previous relationship between the two, particularly the benevolence and continuity of the great king toward the vassal. Here it is demonstrated why the vassal should be loyal to the great king, either because he as a vassal has been favored with sustenance or military assistance or because he has been spared from the severe punishment which he deserves. Such a treaty does not obligate nations other than the vassal except to make sure that they do not hinder the vassal from carrying out the terms of the treaty. Significant themes develop like: the suzerain king is great; he is the initiator in the relationship; he is sovereign; he is irresistible in battle; he is the refuge for the vassal seeking aid and protection; and he is gracious in spite of the vassal's repeated unfaithfulness.

> What the description amounts to is this, that the vassal is obligated to perpetual gratitude toward the great king because of the benevolence, consideration and favor which he has already received . . . the vassal is exchanging *future* obedience to specific commands for *past* benefits which he received without any real *right*.[25]

---

23. Mendenhall, *Law and Covenant in Israel*, 30; Polak, "Covenant at Mount Sinai."
24. Roberts, *First Isaiah*, 469; Kennard, *Biblical Covenantalism*, 1:188.
25. Mendenhall, *Law and Covenant*, 32.

One of the stylistic features, the "I-Thou," emphasizes the personal relationship of obligation and gratitude. This may be in first or third person, but "the covenant form is still thought of as a personal relationship, rather than as an objective, impersonal statement of law."[26] In this, historical and didactive content are used with a rhetorical emphasis to move the will of the vassal to loyalty. Isaiah reflects this need for continued loyalty (Isa 1:18–20; 6:5–9).

The *stipulation* section states in detail obligations imposed upon and accepted by the vassal. The stipulations vary greatly from text to text within Hittite treaties and also within the biblical covenants. The focus of the stipulations section is underscoring how the vassal is to be loyal to the suzerain. The primary duties imposed on the vassal are to: be loyal and trust the great king; be prohibited from enmity of anything within the sovereignty of the great king; pay tribute; provide military assistance; renounce foreign diplomatic contacts; report plots against the great king; extradite fugitives; and indicate succession to the Hittite throne[27] All controversies between vassals are unconditionally submitted to the great king for judgment. Occasionally, it is demanded that the subordinate make a yearly visit before the great king. John Miller identifies that Isa 58:9–14 reflects the idea of casuistic prescriptive stipulations so common in covenant and law texts ("if one does thus-and-so, then . . .").[28] These commands especially involve the poor and vulnerable and correct observance of the Sabbath. However, most of the prophetic charges call Israel or the nations to account for their sins without reflecting the form of covenant stipulations.

Treaty validation provides for the vassal pledging by oath, the treaty being stored in the temple of the vassal's chief deity (literally under the oversight of the gods) and to be read aloud at set intervals before the subordinate.[29] The initial ceremony would often involve the vassal pledging obedience by an oath. The treaty is kept in the temple out of reach of the vassal, for tampering with the treaty was prohibited. The periodic public reading familiarized the entire population with the obligations of the great king and increased the respect for the vassal king by describing the warm relationship which he enjoyed with the great king. Isaiah offers this relationship if Israel repents (Isa 1) and then offers it again as part of the recovery after the Babylonian captivity (Isa 40).

---

26. Mendenhall, *Law and Covenant*, 33.

27. Mendenhall, *Law and Covenant*, 33–34; Beckman, *Hittite Diplomatic Texts*, 3 and the corroborative reading of sixty documents contained therein.

28. Miller, "Concept of Covenant in Deutero-Isaiah," 160.

29. Mendenhall, *Law and Covenant*, 34; Beckman, *Hittite Diplomatic Texts*, 3 and the corroborative reading of sixty documents contained therein.

There is an invocation of the gods of the great king and the vassal to act as *witnesses* to the covenant. These gods are the ones who will enforce the treaty. Within a Jewish monotheism, there are no deities who perform this function, so the witnesses are itemized as standing stones, piles of stones, dominant trees, the people themselves, songs, heaven, and earth. In Isaiah, at least, the witnesses include heaven and earth and Israelites themselves (Isa 1:2; 44:8).[30] Furthermore, the incomparability of Yahweh identifies that Yahweh will not share his place with any idol or impotent godlet, so the witnesses fit within Jewish monotheism (Isa 40–48).

The *Curses and blessings* section helps to ensure loyalty. If the vassal obeys, blessings are promised. The threat of divine retribution as a response to disobedience is the glue that held the Hittite empire together. Nonetheless, some of the Hittite vassals were willing to risk the wrath of the gods and the power of the Hittite armies to achieve independence, as shown by the revolts that frequently broke out upon the death of the great king. However, letters written to the offending vassal threatening them to submit shows that the stipulations were not merely suggestions or wise counsel for the curses were a real threat in disobedience to prescriptive stipulations.[31] Additionally, the fact that the Hittite empire was able to quash these rebellions shows that the covenant stipulations really do prescriptively bind the vassal into a covenant relationship that the great king insists on enforcing to the vassal's demise if necessary.

These treaties were enforced in other ways as well by the Hittite empire. One of the most expedient was to establish a personal bond with a more prominent vassal through a diplomatic marriage. While this is beyond the bounds of the treaty document, Hittite princesses were sent to establish diplomatic relationships with Mittanni, Hayasa, Amurru, and Ugarit in the Hittite documents that Beckman published.[32] Additionally, there is the possibility of a Hittite garrison being established in a vassal's land to protect the vassal from external threat, but also to keep an eye on the vassal and help ensure that these vassals will comply with the terms of the treaty.[33] The fact that ambassadors were sent from the Hittite great king with written letters demanding compliance shows that the suzerainty treaty form was not for

---

30. Miller, "The Concept of Covenant in Deutero-Isaiah," 161.

31. For example, "Letter from Hattusili III of Hatti to Kadashman-Enlil II of Babylon," see #23 in Beckman, *Hittite Diplomatic Texts*, 138–39, introduction and section 4.

32. Gary Beckman identifies which documents and place in the documents addresses this (*Hittite Diplomatic Texts*, 4).

33. One example of this is mentioned in the treaty with Targasnalli of Hapalla, in Beckman, *Hittite Diplomatic Texts*, 70.

mere court guidance;[34] the vassal must comply or suffer the wrath of the great king and his gods.[35] In these Hittite diplomatic correspondences the suzerainty treaty remains binding even though the vassal has violated its terms, and thus the continued threat of covenant curses are extended to the vassal in these letters if the vassal does not quickly respond with repentance. Prophets, such as Isaiah, serve a similar role in calling the vassal to covenant lawsuit and threatening with covenant curses.

With such threats of war and divine wrath, the stipulations show themselves to be binding. Therefore, the vassal is bound by the terms and stipulations of the treaty and the use of a suzerainty treaty as a covenant method conveys this obligatory relation from the great king to the vassal so bound.

If Israel remains faithful in obedience to the terms of the everlasting Mosaic covenant, then they will have everlasting blessing as Yahweh's faithful servants (Isa 56:4–6). However, when Israel rebels, they break this covenant and Yahweh as great king will bring covenant curse upon them (Isa 24:5; 33:8). The *Isaiah Targum* 5.20c reflects this covenant nomism relationship that Yahweh binds on Israel, "The words of the Law are sweet to the ones who do them, and bitterness will come to the wicked, and they will know that in the end sin is bitter to the one doing it."[36] Such a rebellion is as if Israel makes a rival covenant with death, but death cannot rescue them from Yahweh's impending covenant curse (Isa 28:13, 18).[37]

Eventually Yahweh will rescue Israel from his judgment on their rebellion by retaining them within a covenant grant of peace (Isa 54:10). Brueggemann identified the central motifs of Isaiah 55 to be Deuteronomic theology for Israel's repentance, which will be responded to by Yahweh with a faithful word, Davidic kingdom, and covenantal blessings.[38] As the eschatological kingdom begins, Isaiah prophesies that many gentiles will seek instruction in the Law (*twrh*) from Jerusalem so that they would as nations practice peace and not war (Isa 2:2–4).

> In the last days, the mountain of the house of Yahweh will be
> established on the chief mountain and will be raised above the

---

34. Contrary to Walton and Walton, *Lost World of the Israelite Conquest*, 89–93.

35. Beckman provides examples of court correspondence of this nature in *Hittite Diplomatic Texts*, #23 on 138–39 and 142–43; and #30 on 169–73. Cohn-Haft also translates a prayer of Mursilis to placate the Hittite storm god to release his curse from violating such a treaty (*Ancient Near East and Greece*, 177–79).

36. *Tg. Isa.* 5.20c; covenant nomism is discussed by Chilton, *The Glory of Israel*, 13–18.

37. Hays, "The Covenant with Mut."

38. Brueggemann, "Isaiah 55 and Deuteronomic Theology," 191–203, esp. 198.

hills, and all the nations will stream to it. And many peoples will come and say, "Come, let us go up to the house of God of Jacob that he may teach us concerning his ways, and that we may walk in his paths, for the Law will go forth from Zion, and the word of Yahweh from Jerusalem." And God will judge between the nations, and will render decisions for many peoples; and they will hammer their swords into plowshares, and their spears into pruning hooks. Nation will not lift up sword against nation, and never again will learn war. (Isa 2:2-4)

This new commitment to the Law is internalized as a new everlasting covenant relationship which focused upon Israel but extended to the nations because a future righteous servant will continue Davidic covenant blessings into kingdom (Isa 2:3-4; 42:6; 49:8; 55:3; 61:8).[39] This everlasting covenant is also facilitated by the spirit and word in the same manner as Jeremiah's new covenant internalizes and empowers the Mosaic covenant (Jer 31:31-34; Isa 2:3; 59:21; 63:11).

> Yahweh says, this is my covenant with them, my spirit is upon you and my words I have put in your mouth and shall not depart from your mouth, nor from the mouth of your offspring, nor from the mouth of your offspring's offspring, from now and forever, says Yahweh. (Isa 59:21)

Early Judaism reflects this Isaiah emphasis with Yahweh renewing Israel back into the land and promising an everlasting new covenant: "I will make an everlasting covenant with them to be their God and they shall be my people; and I will never again remove My people Israel from the land that I have given them."[40]

The refreshing covenant transformation is empowered by God's spirit, resulting in covenant participants adhering thoroughly to the *torah* (Isa 59:21; Ezek 36:24—37:28; Joel 2:28-29).[41] Furthermore for Qumran and Pharisee alike, the divine spirit will expiate the covenantally righteous person from his iniquity and uncleanness. Such a person is enlightened by the spirit to pure living of the narrow way (Deut 30:6; Isa 59:21; Jer 31:33;

---

39. Anderson, "Exodus and Covenant," 349.

40. Bar 2:33-35; 1QS 4.22; 4Q268 frag. 2 col. 1 6-8; CD B col. 19.12; 1QpHab col. 2.3; col. 11.13; 4Q434 frag. 1 col. 1.4; 4Q437 frag. 1 line 4.

41. *Jub.* 6.17; *Charter of a Jewish Sectarian Association* (1QS; 4Q255-264a; 5Q11) 3.15-4.1; 4.5, 18-23; 1QpHab col. 11.13; *The War Scroll* (1QM, 4Q491-496) 1.1-20; 16.11; 1QH 4, 5, 18; 4Q548 frag. 1 col. 2.9-16; 11Q13 22-25; VanderKam, "Covenant"; Blanton, "Spirit and Covenant Renewal," 137-38.

Joel 2:28-29).[42] For example, Pharisaic *Jubilees* describes Israel as in new covenant returning to Yahweh.

> After this they will return to Me in all uprightness and with all of their heart and soul. And I will cut off the foreskin of their heart and the foreskin of the heart of their descendants. And I shall create for them a holy spirit, and I shall purify them so that they will not turn away from following me from that day and forever.[43]

As such, this new covenant expression is seen as a divine internalization wherein God resolves the problems from Israel's Mosaic covenant rebellion and Yahweh's curse toward Israel's unresponsiveness.

The concept of new covenant was used at Qumran to indicate the faithful or "true Israel" who walk in the proper order of the Qumran Covenanters and obey the previous covenants.[44] In contrast to the Mosaic covenant, the new covenant is for them a new beginning of the faithful keeping of the Mosaic covenant by those who follow Abraham.[45] As such, the new covenant is a sectarian route of repentance so that they return to the Mosaic covenant.[46] Although it is empowering living in the Mosaic covenant, such a new covenant ushers in a new era.[47]

---

42. *Jub.* 1.23-24; *Charter of a Jewish Sectarian Association* (1QS, 4Q255-264a and 5Q11) 3.7-12; 4.22-24; 5.5; *Damascus Document* (CD 4Q268 frag. 1=4Q266 frag. 2 col. 1) ver. 6; 14.1-2; B col. 19, ver. 12-13 here the New Covenant is clearly still Law such as Jer 31:33 Hebrew; 1QpHab 2.3; 11.13 "circumcision of heart's foreskin"; *Odes Sol.* 11.1-3; *4 Ezra* 4.26; 7.50; 9.31; *Ex. Rab.* 19(81c) and *Targum Cant.* 3.8.

43. *Jub.* 1.23, 17-18, and 24-25; Bar 2.35.

44. *Charter of a Jewish Sectarian Association* (1QS, 4Q255-264a and 5Q11) 3.7-12, 26; 4.22-23; 5.5, 21; 9.6; *Damascus Document* (CD 4Q268 frag. 1=4Q266 frag. 2 Col. 1) ver. 6; 6.9, 19; 8.21=19.33-34; 14.1-2; 20.12; B col. 19, ver. 12-13 here the New Covenant is clearly still Law such as Jer 31:33 Hebrew; 19.33; 20.12; 1QpHab 2.3 there is a lacuna where likely בְּרִית stood as referring to new "covenant"; 11.13 "circumcision of heart's foreskin"; *4 Ezra* 9.31; David Noel Freedman and David Miano, "People of the New Covenant," in Porter and de Roo, *The Concept of the Covenant*, 7-26; Craig Evans, "Covenant in the Qumran Literature," in Porter and de Roo, *Concept of the Covenant*, 55-80.

45. CD 1.3-5; 2.14-3.21; 5.20-6.3.

46. *Jub.* 6.17; *Charter of a Jewish Sectarian Association* (1QS; 4Q255-264a; 5Q11) 3.15-4.1; 4.5, 18-23; 1QpHab col. 11.13; *The War Scroll* (1QM, 4Q491-496) 1.1-20; 16.11; 1QH 4, 5, 18; 1QSa; 4Q548 frag. 1 col. 2 9-16; 11Q13 22-25; CD 8.16-18; possibly a reference in *Hab. Pesher* 2.3 "those who betr[ayed] the new [covenant]."

47. *Lev. Rab.* 9.7; 13.3; *Eccles. Rab.* 11.8; *S. of S. Rab.* 2.12, 4; *Tg. Isa.* 12.3 and *Tg. Song* 5.10; *Yalkut Isa.* 26.2; Midrash to Ps 146.7; *b. Sanh.* 51b; *b. Šabb.* 151 b; Batto, "'The Covenant of Peace.'"

RIGHTEOUSNESS[48]

The Hebrew OT primarily develops righteousness through two words: *ṣdq* as "righteousness," meaning "faithfulness to an acceptable order," and synonym *mšpṭ*, which are often in synonymous parallelism (Isa 1:21, 27; 5:7, 16; 9:7 [9:6 MT and LXX]; 16:5; 28:17; 32:1, 16–17; 33:5; 56:1; 59:9, 16–17). Righteousness means "acceptable order of God's Law" (*ṣdq*: Isa 45:23–24; 48:18; 58:2; *mšpṭ*: Isa 28:26; 58:2; Exod 21:1).[49] For example, the concept of righteousness includes proper keeping of the sabbath (Isa 56:1–3; Exod 20:8–11; 31:12–17).[50] While righteousness can mean a virtue of "righteousness" (*ṣdq*: Isa 10:22; 33:15; 45:8; 46:12–13; 48:1; 60:17; *mšpṭ*: Isa 1:17; 10:2; 32:7; 42:3–4; 51:4; 59:8–15; 61:8; and synonymous parallels), often righteousness means "an event of judgment"[51] (*ṣdq*: Isa 5:23; 54:17; 57:12; *mšpṭ*: 3:14; 4:4; 26:8–9; 28:6; 34:5; 41:1; 49:4; 53:8; 54:17). Antonyms to "righteousness" include a range of words for sin and rebellion.

God epitomizes such a condition of righteousness (*ṣdq*) in his dealings with others (Gen 18:22–28; Job 8:3; Pss 4:2; 97:2, 6; Jer 23:6). Yahweh is the righteous one (Isa 5:16; 24:16; 26:7). He does righteous acts (Isa 30:18). God loves righteousness (Isa 61:8) and requires humans to be righteous (Isa 1:17; 56:1).

For the human to be considered righteous, they need to be in a right relationship with God by God initiating the covenant relationship and by the human following obediently within this gracious relationship. This relationship is what E. P. Sanders describes as covenant nomism.

> The "pattern" or "structure" of covenantal nomism is this: (1) God has chosen Israel and (2) given the law. The law implies both (3) God's promise to maintain the election and (4) the requirement to obey. (5) God rewards obedience and punishes

---

48. This orientation to righteousness as "appropriate in Mosaic Covenant," Kennard, *Biblical Covenantalism*, 1:285–89; Tg. Isa. 5.20c; 28.9–10; 32.2; Chilton, *The Glory of Israel*, 13–18, 66, 81–86; Beuken, "*Mišpaṭ*"; Kendall, "Use of *Mišpaṭ* in Isaiah 59"; Whitley, "Deutero-Isaiah's Interpretation of *sedeq*"; Coste, *Righteousness in the Septuagint*; Sweeney, "The Book of Isaiah as Prophetic Torah," 63; and Roy Wells, "'Isaiah' as an Exponent of Torah," 140–55. This covenant emphasis continues: (1) in the synoptics (Kennard, *Messiah Jesus*, 84–86, (2) mystically in early Judaism as a foretaste of eschatological judgment from God (Kennard, *Messiah Jesus*, 305–7), and (3) Paul develops it more extensively as mystical already for the appropriate and retains a not yet expression of eschatological judgment (Kennard, *Messiah Jesus*, 313–21).

49. Peter Enns, "מִשְׁפָּט," in *NIDOTT & E* 2:1142–43; Beuken, "*Mišpaṭ*"; Kendall, "Use of *Mišpaṭ* in Isaiah 59."

50. Gosse, "Sabbath, Identity and Universalism," 365.

51. Peter Enns, "מִשְׁפָּט," in *NIDOTT & E* 2:1143.

transgression. (6) The law provides for means of atonement, and atonement results in (7) maintenance or re-establishment of the covenant relationship. (8) All those who are maintained in the covenant by obedience, atonement and God's mercy belong to the group which will be saved. An important interpretation of the first and last points is that election and ultimately salvation are considered to be by God's mercy rather than human achievement.[52]

As such, it is only possible to be righteous in maintaining a relationship with God in light of admitting any sin that broke the relationship and a wholehearted commitment to covenant obedience. As John Oswalt identifies, "Unless justice is done and righteousness is lived out there can be no shelter from the storm of God's wrath."[53] For Isaiah, God established a foundation stone to provide a standard for righteous faith and behavior as the only route to escape destruction.

> Thus says Yahweh Elohim, "Behold I am laying in Zion a foundation stone, a tested stone, a well-laid precious cornerstone for a sure foundation, he who believes will not be in haste. And I will make justice the measuring-line, and righteousness the level; and hail will sweep away the refuge of lies, and waters will overwhelm the secret place." (Isa 28:16–17)

The statement "reckoned to him as righteousness" is a declaration of acceptance or appropriateness within the covenant arrangement within which a person lives (Gen 15:6; Lev 7:18; 2 Sam 19:19; Pss 32:2; 106:31; Ezek 18).[54] When "righteousness" is used longingly with reference to the future, it takes on the meaning of "vindication" (Ps 71:15–24; especially when *Qal* future is used in Job). The Mosaic covenant is the usual order by which Israel's righteousness is judged (Isa 24:5; 28:26; 48:18; 58:2; Ps 119:106, 142–4). As such, legal justification must reflect the condition of righteousness lived in accordance with the Law (Lev 19:15; Deut 1:16; 16:18–20; 25:1; 1 Kgs 8:32; 2 Chr 6:23). Such righteousness entails pursuing those practices of the Law which retain each other's ontological clean status (Ezek 18:5–18). Any attempt to justify oneself or others wrongly is a cause by which Israel suffered

---

52. Sanders, *Paul and Palestinian Judaism*, 422.
53. Oswalt, "Righteousness in Isaiah," 179–80.
54. 1 Macc 2:52; von Rad, "Faith Reckoned as Righteousness"; contrary to the claim that the word only functions this way in the *Niphal* (Oeming, "Ist Gen. 15.6 ein Beleg"), Achin Behrens ("Gen. 15.6 und das Vorverständnis des Paulus," 329) demonstrates it also functions this way in the *Qal* as in Gen 15:6; 2 Sam 19:19; and Ps 32:2; Jewett, *Romans*, 311–12.

under Mosaic covenant curse (Ezek 16:51-52; Prov 17:15). God grants the description of righteousness for those who operate within the context of faith in the covenant (Gen 15:6). With righteousness identifying the faithful in covenant, Mosaic covenant sacrifice contributes to recovering this righteous covenantal status (Deut 33:19; Ps 4:6). Ultimately, the messianic servant will justify many in his guilt or sin offering (Isa 53:11 MT: "guilt offering" or LXX: "sin offering") and rule the kingdom in righteousness (Isa 9:6; 11:4-5; Dan 9:24).[55]

The LXX presentation of δικαιοσύνην also means "faithfulness to the acceptable order" that God reveals in covenant (LXX: Isa 45:19). The Mosaic covenant is that premier order for Israel within which righteousness indicates appropriateness for covenantal blessing; Israel's blessing is dependent upon covenant nomism (LXX: Isa 61:8). The Davidic king and Israel are to seek and live in consistent righteousness (LXX: Isa 16:5; 56:1). Therefore, God counts it as a sin to legally acquit the wicked (Deut 25:1; Isa 5:23). The king's decisions or a father's instructions are to teach righteousness (LXX: Isa 26:9-10; 38:19). God seeks for righteousness to bless (LXX: Isa 5:7; 61:8). However, Yahweh found rebellion instead of righteousness, or the little bit of righteousness was overwhelmed by sin (LXX: Isa 5:7; 57:12). Yahweh will eventually bless righteous remnant Judah with a new exodus unto kingdom salvation (LXX: Isa 1:26; 26:2; 41:2; 45:8; 46:12; 49:12; 59:17; 58:2; 61:8).[56]

One of the passages including *ṣdq* presents Israel's current setting of occasional righteousness as inadequate "filthy rags," and thus they are blameworthy before God (Isa 64:6 [MT and LXX: 64:5]). Saying it as explicitly as the text does, "what they call *righteous acts* are as corrupt as *menstruation cloths*" during a woman's period.[57] This text identifies that in violating righteousness, there is also a violation of holiness and uncleanness.

Filling out this impurity in priestly documents, such as Leviticus and Ezekiel, the violation of righteousness infects Israel with ontological uncleanness. Jacob Milgrom views the concept of uncleanness through the metaphor of the picture of Dorian Gray, which illustration identifies that violation of righteousness affects the ontology of "clean."[58] Ultimately, sins defile Yahweh's holy name and bring covenant curse (Ezek 43:7-8). Israel pollutes itself and the land with ontological uncleanness by a variety of sins,[59]

---

55. For further discussion see Kennard, *Messiah Jesus*, 293-332 for messianic sacrifice, and 377-414 for messianic rule; *Song of Songs Rab.* 52.2.1-4.

56. Tob 12.9; 14.11; Wis 1.15; *Pss. Sol.* 2.34; 3.4-8; 15.6; *1 En.* 1.8; CD 4.8; 1QS 5.7-11; 1QH 7.12.

57. Oswalt, *The Book of Isaiah Chapters 40-66*, 626.

58. Milgrom, "Israel's Sanctuary."

59. *As. Mos.* 5.3; *Jub.* 33.6-7, 10, 19-20; *Ps. Sol.* 1.8; 2.3; 8.13; *Num. Rab.* 7.1; *Lev.*

which despoil the temple (2 Chr 23:19; 36:14; Ps 79:1; Isa 66:17; Jer 7:30; 32:34; Ezek 5:11; 9:7; 20:7, 18, 30–31; 22:3, 12–17, 24; 23:7, 13, 30, 38; 36:18; 37:23; 43:6–9; Mal 1:11–12).[60] In the novel of *The Picture of Dorian Gray*, Oscar Wilde's adventurer does not age nor suffer the consequences of his adventures; these consequences instead appear on Dorian's painted portrait.[61] Likewise, with regard to Israel's sins, Milgrom speaks of the priestly picture of Dorian Gray, "Sin may not leave its mark on the face of the sinner but it is certain to mark the face of the sanctuary; and unless it is quickly expunged, God's presence will depart."[62] By the time of the prophets, the people and land of Israel were severely polluted by sin-caused impurity and thus precariously sliding toward captivity (Ps 106:38–39; Isa 24:5; Jer 2:7; 3:9; Hos 5:3; 6:10). John Gammie affirms Milgrom's construct of the Dorian Gray picture; however, Gammie also defends that the purification offerings atoned for the individual and not always for only the tabernacle: "Sanctuary and sancta indeed reflected the state of the people's sinfulness precisely because the uncleanness that the former accrued were not removed at every [purification][63] offering."[64] And again later, Rabbinic sources recognized that Israel's disregard for their public promises had brought Israel drought in 66 AD and warned that their noncompliance with Sabbath, sabbatical year, and Jubilee year rendered them impure, tumbling Israel yet again toward impending exile and dispersion.[65] Unfortunately, Israel was unresponsive about their sin and purgation, and suffered captivity and dispersion repeatedly. The answer to sin in Israel is to study and live the Law, thereby returning to righteous living (Pss 19:7–14; 119:9–16).[66]

HOLINESS

Several commentators identify righteousness with holiness from Isaiah 5:16: "Yahweh of hosts will be exalted in judgment; the holy God shows himself

---

Rab. 15.4–5; 16.2, 6; 17.2–3, 6; 18.4; *m. Šebu.* 1.4–5; *t. Šebu.* 1.3; *b. ʿArakhin* 16a; *Tanhuma Mesoraʿ* 15.

60. *As. Mos.* 5.3; *Ps. Sol.* 1.8; 2.3; 8.13; *m. Šebu.* 1.4–5; *t. Šebu.* 1.3–4; *Tos. Kippurim* 1.12; *y. Yoma* 2.2; *b. Yoma* 23a.

61. Wilde, *Picture of Dorian Gray*.

62. Milgrom, "Israel's Sanctuary."

63. Technically, Gammie used *hattaʾt*, which will be explained in this direction in a few pages (Gammie, *Holiness in Israel*, 41–44).

64. Gammie, *Holiness in Israel*, 41.

65. 1QHa 7.29; 12.35; CD 1.3–4; 1QS 2.8; *Y. Taʿan.* 3.3; *b. Šabb.* 33a.

66. *B. Qid.* 30b; *b. Soṭ.* 21a.

holy in righteousness."[67] However, both parallel words for righteousness (*mšpt* and *ṣdq*) are prefaced with a preposition "in" (*b*) as though they refer to an event of judgment, which means that the holy God showed himself to be holy in his righteous judgment. Thus, holy and righteousness do not mean the same thing; rather, God is holy when moral judgments are made.[68]

Holy (*qdš*) is an ontological metaphysical category that means separate.[69] The system of the holy develops categories always applicable to the cult.[70] In Akkadian, *qadašu* and *qadištu* are synonyms for "clean" or "pure," while *qadsutu* means "holy as set apart to god."[71] In Ugaritic, *qdš* means holy ontologically within the categories pertaining to god, such as: shrine, priest, and cult prostitute.[72] Holiness does not mean separate from a lesser level (as Rudolf Otto's *numinous* developed,[73] probably more reflective of a Kantian *noumena* metaphysical idea and followed by Mircea Eilade's sociological dualism informed by broad international religious practice[74]). Instead, *qdš* means separate to its ontological level of being. These levels of being are separated to God as a part of the chain of being in their appropriate closeness to God.[75] Even the biblical concept retains *qdš* as including Canaanite temple prostitutes as holy or set apart for their pagan worship (Gen 38:21–22; Deut 23:17). Likewise, Tyre as a temple prostitute earns holy wages in their corruption (Isa 23:18). So *qdš* is not about morality but an ontological category of being identified in relationship to God as separate or sacred.

---

67. Walter Brueggemann wrongly identifies holiness as a synonym to righteousness ("Justice the Earthly Form of God's Holiness," in *The Covenanted Self*, 48–58; *Isaiah 1–39*, 53).

68. Oswalt, *The Book of Isaiah: Chapters 1–39*, 162; Moberly, "Whose Justice? Which Righteousness?"; Kennard, *Biblical Covenantalism*, 1:259–67, 285–89.

69. Neusner and Chilton, "Sanders's Misunderstanding of Purity," 205–30, esp. 205, 208, 211; Jackie Naudé, "קָדוֹשׁ," in *NIDOTT & E* 3:877; Thomas McComiskey, "קָדוֹשׁ," in *TWOT* 2:786; W. Kornfeld, "קָדוֹשׁ," in *TDOT* 12:522; Gammie, *Holiness in Israel*, 9–11; Wilson, *"Holiness" and "Purity" in Mesopotamia*; *Sifra Qedošim Pereq* 11.21; *Šemini Pereq* 12.3.

70. Neusner, *History of the Mishnaic Law of Holy Things*, esp. 17.

71. Jackie Naudé, "קָדוֹשׁ," in *NIDOTT & E* 3:878; Thomas McComiskey, "קָדוֹשׁ," in *TWOT* 2:787; W. Kornfeld, "קָדוֹשׁ," in *TDOT* 12:523–24.

72. Jackie Naudé, "קָדוֹשׁ," in *NIDOTT & E* 3:878; Thomas McComiskey, "קָדוֹשׁ," in *TWOT* 2:787; W. Kornfeld, "קָדוֹשׁ," in *TDOT* 12:524–25.

73. Otto, *The Idea of the Holy*.

74. Eliade, *The Sacred and the Profane*.

75. The concept of "chain of being" that is referenced is not so much the Western philosophical idea evident in Lovejoy, *The Great Chain of Being*, but rather a Hebrew order of life and holiness as explored by Kennard, *Biblical Covenantalism*, 1:246–67.

The supreme example of holiness of being is that Yahweh is himself holy and thus defines the standard of what holiness means, separate to his category of being (Lev 11:44; 19:2; Num 20:12–13; 27:14; Isa 5:16; 6:3; 57:15).[76] *Qdš* is even used as a synonym for the divine name (Isa 40:25). God is holier than all else (Isa 65:5). Israel is to recognize that holy Yahweh is to be regarded as holy (Isa 5:16). As "Holy One of Israel," God demonstrates himself in judgment (Isa 1:4; 5:16, 24; 30:11; 31:1; 37:23; 47:4) and salvation (Isa 10:20; 12:6; 17:7; 29:19; 30:15; 40:25; 41:14, 16, 20; 43:3, 14–15; 45:11; 48:17; 49:7; 54:5; 57:15; 60:9, 14). All that is Yahweh is holy: he has a holy arm (Ps 98:1; Isa 52:10), a holy word (Ps 105:42), and a holy spirit (Ps 51:11; Isa 63:10–11). All that holy Yahweh touches is holy: Yahweh's heavenly habitation is holy (Isa 63:15), as are the holy city (Isa 48:2; 52:1), the holy mountain (Exod 19:33; Isa 11:9; 27:13; 56:7; 57:13; 65:11, 25; 66:20), holy day (Isa 58:13), and holy people Israel (Isa 11:9; 62:12; Ezek 28:22, 25), holy remnant Israel (Isa 6:13), holy new exodus way unto kingdom (Isa 35:8), holy house (Isa 63:15; 64:11)[77] with holy courts (Isa 62:9; Ezek 42:20). When Israel remained a holy people, they possessed the holy temple and holy cities until their sin brought about captivity (Isa 63:18; 64:10–11 [MT and LXX: 64:9–10]).

When holy Yahweh established a relationship with Israel, then the relationship and Yahweh's personal holy presence demands Israel to be holy as well: "You shall be holy for I Yahweh your God am holy" (Lev 19:2; 11:44–45). Yahweh's holiness sanctifies Israel to be metaphysically separate: "Thus you are to be holy to me, for I Yahweh am holy; and have set you apart from the peoples to be mine" (Lev 20:26). The people make themselves holy by sanctifying themselves or setting themselves apart for Yahweh (Isa 8:13; 13:3; 29:23; 66:17). To enter into Yahweh's presence and to continue in Yahweh's presence as a relationship involving his benefits requires Israel to be holy (Exod 19:10, 14; Num 11:18; Josh 3:5; 1 Sam 16:5; Joel 2:16). While holiness essentially is occupying a separate metaphysical level, it shows itself by doing separate deeds, because each metaphysical level is separate for a purpose which reflects its level. To Israel, Yahweh commands, "You shall consecrate yourselves therefore and be holy for I am Yahweh your God and you shall keep my statutes and practice them; I am Yahweh who sanctifies you" (Lev 20:7–8). Obedience to a morality does not render Israel holy but because they are separated by God for a relationship with him, the implication for Israel is that they should obey his standards. The context develops in which specifics identify Israel as set apart to Yahweh, such as faith (Deut

---

76. Olyan, *Rites and Rank*, 17.
77. *Temple Scroll* (11Q19–21, 4Q524, 4Q365a) 35.8–9; 46.9–12; 52.19.

32:51), or not profaning Yahweh's name (Lev 22:32), or being ready to be involved in Yahweh's sacrifices (1 Sam 16:5). Israel's obedience in the Mosaic covenant is with regard to holiness, and the whole of the Mosaic covenant command system (such as the Decalogue) is dependent upon and contained within holiness (Lev 19:2–37).[78] Furthermore, each respective group in relationship with Yahweh reflects appropriate standards which Yahweh tailors for them. For example, the Levites and other temple leadership set themselves apart for their duties (1 Chr 15:12; 2 Chr 30:17; 31:18). However, with Israel's priestly leadership sinning, they are polluted (pierced through), rendering the leadership unclean (Isa 43:28).

Holiness does not mean moral purity. For example, the garments that Aaron wore set him apart as the high priest, and yet garments have no intrinsic moral value—thus, amoral holiness (Exod 28:3). Yahweh is the one who set Israel apart by his choice—not their works or lifestyle, holiness beneath morality (Exod 31:13). An Israelite's separation could be defiled by a man dying close to him, evidencing no immorality on his part, though he must start his separation again—amoral reduction of holiness to common (Num 6:11). The concept of morality is easily read into a passage like 2 Samuel 11:4, but it should be understood to say Bathsheba had to wait for a time to be legally pure from the "uncleanness" of the sex act. The issue was not her recovery from the sin of adultery, for which the punishment was death. In this context, the word had not yet come concerning David's forgiveness. Therefore, Bathsheba is immoral and becoming holy through the cleansing process. Additionally, idolatry is immoral, yet the people are set apart for a sacred assembly for Baal—immoral holiness (2 Kgs 10:20). As an adjective, *qdš* refers to temple prostitutes separated to their pagan shrines for licentious Canaanite worship—immoral holiness (Gen 38:21–22; Deut 23:17).[79] Furthermore, the enemies of Judah were set apart by God for destruction and captivity—holy common immoral nations (Jer 6:4; 22:7; 51:27–28). Objects and times in themselves have no moral state, which further helps to clarify that holy (*qdš*) does not mean morality. For example, Exodus 28:38 says that the holy things separated by Israel have iniquity transferred to them by the sin of Israel but that a small gold plate on the high priest's turban takes the iniquity away (Exod 28:36). Thus, the idea of holy (*qdš*) does not include moral purity because these amoral objects cannot be in iniquity and morally pure at the same time and in the same manner.

---

78. *Seder Eliyah Rab.* 145; *Sipra Qedošim* par. 1.1; *Lev. Rab.* 24.5; Milgrom, *Leviticus 17–22*, 1602–3.

79. Jackie Naudé, "קָדֹשׁ," in *NIDOTT & E* 3:878; Thomas McComiskey, "קָדֹשׁ," in *TWOT* 2:787; W. Kornfeld, "קָדֹשׁ," in *TDOT* 12:524–25.

Likewise, time can be set apart as holy—amoral holiness. In the creation God set the Sabbath apart as holy in that he stopped his creative work for that day (Gen 2:3; Exod 20:11; 31:17; Isa 58:13) and then called Israel to likewise consider and treat the Sabbath as holy by stopping from their work (Exod 20:8–11; 31:13–17). Childs connects Sabbath with the tabernacle in the book of Exodus: "The first account of the tabernacle closes with the Sabbath command (31:12ff.); the second account of its building begins with the Sabbath command (35:1ff.) . . . The connection between the Sabbath and the tabernacle is therefore an important one."[80] This relationship is reflected within the holiness code, "You shall keep my Sabbaths and revere my sanctuary; I am Yahweh" (Lev 19:30). Isaiah affirms the holiness of keeping the Sabbath as part of keeping the Mosaic covenant, resulting in the Israelite being blessed (Isa 56:2, 4; 58:13).

Often, holiness is described as being *set apart for a purpose*. For example, Jeremiah was chosen to be separate as a prophet of Yahweh (Jer 1:5). Perhaps, with Isaiah's cleansing this pattern also describes Isaiah (Isa 6:7–8). Eleazar was also chosen to be separate so he could keep the ark (1 Sam 7:1). The priests and Levites are chosen to be separate and then their distinctive duties are described (Exod 19:22; 28:41; Lev 6:18, 27; 8:30; 21:8, 15, 23; Num 6:11; 1 Chr 18:14; 2 Chr 5:11; 26:1; 29:5, 34; 30:15, 24; 35:6; 44:19; Isa 43:28). This separateness of priests is set by select covenant grant statements where Yahweh undergirds each priestly line (Num 25; Mal 2:4–5)[81] and through the broader Mosaic covenant as well. Likewise, food was set apart for the purpose of the priests and Levites to eat (Neh 12:47). Leviticus 27:14–19 and 22 identifies vows setting apart a field or a house in *corban* for a purpose. This instruction on vows rendering things holy includes a clause by which the giver may redeem them for one-fifth of the market price. In such a situation the amoral becomes holy and then common without reference to morality or cleanness; so, holiness is distinct from morality and cleanness. Furthermore, Deuteronomy 22:9 urges the farmer to only sow one kind of seed in a field lest he need to separate the produce of the field; the issue is practicality in holiness rather than morality.

These separate categories of holiness have gradation to them. This gradation is evident in comparing two roles, one of which is holy compared to the other. For example, Moses functioning as high priest consecrates the priests (Exod 29; Lev 8; Isa 43:28) and establishes the pattern for the prophets and judges to follow (Deut 18:15–18). Additionally, the gradation is evident by the high priest having stricter obligations regarding cleanness

---

80. Childs, *The Book of Exodus*, 541; Gammie, *Holiness in Israel*, 20.
81. Sir 45.7, 15, 25, 24.

than other priests (Lev 21:1–15). Also deformed priests still have rights to eat food for priests as holy which others can't eat, though in their deformed condition they are prevented from priestly service as common (Lev 21:16–24). Likewise, the first born are separate as God's possession (Exod 13:2; Lev 27:26; Num 3:13; 8:17; Deut 15:19) but the Levites substitute for the first born as a separate group for tabernacle service (Num 8:14–19). The priests and Levites have a greater access to the tabernacle and a greater danger so they must receive danger pay (a tithe) for taking greater risks to keep Israel from being judged (Num 17:12—18:32). The people tithe to priests and Levites; Levites tithe to priests; but priests do not tithe to anyone higher, indicating categories of separateness.

Philip Jenson proposed a grading of holiness to reflect a gradation from very holy to very unclean.[82] For example, his category of very holy (*qdš qdšm*) includes: the holy of holies, high priest, and sacrificial animals offered and not eaten and the Day of Atonement. However clear his system happens to be, his categories don't quite fit the biblical textual description. For example, this category of the very holy is broader than he describes it, and the use of *qdšm* describes a comparison with other things in the context, much like the word for holy (*qdš*). The Holy of Holies is definitely very holy (Exod 26:33–34; 1 Kgs 6:16; 7:50; 8:6; 1 Chr 6:49 [MT and LXX: 34]; 2 Chr 3:8, 10) but so are the incense altar, all tabernacle furniture, the place for priests to eat sacrifice portions, everything designated *corban*, the kingdom temple site, and the Levites' promised land (Exod 30:10; 40:10; Lev 24:9; 27:28; Num 4:19; Ezek 43:12; 45:3; 48:12). The very holy includes Moses, Aaron and his sons, and Aaron's garments (Exod 30:29; 1 Chr 23:13). The category of very holy includes all priestly daily activity, including specifically the daily offerings (burnt, guilt, grain, incense), some of which are eaten by the priests but not by the people (Exod 29:37; 30:36; Lev 6:17 [10], 29 [22], 25 [18]; 7:1, 6; 10:12, 17; 14:13; Num 4:4; 18:9; Neh 7:65). So, Jenson's categories are too conceptually rigid and don't reflect the use of the Hebrew words. Additionally, the previous paragraph developed additional levels of holy (such as deformed priests) which Jenson's scheme does not consider. Furthermore, Jenson conceived of holy and clean as merely separate levels of the same thing, which is contradicted by the word studies here.

Though Jenson is in the current discussion, a superior gradation scheme was presented by Gordon Wenham reflecting that holiness and cleanliness are related but not exactly the same kind of gradations.[83] This

---

82. Jenson, *Graded Holiness*, 36–37.

83. Wenham, *The Book of Leviticus*, 177; *Numbers*, 123; b. *Me'il.* 8b on m. *Me'il.* 2.1; Milgrom, *Leviticus 1–16*, 732; Kennard, *Biblical Covenantalism*, 1:259–67.

discussion in the present chapter follows Wenham's categorization of the gradations in holy and clean as we attempt to reflect more accurately the Hebrew and the biblical text. The concept of holy (*qdš*) is a category of comparison. For example, Levites are common compared to priests but holy compared to Israel.

Separateness (*qdš*) of gradation also has to do with categories we in the West do not normally consider religious but which are identified as holy in the ancient Near East. For example, David and his warriors are separate for military purposes (1 Sam 21:5; Isa 13:3; Jer 6:4; 22:7; 51:27-28; Joel 3:9; Micah 3:5). This reminds us that in the ancient Near East war is a holy activity engaged in for God.

Early Judaism saw God's commitment to Israel as a real holy presence in the holy land and thus Jewish people grounded their everlasting existence in the land on this divine commitment to his holy people.[84] Recognition and alignment with the appropriate degree of holiness is how the Jew should respond under God's rule.[85] Yahweh both grounds Israel's holy condition in the everlasting kingdom and cultivates their morality, for he will lead his holy people in righteousness.[86]

CLEAN AND UNCLEAN

"Clean" (*thr*) is a measure of what is "cult appropriate" in light of one's relationship with Yahweh, in contrast to "unclean" (*tm'*) which is "inappropriate for the cult" (Lev 10:10; 11:47; 14:57; 20:25; Num 5:28; Deut 12:15, 22; 15:22; Job 14:45; Eccl 9:2; Ezek 22:26; 44:23). Clean (*thr*) occurs once in Isaiah 66:17 as an impotent attempt to purify the people and is thus condemned.[87] Unclean (*tm'*) occurs half a dozen times in Isaiah. For example, idolatrous images are unclean as menstruation (*dwh*) objects[88] and should be destroyed (Isa 30:22). Furthermore, the exodus plan to travel toward kingdom bans unclean humans from both the new exodus travel and from Zion as the kingdom center (Isa 35:8; 52:1, 11). As a result, confession by a rebel is still unclean in that it is a lie, but the confession of "unclean lips" by Isaiah in repentance is welcomed and forgiven (Isa 6:5; 64:6 [MT and LXX: 64:5]).

---

84. *Temple Scroll* 48.7, 10; 51.8.10; 1QH 4.25; 7.10; 1QM 3.4; 1QS 2.25; 5.13, 20; 8.17-23; 9.8; 1QSa 1.12; 2.9; CD 20.2, 5, 7, 24; *T. Job* 33.4-7; *T. Dan.* 5.11-13.

85. *Sifra* 207.2.11, 13.

86. *Pss. Sol.* 17.21-28; *Jub.* 15.30-31.

87. Neusner, *Idea of Purity in Ancient Judaism*, 26.

88. Oswalt, *The Book of Isaiah: Chapters 1-39*, 1:558.

With Isaiah's cleansing, he is appropriate to be in the heavenly temple throne room and to carry out God's purposes for him.

Two-fifths of all Rabbinic writings develop the issue of uncleanness and purification.[89] Jacob Neusner develops that they have to do with an "ontological ritual purity."[90] As such, clean is that part of the Hebraic world view that has to do with one's relationship to metaphysical purity for cultic purposes. That is, clean qualifies admission to sacred space.[91] However, in later prophets this ontological condition shows that it is significantly affected by morality in covenant as well. That is, sometimes unclean is sin and oftentimes it is not, but uncleanness always keeps something or someone from being connected in a cultic relationship with Yahweh. Furthermore, while rebellious sin causes such uncleanness, not all uncleanness is caused by sin. So, captivities and dispersions are caused by rebellion drawing Israel into unrecoverable uncleanness.

Throughout the ancient Near East there are cognates and synonyms that identify observable and religiously clean or cultic appropriateness.[92] While the Egyptian idea may be rooted in washing for ceremonial purposes; the Mesopotamian, Ugarit, and Hittite idea is more related to unmixed purity and brilliance. In observational use, the Hebrew *thr* describes a pavement made of sapphire as "clear and gleaming" as the sky (Exod 24:10). Likewise, *thr* describes the gold as "pure" for building the tabernacle, tabernacle furniture, and temple (Exod 25:11-39; 28:14-36; 30:3, 35; 31:8; 37:2-24; 39:15-37; Lev 24:4-7; 1 Chr 28:17; 2 Chr 3:4; 9:17; Job 28:19).[93] This use of *thr* indicates that the word conveys a metaphysically real quality of cultic appropriateness. Likewise, the incense burned there must be pure (*thr*, Exod 30:35; 37:29). In fact, Malachi 3:3 uses the Piel of *thr* twice for purifying precious metals and then metaphorically for purifying the Levites, so that they might function appropriately in the cult.

Being "unclean" essentially means being in a metaphysical condition of inappropriateness for cult participation and for being in close proximity

---

89. *Makhširin; Tohorot; 'Uqsin; Kelim; Parah; Miquaot; Tebul Yom; Yadayim*; and *Hagigah*.

90. Neusner, *Idea of Purity in Ancient Judaism*, 1; extending this, Josephus (*Ag. Ap.* 2.203; *Ant.* 3.266-68; 18.117-8) and Philo (*Good Person* 4; *Cherubim* 94-95; *Worse* 20) view clean and unclean through a Platonic worldview affecting the ontology of the soul. Neusner does not embrace such Platonism, but rather ties it to more of an ontological geometry of the real (*Idea of Purity in Ancient Judaism*, 16); Wilson, *"Holiness" and "Purity" in Mesopotamia*; Harrington, *Impurity Systems*.

91. Olyan, *Rites and Rank*, 17.

92. Richard Averbeck, "טָהֵר," in *NIDOTT & E* 2:339; Edwin Yamauchi, "טָהֵר," in *TWOT* 1:343; Helmer Ringgren, "טָהֵר," in *TDOT* 5:288-90.

93. 1QM 5.10-12.

to Yahweh. Such uncleanness is not sin, for the condition may be caused naturally without doing any inappropriate deed (Isa 6:5). Such a condition simply presents itself and needs to be noticed and appropriately acted upon, or it excludes people from cultic participation (Isa 1:16). If such practice is ignored, then it becomes a further indication of rebellion. If a priest considers a person or object as perpetually unclean then that person must dwell perpetually outside the camp (Lev 13:3, 45–46; 14:8–11; Num 5:2–4; Isa 35:8; 52:1, 11),[94] and perpetually unclean objects must be destroyed as inappropriate (Isa 30:22). For example, idols are unclean and should be destroyed (Isa 30:22). Likewise, the unclean will be banned from living among the camp of the new exodus way unto kingdom and its capital, Zion (Isa 35:8; 52:1, 11). Such severity about living outside the camp reflects that in the exodus camp it is as though Israel is perpetually on pilgrimage, being in close proximity to the tabernacle and the functioning cult. While all Jewish teaching excluded such unclean people and things from the temple and cult, once Israelites spread throughout the land, the leper could live within the land since they were later permitted to attend synagogue (2 Chr 23:19).[95] However, lepers were a social and religious pariah, needing to avoid social settings and to call out "unclean, unclean" so that other Israelites would not touch them inadvertently and become themselves unclean (Lev 5:3; 13:11, 33, 45–46; Num 5:2–4; 1 Sam 20:26).[96] Additionally, the leper was to have torn clothes and disheveled hair, which are the signs of mourning a death (Lev 10:6; 13:45–46).[97] In this case, the leper is mourning his own death because such illnesses draw the victim into the shadowland between life and death.

Uncleanness is a communicable disease which is transferred by touch and close proximity. For example, contact with the blood of birth or menstruation or with bodily discharges renders one ontologically unclean and thus restricted to set areas (Isa 30:22; 64:6 [LXX: 64:5]; Lev 12:2; 15:2–33; Num 5:2; Deut 23:10; Ezek 22:10; Luke 2:22–23).[98] In such a condition, Je-

---

94. CD 13.5–6; 11QT 46.16–18; 48.14–17; 4QThrA1 1–3; 4QMMT 71–72; b. 'Arak. 15b–16a; Lev. Rab. 17.3; m. Neg. 3.1; 4.7–10; Sifra, Mes. Neg. 1.1; m. Kel. 1.7; b. Yom. 16a, 30b.

95. M. Neg.; Strack and Billerbeck, Kommentar zum Neuen Testament, 4:752; 11QTS 45–53; Yadin, The Temple Scroll, 1:277–343.

96. CD 15.7–8; 11QT 45.17–46.2; 48.14–49.4; m. Neg. 3.1; 11.1; 12.1; 13.6–12; Josephus, Ag. Ap. 1.31; Targum on 2 Chr 26.21; Strack and Billerbeck, Kommentar zum Neuen Testament, 4:745–63.

97. 4QThrA1 3; Sifra Taz. Neg. 12.12–13; b. 'Arak. 16b; b. Pesah. 67a; Josephus, Ant. 3.264; Ag. Ap. 1.281.

98. While the biblical text does not identify woman's uncleanness and the need and means to be purified to Adam and Eve, Jub. 3.8–14 traces the laws of purification to

sus and Mary were cleansed from their uncleanness according to the Law, and obviously neither had sinned in the birthing process to become unclean (Luke 2:22-23). Humans and animals that even ignorantly touch or eat an unclean thing become unclean and continue to communicate uncleanness by touch to other things (Lev 5:2-3; 7:19-21; 11:4-8, 24, 39, 44, 47; 15:4-12, 19-27; 17:15; 18:19; 20:25; 22:4-8; Num 19:11, 16, 22; Hag 2:12-13).[99] In fact, on rare occasions like the death of a human within a tent, everyone who enters the tent and all open vessels in the tent are rendered unclean as by an airborne contaminant (Num 19:14-15, 18).[100] Such transferability of uncleanness renders the derived unclean object unclean by proximity but often not as unclean as the source. For example, sometimes the source is permanent in uncleanness like the dead or a kind of animal. Other times, the remedy of an unclean source may be just more severe (like washings, seven days, and two sacrifices) than the remedy of derived uncleanness (washing and one day, Lev 15:4-27). However, various instances of derived uncleanness from the same source are equally unclean and have the same remedy. There are different levels of derived uncleanness: touching a dead body requires seven days to remedy and touching an unclean thing requires one day to remedy (Num 19:11-12; Lev 15:4-27).[101] However, there are some things (like clay pots and stoves) that have an especially porous quality with regard to uncleanness and can never be purified, but must be destroyed to remove their uncleanness (Lev 11:33-35; 15:12). In contrast, there are some things (like water and seed) that have an especially resistant quality with regard to uncleanness, such that even a dead body touching them does not render them unclean (Lev 11:36-37).

The rabbis present uncleanness as communicable through a spiritual process akin to demonization for those pagans who have such within their

---

their time. While Num 5:2 excludes those with flow as outside the camp in rabbinic treatment, it is possible to quarantine the unclean (11QT 48.14-17; *m. Nid.* 7.4; *ARN A* 2.3; *Tg. Ps.-J.* on Lev 12:2; Josephus, *Ant.* 3.261). Because of this, all women are banished from the sacrificial court (Lev 12:6; 15:29; 11QT 45.7-10; CD 12.1-2; *m. Kel.* 1.8; *b. Yom.* 16a) and the sexually unclean are kept from the temple until they wash and the next day arrives (Lev 15:16-18; 11QT 45.7-10, 16-18; 4QOrdc 7-8; CD 12.1-2; *m. T. Yom.* 2.2-3; *m. Zab.* 5.10-11; *Sifra Shem. Sher.* 8.9; *Sifra Mes. Zab.* 2.8).

99. CD 7.3; 4QThrA1 4-5; *m. Zab.* 2.4; 5.6.

100. 11QT 49.5-7; 11-17; CD 12.15-18; *m. Kil.* 2.1; 11.2; *m.'Ohal.* 5.5; *Sipra Num.* 126; *b. Mo'ed Qaṭ.* 15b. Furthermore, the dead are not to be buried within a wall city, or it renders the city unclean (Num 5:2; 11QT 48.11-14; *m. Kel.* 1.7).

101. 11QT 47.7-18; 49.5-7; 11-17; 50.4-9; 51.1-5; 52.13-21; CD 12.15-18; *m. Kil.* 1.5; 2.1; 11.2; *m. 'Ohal.* 5.5; *m. 'Ed. Ṭehar* 6.3; *t. 'Ed. Ṭehar* 2.10; *Sifr. Num.* 126[162]; 127[165]; *b. Mo'ed Qaṭ* 15b; *Pal. Tg.* Num. 19:13, 16; *m. Ḥul.* 9.1, 5; *m. Ṭehar.* 1.4; *m. Zabim* 5.3; cf. *Parah; Miqvaot; Tebul Yom; Yadayim;* and *Hagigah.*

worldviews, but for a Jewish audience with a fuller biblical worldview, the communicability of uncleanness is merely grounded in the declaration or fiat of God. For example, Rabban Yohanan to the pagans says, "A man who is defiled by contact with a corpse—he, too, is possessed by a spirit, the spirit of uncleanness."[102] However, his Jewish disciples recognized that this was a simplistic answer, so they asked him again to explain communicable uncleanness. In response, the Jewishly informed Rabban Yohanan indicated that defilement and cleansing were ultimately grounded in God.

> By your lives, I swear: the corpse does not have the power by itself to defile, nor does the mixture of ash and water have the power by itself to cleanse. The truth is that the purifying power of the Red Cow is a decree of the Holy One. The Holy One said: "I have set it down as a statue, I have it as a decree. You are not permitted to transgress my decree. 'This is the statue of the Torah (Num. 19:1).'"[103]

So once again, within a Jewish worldview, the concepts of clean and unclean are held in metaphysical place by God's power and fiat. However, rabbinically some uncleanness is more culpable—that which is voluntary, foreseeable, and preventable.[104]

Jonathan Klawans delineates specific differences between moral (mostly developed within the section on righteousness) and ritual defilement.[105] However, in Isaiah uncleanness is parallel to the moral idea of unrighteousness and will thus be condemned (Isa 30:22; 64:6 [LXX: 64:5]; 66:17). Thus, the confession that Isaiah and Israel have unclean speech is an admission that Israel is rebellious, and Isaiah repents by including himself with his people as also part of the problem (Isa 6:5; 64:6 [LXX: 64:5]).

Beyond Isaiah, priestly documents (Lev; Num; Ezek) view uncleanness as an airborne contaminant. Jacob Milgrom led a reappraisal of the effect of the concept of ontological uncleanness through his metaphor of the picture of Dorian Gray. The Oscar Wilde novel *The Picture of Dorian Gray* portrays an individual adventurer who did not age or suffer the consequences of his adventures, for they all were marked upon his picture until he and his portrait met in his self-destruction.[106] One may say of the priestly

102. Rabban Yohanan, *Pesiq. Rab. Kah.* 4.7.
103. Rabban Yohanan, *Pesiq. Rab. Kah.* 4.7; Num 17:14; 19:16, 18; 11QT50.4-9; *Pal. Targ.* Num 19:13, 16; *Sif.* Num 127; *m. 'Ed.* 6.3; *m. Kel.* 1.5; *t. 'Ed.* 2.10.
104. 4QThrA1 1; *m. Baba Qamma* 1.4; *b. Arak.* 15b-16a; *Lev. Rab.* 17.3; Neusner, *Handbook of Rabbinic Theology*, 473-80.
105. Klawans, *Impurity and Sin*, 26.
106. Wilde, *Picture of Dorian Gray*.

picture of Dorian Gray that uncleanness may not leave its mark on the face of the unclean but it is certain to mark the face of the sanctuary; and unless it is quickly expunged, God's presence will depart.[107]

For Israel to ignore this warning and to become unclean defiles the tabernacle, putting themselves at risk to be cut off in covenant curse (Lev 15:31; Num 19:13).[108] This defilement of the tabernacle expands to defile the holy place and altar as well (Lev 16:16, 18; Num 19:20). For example, high-handed unrepentant sin, such as refusing to purify oneself after touching a dead body, defiles both the tabernacle and the holy place (Num 19:13, 20). Some might think that the tabernacle and the holy place are interchangeable on the basis of Numbers 19:13, 20, but they are better seen as different aspects of the tabernacle as is apparent in Leviticus 16:16–20 where the effect of uncleanness is developed again and the holy place, the tent of meeting, and the altar are all distinguished. In recognizing this, Jacob Milgrom presents uncleanness defiling the tabernacle in three stages.[109] First, the individual's inadvertent misdemeanor or severe physical impurity defiles the courtyard altar, which is cleansed by daubing its horns with the blood of the purification offering (Lev 4:25, 30; 9:9). Second, the inadvertent misdemeanor of the high priest or the entire community pollutes the Holy of Holies, which is purged by the high priest placing the purification offering blood on the inner altar and before the veil that divides the holy place from the Holy of Holies (Lev 4:5–7, 16–18). Third, high-handed, unrepentant sin not only pollutes the outer altar and penetrates into the holy place, but also pierces the veil to the Holy of Holies and the holy ark, the throne of God on earth (Lev 16:16; Num 19:20; Isa 37:16). Since the high-handed, rebellious sinner is barred from bringing a purification offering (Num 15:27–31), the uncleanness wrought by his offense must await the cleansing of the sanctuary on the Day of Atonement, which consists of two steps: cleansing the tent and the outer altar, and cleansing the people with atonement (Lev 16:16–19, 30; Isa 52:15 "sprinkle" people with blood and Isa 53:10 MT "guilt offering" or LXX "sin offering"). Thus, all that is most holy is cleansed on the Day of Atonement with the purification-offering blood. Thus, the graduated cleansings of the sanctuary lead to the conclusion that the severity of sin and uncleanness varies in direct relation to the depth of its penetration into the sanctuary.

Milgrom summarizes this sanctuary contamination through three laws: first, "*Sancta contamination varies directly with the charge (holiness)*

---

107. Similar point to that made by Milgrom, "Israel's Sanctuary."
108. *As. Mos.* 5.3; *Pss. Sol.* 1.8; 2.3; 8.13; *m. Šebu.* 1.4–5; *t. Šebu.* 1.3.
109. Milgrom, *Numbers*, 445–46.

of the sanctuary, the charge of the impurity, and inversely with the distance between them."[110] This law is an application by Milgrom of Mesopotamian contamination of the cult through airborne impurity. However, Yahweh's cult is extremely holy, so it is highly sensitive to contamination in the camp (Deut 23:15). Thus, there are repeated warnings to not pollute the sanctuary, which would bring destruction from Yahweh (Lev 12:4; 15:31; 20:1–4; Num 19:13, 20). By observation and comparison, Milgrom proposes a second law: "*Impurity displaces an equal amount of sanctuary holiness.*"[111] Holiness is being treated as an ontological thing which can be displaced. God will tolerate inadvertent wrongs which contaminate the outside alter and shrine for they can be purged through purification offerings (Lev 4:1–35). However, there is no sacrifice for defiant and rebellious acts, so the nation must purify the sanctuary of these on the Day of Atonement (Lev 16, especially verses 10, 16, 20–22; Num 15:30). To not comply with such purgation forces God's departure from the contaminated temple as a result of Israel's sin (Ezek 5:11; 8:6; 23:38–39; 24:21; 37:26–28; 48:8, 10, 21; and the similar vocabulary of 39:24 with Lev 16:16). With such divine departure, judgment, captivity, and destruction of Israel will ensue. God promises to only return at his initiation of an everlasting covenant of peace (the New Covenant) that makes Israel responsive to God's presence and Yahweh's holy temple placed within the nation (Ezek 11:16; 37:26–28; 48:8, 10, 21). Milgrom summarizes his third purity law in the following paragraph:

> Thus, the pre- and post-ablution periods offer a new criterion for comparing the realms of the sacred and the common, to wit: *(a) The sacred is of greater sensitivity to contamination than the common by one degree, and (b) each purification stage reduces contagion to both the sacred and the common by one degree.* There are three possibilities to contaminate an object: from afar, by direct contact, or at home. Specifically, a severely impure person contaminates a common object by direct contact and a sacred object from afar. After the ablution, he is no longer contagious to the common object but can contaminate a sacred object by direct contact (but not from afar). Finally, after the last stage of purification he is no longer contagious even to sancta.[112]

---

110. Milgrom, "Priestly Laws of Sancta Contamination," 137–46, esp. 142.

111. Milgrom, "Priestly Laws of Sancta Contamination," 142–43.

112. Milgrom, "Priestly Laws of Sancta Contamination," 145; "Priestly Impurity System."

Such a summary for how uncleanness contaminates and is purified is warranted by the biblical examples, Josephus, and tannaitic sources (Lev 11–16).[113] The purgation is accomplished through repentance, time, and the appropriate sacrifice.[114]

Furthermore, any form of uncleanness defiles the land. For example, a dead body hanging overnight defiles the land which Yahweh gives Israel as an inheritance (Deut 21:23). Likewise, by not killing murderers by capital punishment, the land is defiled and threatens Yahweh's continuing dwelling with Israel (Num 35:34). Furthermore, for Israel to flagrantly defile themselves by sensuality and pagan worship defiles the land and places Israel at risk of Yahweh's covenant curse in the same manner as he cursed the people of the land for their idolatry (Lev 18:24–30).

The means of purification involves washing in specially prepared water and fulfilling the time of uncleanness. Isaiah offered this practice metaphorically as removing sin and practicing justice (Isa 1:16–17). The ritual cleansing stages establish gradations of uncleanness while the person or object has completed part of the process (such as the washing) without finishing the process (such as the whole time allotted).[115] The water to remove impurity is prepared by mixing the ashes of the red heifer burnt offering, cedar wood, hyssop, and scarlet material together in the water (Num 19:1–10). Those involved in preparing this water for cleansing become clean, namely the priest who sacrifices this offering and the man who gathers the ashes (Num 19:7, 10). The unclean utilize the water for cleansing to wash themselves and their clothes and are unclean until evening. Anyone who touches or is inside a tent with a dead body is required to purify himself by washing in the water for cleansing on the third and seventh day and is unclean until the seventh day (Num 19:11–13, 18–19).[116] The one who sprinkles the water for cleansing shall be unclean till evening and then he too must wash himself and clothes in the water for cleansing (Num 19:21–22). The one who refuses to cleanse himself through the water of cleansing defiles the tabernacle and is destined to be cut off.

Sacrifice is only to utilize clean offerings and sites. For example, Noah sacrificed only clean animals (Gen 8:20). Furthermore, the purification offering is a clean sacrifice with the ashes poured out outside the camp in a clean place (Lev 4:12; 6:11). There is no alternative altar for cleansing than

113. M. Kelim 1.4; m. Neg. 13.7, 11; Josephus, Ag. Ap. 1.31; Ant. 3.264.

114. Kennard, Biblical Covenantalism, 1:289–313.

115. Num 31:19; 11QT 49.13–17; b. Mo'ed Qaṭ. 15b; Thomas Kazen, "4Q274 Fragment 1 Revisited."

116. 11QT 49.5–7; 11–17; CD 12.15–18; m. Kelim 2.1; 11.2; m. 'Ohal. 5.5; Sifr. Num. 126; b. Mo'ed Qaṭ.15b.

the tabernacle, or Israel is under threat of being cut off (Josh 22:16–20). Doing any ritual as a priest or eating a sacrifice or touching a holy gift in an unclean ontological condition or place threatens the cult with uncleanness, thus rendering the one guilty cut off from the people (Lev 7:19–21; 10:9–10, 14; Num 18:11, 13; Deut 26:14). If someone was clean and skipped Passover, then they are without excuse and shall be cut off (Num 9:13–14). On the other hand, when the ignorant ate Passover in an unclean condition, merciful Yahweh atoned for them in response to Hezekiah's revival and prayer on their behalf (2 Chr 30:17–19). However, it is far better to operate as in Zerubabel's revival by first cleansing all the people so that they could participate in Passover (Ezra 2:20–21).

Within the Mosaic covenant, Yahweh demands that Israel be kept clean and holy (Lev 11:44–45). Only clean people can participate in cultic functions (Lev 7:19–20; 1 Sam 20:26; Ezra 6:20; and an exception in 2 Chr 30:17–19 which has God supernaturally cleanse Israel also supports the rule). If Israel does not deal with their uncleanness, then it becomes a sin. For Israel to ignore this mandate and to become unclean defiles the tabernacle and puts Israel at risk to be cut off in covenant curse (Lev 15:31; Num 19:13). This defilement of tabernacle from Israel's uncleanness includes the holy place and altar as well (Lev 16:16, 18; Num 19:20). Ultimately, sins defile Yahweh's holy name and bring covenant curse as was previously developed (Deut 28:15—29:29; Ezek 43:7–8). For example, a high-handed unrepentant sin, such as refusing to purify oneself after touching a dead body, defiles both tabernacle and holy place (Num 19:13, 20). Furthermore, one of the sins for which Israel is condemned to the Babylonian captivity is the sin of the priest's failure to teach the people and to practice the difference between clean and unclean (Ezek 22:26; Hag 2:11–14).

Whatever standard God sets metaphysically for clean becomes what is appropriate. The ontologically unclean cannot be rendered clean by human means (Job 14:4). No attempt at viewing or externally fulfilling purifying rituals can transform the metaphysically unclean into clean status (Prov 30:12; Isa 66:17).

Verbally, words that are refined and helpful are "pure" (*thr*, Ps 12:6; Prov 15:26). Obedience to such "pure" (*thr*) teaching preserves a person from sin, allowing them to continue to be ontologically clean (Ps 12:6–7), whereas lying words are "unclean" (*tm'*) but can be forgiven through Yahweh's refining process (Isa 6:5). However, if a life habituates to sin, no amount of claiming such an ontological clean status can remove a person's sins (Prov 20:9).

Metaphorically, "pure" (*thr*) refers to the condition of having one's sins atoned for and forgiven, returning them to ontological clean status (Lev

16:30; Ps 51:7, 10; Isa 1:16; 6:7; Ezek 24:13). This recovered condition is accomplished nationally at the Day of Atonement (Lev 16:30). An Israelite is individually recovered by the purification offering or guilt offering (Lev 4:20, 26, 31, 35; 5:10, 13; Isa 53:10). However, if an Israelite has committed high-handed sin there is no purification offering available, so merciful Yahweh may yet cleanse and forgive without utilizing a sacrifice if the Israelite is truly repentant (Ps 51:2, 7, 10). In contrast, if an Israelite accused of sin passes the test of the waters of curse, she should be considered morally and ontologically clean without needing additional divine mercy through a sacrifice (Num 5:28).

Israel's ontological uncleanness includes sins of violating the temple by means of idols, idolatrous practices, violation of kosher, adulterous trusting of gentile power rather than Yahweh's, and the presence of dead or unclean within the temple (2 Chr 23:19; 36:14; Ps 79:1; Isa 66:17; Jer 7:30; 32:34; Ezek 5:11; 9:7; 20:7, 18, 30–31; 22:3, 12–17, 24; 23:7, 13, 30, 38; 36:18; 37:23; 43:6–9; Mal 1:11–12).[117] These metaphorical descriptions must not reduce "clean" to "moral" and "unclean" to "sin," but rather they show that metaphysical cleanness is porous and prone to be affected by the virus of vice and sin, resulting in the ontological infection of uncleanness. Cleansing from such practices and their resultant uncleanness requires the removal of all idols and the avoidance of such practices (Gen 35:2; Josh 22:17; Ezek 24:13). One of the goals of the reformers in Israel was to recover the temple as clean (2 Chr 29:16) and to defile pagan idols by eradicating idolatrous practices from Israel (2 Kgs 23:8, 10, 13, 16; Isa 30:22; Jer 19:13; Ezek 37:23). The final defilement of the first temple was its destruction by the Babylonians (Ps 79:1). Israel had to go through the Babylonian captivity before they would be cleansed again; their ontological uncleanness brought about judgment (Ezek 24:13–14; 36:18; 43:8; Micah 2:10). At the dedication of the second temple, Israel separated themselves from the uncleanness of their Gentile neighbors in order to seek the Lord (Ezra 6:21; Neh 12:30; 13:30).

Early Judaism clarified aspects in the biblical teaching to fill in gaps and to continue the biblical tradition into aspects of graded impurity.[118] For example, after one's purification, washing the person was considered to be not as unclean as before, but uncleanness remained with a person until the *time* for purification *was over* (usually as the sun goes down), and then they were clean.[119] So those who were in process of being cleansed needed to be

---

117. *As. Mos.* 5.3; *Pss. Sol.* 1.8; 2.3; 8.13; *m. Šebu.* 1.4–5; *t. Šebu.* 1.3.

118. Harrington, *Impurity Systems*, 114.

119. 11QT 45.9–10; 49.20–21; 50.12, 15–16; 51.3, 5; 4QMMT 13–17; 59–67; 4Q274 frag. 1; 4QThrA1 5–6 in contrast to *m. T. Yom* 2.1–2; Harrington, *Impurity Systems*, 64–65; Kazen, "4Q274 Fragment 1 Revisited."

careful not to become defiled by those who were not becoming clean because time contributed toward cleansing as well as the washings. Additionally, statements that a person is "pure" after they are healed and washed do not indicate that the subsequent sacrifices have no atonement role for the individual (Lev 15:13); rather the individual is "pure enough" for that stage of the purification process ("pure enough" for the healed leper to enter the camp but not his tent until a priest announces him "pure" on the seventh day and again after sacrifices on the eighth day, Lev 14:8–9, 20).[120]

In a few instances the rabbis were more concerned about issues of remaining clean than remaining righteous, which extends beyond the biblical pattern.[121] While concerned for righteousness, often sectarian Judaism went beyond the purity standards of the Bible and the rabbinics. For example, Israelites do not need to purify themselves to eat common food (Mark 7:2; Luke 11:37–41).[122] Likewise, where the Bible is silent, sectarians and some rabbinics consider contact with outsiders, especially gentiles, as rendering them unclean (Acts 10:28; 11:3).[123] Many Christians are concerned about justification for salvation to the neglect of sanctification accomplished in atonement. However, Isaiah's servant of Yahweh sprinkles the nations in atonement 1) sanctifying them so that those who align with the servant are saints, and 2) justifying them so that those who align with the servant are forgiven (Isa 52:15). Positional justification and sanctification identifies believers in Yahweh's servant as appropriately belonging within God's kingdom as it is formed in the wake of this atonement.

Eventually in kingdom, God will supernaturally and directly cleanse the nation Israel from their sins of idolatry so they will be metaphysically clean (Isa 35:8; 52:1, 11, 15) and responsive with a new covenant heart transformation (Ezek 36:25–26, 33; priests cleansed, Mal 3:3; and the high priest cleansed as well, Zech 3:3–5). In such a clean status, Levitical priests of Israel will offer sacrifices in the cleansed temple in clean vessels and obtain atonement and forgiveness (Isa 66:20; Jer 33:18; Ezek 43:18—44:31; 45:4–5; Mal 1:11). In that era of kingdom, the priests will teach the people the difference between holy and common, and clean and unclean (Ezek 44:23).

---

120. Contrary to Milgrom, "The Preposition מִן in the חַטָּאת Pericopes," 161–62; consistent with Gane, "Private Preposition מִן"; Kazen, "4Q274 Fragment 1 Revisited."

121. An odd discussion about the uncleanness of a knife as more grievous than murder (*t. Yoma* 1.12).

122. For example, Israelites do not need to purify themselves to eat common food except among the sectarians (4QThrA1 3; 4QOrdc 7–9).

123. Josephus, *War* 2.150, 229; *Ant.* 12.145; 14.285; 1QM 9.8–9; *m. Pesah.* 9.8; *m. Ṭehar.* 5.8; 7.6; *m. Nid.* 7.3; *t. Nid.* 9.16; *t. Zabim* 2.1; *Sifr. Taz. Neg.* par. 1.1; *M. Zabim.* par. 1.1; *b. Šabb.* 83a, 127b; *b. Nid.* 69b.

DEUTERONOMIC HISTORY

In Isaiah, Deuteronomic history captures historical material responding to the suzerainty treaty to Israel's situation.[124] If Israel remains faithful in obedience to the terms of the everlasting Mosaic covenant, then they will have everlasting blessing as Yahweh's faithful servants (Isa 56:4-6; Deut 28:1-14). However, when Israel rebels, they break this covenant and Yahweh as great king will bring covenant curse upon them (Isa 24:5; 33:8; Deut 28:15—29:28).

The first narrative section in Isaiah is the account about the sign-child provided to evil King Ahaz and Judah under him. The events of the narrative occurred around 737-732 BC (dated on the basis of the kings warring in Isa 7:1-2, namely: Ahaz, 741-725 BC; Rezin, 740-732 BC; and Pekah, 737-732 BC). The date for the sign prophecy also can be calculated by noticing when the predictions were realized and calculating back to when the prophecy must have been said to make it fit. On the basis of the descriptions in Isa 7:15, the prophecy would be within 736-735 BC. This date of prophecy would also be within 735-734 BC based on the descriptions in Isa 8:4. Therefore, Isaiah presents this sign prophecy as likely occurring around 735 BC.

The setting for the narrative is that the Arameans were camping in Ephraim, causing Ahaz and Judah to fear impending invasion (Isa 7:2).[125] Yahweh prompted Isaiah to go with his son Shearjashub ("a remnant will return") to meet Ahaz at the upper pool by the highway around the laundryman's field (Isa 7:3). This location around Jerusalem cannot be placed exactly today as it could in Isaiah's day, but it is outside Hezekiah's wall, based on Josephus identifying that the later Assyrian camp was on the western hills and the meeting of Rabshekah of Assyria with Judah's representatives occurred at the same pool (such as perhaps the later Tower Pool; Isa 36:2-22).[126] Some others identify this pool as perhaps the Gihon spring or near the pool of Bethesda.[127]

Isaiah met Ahaz and offered any sign that Ahaz would choose for reassurance that Rezin and Pekah would not ultimately threaten Judah (Isa 7:4-11). Yahweh was promising peace for Judah's faithfulness. Ahaz refused to ask for a sign, pretending a false spirituality. This refusal to ask a sign was seen by Isaiah and God as further rebellion on Ahaz's part. Isaiah's change

---

124. Bright, "Faith and Destiny."

125. Josephus, *Ant.* 9.243-57 develops Ahaz's reign.

126. "Monument of the Fuller" on the north side of Jerusalem, Josephus, *Ant.* 5.303; *War* 5.7.3, and 5.4.2; Ussishkin, "Sennacherib's Campaign to Judah," 95; Boutflower, *The Book of Isaiah*, 269.

127. Dalman, *Jerusalem und seine Gelände*, 38-40; Young, *The Book of Isaiah*, 1:271.

from "your God" (Isa 7:11) to "my God" ominously indicts Ahaz in rebellion (Isa 7:13). Even so, Yahweh provides him with a sign (Isa 7:13). Isaiah reassured Ahaz that within sixty-five years or about 669 BC Ephraim will be no more; in fact Esar-haddon carried away Manasseh and resettled a foreign ruling class of colonists in Ephraim by then (Isa 7:8; Ezra 4:2, 10).[128] To encourage Ahaz and Judah to believe, a sign is provided for them, to provide a timeline for measuring God's encouraging rescue from the momentary threat (Isa 7:14). Because the sign is offered to the plural group surrounding Ahaz, faith is not just passive, nor making political arrangements to Assyria, but it is in Judah's trust of Yahweh's instruction and timing that Yahweh will fight for Judah and deliver them.[129] The narrative provides no evidence of Judah's faithfulness, so their deliverance could be understood as a measure of Yahweh's mercy before they go too far.

In the wake of the previous narrative, the historical material about Hezekiah concludes the section developing Assyria, providing a sample of Deuteronomic history reflecting the blessing and curse under the Mosaic covenant (Isa 36–39).[130] The accumulated Assyrian documents and reliefs of this era show severe curse from Assyrian conquests, including piles of severed heads of their opponents.[131]

Sennacherib subdued the coast and then came inland, sieging Lachish in 701 BC, when Hezekiah was tempted to depend upon Egypt's aid (Isa 20:1–6; 30:1–5; 31:1–3; 36:1, 6). This would mean that Hezekiah's accession to the throne was around 715 BC, later than many commentators would place it.[132]

During the siege of Lachish, Sennacherib sent commander Rabshakeh and a large army to Jerusalem to meet Hezekiah's representatives (Eliakim, Shebna, and Joab) at the same location where Isaiah had met Ahaz (Isa 7:3; 36:1–3; 2 Kgs 18:17–37). This location around Jerusalem cannot be placed exactly today as it could in Isaiah's day, but it is outside Hezekiah's wall, based on Josephus identifying that the later Assyrian camp was on the western hills, with the pool (such as the later Tower Pool) being where Rabshekah of Assyria met Judah's representatives (Isa 36:2–22).[133]

---

128. Young, *The Book of Isaiah*, 1:275–76.

129. Wong, "Faith in the Present Form of Isaiah."

130. Josephus, *Ant.* 10.2.1 and 10.2.12–34 develops Hezekiah's reign, and Hillel II considers him to be a messiah (*b. Sanh.* 99a).

131. Lewis, "'You Have Heard.'"

132. J. J. Roberts, *First Isaiah*, 451.

133. "Monument of the Fuller" on the north side of Jerusalem, Josephus *Ant.* 5.303; *War* 5.7.3 and 5.4.2; David Ussishkin, "Sennacherib's Campaign to Judah: The Archeological Perspective with an Emphasis on Lachish and Jerusalem," In *Sennacherib at the*

Rabshakeh disparaged Hezekiah's dependence upon Egypt, much as Sargon II had done with Ashdod ten years previously (Isa 36:4-6).[134] Presumably, Egypt had engaged the Assyrians at Eltekeh, but Laichish and Egypt failed to stop the Assyrian attack (Isa 37:8). At this point Sennacherib's siege-forces claimed to have Hezekiah captured in Jerusalem "like a bird in a cage"[135] (Isa 36:12-20). Brevard Childs develops that Rabshakeh's taunt of impending judgment reflects a challenge to Deuteronomic theology with his repeated denigration of Yahweh, "trust" ($bṭḥ$), and "save" ($nṣl$).[136] Rabshakeh makes three points: Egypt can't help (Isa 36:4-6, 8-9), Yahweh neither has the strength nor the will to support Hezekiah, who had destroyed alters (Isa 36:7, 10, 18-20; 37:10-12), and the people of Judah will not support Hezekiah when Assyria has the brute force to win (Isa 36:14-21).[137] Ultimately, Hezekiah recognized that Assyria is challenging Yahweh's strength (Isa 36:18-20).

When Hezekiah heard the boastful Assyrian taunt, he repented, tore his clothes, and covered himself with sack-cloth in mourning, entered the temple to pray for the remnant that was left, and spread Assyria's taunt letter out before Yahweh (Isa 37:1-4; 14-20). Hezekiah's prayer essentially asked for Yahweh to deliver Judah from Sennacherib so that all the nations might know that Yahweh is God (Isa 37:20). Hezekiah's prayer reflects his Deuteronomic religious reforms and his trusting in Yahweh (2 Kgs 18:3-6; 2 Chr 29:3-21).[138] Isaiah responded that Hezekiah need not fear Rabshakeh's blasphemy, for Sennacherib will return to Assyria and be killed by sword in his own land because he arrogantly challenged Yahweh (Isa 37:6-7, 21-29). Isaiah's response polemicizes Gilgamesh and Enkidu's invasion of the cedar forest as impotent desecration before Yahweh's might (Isa 37:23-24).[139] Hezekiah was provided with a sign indicating that Judah might be challenged for two years but in the third spring they are to plant and eat their crops because the Assyrian threat will be past since the zeal of Yahweh the general will defend a remnant in Jerusalem for David's sake (Isa 37:30-35). Isaiah describes that the angel of Yahweh killed 185,000 of Sennacherib's troops (Isa 37:36), an event that Herodotus recounts as a plague that felled Assyria

---

Gates of Jerusalem, edited by Isaac Kalim and Seth Richardson, 95; Charles Boutflower, *The Book of Isaiah Chapters [1-XXXIX] In Light of the Assyrian Monuments*, 269.

134. Fuchs, *Die Annalen*, 81-96; K.1668b+D.T.6 VII.b lines 30-33; J. J. Roberts, *First Isaiah: A Commentary*, 453.

135. *Esar* 582-84; *Annals of Assyrian Kings*, In *AfOB* 9, 58, lines 12-18.

136. Brevard Childs, *Isaiah and the Assyrian Crises*, 89, 99-100.

137. Oswalt, *The Book of Isaiah: Chapters 1-39*, 634.

138. Roberts, *First Isaiah*, 469.

139. *Gilgamesh* 5.262-65, 289-97; Roberts, *First Isaiah*, 469-70.

when it was near the border of Egypt.[140] Sennacherib returned to Nineveh and was killed by his sons in the temple of Nisroch as Isaiah had predicted (Isa 37:7, 37–38).[141]

Before Sennacherib left, Hezekiah became mortally ill and was expected to die but, through his tears, he prayed to Yahweh with a confession of trust, "Remember I have walked before you in truth with my whole heart and have done good in your sight" (Isa 38:1–3, 6). Isaiah was sent to Hezekiah with a promise of covenant blessing including fifteen more years of life and deliverance from Assyrian siege (Isa 38:4–7). Yahweh even provided the sign Hezekiah requested, enabling the sun's shadow to go back ten steps on the stairs to reassure Hezekiah of this healing and deliverance (Isa 38:7–8, 22; 2 Kgs 20:8–10). Perhaps 2 Chronicles 32:31 identifies this sign to be a local phenomenon of refraction for the Babylonian emissaries to ask about it.[142] However, Isaiah does not explain how the movement of the shadow was accomplished, simply that it happened and that Hezekiah was encouraged.

Hezekiah's faithfulness to trust Yahweh strongly contrasts with Ahaz's refusal. Hezekiah responds to the promised healing with a lament about his nearness to *sheol* and a petition for healing and forgiveness. As Hezekiah is praying, his prayer confidently confesses his trust and praise to Yahweh for saving them from death. This worship of Yahweh continues with public singing and musical instruments (Isa 38:10–20).

In the wake of Hezekiah's healing, Babylonian emissaries from Merodach-baladan came and Hezekiah foolishly showed them the wealth of the temple and his house (Isa 39:1–4). Such an attitude demonstrated some degree of self-sufficiency such that Isaiah responded from Yahweh that all that they have seen, Babylon will take away into captivity (Isa 39:5–7; 2 Kgs 20:17–18). Hezekiah callously responded to this covenant curse by expressing that this was good because he selfishly thought at least there will be peace and truth in his own days (Isa 39:8). However, it meant that in 598 BC Babylon stripped the temple and deported Jehoiachin and his household to Babylon (2 Kgs 24:12–16).[143]

These narrative sections fit within a Deuteronomic history or covenant nomism in which Judah's faithfulness to the Mosaic covenant begets blessing from Yahweh. However, if the king considers himself self-sufficient, then the nation is on a trajectory for covenant curse from Yahweh.

---

140. Perhaps bubonic plague caused by rats, Herodotus, *Hist.* 2.141; Roberts, *First Isaiah*, 471–72.

141. "Sennacherib's Campaign Against Jerusalem," in *ANET*, 309a; Roberts, *First Isaiah*, 473.

142. Oswalt, *The Book of Isaiah: Chapters 1–39*, 678.

143. Clements, *Isaiah and the Deliverance of Jerusalem*, 66.

CHAPTER 6

Sin and Judgment

ISAIAH DOES NOT DISCUSS sin abstractly. Humans do sin, and in response God brings judgment upon them. In Isaiah's expression, sin and judgment are tied together and must be developed together.

ISRAEL'S SIN: BREACH OF COVENANT

In their rebellion, Yahweh's vassals broke covenant with him. In Isaiah, sin is against God and essentially a rebellion of those obligated to obey.[1] Eichrodt records that "Isaiah describes sin as rebellion against the divine Lord, a rupture of the relationship of *pietas* between a father and his children arising from pride and lack of faith, which will not allow themselves to be set right by the transcendent of God."[2]

Words for Sin

Pšʿ means "rebellion" and a "violation of a standard."[3] Such rebellion is the primary sin of Israel in the book of Isaiah (1:2; 24:20; 43:25; 44:22; 50:1; 53:5, 8; 57:4; 58:1; 59:12, 20). Israel is Yahweh's child who rebelled against him (Isa 1:2). In their rebellion, Israel does not even acknowledge their dependence upon Yahweh; Yahweh owns them, and Israel does not respond

---

1. Snaith, *The Distinctive Ideas of the Old Testament*, 75, 79–86.
2. Eichrodt, *Theology of the Old Testament*, 1:375; Isa 1:2, 4; 2:6; 5:12, 21, 24; 9:8; 28:1, 10, 14, 22.
3. BDB 833.

with the very submission animals have for their masters (Isa 1:3). Such ignorance and lack of understanding is itself also sin.[4] Israel maintained a persistent rebellion against God in spite of compounding ill effects (Isa 1:5-9; 31:6). Israel had been choosing rebellious deeds since the nation's inception, thus showing their unfortunate consistent character (Isa 1:28; 46:8; 48:8; 57:4; 58:11). Even their leaders were rebellious against God (Isa 43:27). In response, Israel confessed (Isa 59:12-13):

> Our offenses are many in your sight, our songs testify against us
> Our offenses are ever with us, and we acknowledge our iniquities:
> Rebellion and treachery against Yahweh, turning our backs on our God,
> Fomenting oppression and revolt, uttering lies our hearts have conceived.

They rejected the Law of Yahweh (Isa 5:24) and resisted the message of the prophets from the Holy One of Israel (Isa 30:8-11). For their rebellion, they were divorced from God in the judgment of the captivity (Isa 50:1). In addition, the others of the earth were guilty in rebellion to the degree that when they were judged by Yahweh, they will not rise again (Isa 24:20; 66:24). The remedy is only through divine forgiveness (Isa 43:25; 44:22) based on the sacrificial death of the servant (Isa 53:5, 8, 12). This redemption only extends to those who repent of their rebellion (Isa 59:20).

Another word developing the theme of rebellion is *sr*, meaning "turning aside and departing," as in apostasy.[5] Israel persisted in their revolt against Yahweh (Isa 1:5; 31:6; 59:13). Yahweh responded by turning away, removing their support and protection, and fighting against them (Isa 1:16; 3:1; 5:5). They refused or "resisted" (*mn*) to obey Yahweh's commands (Isa 1:20).[6] Israel rebelled, contentiously defying Yahweh's glorious presence, which grieves the holy spirit[7] (Isa 1:20; 3:8; 63:10). Yahweh responded by fighting against them (Isa 63:10) and sending his servant who did not rebel (Isa 50:5).

A further word related to this concept, *ḥṭ'*, means "miss the mark" or "fall short of the divine standard."[8] The term essentially does not have to have a moral significance, as in one who does not live to the kingdom norm of a hundred years (Isa 65:20). However, usually the term refers to moral rebellion or "sin" in the book (Isa 43:27; 58:1). Israel is characterized by

---

4. Watts, *Isaiah 1-33*, 27.
5. BDB 693-94.
6. BDB 549.
7. BDB 598.
8. BDB 306-8.

sin (Isa 1:4, 18, 28; 33:14; 59:12), even openly (Isa 3:9). Babylon and Isaiah are identified as guilty (Isa 6:7; 13:9), but Israel is the one most charged with guilt in rebelling against God's covenant plan. Yahweh declares, "Woe to the obstinate children . . . to those who carry out plans that are not mine, forming an alliance, but not by my spirit, heaping sin upon sin" (Isa 30:1; 5:18; 42:24). This alliance is likely Israel's dependence upon Egypt during the threat from Assyria. Israel drew sin to themselves "by soliciting temptation, drawing it out by obstinate persistency in evil and contempt of divine threatenings"[9] (Isa 5:18). Sin separated Israel from Yahweh (Isa 59:2). God carried the burden of someday judging Israel (Isa 27:9; 43:24; 64:5). Their sin was paid for through the captivity and thus forgotten by God (Isa 38:17; 40:2). Eventually, the messianic servant bore this burden of sin (Isa 53:12). Because Israel was forgiven, they were encouraged to return to Yahweh (Isa 44:20).

Similar words for rebellion include *'nn*, often occurring in a parallel construction with the following (Isa 1:4; 5:18). The essential meaning of the word is "iniquity, crookedness, and guilt."[10] *Šḥt* is used for "corrupt and destructive behavior"[11] (Isa 1:4; 11:9; 36:10; 37:12; 31:13; 54:16; 65:8, 25). *Rʿ* is used for "evil," often when there is a harmful, injurious, and wicked quality (Isa 1:4, 16; 3:9, 11; 5:20; 7:5; 13:11; 31:2; 32:7; 33:15; 47:10; 56:2; 57:1; 59:7, 15; 65:12; 66:4). *Ršʿ* signifies "wickedness," particularly in describing the character of an individual[12] (Isa 3:11; 5:23; 11:4; 13:11; 14:5; 26:10; 48:22; 53:9; 55:7; 57:20–21; 58:4, 6).

Specific Sins within Israel's Breach of Covenant

Idolatry was sternly opposed by Yahweh in the Ten Commandments (Deut 5:8–10); however, Israel learned the practices of the nations in the land. For example, the established Canaanite high places were only removed during the reign of good kings (Isa 36:7) and at other times there is clear syncretism at these sites. Isaiah clearly intimates that the land is full of idols (Isa 2:8). Offerings and sacrifices occur in orchards ("garden" Isa 65:3; 66:17), especially at sacred trees (Isa 1:29–30; 2:8; 57:5; 2 Kgs 16:4; Hos 4:13; Jer 2:20; 3:6–13; 17:2; Ezek 6:3). Otto Kaiser describes this worship.

---

9. Alexander, *Prophecies of Isaiah*, 137; Nagelsbach, "The Prophet Isaiah," 6:101.
10. BDB 730–31.
11. BDB 1007–8.
12. BDB 957–58.

They gather under trees which have grown in a striking way, for Canaanite fertility cults, with rites which in Israel's eyes are obscene. Holy terebinths of this sort were venerated in Palestine as late as the Christian era. Relics of tree worship in a changed form can still be seen at the present day among the Arabs. The "gardens" are sanctuaries for the cult, in which the alternation between death and life, between the summer heat and the spring, is meant to be made present and brought about. In them the Egyptian and Phoenician divinities Osiris and Adonis may have been venerated (Isa 65:3; 66:17). Terebinths are deciduous trees and consequently provide a striking symbol of the process of a god, his journey into kingdom of the dead and resurrection in the spring. The prophet accepts these views, but only in order to firmly oppose them: those who worship these gods will themselves wither (1:30). But this withering will not be followed by a resurrection; they will ultimately be like trees and gardens whose water supply has dried up (Pss 1:3; 52:8; 90:5ff; 92:12f; Job 15:30ff; 18:16; Isa 40:6; 53:2).[13]

There was even the offering of meal and drink to fortune, the Assyrian god of good luck (Isa 65:11). To this idolatry Yahweh responds by showing the insufficiency of idols, for he is incomparable to them. Humans were made in the image of God with vitality and procreation; idols are made in the lifeless image of humans (Isa 44:13; Rom 1:23). Isaiah sarcastically describes idols as *elihim*, representing the pagan gods as "godlets," or "good-for-nothing-ones" (Isa 2:8, 18, 20; 10:10ff; 19:1, 3; 31:7; 40:18–20; 41:6–7, 28–29; 44:9–20; 45:16–20; 46:1–2, 5–7).[14] The word could also mean that idols are utterly worthless (Isa 41:24, 29; 44:9–20; 57:11–13; Zech 11:17; Job 13:4). In fact, Isaiah identifies that the false gods are "empty winds" or "farts" (Isa 41:29; 26:18), which means that these false gods cannot accomplish anything. Idolaters are detestable to Yahweh, "You are less than nothing and your works are utterly worthless. He who chooses you is detestable" (Isa 41:24). On this basis the idol worshipers should be ashamed. Those who make idols are nothing (Isa 44:9). They are ignorant, with blinded eyes and deluded hearts (Isa 44:18–20). Idols cannot give counsel (Isa 41:26–29). They are a continual irritation to Yahweh (Isa 65:5). Yahweh shall pay idolaters back fully for their sins and their father's sins by totally shaming them through the captivity (Isa 42:17; 65:6–7; Deut 29:16–18, 26). Idolaters were left fearful in judgment as godless (Isa 33:14). Yahweh offered to deliver those who turn to him by defiling and destroying the idols (Isa 30:22; 31:7).

---

13. Kaiser, *Isaiah 1–12*, 22.
14. Vos, *Biblical Theology*, 236; Oswalt, *The Book of Isaiah*, 1:123.

Such idolatry was greatly cured among remnant Israel in their return from the Babylonian captivity.

Divination and spiritualism were additional sins practiced within this idolatry (Isa 2:6; 57:3; Deut 18:9–13). Idolatrous symbols and offerings are everywhere in Israel (Isa 57:5–10). Additionally, Israel pridefully consults the dead through mediums (Isa 8:19; 65:4–5). Such consultation is a mockery to Yahweh (Isa 57:4). They participate in sex orgies among the oaks (Isa 57:5, 8). They also sacrificed their children in ravines (Isa 57:5), probably to Molech (2 Kgs 23:10) or Baal (Jer 19:5). Yahweh will pay Israel back for their sins through famine and destruction (Isa 8:21–28; 65:8, 11–12, 15).

Outward religiosity does not match the inward reality of obedience (Isa 29:13; 58:2–5; Zech 7; Matt 15:8). Such hypocritical worship is detested and opposed by Yahweh (Isa 1:1–15; 29:1; Ps 50:7–15; 51:16). Yahweh does not oppose the temple cult or prayer but does oppose superficial spirituality (Isa 1:13–15). Yahweh makes it clear that "these people come near to me with their mouth to honor me with their lips, but their hearts are far from me. Their worship of me is made up only of rules taught by men" (Isa 29:13). Such outward rituals are meaningless, and their prayers are not heard (Isa 1:10–15).

Additionally, Israel is condemned in their unbelief. For example, Ahaz rebels in refusing to ask for a sign when Yahweh offers it to him (Isa 7:12). God offers a sign anyway. Prophecies are given ahead of time to prompt Israel in their stubborn unbelief (Isa 48:3–8). However, Israel's lack of trust in Yahweh is evidenced through their self-sufficiency with unrepentant revelry and in their establishing alliances with other nations (Isa 22:4, 11–13; 28:1; 29:17—30:17; 31:1–5). Israel is repeatedly hard hearted, not learning anything from Yahweh's miraculous deliverance, for he has spiritually blinded them (Isa 6:9–13; 29:9–12). In blindness, Israel obstinately pursues its own way (Isa 65:2). Israel will stumble and be judged by God (Isa 8:14–15). Their condemnation includes the guarantee that they will not be forgiven by Yahweh (Isa 22:14). A specific condemnation is exiling the palace steward Shebra and replacing him with Eliakim, son of Hilkiah (Isa 22:15–25). Yahweh allows Israel to entangle themselves with legalistic condemnation (Isa 28:9–13). Those who rely upon foreign alliances instead of the Lord will be judged with destruction (Isa 28:2–4, 11; 29:15, 16; 30:1–7, 12–17; 31:1–3). In this manner, they have made a covenant with death which will be annulled by Yahweh, bringing their complete destruction (Isa 28:15, 18).

This lack of faith is mirrored by the vice of pride. Israel and the nations are condemned for their pride (Isa 2:6–21; 3:16—4:1; 5:21; 9:8; 10:5–15; 13:11, 19; 16:6; 23:9; 24:21; 25:11; 28:1). Such pride breeds self-sufficiency and complacency as Goldingay develops.

> Pride means a majesty that can express itself in self-confidence and self-assertiveness rather than submission to God and to other people. Isaiah comments on the loftiness in the way Judah looks about (Isa 2:11; 5:15). It does so with a kind of justified pride. Yet that exaltedness in its gaze (lit. "eyes") compromises the facts about who has the really majestic gaze, who is entitled to look about with true *kābod* [Hebrew meaning: glory or weightiness]. "Their tongue and their deeds are against Yhwh, rebelling against his majestic gaze" (Isa 3:8). "The regard of their face [*or* their regard of other people's faces] witnesses against them" (Isa 3:9). The way they look at people issues in not treating people equally (cf. Deut 1:17; 16:19). There is a link between how they look at themselves in their impressiveness, how they look at other people in light of how impressive they are and how they thereby compromise the majesty of Yhwh. But "Yhwh Armies has a day against everything exalted and high, against everything lofty, and it will drop down" (Isa 2:12). That includes impressive things such as Lebanese cedars, Bashan oaks, high mountains, tall towers, fortified walls, Tarshish ships: all of these. "Human loftiness will bow, the exaltedness of people will drop down; Yhwh alone will tower on that day" (Isa 2:17).[15]

Their pride will be crushed under Yahweh's judgment. Furthermore, these prideful traits resist repentance.

The lead rebels, such as Ahaz and Shebra, corrupt the nation (Isa 7:12; 22:15–25), resulting in the judges being corrupt (Isa 5:23). These leaders have no conception of their office; they act for their own advantage rather than serving others (Isa 56:11–12). The elders are blind and mislead Israel into doing its own rebellious thing (Isa 56:9–12). These leaders will be killed (Isa 3:14–15).

Israel's leaders oppress the people (Isa 3:14–15; 9:19–21; 10:1–4; 30:12). They exploit workers (Isa 58:3). Quarrelling and violence are the lifestyle of Israel's leadership (Isa 58:9). They do not know peace and justice (Isa 59:8–9, 14), especially during the reign of Manasseh (Isa 59:1–15), as they participate in murder (Isa 59:3, 6–7). They pay no attention to the death of the righteous (Isa 57:1–2). In hard times there is even cannibalism (Isa 9:19–21; Deut 28:53–57).

Israel loves and pursues materialism. Israelites add to their list of vices excessive accumulation of land and houses, which force people into homelessness (Isa 2:7; 5:8; 22:15–18; Deut 17:16–17). They exploit workers (Isa 58:3). They love bribes (Isa 1:23; Deut 16:19). Society women drive

---

15. Goldingay, *Old Testament Theology*, 3:530.

this materialism by pursuing female luxury (Isa 3:16—4:1). These society women multiply beauty techniques with makeup, jewelry, fancy hair styles, robes, and hair coverings, all to attract and beg for the man they want. They feel secure and complacent (Isa 32:9, 11). Yahweh judges them with disease, making the women bald (Isa 3:17; Deut 28:21-22, 27, 35, 58-63). They formerly possessed items of beauty which are now replaced in captivity by bonds, marring, and mourning (Isa 3:18-24, 26: 32:11-13). Their men will die in battle (Isa 3:25-26). Their houses will be vacant and lacking productivity (Isa 5:9-10). Their city will be destroyed (Isa 32:12-14). They will be disgraced (Isa 4:1) and will fear (Isa 32:10-11).

Rebellious Israel is inhabited with fools and scoundrels whose mind concentrates on evil schemes (Isa 32:5-7). They solicit temptation (Isa 5:18). They are involved in deception, calling evil good and good evil (Isa 5:20; 59:3-4, 13, 15) in their false wisdom (Isa 29:13-14). They speak lies and folly, which spreads error concerning Yahweh and wrongly destroys the needy (Isa 6:5; 9:15, 17; 32:5-7). They make untrue and unrighteous oaths in Yahweh's name (Isa 48:1). Drunkenness increases their lack of regard for the deeds of Yahweh (Isa 5:12, 22; 28:1, 3, 7-8). They are proud and will be swept away into captivity (Isa 5:21). As scoffers, they speak meaningless sounds and, swept into captivity, they will hear languages meaningless to them (Isa 28:10).

All these sins are a breach of the Mosaic covenant in many respects. Isaiah defines sin contextually as going astray by doing one's own thing (Isa 53:6). Even those who act righteously confess that they are as one who is unclean (Isa 6:5). They admit that their righteous acts are like rags a woman wore in her menstrual period to catch her blood flow (Isa 64:6). Such filthy rags of sin spur God's anger to certain judgment. Vriezen summarizes Israel's sin as unbelief and pride.

> In fact for Isaiah, all sins are rooted in failure to recompense god, failure to believe, and willful rejection of him. These failures Isaiah sees in all spheres of life, military and civil, profane and cultic, among high and low, priest and prophet. By these people god is not known as the living god who is the holy, glorious, and mighty one. Therefore, they wander into all sorts of ways but they do not choose the only way, the way of revelation. Proud and defiant, their lives come into conflict with god, and they shall perish.[16]

---

16. Vriezen, "Essentials of the Theology of Isaiah," 135.

COVENANT LAWSUIT

Israel was given the opportunity to obey Yahweh, their suzerain. If they had obeyed, they would have had national prosperity over other nations (Deut 28:1). Both city and country would have been blessed at all times (Deut 28:3, 6). Families, children, crops, livestock, and the preparation of food would have been blessed (Deut 28:4–5). However, Israel did not obey Yahweh, so curses came upon them, beginning with the covenant lawsuit.

In rebellion, Isaiah reflects a covenant lawsuit Yahweh has against Judah and Israel on the basis of the Mosaic covenant (Isa 51:5; 59:15).[17] With the Mosaic covenant as a suzerainty treaty, Yahweh bound his elected Jewish forefathers during the exodus from Egypt (Isa 10:26; 11:16). Under this arrangement the Jews are already in the Mosaic covenant which means that they need to obey to be blessed, for if they disobey they will be cursed. This Mosaic covenant served as a covenant nomist arrangement within which Yahweh graciously folded Israel into his plans. The Mosaic covenant continued to bind the generation of Jews in Isaiah's day under the threat of suzerainty treaty covenant curse. Unfortunately, Judah and Israel stubbornly did evil in breaking God's covenant commands; so, Yahweh brought disaster upon them with no preventative option (Isa 1:7–10). They were swept away into captivity and death for their violation of the Mosaic covenant.

Isaiah's prophetic exhortation responds to the suzerainty treaty stipulations as did diplomatic correspondence which follows a disobedience to the treaty stipulations, threatening devastation for the vassal from the great king if the vassal does not quickly comply with what the suzerainty treaty demanded in the stipulations section. For example, the "Letter from Hattusili III of Hatti to Kadashman-Enlil II of Babylon" threatens Babylon with a devastating military campaign if they do not swiftly submit to the terms of the suzerainty treaty.[18] The analog for such diplomatic correspondence in the OT is the prophets, calling Israel back to faithfulness on the basis of the suzerainty treaty of Deuteronomy. To the extent that the great king is powerful, the vassal should fear and comply with the terms of the suzerainty treaty. To the extent that the vassal's disobedience is answered by diplomatic correspondence (or prophets), the vassal should immediately and fully

---

17. Nielsen, *Yahweh as Prosecutor and Judge*. Early Jewish rabbis continue to have problems with Isaiah's denunciations of Judah (*Pirke de Rav Eliezer* 11.8; *Lev R.* 6.6; *b. Meg.* 10b; Blenkinsopp, *Opening the Sealed Book*, 49).

18. An example is the "Letter from Hattusili III of Hatti to Kadashman-Enlil II of Babylon," see #23 in Beckman, *Hittite Diplomatic Texts*, esp. 138–140, with the lawsuit in section 4 while offering positive benefits in section 5 followed by negative consequences in section 6 and following if they do not repent; Thompson, *The Book of Jeremiah*, 169.

submit to the stipulations of the suzerainty treaty. To not comply would bring the experience of covenant curse.

Some claim that the genre of covenant lawsuit reflects concerns of the Babylonian Akitu new year's festival playacting a royal and priestly atonement.[19] There is no evidence that the genre of covenant lawsuit emerges from such a Babylonian context and Mowinckel's view is largely in disrepute. For example, there is no implication that a king in Judah will carry the sin for the people and atone for them in a cultic setting. Such atonement roles are subsumed to Yahweh's servant, which is a different development in Isaiah than the Davidic king.

The covenant lawsuit or complaint pattern (*rib*) is as follows in the prophets and the ancient Near East, as illustrated by Isaiah 1.[20]

First, there is a *call of witnesses* (heaven and earth) to hear and testify (Isa 1:2-4, 10; also 2:2-4; 41:1; 42:18; 48:12-14a; 57:3; 58:1; 66:1a). The suzerain calls the witnesses to the original treaty for the purpose of hearing the charges, "not to act as judges but simply to testify that they had been

---

19. Those advocating for this liturgical connection include: Engnell, *The Call of Isaiah*, 40; "Studies of Divine Kingship," 35; Köhler, *Die hebräische Mensch*, 143-71; Mowinckel, *Psalms in Israel's Worship*, 1:94-95.

20. The leadership of priests, kings (literally "shepherds"), and prophets walk away from Yahweh in not correcting the people but instead encouraging their departure to Baal all the more (Jer 2:8). Such a rebellious response draws Yahweh to *contend* against Israel in trial (Jer 2:9, two times *'rîb*). This rebellion is truly outrageous with no near parallels elucidated. Mendenhall, "Ancient Oriental and Biblical Law," 26-46; Gemser, "The *rîb*-Controversy-Pattern"; Huffmon, "The Covenant Lawsuit in the Prophets"; Gunkel and Begrich, *Einlietung in die Psalmen*, 329; Harvey, "Le Riv-Pattern"; *Le plaidoyer prophétique*, 54, 80-81; G. Ernest Wright, "The Lawsuit of God," 53 with support from 33-36 and 41-58; Bright, *Jeremiah*, 89; Limberg, "The Root רִיב and the Prophetic Lawsuit Speeches," esp. 297 and 301; Martin, "Forensic Background to Jeremiah III 1"; Boyle, "Covenant Lawsuit of the Prophet Amos"; Miller, "Concept of Covenant in Deutero-Isaiah," 50-54, 64, 163, 183-92; Suganuma, "Covenant Rib Form"; Harrison, *Jeremiah and Lamentations*, 24; Ramsey, "Speech Forms in Hebrew Law"; Nielsen, *Yahweh as Prosecutor and Judge*, 15-17, 27-32, 62-71; Owens, "Jeremiah, Prophet of True Religion," 372; Michael deRoche overreacts against a legal *sitz im leben* for one of confrontation in covenant, but it is helpful to remember that suzerainty warnings of covenant violation are not modern law courts, for the great king is prosecutor, judge, and general all in one to do as he pleases ("Yahweh's *rîb* against Israel"); Fensham, "Common Trends in Curses," 157; von Waldow, "The Message of Deutero-Isaiah," 270-72, 280-81; Schoors, "The *Rîb*-Pattern in Isaiah XL-LV"; *I Am God Your Saviour*, 189-244; Merrill, "Literary Character of Isaiah 40-55," 150-53; Bovati, "Le Language Jardique du Prophete Isaïe"; Harner, *Grace and Law in Second Isaiah*, 137-44; Dijkstra, "Lawsuit, Debate and Wisdom Discourse"; Williamson, "Isaiah 1 and the Covenant Lawsuit," 393-406; Mihinovich, "Form Criticism and *rîb* in Isaiah"; Kennard, "Covenant Lawsuit" in Jeremiah, in *Biblical Covenantalism*, 2:73-79.

witnesses of the original oath which the vassal has now broken."[21] Wright explains, "The Suzerain is himself the real Judge, Plaintiff, and Jury; he is the one who has been violated, and since there is no power above him he wields power himself, both accusing and sentencing."[22] The heavens and the earth often are part of this testimony against the indicted, as witnesses (Isa 1:2; also 42:18; 44:23; 45:8; 48:12–14a; 49:13; 57:3; 58:1; 66:1a; Jer 2:4–6; Mic 6:1–8). In such a situation, the frequent use of "say" followed by quoted speech (Isa 1:2, 10–11, 28; 2:3; 3:10, 16; 5:19) and the use of interrogative particles (Isa 1:12; 5:4) indicate a lawsuit context.[23]

Secondly, there is an *introduction to the case* at issue articulated by the divine judge and prosecutor or by his earthly official. Yahweh declared that Israel walked away from God and became empty (Isa 1:11–12; also 2:5; 5:1–2; 42:19; 48:14b–c; 57:4; 66:16).

Third, there is a *historical indictment* which develops the past benevolence of Yahweh and indicts the people in their sins, especially murder (Isa 1:13–15; also 2:6; 5:3–7; 41:2–3; 42:20–24b; 48:15–16; 50:1; 57:5–10; 58:2–3a; 66:2). In Isaiah, the focus of this section is upon Yahweh's generosity to bring Israel out of Egypt and to plant them in the fruitful promised land. In response, Israel walked away from God in rebellion and defiled the land.

Fourth, the covenant lawsuit *indictment declares the people's guilt*; Israel has left their God for an impotent strategy that will not hold water (Isa 1:15c; also 2:7–9; 5:8, 18–23; 42:24c–d; 50:1; 57:11; 58:3b–4; 66:3a–b). This element is most commonly found in prophecy since it is the basis of the prophet's mission. It is often a quotation of the word of God, which is then expanded, interpreted, and defended.

Fifth, the *sentence of the people*'s condemnation in this instance offers the possibility for repentance (Isa 1:16–20; also 55:6–7). Though Israel is declared to be a condemned people (as Sodom and Gomorrah), repentance is possible (Isa 1:9).[24] If Israel would come to Yahweh and obey, then their sin would be turned from its scarlet murder to whiter than snow. In such a murderous condition it does them no good to raise bloody hands in prayer, or to grieve their impotence in removing the blood from their hands (Isa 1:15).[25] The only remedy is real repentance and learning to do good, especially to the vulnerable in society (orphans, widows, and those crushed by

---

21. Wright, *Terminology of Old Testament Religion*, 404.
22. Wright, *Terminology of Old Testament Religion*, 47.
23. Craigie et al., *Jeremiah 1–25*, 21.
24. Vriezen, "Essentials of the Theology of Isaiah," 138.
25. Akin to lady Macbeth's sleepwalking scene, crying, "Out, damned spot! Out I say!" Shakespeare, *Macbeth*, act 5, scene 1, line 39.

injustice [Isa 1:16–17]). At other instances Israel's guilt is declared: Israel left their glory for an impotent strategy that will not profit, so Yahweh floods them with covenant curses (Isa 2:10–22; 5:9–17, 24–30; 42:25; 48:17–19; 57:12–13; 66:3c–4).

At times within this curse, Yahweh expressed an emotional sigh "woe" (*hoy*) to indicate impending curse and death mourning (Isa 1:4, 24; 3:9, 11; 5:8, 11, 18, 20–22; 10:1, 5; 16:4; 17:12; 18:1; 29:1, 15; 30:1; 31:1; 45:9–10).[26] Occasionally, the word is used as an indication for excitement and reversal of the circumstances (Isa 55:1; 5:8, 11; 10:5).[27]

Yahweh accuses Judah and Israel of a host of sins, all of which can be found set out in the stipulations of the Mosaic covenant. Because Israel has done the moral-"evil" (*rʿ*: Isa 1:4, 16; 3:9, 11; 5:20; 7:5; 13:11; 31:2; 32:7; 33:15; 47:10; 56:2; 57:1; 59:7, 15; 65:12; 66:4) of rebellion, Yahweh will bring on them the calamity-"evil" (*rʿ*: Isa 3:9, 11; 31:2; 45:7; 47:11) of covenant curse. Violating the first and second commands, Israel worshiped false gods instead of Yahweh (Isa 1:29–30; 2:8; 57:5).[28] Violating commandments six through nine of the Decalogue, Israel was deceptive, stealing, murderous, adulterous, and swearing falsely (Isa 5:20; 6:5; 9:15, 17, 19–21; 32:5–7; 58:3; 59:3–4, 6–7, 13, 15).[29] They refused to serve Yahweh because their leadership ruled them without regard to Yahweh's commands (Isa 3:14–15; 5:23; 7:12; 9:19–21; 10:1–4; 22:15–25; 30:12; 56:11–12; 58:3). The people selfishly and unjustly amassed wealth, not caring for the needy (Isa 2:7; 5:8; 22:15–18).[30] It is on account of all these sins in Yahweh's Mosaic covenant relation with them that Israel is swept away into captivity, calamity, and death.

ISRAEL'S JUDGMENT: COVENANT CURSE

Israel was given the opportunity to obey Yahweh, their suzerain. If they would have been faithful, then they would have national prosperity over other peoples for all time (Deut 28:1–6). However, Israel did not obey but broke covenant, so covenant curses were brought down upon them. The city and the country were cursed in disobedience (Deut 28:16). The children,

---

26. Gerstenberger, "Woe-Oracle of the Prophets," esp. 251–53, 258–59, 263; Janzen, *Mourning Cry and Woe Oracle*, 1, 3, 35, 51, 83; Brueggemann, *The Covenanted Self*, 94, with 138 n. 7.

27. Gerstenberger, "Woe-Oracle of the Prophets," 251; Janzen, *Mourning Cry and Woe Oracle*, 35.

28. Jer 2:8, 11, 28; 7:9; 8:19; 10:8, 11, 14; 11:12, 17; 16:18, 20; 18:15; 32:35.

29. Jer 3:6–11; 7:8–9; 8:5, 8, 10; 9:2–6; 13:26–27.

30. Jer 5:27–28; 7:5–6; 8:10; 17:11.

crops, livestock, and preparation of food were cursed in rebellion (Deut 28:17–18). All Israel was cursed in covenant curse (Deut 28:19).

Much of this curse is expressed verbally by Isaiah, echoing covenant curse statements in Deut 28. However, Isaiah also utilized nude personal drama, acting out impending curse to convey the depth of enslavement and deportation (Isa 20:3–4). To dramatize this curse of conquest and exile, Isaiah went about nude for three years as he delivered some of the prophetic texts (Isa 20:3–4).

In disobedience, covenant curse will come from Yahweh. Delbert Hillers made an extensive study of treaty curses in the ancient Near East in which he noticed many of the following parallels to ancient Near Eastern curses within the book of Jeremiah.[31] Kennard has added Isaianic support for Hillers's categories and added several additional categories for judgment in covenant curse.

1. The people and the land are destroyed by conquest (Isa 1:7–9; 3:24; 15:3; 22:12; 28:15).[32]

2. War and captivity will come against you (Isa 1:7–9; 3:14–15, 25–26; 7:18; 8:4).[33]

3. Land destroyed by enemies and plundered (Isa 3:14–15, 25–26; 5:26–30; 7:18; 8:4; 42:18–25).[34]

---

31. Hillers, *Treaty-Curses*, 29, 44–71, 76, 88; list modified by Kennard's own study of Jeremiah and Isaiah. Some metaphors are not duplicated in Jeremiah, such as becoming malt from husks (Beckman, *Hittite Diplomatic Texts*, 48, 52).

32. Beckman, *Hittite Diplomatic Texts*, 17, 29, 33, 40, 48, 52, 58, 64, 69, 86, 92, 112, 122; also other futility curses: *Sefire* I.4.19; Deut 28:15–20, 25, 49–50, 53, 57; Jer 2:12, 30; 4:6, 13, 20, 26; 5:10; 6:19; 7:33; 8:16; 9:11; 10:18; 11:22; 12:11–12; 13:14; 14:18; 15:8, 11, 14; 16:4; 17:18; 18:7, 16, 21; 19:8; 26:10–15; 34:22; 41:3; 45:5; 46:22–23; 50:26; 51:1–4, 55–56; Hos 4:10; 5:6; 8:7; 9:12, 16; Amos 4:4; 5:11; 8:12; Mic 3:4; 6:14–15; Zeph 1:13; Hag 1:6; Mal 1:4; CD 1.16–18; 3.10–11; 8.1; 4Q463 1 1; Hillers, *Treaty-Curses*, 28–29. This destruction entails the covenant curse of death, which is the point of the Isaiah 28:15 covenant with death rather than Christopher B. Hays's explanation, selling out in pagan worship to the Egyptian god of death ("Covenant with Mut"). Fensham also makes connections with *kudurru* or boundary stone curses ("Common Trends in Curses," 167).

33. Beckman, *Hittite Diplomatic Texts*, 139; Deut 28:20, 25, 49–50, 53, 57; Jer 4:5–6, 13, 29; 5:15–17; 6:23; 11:22; 15:2; 18:17, 21; 19:9; 21:4–7; 41:4–18; 46:3–5; 49:37; 50:13–15; 51:1–4; 52:4–16.

34. Beckman, *Hittite Diplomatic Texts*, 17, 29, 33, 40, 48, 52, 58, 64, 69, 86, 92, 112, 122, 139; also other futility curses: *Sefire* I.4.19; "Laws of Hammurabi," 50.81–91, in Roth, *Law Collections*, 138–39; Deut 28:20–22, 25, 27, 35, 49–50, 53, 57–63 parallel to 7–11, 67; 29:19–23; Jer 4:5–6, 13, 29; 5:15–17; 6:23; 11:22; 15:2; 18:17, 21; 19:9; 21:4–7; 41:4–18; 46:3–5; 49:37; 50:13–15; 51:1–4; 52:4–16; Hos. 4:10; 5:6; 8:7; 9:12, 16; Amos 4:4; 5:11; 8:12; Mic 3:4; 6:14–15; Zeph 1:13; Hag 1:6; Mal 1:4; Hillers, *Treaty-Curses*, 28–29.

4. Land became desolate with possessions benefiting another (Isa 3:18–26; 5:9–10; 6:11–12; 13:9; 32:10–14; 44:26; 49:19; 51:3).[35]

5. Land destroyed by plague and disease (Isa 1:5–6; 3:17).[36]

6. Drought (Isa 1:30; 8:21–22; 65:8, 11–12, 15).[37]

7. Crops produce little with abundant weeds (Isa 5:10; 7:23–25; 9:18 [MT: 9:17]; 10:17; 27:2–5; 32:12–13; 65:21).[38]

8. The land will be a dwelling for threatening carnivorous animals (Isa 5:29–30; 7:18; 35:9; 51:8; 56:9).[39]

9. The people are cursed to eat the flesh of their sons and daughters (Isa 9:19–20; 49:26).[40]

10. Removal of joyful sounds (Isa 10:10; 24:8, 11; 32:13).[41]

---

35. Deut 28:30–35, 49–52; Lev 26:31–32.

36. The plague curses are broadly parallel to the plagues of the exodus (Deut 28:21–22, 27, 35, 60–61; 29:22; Exod 7–11). Plague and infirmity are also a curse under the "Laws of Hammurabi," 51.50–65, in Roth, *Law Collections*, 139–40; some similarity of illnesses with *VTE* sect 38a–40, 56, 60, 72–73.

37. Deut 28:22–24; 29:19; Wiseman, *Vassal-Treaties*, 90, col. 7, lines 528–30 (*VTE* sect 63–64), says, "There is no fertility in iron ground and no rain or dew comes from bronze skies," with reference to drought; Walton and Matthews, *Genesis–Deuteronomy*, 263; Basil the Great, *Exegetical Homilies* 3.8; Lienhard, *Exodus, Leviticus, Numbers, Deuteronomy*, 323. Elijah claimed this drought curse when Israel rebelled (1 Kgs 17:1), and an ample rain blessing of Deut 28:12 came when the prophets of Baal were killed (1 Kgs 18:44–45). Drought is also a curse under the "Laws of Hammurabi," 50.64–71 (with often famine following, 49.53–54, 66–67, 80), in Roth, *Law Collections*, 136–38; also drought curse in *VTE* sect 63–64, with famine *VTE* sect 47, 56, 62, 74, 85; Fensham also makes connections with *kudurru* or boundary stone curses ("Common Trends in Curses,"168).

38. Lev 26:26; Deut 28:30, 39; Amos 5:11; Zeph 1:13; Prinsloo, "Isaiah 14:12–15"; Blenkinsopp, *Isaiah 1–39*, 208.

39. *Sefire* I.A.31; II.A.9, 30–32; Aramaic "Treaty between Bar-Ga'yah and the King of Arpad," *Sephire* 1.27; Fitzmyer, *Aramaic Inscriptions of Sefire*, 44–45; "Aramaic Inscriptions of Sefire I and II," 181, 185; *Gilgamesh Epic* 12.93–94; Deut 28:38–42; 32:24; Lev 26:22; Jer 2:14–15; 4:7; 5:6; 8:17; 10:22; 12:9; 48:40; 49:19, 22, 33; 50:44; 51:37; Lam 3:10–11; Hos. 2:20; 5:12, 14; Hillers, *Treaty-Curses*, 28–29, 54–56.

40. *AshN* rev. 4.10–11; Openheim, "'Siege-Documents' from Nippur," esp. 79 n. 34; Wiseman, *Vassal-Treaties*, 62, 70, and 72, col. 6, lines 448–50, 548–50, and col. 7 line 572; Hillers, *Treaty-Curses*, 62–63; Deut 28:53–57; 49:26; Jer 19:9; Lam 4:10; Ezek 5:10; Zech 11:9.

41. *Sefire* I.A.29; Ashurnirari treaty 4.19; Rassam Cylinder 6.101–3; *Ludlul bēl nēmeqi* I.101–2; Era Epic I.2; Jer 7:34; 9:10, 17–19; 14:2; 16:5, 9; 25:10; 33:11; Lam 5:14–15; Ezek 26:13; Amos 8:10; Hillers, *Treaty-Curses*, 57–58; Lambert, *Babylonian Wisdom Literature*, 36; Borger and Lambert, "Ein neuer Era-Text aus Ninive," esp. 141; blessing indicated by joy returning Isa 9:3; 29:19; 35:1–2, 10; 51:11; 55:12; 60:15; 61:7; 65:18; 66:5, 10.

11. Removal of peace because God must bring it back (Isa 43:27–28; 48:22; 57:18, 21; 59:18; 66:6).[42]

12. Removal of the sound of millstones (Isa 47:2).[43]

13. Stripped like a prostitute (Isa 1:21; 3:17; 20:3–4; 23:15–18; 47:3).[44]

14. Becoming a prostitute (Isa 23:15–18).[45]

15. Breaking of weapons (Isa 9:4–5; 14:5, 25; 58:6).[46]

16. Breaking the scepter (Isa 9:3; 14:5, 29).[47]

17. Divorced from God (Isa 50:1).[48]

18. Contaminated water (Isa 15:9).[49]

19. Incurable wound (Isa 1:5–6).[50]

---

42. Beckman, *Hittite Diplomatic Texts*, 139; Jer 6:14; 8:11, 15; 12:12; 14:19; 16:5; Lam 3:17.

43. *Esar* 443–45; Hillers, *Treaty-Curses*, 58; Jer 25:10.

44. Hillers (*Treat-Curses*, 58–60) develops two curses together: 1) Becoming a prostitute, which is the next category, and 2) Being stripped like a prostitute: *Sefire* I.A.40–41; Deut 28:48; Ezek 16:37–38; 23:10, 29; Hos 2:5, 12; Nah 3:5.

45. Similar pattern to Isa 20:2–4; *AshN* rev. 5.9–11; *Gilgamesh Epic* 7.3.6–22; Jer 13:22, 26–27; Lam 1:8; Amos 7:17; Hillers, *Treaty-Curses*, 58–60.

46. *Sefire* I.A.38–39; *Baal* rev. 4.18; *Esarhaddon* 543, 573–75; "Code of Hammurabi," rev. 28.3–4; "Hittite Soldier's Oath," in *ANET*, 354; King, *Babylonian Boundary Stones*, p. 23 text 3.16; p. 47 text 4.21–22 (boundary stones); Kupper, *Correspondence de Kibria-Dagon*, #15, lines 7–8; Wiseman, *Allah Tablets*, p. 25 #1 line 17; Budge and King, *Annals of the Kings of Assyria*, 1:107, line 80 ("Inscription of Tiglath-Pileser 1"), p. 172 lines 19–21 ("Inscription of Ashurbanipal"); *AfOB* 9 p. 44 line 75 (Inscription of Esarhaddon); *Vordeasiatische Bibliothek*, 7:322–3 line 5, 7:194–5 line 25 ("Inscriptions of Ashurbanipal"); Hirsch, "Die Incriften der Könige von Agade," 43, lines 36–44 ("Inscription of Sargon of Akkad"), p. 45 lines 47–55; p. 46 lines 22–30; Hillers, *Treaty-Curses*, 60–61; 1 Sam 2:4; Jer 49:35; 51:56; Ezek 39:3; Hos 1:5; 2:20; Zech 9:10; Pss 46:10; 76:4.

47. Curse from *Shsmshi-Adad treaty* 22; "Code of Hammurabi," rev. 26.45–51; *ANET*, 179; Hillers, *Treaty-Curses*, 61; Jer 48:17; Zech 10:11; Ps 89:45; *Sir.* 32.23.

48. Hosea graphically illustrates the marriage and divorce by God of prostituting Israel. Hosea 2:19–20 (English), 21–22 (Hebrew) resolves this divorce, though many Jews consider this statement as a reflection of the Exodus Mosaic covenant. Jer 3:8; A curse of prostitution is recorded in *Ashur-Nerari 5 Treaty with King of Arad* rev. 5.9, 12–13; Parpola and Watanabe, *Neo-Assyrian Treaties and Loyalty Oaths*, 12, rev. 5.9.

49. *Esar* 521–22; Hillers, *Treaty-Curses*, 63–64; Jer 8:14; 9:14; 23:15.

50. *Baal* rev. 4.3–4; *Esar* 643–45; "Code of Hammurabi," rev. 28.50–69; *AfOB* 9, 99, lines 40–41; Hillers, *Treaty-Curses*, 64–66; Jer 8:22; 10:19; 14:17, 19; 15:18; 30:12–15; 46:11; 51:8–9; Ezek 30:21; Hos 5:13; Mic 1:9; Nah 3:19; the theme is reversed to prophecy renewal: Jer 30:17; 33:6; Isa 58:8.

20. Warriors become like women, losing strength and virility (Isa 13:8; 19:16).[51]

21. Trapped like a bird (Isa 8:14; 28:13).[52]

22. No burial (Isa 5:25).[53]

23. Storm (Isa 4:6; 25:4; 28:2; 29:6).[54]

24. Wildfire (Isa 1:7; 5:24; 9:5, 18–19; 10:16–17; 26:11; 29:1–4, 6; 30:14, 27, 30, 33; 33:11–14; 37:19; 44:16, 19; 47:14; 64:11; 65:5; 66:15–16, 24).[55]

25. Flood (Isa 8:7; 28:2, 17–22).[56]

26. Earthquake (Isa 22:10; 30:13–14).[57]

27. Wives ravished (Isa 3:18–24, 26; 13:16; 32:11–13).[58]

28. Confusion[59] and Blindness[60] (Isa 6:9–11; 24:10; 28:10; 29:9–10; 30:3; 34:11; 42:18–20; 43:8; 44:18; 45:16; 51:17–23; 57:16; 59:9–10; 63:17).[61]

---

51. *Ashur-Nerari 5 Treaty with King of Arad* rev. 5.9, 12–13; Parpola and Watanabe, *Neo-Assyrian Treaties and Loyalty Oaths*, 12, rev. 5.9; an old Babylonian prayer in Gelb, *Assyrian Dictionary*, Z:110b; Hittite prayer to Ishtar, lines 25–29, in Sommer, "Ein hethitisches Gebet," 98; "Hittite Soldiers' Oath," in *ANET*, 354, obv. 2.48–49, 51–53, rev. 3.1; *Era Epic* 4.55–56, in *AfOB* 9, 99; Hillers, *Treaty-Curses*, 66–68; Jer 22:23; 50:35–38; 51:30; Mic 4:10; 2 Sam 3:29; Ps 48:7.

52. *Esar* 582–84; "Annals of Assyrian Kings" describes Hezekiah surrounded in Jerusalem "like a bird in a cage," in *AfOB* 9, p. 58 lines 12–18; *Era Epic* 4.18–19; Hillers, *Treaty-Curses*, 69–70; Deut 28:23; Jer 5:26; 48:43–44; 50:24; Ezek. 17:15–21; Hos 7:12; similar to: Josh 23:13.

53. *Esar* 426–27, 483–84; *Maqlu* 4.42–44 and 8.85–89, in King, *Babylonian Boundary Stones*, p. 47 #4.19–20; p. 62 #2.14–19, 24–25; p. 127 #6.54–55; *AfOB* 9, p. 58 line 6; Hillers, *Treaty-Curses*, 68–69; 1 Kgs 14:11; 2 Kgs 9:10, 36; Jer 7:33; 8:2; 9:21; 14:16; 16:4, 6; 15:33; 22:19; 25:33; 34:20; 36:30; Ezek 39:17–20; Pss 79:2–3; 83:11.

54. Jer 4:13.

55. Jer 7:20; 15:14; 17:4, 27; 20:9; 43:12–13; 44:6; 49:27; 51:58.

56. Beckman, *Hittite Diplomatic Texts*, 52; *Esar* 488–89; 442; *Esarhaddon Annals* episode 5 and 7, in *AfOB* 9, p. 13–14; p. 32 line 12, p. 48 line 69, p. 65 line 10; Hillers, *Treaty-Curses*, 70–71; Jer 46:7–8; 47:2; Amos 8:8.

57. Jer 4:24; 8:16.

58. VTE sect 42; *Assur-nerari-Matiilu Treaty* SSA 2 2 v 1–13 and SSA 2 5 iv18'–19'; Crouch, *Israel and the Assyrians*, 63–64; *Esar* 521–22; Hillers, *Treaty-Curses*, 63; Deut 28:30; 2 Sam 12:11; 16:20–22; Jer 8:10.

59. Deut 28:20, 28–29, 34; Not a curse found in the Hittite suzerainty treaties but present in "Laws of Hammurabi," epilogue 49.98; 50.2–6 in Roth, *Law Collections*, 136, 140; Zehnder, "Building on Stone?," 525 has one text listed incorrectly.

60. Wiseman, *Vassal-Treaties*, 60, col. 6 line 423–24; VTE sect 40.

61. Deut 28:20, 28–29, 34, 45–48, 65–67; Craig Evans compares the MT developing divine caused obduracy (Israel's thinking is "made fat" by Yahweh, Isa 6:10) that early

29. Terror (Isa 28:19; 33:13-14).

30. Futility (Isa 5:9-10; 7:18; 35:9; 51:8; 56:9).[62]

This multitude of covenant curse metaphors is coupled with other devastating descriptions of demise for Israel or other people as they violate the terms of covenant. The destruction and warfare emphasis are present in covenant curses as within the prophets. However, the biblical prophets write and speak with more metaphors to render vivid the imagery to motivate Israel's repentance. Eichrodt describes Israel's condemnation of confusion in their rebellion.

> The breach of a relationship of trust so personal as that of marriage can result only in the divorce of the wife; for here the inner alienation both becomes externally visible and is worked out to its logical conclusion. The man who, when all natural supports are reeling, refuses to find his foothold on the rock of the promise cannot but stagger, slip and fall (Isa 7:9; 8:12-15). Deliberate disregard of divine truth, habitual failure to listen to God's warning, inevitably lead to that deadness in regard to God's operations which at the decisive moment notices nothing, but in a stupor, asleep, or drunk lurches irremediably toward the approaching disaster (Isa 28:11-12; 29:9-10; 6:9-10).[63]

Judah and Israel are swept away in the experience of the devastation of covenant curse. Perhaps even the rebels experience everlasting punishment that is loathsome to all humans (Isa 66:24).

Judaism softens (Qumran, LXX, Rabbinics, Targums, and Vulgate: Israel "will be appalled" at their continuing extent of judgement experience) with the NT Gospels and Acts largely following the LXX (Evans, *To See and Not Perceive*, 43, 55-58, 62, 70-71, 93, 106, 115, 134).

62. Futility curses: *Sefire* I.4.19; Hos 4:10; 5:6; 8:7; 9:12, 16; Amos 4:4; 5:11; 8:12; Mic 3:4; 6:14-15; Zeph 1:13; Hag 1:6; Mal 1:4. One special case of futility curse is that of devouring animals: *Sefire* I.A.31; II.A.9, 30-32; *Gilgamesh Epic* 12.93-94; Deut 28:38-42; 32:24; Lev 26:22; Jer 2:14-15; 4:7; 5:6; 8:17; 12:9; 48:40; 49:19, 22; 50:44; Lam 3:10-11; Hos 2:20; 5:12, 14; Hillers, *Treaty-Curses*, 28-29, 54-56; Aramaic "Treaty Between Bar-Ga'yah and the King of Arpad," *Sephire* 1.27; Fitzmyer, *Aramaic Inscriptions*, 44-45; "Aramaic Inscriptions of Sefire I and II," 181, 185; Beckman, *Hittite Diplomatic Texts*, 17.

63. Eichrodt, *Theology of the Old Testament*, 2:432.

CHAPTER 7

Motifs of Judgment

THERE ARE A VARIETY of pictures which make the consequences of judgment more vivid. This chapter explores the most developed of these motifs in Isaiah.

MINISTRY OF HARDENING

Judgment is certain within the context of Israel breaking covenant. Especially once Yahweh's patience is used up and repentance is no longer available, Yahweh puts Israel in a state of mind that guarantees that they will be judged sooner. This state is one of hardening the unbeliever's heart (Isa 6:9–10). Once Israel resists with this level of rebellion, Yahweh and Isaiah's seer ministry will continue to prepare Israel in their blindness and rebellion until they are fully judged and lying desolate (Isa 6:11–13).[1] Yahweh's agents of judgment—plague, drought, and respective nations—will each destroy the other in subsequent judgment. The goal of this ministry of hardening and judgment is to purify Israel and the nations by removing all but a remnant (Isa 6:13).

---

1. Carroll, "Blindsight and the Vision Thing." Unfortunately, generations later during Jesus' ministry, Israel was still filling out this pattern of blindness so that Jesus' parabolic ministry also prepared them to be swept into judgment under the Romans, as such Paul justifies his gentile ministry (Matt 13:13–17; Mark 4:11–13; Luke 8:10; John 12:39–41; Acts 28:24–28).

YAHWEH'S DEFEAT OF THE SEA-MONSTER: RAHAB OR LEVIATHAN

Rahab and Leviathan are the anti-creation chaos monsters associated with the sea, which swallow up life but flee from victorious Yahweh (Isa 27:1; 51:9; Ps 104:26).[2] Creation accounts had presented them as Yahweh's play toys among the creation, so no real threat (Gen 1:21; Ps 104:26).[3] However, Rahab and Leviathan were a seven-headed chaos dragon named *Ltn* from ancient Canaanite, Ugaritic, and Hittite mythology whose heads were crushed by Yahweh (Ps 74:14).[4] There are two sequential features of the myth: destroying and controlling. As such, Thomas Hobbes utilized this *Leviathan* metaphor to describe challenging absolute power.[5] In Isaiah 51:9, Yahweh cut Rahab in pieces and pierced the dragon (Ps 89:10; Isa 51:9). In the myth of the chaos monster, the restraining monster is vanquished and caught, and its body is broken into pieces and the vital fluids, essential for life, are released (Job 41:1; Ps 89:10). The hero in the myth must then bring these forces under control in an organized form which signifies the defeat of chaos.[6] Much of this myth should not be imported because it is a case of borrowed imagery and not borrowed theology.[7] Yahweh existed before all else and created everything else (Isa 44:6; 45:6–7). This imagery is utilized to express Yahweh's triumph over chaos in creation. Isaiah utilizes this imagery as picturing the judgment and control of the sea in the exodus. In this myth,

---

2. Baal cycle 67.1.1–3; 'Anat 3.35–39; 2 Esd. 6:52; 2 Bar. 29:3–8; KTU 1.5.i 1–3 rather parallel to Isa 27:1; Schunck, "Jes. 30, 6–8 und die Deutung der Rahab im AT," 48–56; Oswalt, "Myth of the Dragon," 163–72; Sawyer, *Isaiah*, 1:223–25; Blenkinsopp, *Isaiah 40–55*, 332; Childs, *Isaiah*, 196–97; Barker, *Isaiah's Kingship Polemic*, 128–70; Waltke, *Creation and Chaos*, 10.

3. B. 'Abod. Zar. 3b identified that God played with his created chaos monster "three hours a day"; Blenkinsopp, *Isaiah 1–39*, 372.

4. Waltke, *Creation and Chaos*, 12; Ugaritic text: Baal cycle 67.1.1–3, 27–30 says, "When thou smites Lotan [=Leviathan] the evil dragon, even destroyest the crooked dragon, the mighty one of the seven heads ... Thou hast broken the sea with Thy might, even smashed the heads of the monster on the waters, Thou hast crushed the heads of Leviathan, even given him as food for the people"; 'Anat 3.35–39, in *ANET*, 125–26; *ANEP* no. 670; Ps 74:13–14. Gordon ("Leviathan: Symbol of Evil," esp. 4) describes an Ugaritic seal where heroes destroyed a seven-headed dragon, four of whose heads are already dead while the other three are still alive and fighting. The seal shows that the myth was current in the Semitic world by the middle of the third millennium; Wakeman, *God's Battle with the Monster*, 79; Barker, *Isaiah's Kingship Polemic*, 128–70.

5. Hobbes, *Leviathan*.

6. Wakeman, *God's Battle with the Monster*, 7–24, 50; Waltke, *Creation and Chaos*, 6.

7. Allen, "The Leviathan-Rahab-Dragon Motif," 63; McKenzie, "A Note on Psalm 73 [74]:13–15," 281; Waltke, *Creation and Chaos*, 13–14.

Egypt is called Rahab (Isa 30:7; Ps 87:4) and during the exodus the sea is divided for safe passage after Rahab's defeat (Isa 51:9–10). Bernard Anderson says of this Red Sea crossing event, "It was then that Yahweh slew the monster Rahab, separated the Great Deep (*tehom Rabbah*), so that the people could pass through (Isa 44:27), rebuked the rebellious sea (*yam*; Isa 5:10)."[8] Eichrodt says that this imagery portrays the classic struggle between God and chaos in which all must choose sides; Israel is judged as they choose the side of chaos.

> By adopting the mythological concepts of the Chaos-monster and its slaying at the hands of the Creator of the universe, and transferring them to the subjugation of tyrant nations and their rulers by Yahweh (Isa 17:12–13; 14:12–21; Nahum 1; Ezek 38), they sketch the evil in man in the lineaments of a demonic cosmic power comprising in itself all that rejects God, and striving with the God of Israel for the dominion of the earth. Looked at in this way, the sin of Israel can be seen for the first time in its full impact as a taking sides in a cosmic conflict; the people whom God has chosen enter the struggle against him on the side of the nations whom he despises, and thus logically incur the same fate as has been prepared for the rest.[9]

After the judgment and control are achieved over the monster, the victor is recognized as the king.[10] This imagery depicts Yahweh's triumph at creation and in history over; Israel's enemies and in the future over the ultimate figure of chaos, Leviathan, in establishing the kingdom (Isa 27:1). In the ancient Ugaritic mythology, Leviathan is a being Baal slays, and Mot promises to destroy him.[11] The one who slays and destroys Leviathan has great power. In Isaiah, Yahweh is the one who conquers Leviathan. Yahweh even prophesies the destruction of Mot, whose name means death (Isa 25:7–8; 26:19). Waltke summarized this motif, "As the Creator of the cosmos, He triumphed prior to creation, as Creator of history he triumphs in the historic present, and as Creator of the new heavens and the new earth he will triumph in the future."[12]

---

8. *KTU* 1.2.iv; 1.3.iii; 1.5.i; *ANET*, 130–31; Anderson, *Creation Versus Chaos*, 128.

9. Eichrodt, *Theology of the Old Testament*, 1:378.

10. Wakeman, *God's Battle with the Monster*, 50, "Once the monster's powers have been incorporated into the cosmos, the god to whom such achievement is ascribed is ordained 'the king of the gods.'"

11. Gray, *Legacy of Canaan*, 56–57.

12. Waltke, *Creation and Chaos*, 15.

CREATION-REVERSAL

Yahweh created the world formless (*tohu*) or void (*bohu*; Isa 45:18; Gen 1:1–2, 26). With the fall of humans there is the return to chaos as an outgrowth of sin (Gen 3:14–19; 4:7–8, 23–24; 6:5–7). The chaotic state of the world includes many forms of sin and rebellion with all its vanity (Isa 29:21; 40:17, 23; 41:29; 44:9; 45:18; 59:4). Such a state of sin is irrational in its chaotic opposition to the king. Yahweh judges the rebellious earth with the measuring line which determines chaos (*tohu*) or desolation (*bohu*; Isa 34:11). As a result of his judgment there remains the confusion of desolate ruins (Isa 24:10). Because Yahweh set the covenant standard openly, Judah cannot remedy her rebellious condition by seeking Yahweh secretly; repentance must usher in righteous choices to protect the vulnerable (Isa 45:19).

FALL-CURSE

The fall of humans into sin changes the blessings of God's creation into a framework of curse amid God's blessing (Gen 1:22, 28; 2:3 to 3:14, 17; 4:11). In the day the first forefather sinned, humans died spiritually, and physical death grew out of this (Gen 2:17). This initial rebellion fostered a continuing legacy of leadership rebellion and judgment (Isa 43:27–28). The fall included the expression of the futility of life in the world. In the wake of such sin, in conditions of marriage and occupation there will be frustration and futility (Gen 3:16–19; Isa 3:18–26; 5:9–10; 6:11–12; 7:18; 9:19–20; 13:9; 32:10–14; 35:9; 49:26; 50:1; 51:8; 56:9).[13] This futility is especially seen in Isaiah by the hardness of heart, sin, and judgment. All these twisted character and consequences shall be reversed in the establishment of the kingdom.

DIVORCE

One metaphor for judgment is that of Yahweh divorcing Israel (Isa 50:1–3; Jer 3:1, 8). The imagery is truly frightening because in the finality of divorce, the divorcing partner is banned in the Mosaic covenant from marrying his

---

13. Futility curses: *Sefire* I.4.19; Hos 4:10; 5:6; 8:7; 9:12, 16; Amos 4:4; 5:11; 8:12; Mic 3:4; 6:14–15; Zeph 1:13; Hag 1:6; Mal 1:4. One special case of futility curse is that of devouring animals: *Sefire* I.A.31; II.A.9, 30–32; *Gilgamesh Epic* 12.93–94; Deut 28:38–42; 32:24; Lev 26:22; Jer 2:14–15; 4:7; 5:6; 8:17; 12:9; 48:40; 49:19, 22; 50:44; Lam 3:10–11; Hos 2:20; 5:12, 14; Hillers, *Treaty-Curses*, 28–29, 54–56; Aramaic "Treaty Between Bar-Ga'yah and the King of Arpad," *Sefire* 1.27; Fitzmyer, *Aramaic Inscriptions*, 44–45; "Aramaic Inscriptions of Sefire I and II," 181, 185; Beckman, *Hittite Diplomatic Texts*, 17.

divorced again (Deut 24:1-4).[14] This divorce is identified as happening when Israel was "sent off" (šlttyh) into slavery (Isa 43:14; 50:3), though šlttyh clearly elsewhere identifies "divorce" (Deut 24:1-4; Jer 3:1, 8). Such judgment divorce is cause for mourning. Eventually, Yahweh called the rebellious, forsaken wife Israel back to him with redemptive loyal love (Isa 54:5, 8; 63:4, 9).

KINGDOM OF DARKNESS

Yahweh did not speak in secrecy of darkness but clearly for all to hear (Isa 45:19, 3). Darkness in Isaiah is viewed as a manner of life and a picture of God's judgment. As a manner of life, the people are the ones who exist within this sinful futile realm (Isa 9:2; 29:18). The utter depravity of humanity is pictured in that "darkness covers the earth and thick darkness is over the peoples" (Isa 60:2). The populace is unredeemed by God in this realm of unrepentant darkness.

> So justice is far from us, and righteousness does not reach us. We look for light, but all is darkness; for brightness, but we walk in deep shadows. Like the blind we grope along the wall, feeling our way like humans without eyes. At midday we stumble as if it were twilight; among the strong, we are like the dead . . . for our offenses are many in your sight. (Isa 59:9-12)

Within the realm of darkness, there is a great temptation to rationalize and call darkness light and call light darkness. Yahweh severely warns that those who reverse truth for fake news are under impending judgment (Isa 5:20). Yahweh judges those liars by creating more darkness and hardening such rebels in their hearts and blinding them in their darkness (Isa 6:10; 45:7). In Isaiah 45:7, the parallelism shows that this darkness pictures disaster (ra' based on contrast in the parallelism in the verse and context of God's judging), not moral evil. In judgment there is darkness and distress (Isa 5:30). What light remains is darkened by clouds (Isa 5:30). Babylon is the recipient of this darkness (Isa 47:5). In the day of salvation this darkness is exchanged for the brightness of seeing light (Isa 29:18; 42:7; 49:9; 58:10).

---

14. *Lam. Rab.* 1.3 challenges Israel to produce its nonexistent divorce paper; Goldingay, *The Message of Isaiah 40-55*, 395.

FLOOD AS DESTRUCTION

One of the metaphors used for judgment is a flood (Isa 8:7; 28:2, 17–22).[15] As a polemic to Baal who did not want windows in his house because one could slip in and destroy his house and kingdom, Yahweh has great window grates through which he dumps water out for his flood of judgment (Isa 24:18; previously Gen 7:11). The imagery of a heavy storm pours out flooding water in judgment (Isa 28:2, 17–19). Yahweh causes the flood of the Assyrian army to overflow its banks and completely overtake Aram and the northern kingdom, Ephraim. As for Judah, the flood shall sweep up to their necks, nearly destroying it all except for Jerusalem, which was graciously spared (Isa 8:7–8; 20:28; 59:9; previously Gen 6:17 everything destroyed but in Gen 6:8 Noah found Yahweh's grace). Yahweh promised to be with Israel in the midst of the flood just as he was with them during the exodus (Isa 43:2). Yahweh also causes the flood judgment to cease by rebuking the opposing forces, "Although the peoples roar like the roar of surging waters, when he rebukes them as they flee faraway" (Isa 17:13; previously Ps 104:7). God dries up the flood, thus stopping the judgment (Isa 44:24–27; previously Gen 8:13–14). The imagery of the great flood is utilized because it clearly shows the severity of the judgment. As with Noah when the flood judgment had ceased Yahweh promised that he would not judge the earth with a flood (Gen 9:11), now he promised that he would not break off his covenant of peace with his people (Isa 54:8–9). In the wake of this judgment, God initiates that he will never again judge the earth with treaty curses after he restores Jerusalem (Isa 62:8; Lev 26:16; Deut 28:31, 33).

FIRE AS DESTRUCTION

Fire is often tied to God in his judgment (Isa 1:7; 5:24; 9:5, 18–19; 10:16–17; 26:11; 29:1–4, 6; 30:14, 27, 30, 33; 33:11–14; 37:19; 44:16, 19; 47:14; 64:11; 65:5; 66:15–16, 24).[16] The imagery comes out of that of a storm where the fire is the bolt of lightning (Isa 29:6; 30:27, 30; 64:2–3). Such imagery develops the concept of the warrior god judging.

> See, Yahweh is coming with fire and his chariots are like a whirlwind; he will bring down his anger with fury and his rebuke with flames of fire. For with fire and with his sword Yahweh

---

15. Beckman, *Hittite Diplomatic Texts*, 52; *Esar* 488–89; 442; *Esarhaddon Annals* episode 5 and 7, in *AfOB* 9, p. 13–14; p. 32 line 12, p. 48 line 69, p. 65 line 10; Hillers, *Treaty-Curses*, 70–71; Jer 46:7–8; 47:2; Amos 8:8.

16. Jer 7:20; 15:14; 17:4, 27; 20:9; 43:12–13; 44:6; 49:27; 51:58.

will execute judgment upon all humans, and many will be those slain by Yahweh (Isa 66:15–16).

Yahweh judges sin with his holiness. Sin causes destruction by fire but God's wrath destroys all the more (Isa 65:5).

> Surely wickedness burns like a fire; it consumes briers and thorns, it sets the forest thickets ablaze, so that it rolls upward in a column of smoke. By the wrath of Yahweh Almighty the land will be scorched and the people will be fuel for the fire. (Isa 9:18–19)

> Yahweh Almighty will send wasting disease upon his sturdy warriors; under his pomp a fire will be kindled like a blazing flame. The light of Israel will become a fire, their Holy One a flame; in a single day it will burn and consume his thorns and his briers. The splendor of his forests and fertile fields it will completely destroy. (Isa 10:16–19)

The fire of God consumes its object in judgment (Isa 1:7; 5:24; 9:5, 19; 7:14; 64:11). Though Israel experiences this judgment, it is reserved for Yahweh's enemies (Isa 26:11). Additionally, an abundance of fire is reserved for the false gods in a pit (Isa 30:33). Everlasting burning is the ultimate fire judgment which Yahweh holds out for his enemies (Isa 33:11–12, 14; 66:24). For Israel it is Yahweh's desire that the fire serve as cleansing (Isa 6:6–7) and guidance (as the pillar of fire in the exodus, Isa 4:5). Yahweh promises to be with his people in the midst of the fire judgment and to deliver them (Isa 43:2; Dan 3:24–26).

EARTHQUAKE AS DESTRUCTION

Earthquake is a regular metaphor for covenant judgment (Isa 22:10; 30:13–14).[17] In its day, Babylon figuratively shook the earth and made kingdoms tremble (Isa 14:16). Even more than this conquest, Yahweh makes the kingdoms tremble in his judgment (Isa 23:11; 64:2). In the day of Yahweh, Babylon and Israel shall be judged with the shaking of heaven and earth (Isa 13:13; 64:1). This shaking comes out of the storm of judgment which also produces the fire and flood (Isa 29:6; Ps 18:7; 46:2; Jude 5–7). Such earthquake imagery may emerge out of a historical earthquake during Uzziah's reign (Amos 1:1; Zech 14:5). Leupold describes the earthquake event of Isaiah 5:25 in Jerusalem.

---

17. Jer 4:24; 8:16.

> Such letting loose of the forces of nature was not regarded as nature working autonomously. God's anger was manifesting itself: He was stretching forth his hand against his people. He smote them by touching the mountains and making them quake. The earthquake must have been unusually disastrous, for dead bodies lay about like refuse in the streets of the city for some time thereafter. For Israel of old, the anger of God was a very real thing to be viewed with extreme seriousness. But this earthquake was merely the forerunner of other judgments to come.[18]

The cataclysmic earthquake caused by Yahweh is described by Isaiah as shaking and splitting the earth in response to rebellion.

> The floodgates of the heavens are opened, the foundations of the earth shake. The earth is broken up, the earth is split asunder, the earth is thoroughly shaken, the earth reels like a drunkard, it sways like a hut in the wind; so heavy upon it is the guilt of its rebellion that it falls—never to rise again (Isa 24:18–20).

Humans respond in utter fear at the splendor of Yahweh as he rises to shake the earth. During earthquake judgment, humans flee to caves to escape from his exposing judgment (Isa 2:19, 21).

DAY OF YAHWEH AS DESTRUCTION

The day of Yahweh is a broadly encompassing concept identifying God's immediate presence and activity judging and restoring the earth.[19] As Dale Wheeler describes the day of Yahweh as the time in which "Yahweh, as Covenant Sovereign, intervenes in human history to execute the Covenant curses (and blessings!) upon the disobedient vassals, be they Israelite or Gentile."[20] In this capacity Yahweh expresses the role of warrior in theophanic war.[21] Gary Smith describes the day of Yahweh as that day when "God will muster his armies, shake the heavens and the earth, and destroy

---

18. Leupold, *Exposition of Isaiah*, 1:122.

19. "Day of Yahweh" is not merely a metaphor of "holy war" as Gerhard von Rad proposed ("Origin of the Concept of the Day of Yahweh," 97–72); it is a fuller concept of God's presence and action of blessing and judgment as Meir Weiss demonstrates ("Origin of the 'Day of the Lord'").

20. Wheeler, "Covenant Lawsuit in Isaiah 1," 45.

21. von Rad, "Origin of the Concept of the Day of Yahweh"; Cross, "Divine Warrior in Israel's Early Cult"; Meir Weiss, "Origin of the 'Day of the Lord,'" 29–60; Watts, *Isaiah 1–33, 34–35*; Cerny, *The Day of Yahweh*, 87, 93; Everson, "The Days of Yahweh."

the arrogant sinners on earth."[22] By this encompassing emphasis, the day of Yahweh often describes an eschatological judgment in which Yahweh expresses his vengeance directly and Yahweh alone will be exalted (Isa 2:11–12; 61:2). At times it is referred to as "that day" in close proximity to Yahweh Almighty (Isa 2:12, 20; 3:1, 7, 15, 18; 4:1–2). In the fury and anger of judgment, the day of Yahweh can encroach into history as when Babylon was judged (Isa 13:9).

ESCHATOLOGICAL JUDGMENT

As a segment of the judgment of Yahweh, there is a climactic judgment in which all stages of judgment find ultimate fulfillment. The proud rebels will greatly fear Yahweh as he brings them low (Isa 2:6; 13:6–8). Yahweh alone will be exalted (Isa 2:11). Earthquakes, fire, and flood imagery reach their peak in this time. Cruel wrath and fierce anger are manifested from Yahweh (Isa 13:9, 13). Yahweh's wrath makes Israel's enemies drunk so that they stager (Isa 34:2; 51:17; 63:6).[23] This destruction is prefigured by the severity of Assyria's destruction of Babylon (Isa 13:1–5, 17–22).[24] Israel will be severely judged with the destruction of Jerusalem and the temple (Isa 27:9–10). Vegetation will be stripped from the land as great numbers of sinners are destroyed (Isa 13:9, 14–16; 24:5–6, 17–18; 27:10–11; 34:3, 5–7; 63:1–6; 66:15–17).[25] The heavens and the earth will be shaken (Isa 13:13; 24:18–20). While stars are visible, the sun and moon will be darkened (Isa 13:10; 24:23). Then stars will dissolve and fall (Isa 34:14). The whole earth will be devastated in the final destruction of gentile powers which avenges Yahweh's people (Isa 24:1–13, 19–20; 25:1–3, 5, 7, 10–12; 35:4). Such everlasting destruction renders many areas as sparse as an unclean desert (Isa 34:8–15). Heavenly powers and earthly kings will be imprisoned by Yahweh (Isa 24:21–22). This judgment is so severe that all people will honor Yahweh (Isa 25:3). Only a remnant will be left of all the nations (Isa 24:6). This remnant will rejoice and praise God at Yahweh's concluding of eschatological judgment (Isa 24:14–16). In this era, almighty Yahweh will reign on Mount Zion in the kingdom he establishes (Isa 24:23).

22. Smith, *Isaiah 1–39*, 322.
23. Parallel to Rev 14:18–19; 19:13–16.
24. Parallel to Rev 17–18.
25. Parallel to Rev 19:13–15.

SHEOL

Biblical Judaism from Abraham to David focused on faithfully living within the appropriate covenant and realizing the blessing in this life (Deut 30:6, 15–16, 19). When brief mentions of afterlife present themselves, they are vague but encouraging, as "gathered to your forefathers" (Gen 25:8, 17; 35:29; Judg 2:10; 2 Kgs 22:20; 2 Chr 3:28). This comment of "gathered to your forefathers" includes being buried where the forefathers were buried (Gen 49:29, 33) but there is more to it than this because those who die and are not buried where one's family is buried are still "gathered to their forefathers" (Num 20:24, 26; 27:13; 31:2; Deut 32:50). By the tenth century BC this ambiguity develops further to the concept of *sheol*.

Sheol refers to a grave beneath the earth's surface (Gen 7:11; 8:2; 49:25 Job 38:16; Pss 69:16; 71:20; 88:5; Jonah 2:3)[26] toward which a person and not merely a body is heading (Gen 37:35; 42:38; 44:29, 31; 1 Sam 2:6; 1 Kgs 2:6, 9).[27] By extension, *sheol* is conceived of as a cavernous pit which swallows judged humans alive (Num 16:30, 33; Ps 55:15). Metaphorically, *sheol* means 1) the deepest low as the opposite of high (Isa 7:1; 14:9; Ps 139:8; Job 11:8; Amos 9:2), and 2) as parallel with destruction of this life (Ps 88:3; Prov 15:11; 27:20). That is, *sheol* develops into a place beneath the earth's surface where people descend in death (Gen 37:35; Job 7:9; Isa 14:9; Ezek 31:15, 17; 31:27). All humans (Isa 5:14), both good (Gen 37:35) and evil (Num 16:30), go into this place of afterlife.[28] People generally go to *sheol* against their will (*wryd* in Hiphil and Piel: Gen 42:38; 44:29, 31; 1 Sam 2:6; 1 Kgs 2:6; Ezek 31:16), brought there by Yahweh (1 Sam 2:6; Isa 26:19). As the place of death, it is approached through gates covered with dust (Job 17:16; Isa 38:10).

> If I look for *sheol* as my home,
> I make my bed in the darkness;
> If I call to the pit, "You are my father;"
> To the worm, "my mother and my sister";
> Where now is my hope?
> And who regards my hope?

26. Johnson, *Vitality of the Individual*, 88; Tromp, *Primitive Conceptions*.

27. *Elephantine papyri* 71.15.

28. Early patristic views of purgatory develop to rescue people from *sheol* through misinterpreting Isa 66:24 "fire not quenched," 1 Cor 3:10–15 "refining fire," 1 Pet 3:19, and Eph 4:9–10 (Origen, "Homily 16," in *Homilies on Jeremiah and 1 Kings*, 28, in Migne, *Patrologia graeca*, vol. 13, col. 415 C-D; "Homily 6 on Exodus," sect. 4, in Migne, *Patrologia graeca*, vol. 12, col. 334–35; Gregory Nyssa, "Sermon on the Dead," in Migne, *Patrologia graeca*, vol. 13, 445, 448; Augustine, *Enchir.* 69; 93; 111–13; *Civ.* 20.22; 21.9.2, 10.1, 16, 26.2; Gregory the Great, *Dial.* 4.39).

> Will it go down with me to *sheol*?
> Shall we together go down into dust? (Job 17:13–16).[29]

Those who go into *sheol* do so in a shadow-like existence of forgetfulness of their former selves (Ps 88:13; Eccl 9:5). Yahweh killed the dead rulers, removing their memory by sending them to *sheol* (Isa 26:13). All the dead go to *sheol*, for it is the great equalizer (Isa 5:14–15). The dead are not able to take anything from this life with them into *sheol* except their decaying bodies (Eccl 5:14). The dead are laid out on death beds or thrones (Isa 14:9, 11), with worms and maggots covering their bodies (Isa 14:11). *Sheol* is a place of torment (Isa 50:11). The dead are conscious in their shade existence (Isa 14:9). However, those in *sheol* generally do not know the events in the world above (Job 14:21; Eccl 9:5), though those in *sheol* may be aware of catastrophes and join in lamentation over them (Jer 31:15). This concept of *sheol* has implications, namely:

1. In the OT praising God is reserved for the living and thus not expected to occur in *sheol* (Pss 38:18–19; 115:17).

2. Any dead conjured up can do no more than chirp[30] as a bird (Isa 8:19; 10:4; 29:4), so a more cogent conjured Samuel was likely divinely enabled and announced divine judgment upon Saul (1 Sam 28:11–19).

3. David says of his and Bathsheba's child, "I shall go to him, he will not return to me" (2 Sam 12:23). This does not develop infant or fetal salvation but the recognition that the dead child has gone to *sheol* and David will join him in *sheol* when he also dies.

4. *Sheol* is personified as a fearsome enemy in illness or instances of risk, dragging victims down with ropes into its own mouth (2 Sam 22:6=Pss 18:4; 141:7; Job 24:19). It is a cruel despot carrying out evil designs because of irresistible power (Ps 89:48; Song 8:6).

In contrast to these disturbing images of *sheol*, Isaiah hints that there is a better program for the righteous, namely the righteous die in peace with God swallowing up death (Isa 25:8; 57:20), which may hint that the righteous continue to live (Isa 26:19). However, Isaiah writes before a clear resurrection view begins to be developed by Dan 12:2 and early Judaism.

---

29. Similar to *Gilgamesh Epic* 7.4.30–40; Segal, *Life After Death*.

30. Speech of the dead is that of bird chirping (Oswalt, *The Book of Isaiah: Chapters 1–39*, 685).

CHAPTER 8

The Nations in Judgment

SOVEREIGN GOD CONTROLS THE events of history, judging the nations (Isa 14:24–25; 22:11; 23:8–9) and utilizing them as his tools (Isa 7:17–20; 13:3; 39:6–7).[1] When God uses the nations, such as Assyria or Babylon, to bring judgment on Israel, then Yahweh turns the great gentile army into a "people made holy for me" (Isa 13:3).[2] This is an important idea because when Israel is defeated by the nations it is not because Yahweh gets overwhelmed, it is because Israel's defeat is part of Yahweh's plan (Isa 45:6–7). While these nations become part of Yahweh's holy army, Yahweh brings judgment upon Israel. However, judging Israel is not the emphasis of Isaiah's development with regard to the nations. Instead, Isaiah's emphasis is Yahweh's sovereignty by the divine judging of these same nations.

Every prophet of the OT, except Hosea, contains judgment oracles against the nations surrounding Israel (Isa 13–27; Jer 46–51; Ezek 25–31; Amos 1–2). Most of these oracles were never heard by those nations,[3] which means that the prophecy guarantees what is said will be realized, and that the benefit of hearing these judgments is primarily an encouragement for the Jewish audience that would have heard them. John Hayes identified that these prophetic oracles fulfilled a role of denouncing one's enemies to the leader of the other side, such as the king of Israel (Num 22–24; 1 Sam

---

1. Bright, "Faith and Destiny," 3–5, 11; Davies, "Destiny of the Nations."

2. Goldingay, *Old Testament Theology*, 3:575.

3. This condition that the people who are judged do not hear the prophet's judgment is similar to how extra-biblical oracles function ("State Archives of Assyria" 9 2.3, 3.2, and 8, easily accessible in Hays, *Hidden Riches*, 248, 266, 258).

15:2-3; 1 Kgs 20:26-30; Isa 7:5-7).[4] Such cursing was part of a royal theology battle plan declared by a prophet or priest articulating the words of a deity concerning the opponents' destruction (Isa 13:2-4). Usually these nations are condemned for their pride (Isa 13:11, 19; 16:6; 23:9; 24:21; 25:11; 28:1), as Israel had been (Isa 2:6-21; 3:16—4:1; 9:8; 10:5-15). The nations are also condemned for evil (Isa 13:11; 14:5-6, 20) and abuse of Israel (Isa 25:4; 26:21). Furthermore, the nations are also condemned because Israel depended upon them as a greater security than Yahweh himself (Isa 18:2; 19:18-22; 20:6). These consequences additionally admonish Judah so that they would trust Yahweh, honoring the name of God and showing the impotence of pagan deities.[5] Imbedded within these oracles of judgment are hopeful reminders of Yahweh's salvation for Israel which in its generosity includes even nations (Isa 14:1-2; 16:5; 18:7; 19:18-25; 23:17-18). Yahweh will eschatologically transform the hearts of humankind (Isa 2:1-5; 11:10-16; 19:18-25). The nations will ultimately submit to the Davidic king (Isa 9:6-7; 11:4, 10, 14-15; 15:5; 25:6—27:13), bringing tribute to Jerusalem (Isa 14:1-2; 18:7; 23:15-18; 45:14; 60:5-7, 11, 13, 16; 61:6; 66:12) and worshiping Yahweh in Israel's salvation (Isa 2:1-4; 19:18-25; 25:6-10a; 42:1-4; 45:22-25; 49:6; 51:4-6; 55:3-5; 56:3-8; 66:18-24).[6]

Isaiah 13-35 develops Yahweh as sovereign in bringing judgment upon the nations. These judgment oracles are a unit, with many of them introduced by the "burden" (*ms'*) that lands on each of these nations to judge them (Isa 13:1; 15:1; 17:1; 19:1; 21:1, 11, 13; 22:1, 25; 23:1). Some of the oracles do not begin with the term "burden" but it is better to literally include them within the previous burden: Cush as within Isa 17:1 Damascus, Philistia as within Isa 13:1 Babylon, and Dumah and Arabia as within Isa 21:1 Babylon.[7] However, in this theology, the places will be presented separately since no clear rationale for these relationships is developed in the Isaiah text.[8]

The most prominent oracles in the section are against Babylon and Assyria (who threaten Judah), and Egypt (because Israel hopes Egypt will come to Israel's aid). Because these oracles are not presented to the nations

---

4. Hayes, "Usage of Oracles against Foreign Nations," esp. 83-86; *War Scroll* 13.2-6; Sumerian *Curse of Agade*, in Kramer, *The Sumerians*, 62-66; Malamat, "Prophetic Revelations in New Documents."

5. Raabe, "Why Oracles against Nations?"; Smith, *Isaiah 1-39*, 288.

6. Helpful summary by Graham Davies, "Destiny of the Nations," 104-5, whereas in the rest of the article (93-120) he argues for the unity of the book of Isaiah.

7. For this pattern of including Cush: Clements, *Isaiah 1-39*, 163-66; Philistia: Sweeney, *Isaiah 1-39*, 229; Dumah and Arabia: Childs, *Isaiah*, 148.

8. Following Smith, *Isaiah 1-39*, 289.

themselves, there is very little development of the nations' sins, apart from the summaries in the previous paragraph. The focus is on the nations' destruction, which provides a measure of encouragement to Judah that Yahweh will fight on their behalf even when Israel is rebellious and will themselves be judged. Perhaps the brief mention that nations do evil to Israel (Isa 13:11; 14:5-6, 20) and abuse Israel (Isa 25:4; 26:21) provides some encouragement to Judah that Yahweh takes notice of them. Also the brief mention of nations judged because Israel was depending upon them for security rather than upon Yahweh (Isa 18:2; 19:18-22; 20:6) provides a hint to Judah that the nations cannot provide this security; Judah must trust Yahweh.

Assyria and Damascus were to be destroyed by Yahweh's armies (Isa 17:1-3, 9; similar language: 1:7-9; 28:15).[9] Some of the burdensome features date as being given in a context which appears while Assyria was conquering Judah during 704-701 BC.[10] This conquest was accomplished under Nebuchadnezzar's Babylonian coalition, destroying Nineveh in 612 BC. Assyria was threshed and harvested (Isa 17:4-6, 11) and plundered (Isa 17:14; similar language to Judah: Isa 3:14-15, 25-26; 7:18; 8:4; 42:18-25).[11] Part of the plunder was that their idols were forsaken (Isa 17:7-8; similar to language about Egypt: Isa 19:1). This destruction blew them away like chaff (Isa 17:13; similar language to Judah: Isa 4:6; 25:4; 28:2; 29:6).[12] The devastation was so extreme that the populous was terrorized (Isa 17:14; similar language to Judah: Isa 28:19; 33:13-14). The land was left to famine (Isa 17:4) and with ruins so extreme that shepherds would bring their flocks to graze (Isa 17:2).

Isaiah announced "Fallen, fallen is Babylon" (Isa 21:9), for Babylon was to experience a historical expression of the day of Yahweh (Isa 13:6, 9), even metaphorically removing heavenly light (Isa 13:10), brought about

---

9. Similar metaphors are used in: Beckman, *Hittite Diplomatic Texts*, 17, 29, 33, 40, 48, 52, 58, 64, 69, 86, 92, 112, 122; also other futility curses: *Sefire* I.4.19; Jer 2:12, 30; 4:6, 13, 20, 26; 5:10; 6:19; 7:33; 8:16; 9:11; 10:18; 11:22; 12:11-12; 13:14; 14:18; 15:8, 11, 14; 16:4; 17:18; 18:7, 16, 21; 19:8; 26:10-15; 34:22; 41:3; 45:5; 46:22-23; 50:26; 51:1-4, 55-56; Hos 4:10; 5:6; 8:7; 9:12, 16; Amos 4:4; 5:11; 8:12; Mic 3:4; 6:14-15; Zeph 1:13; Hag 1:6; Mal 1:4; CD 1.16-18; 3.10-11; 8.1; 4Q463 1 1; Hillers, *Treaty-Curses*, 28-29.

10. Gary Smith, *Isaiah 1-39*, 289.

11. Similar metaphors are used in Beckman, *Hittite Diplomatic Texts*, 17, 29, 33, 40, 48, 52, 58, 64, 69, 86, 92, 112, 122, 139; also other futility curses: *Sefire* I.4.19; "Laws of Hammurabi," 50.81-91, in Roth, *Law Collections*, 138-39; Deut 28:20-22, 25, 27, 35, 49-50, 53, 57-63 parallel to 7-11, 67; 29:19-23; Jer 4:5-6, 13, 29; 5:15-17; 6:23; 11:22; 15:2; 18:17, 21; 19:9; 21:4-7; 41:4-18; 46:3-5; 49:37; 50:13-15; 51:1-4; 52:4-16; Hos 4:10; 5:6; 8:7; 9:12, 16; Amos 4:4; 5:11; 8:12; Mic 3:4; 6:14-15; Zeph 1:13; Hag 1:6; Mal 1:4; Hillers, *Treaty-Curses*, 28-29.

12. Similar metaphor: Isa 11:4; 30:28; 33:11; Jer 4:13; *Enuma Elish* 1.105; 2.95-105.

by the Medes (Isa 13:17; 21:2), to bring destruction upon their empire (Isa 13:6, 9; 14:22; 21:9; similar language: Isa 1:7-9; 28:15).[13] It is possible that the prophet floats this language during the Assyrian conquest of Judah (704-701 BC) when Judah may have been tempted to depend upon Babylon to diminish the Assyrian threat. No exact date is predicted but Isaiah says that it could "soon come" (Isa 13:22). However, the overthrow of Nineveh occurred in 612 BC, and Babylon began to be dominated by the Medes (Isa 13:17).[14] The walls were still standing in the wake of Cyrus's conquest in 539 BC, but they were also destroyed by 518 BC. Xerxes ruined the temple to Belus. As Seleucia rose, Babylon declined. The Medes killed Babylonians in conquest (Isa 13:18), ravished their wives (Isa 13:16; similar language to: Isa 3:18-24, 26; 32:11-13),[15] killed their kids (Isa 13:16, 18), and plundered their houses (Isa 13:16-17; similar language to Judah: Isa 3:14-15, 25-26; 7:18; 8:4; 42:18-25),[16] and smashed their idols (Isa 21:9; similar language to Assyria: Isa 17:7-8). Babylon was a threshed people (Isa 21:10) as in the wake of an earthquake (Isa 13:13; similar language to Isa 22:10; 30:13-14),[17] leaving them like Sodom and Gomorrah (Isa 13:19). Such a complete conquest terrorized Babylon (Isa 13:8; 21:3-4; as elsewhere in conquest: Isa 28:19; 33:13-14) so that their heart and hands melted (Isa 13:7). With such pain as a woman in labor (Isa 13:8; 21:3), the people flee their hunters (Isa 13:14-15). This leaves the land of Babylon with no inhabitants, so it becomes a desert where shepherds bring their flocks and desert creatures dwell (Isa 13:20-22; 14:23; as elsewhere: Isa 5:29-30; 7:18; 35:9; 51:8; 56:9).[18] To make

13. Similar metaphors are used in Beckman, *Hittite Diplomatic Texts*, 17, 29, 33, 40, 48, 52, 58, 64, 69, 86, 92, 112, 122; also other futility curses: *Sefire* I.4.19; Jer 2:12, 30; 4:6, 13, 20, 26; 5:10; 6:19; 7:33; 8:16; 9:11; 10:18; 11:22; 12:11-12; 13:14; 14:18; 15:8, 11, 14; 16:4; 17:18; 18:7, 16, 21; 19:8; 26:10-15; 34:22; 41:3; 45:5; 46:22-23; 50:26; 51:1-4, 55-56; Hos 4:10; 5:6; 8:7; 9:12, 16; Amos 4:4; 5:11; 8:12; Mic 3:4; 6:14-15; Zeph 1:13; Hag 1:6; Mal 1:4; CD 1.16-18; 3.10-11; 8.1; 4Q463 1 1; Delbert Hillers, *Treaty Curses*, 28-29.

14. Young, *The Book of Isaiah*, 1:427.

15. VTE sect 42; *Assur-nerari-Matiilu Treaty* SSA 2 2 v 1-13 and SSA 2 5 iv18'-19'; Crouch, *Israel and the Assyrians*, 63-64; Esar 521-22; Hillers, *Treaty-Curses*, 63; Deut 28:30; 2 Sam 12:11; 16:20-22; Jer 8:10.

16. Similar metaphors are used in: Beckman, *Hittite Diplomatic Texts*, 17, 29, 33, 40, 48, 52, 58, 64, 69, 86, 92, 112, 122, 139; also other futility curses: *Sefire* I.4.19; "Laws of Hammurabi," 50.81-91, in Roth, *Law Collections*, 138-39; Deut 28:20-22, 25, 27, 35, 49-50, 53, 57-63 parallel to 7-11, 67; 29:19-23; Jer 4:5-6, 13, 29; 5:15-17; 6:23; 11:22; 15:2; 18:17, 21; 19:9; 21:4-7; 41:4-18; 46:3-5; 49:37; 50:13-15; 51:1-4; 52:4-16; Hos 4:10; 5:6; 8:7; 9:12, 16; Amos 4:4; 5:11; 8:12; Mic 3:4; 6:14-15; Zeph 1:13; Hag 1:6; Mal 1:4; Hillers, *Treaty-Curses*, 28-29.

17. Jer 4:24; 8:16.

18. Curse statements elsewhere: *Sefire* I.A.31; II.A.9, 30-32; Aramaic "Treaty

Babylon a desert includes destroying houses, wives, and infants (Isa 13:16). Carol Dempsey explains, "The guilty parties are those among the Babylonian who wield power, and yet the innocent among their families will be made to suffer too in order to exacerbate the suffering of the powerful."[19]

In this conquest, a taunt is announced against the king of Babylon (Isa 14:4-21). The Babylonian king is described as speaking with language familiar to the Akitu new year's festival as he stands atop the top platform of the ziggurat, called "heaven" (Isa 14:12-13), so that as the Babylonian king, he is an arrogant human who could be called a bright star in the East (Isa 14:12, 16).[20] The prideful statements that the king's "I wills" describe are consistent language with the Akitu volitional statements of the high priest and the king's confessions, though there is no exact match in these comparative documents (Isa 14:13-14).[21] Nevertheless, the oppressing Babylonian king is declared to be thrust down as a "human" ('yš; ἄνθρωπος) corpse and fallen[22] into *sheol*, with his ruling scepter destroyed (Isa 14:4-6, 12, 15-17). With his removal there is rest from his destruction and removal of trees to fund his building projects (Isa 14:7-8). *Sheol* and its inhabitant dead kings rise up from their death beds to welcome the king of Babylon to their

---

Between Bar-Ga'yah and the King of Arpad," *Sephire* 1.27; Fitzmyer, *Aramaic Inscriptions of Sefire*, 44-45; "Aramaic Inscriptions of Sefire I and II," 181, 185; *Gilgamesh Epic* 12.93-94; Deut 28:38-42; 32:24; Lev 26:22; Jer 2:14-15; 4:7; 5:6; 8:17; 10:22; 12:9; 48:40; 49:19, 22, 33; 50:44; 51:37; Lam 3:10-11; Hos 2:20; 5:12, 14; Hillers, *Treaty-Curses*, 28-29, 54-56. Babylon is described as a desert by Strabo (*Geogr.* 16.1) and Pausanius (Young, *The Book of Isaiah*, 1:427).

19. Dempsey, *Isaiah*, 33.

20. There is no allusion to Satan's fall as Tertullian (*Marc.* 5.17), Origen (*Princ.* 1.5.5), and Gregory the Great (*Epist.* 18 and 22) propose to make sense of the Vulgate Isa 14:12 "light bearer, morning light" (Latin Vulg.: "Lucifer, qui mane oriebaris") as a name, and the unrelated later description in Luke 10:18 of Satan falling from heaven while Jesus' seventy disciples cast out demons. Isaiah 14's context identifies the fallen to be "human" (MT: 'yš; LXX: ἄνθρωπος; but absent in Vulgate permitting a non-human fulfilling this role among Vulgate authoritative traditions) in *sheol* (Isa 14:15-16). This text should be understood as the Babylonian king, not a spiritual angel named Satan.

21. Cuneiform tablets 22 and 23 of day five of the *Babylonian Akitu Festival*, lines 417-33, easily accessible in Hays, *Hidden Riches*, 152. Additional mythologies include parallels with Ishtar in *sheol* (*ANET*, 52-57, 106-9), Gilgamesh (van Leeuwen, "Isa 14:12 ḥoleš 'al gwym and Gilgamesh"), or worship of Baal (Goldingay, *Isaiah*, 103; Keowen, *History of the Interpretation of Isaiah*).

22. To "fall from heaven" is to fall from a great political height (Dan 8:10; Cicero, *Att.* 2.21; *Phil.* 2.41; Horace, *Epod.* 17.41; Herodotus, *Hist.* 3.64), though the Babylonian Akitu festival is carried out on the top platform of a Babylonian ziggurat called "heaven" and such a fall from heaven could also allude to the removal from living royalty, and thus removal from effecting recovery for Babylon. There is no allusion to a fall of Satan, as misinterpretation of the Latin text fostered.

maggot covered existence among the worms (Isa 14:9-11, 18). As a killed and trampled corpse, he has destroyed his people and is to be forgotten as a rejected branch for burning (Isa 14:19-21).

Isaiah dramatically walks naked and barefoot for three years to indicate that three years after Sargon captured Ashdod,[23] or about 712 BC, Egyptian cities would be destroyed and Egyptians would be walked naked to Assyria (Isa 19:4, 10-15; 20:3-6; 27:12-13; similar language: Isa 1:7-9; 28:15).[24] There is no record of Assyrian invasion of Egypt until the rebellions of 671 and 667 BC.[25] However, the oracle is clear that such judgment is not due to humans, for Yahweh rode the clouds in judgment against Egypt for Judah's considered dependence upon Egypt with the rising Assyrian threat (Isa 19:1). Egypt would not have been a strong ally in any case, because Isaiah describes them as "empty do nothings" (Isa 30:7, *riq*).[26] Assyrian Rabshakeh describes Egypt's impotence as a "broken reed of a staff" that cannot support their own weight, nor Judah's (Isa 36:6). Assyrian captivity terrorized the Egyptians until they became like women (Isa 19:1, 16-17; as elsewhere in conquest: Isa 28:19; 33:13-14). Egypt laments their destruction (Isa 19:8-10). In this condition idols are forsaken and drought occurs (Isa 19:1, 6-7; as describing Assyria, Isa 17:7-8, also a covenant curse in Deut 28:23-24; 29:19).[27] In the wake of this invasion Isaiah identifies that there will be five cities worshiping Yahweh near the Egyptian border and praying to savior Yahweh to protect them (Isa 19:18-25). These five cities in Egypt will be allied with Yahweh and will speak a Canaanite dialect (Isa 19:18). There will be an altar in Egypt and a monument on their border as a testimony to Yahweh (Isa 19:19-20). Attempts to identify these five cities have been unsuccessful, though some point to Heliopolis and Beth-Shemesh (Gen 41:45, 50; 46:20; Jer 43:13).[28] These are not Jewish cities in Egypt, meaning that the Jewish temples in Elephantine and in Alexandria don't fit this description

---

23. *ANET*, 286, 249-62.

24. Similar metaphors are used in: Beckman, *Hittite Diplomatic Texts*, 17, 29, 33, 40, 48, 52, 58, 64, 69, 86, 92, 112, 122; also other futility curses: Sefire I.4.19; Jer 2:12, 30; 4:6, 13, 20, 26; 5:10; 6:19; 7:33; 8:16; 9:11; 10:18; 11:22; 12:11-12; 13:14; 14:18; 15:8, 11, 14; 16:4; 17:18; 18:7, 16, 21; 19:8; 26:10-15; 34:22; 41:3; 45:5; 46:22-23; 50:26; 51:1-4, 55-56; Hos 4:10; 5:6; 8:7; 9:12, 16; Amos 4:4; 5:11; 8:12; Mic 3:4; 6:14-15; Zeph 1:13; Hag 1:6; Mal 1:4; CD 1.16-18; 3.10-11; 8.1; 4Q463 1 1; Hillers, *Treaty-Curses*, 28-29.

25. Watts, *Isaiah 1-33* (rev. ed.), 322.

26. BDB 938.

27. Elijah claimed a drought curse when Israel rebelled (1 Kgs 17:1) and the ample rain blessing of Deut 28:12 when the prophets of Baal were killed (1 Kgs 18:44-45). Drought is also a curse under the "Laws of Hammurabi," 50.64-71 (with often famine following, 49.53-54, 66-67, 80), in Roth, *Law Collections*, 136-38.

28. Gottwald, *All the Kingdoms of the Earth*, 225-27.

as perhaps Onias's temple in Leontopolis involving Egyptians might.[29] Yahweh will be known to the Egyptians and Assyrians such that there will be a highway between them, enabling them to all worship Yahweh together (Isa 19:21-25). However, there is not enough archeological evidence at the time of this writing to identify which five cities are alluded to here.

Isaiah summarizes the other nations' destructions in redundant terminology. Moab will be destroyed within three years (Isa 15:1; 16:4, 14; 25:10). Moabites will be killed (Isa 15:9) and left mourning (Isa 15:2-5, 8; 16:7, 9-12). The land of Moab will be plundered with drought and withering crops (Isa 15:6-7; 16:8). Philistia will be destroyed, leaving the mourners to flee from continuing famine (Isa 14:29-31). Edom feels the threat of near destruction (Isa 21:11-12), and Arabia is concerned as fugitives flee across their land (Isa 21:13-17).[30] Ethiopia will be harvested (Isa 18:5). Tyre and Sidon will be destroyed (Isa 23:1-18). Tiglath-Pileser's army swept over Tyre, Sidon, Philistia, Moab, and the trans-Jordan (1 Chr 5:26) with continued records of vassal kings of Moab and Judah, and with Edom and Ammon paying tribute to Assyria in 730s and 720s BC.[31] These nations banded together as a coalition with King Azuru of Ashdod and supported by King Pir'u (Pharoah Bocchoris) of Egypt when the northern tribes of Israel fell in 722-21 BC; but Sargon defeated Ashdod, making it an Assyrian province in 712-711 BC.[32] Assyrian records continue to list these nations as vassals paying tribute to Sennacherib (701 BC) and Essarhaddon (681-669 BC),[33] even providing building materials for Essarhaddon's palace in Ninevah.[34] Under Ashurbanipal (669-630 BC) Arabian tribes flooded this region and East Syria but they were repulsed, with Arab chief Ammuladi of Kedar being captured in Moab and taken hostage to Ninevah (probably Jer 48).[35] Moab ceased to be an autonomous nation, and the Arab fugitives fled in southernly directions (Isa 15:5, 7; 16:1-4; fulfilling 21:13-17; Jer 48:4-6, 28, 34, 45). However, there is still a king in Moab as late as 598 BC (Jer 27:3). When Zedekiah of Judah rebelled around 587 BC, Jerusalem was destroyed, with many fleeing to Moab until governor Gedaliah was appointed and brought stability to the region (2 Kgs 24:17-20; Jer 40:11-12).

29. Josephus, *Ant.* 13.2; LXX alternative reading "city of righteousness"; 1QIsa^a reading; Baruq, "Is 19:18 et Leontopolis," *DBS* 5 (1952) 336-70.

30. A. A. Macintosh nicely surveys rival eighth- and sixth-century views to fulfill these Isaiah prophecies (*Isaiah xxi: A Palimpsest*).

31. *ANET*, 282-84.

32. *ANET*, 286-87.

33. *ANET*, 287-88.

34. *ANET*, 291.

35. *ANET*, 298.

Near the climax of judgment on the nations, but before Tyre and universal judgment is proclaimed, there is an odd prophecy laced with questions at the valley of vision in Jerusalem (Isa 22). In light of all this judgment, Yahweh asks Jerusalem, "What is the matter with you?" (Isa 22:1–2). As Yahweh conquers, don't try to comfort Yahweh in his mourning (Isa 22:3–11). Judah does not depend upon Yahweh, so its iniquity will not be forgiven (Isa 22:11, 14). Jerusalem should repent and mourn, but in these judgments on the nations they instead celebrate (Isa 22:2, 12–13). Yahweh warns that Jerusalemites cannot escape judgment by strengthening the walls or providing new sources of water, nor by making tombs for themselves for death will destroy them in open field (Isa 22:9–11, 15–18). Yahweh will depose leadership and raise leadership, but all Jerusalem will fail because Yahweh has spoken (Isa 22:15–22).

National judgments climax with a universal section (Isa 24–27), which Duhm called "Isaiah's apocalypse"[36]—the whole world is targeted for destruction under Yahweh's curse (Isa 24:1, 3, 21; 26:14). The section is not actually apocalyptic in genre since it utilized the same metaphors in a similar manner as elsewhere in Isaiah's judgments.[37] Furthermore, there is no visionary journey through these images and no role for angels expounding on the context as is so common among early Jewish apocalyptic literature. However, the novelty of the section is that it mostly resists mentioning any specific locales, except Moab and the whole Middle East from the Euphrates to Egypt (Isa 25:10; 27:12–13), which leaves the section rather universal under Yahweh's judgment.

The conquest language and removal of lights from the sky (Isa 13:10; 34:4) is reapplied by Jesus to refer to eschatological sky signs similar to Joel 2:10 just prior to the Son of Man coming on the clouds (Isa 27:13) in Jesus' second coming to establish kingdom (Matt 24:29; Mark 13:24–25).

There are several reasons for this universal judgment of nations. First, the nations have violated the "everlasting covenant" (Isa 24:5–6), which is best understood as the Mosaic covenant or Law on the basis of the use of "*torah*" and "stipulations" (*twrh* and *ḥqh*) in the OT mostly referring to the everlasting Mosaic covenant (Isa 21:5; Exod 12:14; 27:21; 28:43; 31:13–17; Lev 6:22; 10:9; 16:29–34; 23:41) rather than other everlasting covenants— the Noahic (Gen 9:12, 16) and Abrahamic (Gen 13:15, 17:7–8, 13, 19; 48:4).[38] However, since the Mosaic covenant was made by Yahweh with

---

36. Duhm, *Das Buch Jesaia*, 172–94.

37. Johnson, *From Chaos to Restoration*, 100.

38. Kennard, *Biblical Covenantalism*, 1:134–35; Polaski, "Reflections on a Mosaic Covenant."

Israel, the violation of this covenant by those who were not party to the Mosaic covenant means that they beget the covenant curses through their abuse of protected Israel within this covenant. Second, the nations' pride is listed as a reason for these judgments, thus challenging Yahweh's sovereignty (Isa 24:21 "height in height"; 25:11). Additionally, they specifically violated features that the Mosaic covenant addressed, namely putting the vulnerable at risk (Isa 25:4; Exod 22:22; Deut 24:17) and committing iniquity and murder (Isa 26:21; Exod 20:13; Deut 5:17; 19:15). For these reasons, the nations are judged as a whole.

The curses that Yahweh brings upon the nations broadly fit within the pattern of covenant curses elsewhere in Isaiah and in ancient Near Eastern international diplomatic texts:

1. Devastation of the earth (Isa 24:1, 3; 25:2, 12; 26:5, 14; compared with Judah: Isa 1:7–9; 3:14–15, 25–26; 7:18; 8:4; 28:15).[39]

2. Reversal of conditions (Isa 24:2, 7–13).[40]

3. Land destroyed by enemies and plundered (Isa 13:16; 14:21; compared with Isa 3:14–15, 25–26; 5:26–30; 7:18; 8:4; 42:18–25).[41]

4. Wives ravished (Isa 13:16; compared with Isa 3:18–24, 26; 13:16; 32:11–13).[42]

5. Children dashed to pieces (Isa 13:16, 18; 14:21; compared with Isa 49:26).[43]

---

39. Beckman, *Hittite Diplomatic Texts*, 17, 29, 33, 40, 48, 52, 58, 64, 69, 86, 92, 112, 122, 139; also other futility curses: *Sefire* I.4.19; Jer 2:12, 30; 4:5–6, 13, 20, 26, 29; 5:10, 15–17; 6:19, 23; 7:33; 8:16; 9:11; 10:18; 11:22; 12:11–12; 13:14; 14:18; 15:2, 8, 11, 14; 16:4; 17:18; 18:7, 16–17, 21; 19:8–9; 21:4–7; 26:10–15; 34:22; 41:3–5; 45:5; 46:22–23; 49:37; 50:13–15, 26; 51:1–4, 55–56; 52:4–16; Hos 4:10; 5:6; 8:7; 9:12, 16; Amos 4:4; 5:11; 8:12; Mic 3:4; 6:14–15; Zeph 1:13; Hag 1:6; Mal 1:4; CD 1.16–18; 3.10–11; 8.1; 4Q463 1 1; Hillers, *Treaty-Curses*, 28–29. This destruction entails the covenant curse of death, which is the point of Isaiah 28:15 covenant with death rather than Christopher B. Hays's explanation selling out in pagan worship to the Egyptian god of death ("Covenant with Mut").

40. Deut 28:15–19 as compared to 28:1–6.

41. Beckman, *Hittite Diplomatic Texts*, 17, 29, 33, 40, 48, 52, 58, 64, 69, 86, 92, 112, 122, 139; also other futility curses: *Sefire* I.4.19; "Laws of Hammurabi," 50.81–91 in Roth, *Law Collections*, 138–39; Deut 28:20–22, 25, 27, 35, 49–50, 53, 57–63 parallel to 7–11, 67; 29:19–23; Jer 4:5–6, 13, 29; 5:15–17; 6:23; 11:22; 15:2; 18:17, 21; 19:9; 21:4–7; 41:4–18; 46:3–5; 49:37; 50:13–15; 51:1–4; 52:4–16; Hos 4:10; 5:6; 8:7; 9:12, 16; Amos 4:4; 5:11; 8:12; Mic 3:4; 6:14–15; Zeph 1:13; Hag 1:6; Mal 1:4; Hillers, *Treaty-Curses*, 28–29.

42. *VTE* sect 42; *Assur-nerari-Matiilu Treaty SSA* 2 2 v 1–13 and *SSA* 2 5 iv18'–19'; Crouch, *Israel and the Assyrians*, 63–64; *Esar* 521–22; Hillers, *Treaty-Curses*, 63; Deut 28:30; 2 Sam 12:11; 16:20–22; Jer 8:10.

43. *AshN* rev. 4.10–11; A. L. Openheim, "'Siege-Documents' from Nippur," esp. 79 n. 34; Wiseman, *Vassal-Treaties*, 62, 70, and 72, col. 6, lines 448–50, 548–50, and col. 7

6. Earth mourning destruction (Isa 24:4, 7, 11; compared with Isa 10:10; 24:8, 11; 32:13).[44]

7. Earth burned (Isa 24:6; 26:11; 27:4, 11; compared with Isa 1:7; 5:24; 9:5, 18–19; 10:16–17; 26:11; 29:1–4, 6; 30:14, 27, 30, 33; 33:11–14; 37:19; 44:16, 19; 47:14; 64:11; 65:5; 66:15–16, 24).[45]

8. Decay (Isa 24:7).

9. Trapped in a snare (Isa 24:17–18; compared with Isa 8:14; 28:13).[46]

10. Earthquake (Isa 24:19–20; compared with Isa 22:10; 30:13–14).[47]

11. Prisoners (Isa 24:22; compared with Isa 1:7–9; 3:14–15, 25–26; 7:18; 8:4).[48]

12. Storm (Isa 25:4; compared with Isa 4:6; 25:4; 28:2; 29:6).[49]

13. Wind blows away (Isa 27:5; similar language to Assyria: Isa 17:13).[50]

14. Death (Isa 26:14; 27:7; similar language to Moab: Isa 15:9).

15. Drought (Isa 25:5; compared with Isa 1:30; 8:21–22; 65:8, 11–12, 15).[51]

16. Labor pain (Isa 26:17–18; similar language to Babylon description: Isa 13:8; 21:3).

---

line 572; Hillers, *Treaty-Curses*, 62–63; Deut 28:53–57; Ps 137:8; Hos 10:14; Nah 3:10.

44. *Sefire* I.A.29; *Ashurnirari treaty* 4.19; *Rassam Cylinder* 6.101–3; *Ludlul bēl nēmeqi* I.101–2; *Era Epic* I.2; Jer 7:34; 9:10, 17–19; 14:2; 16:5, 9; 25:10; 33:11; Lam 5:14–15; Ezek 26:13; Amos 8:10; Hillers, *Treaty-Curses*, 57–58; Lambert, *Babylonian Wisdom Literature*, 36; Borger and Lambert, "Ein neuer Era-Text aus Ninive," esp. 141.

45. Jer 7:20; 15:14; 17:4, 27; 20:9; 43:12–13; 44:6; 49:27; 51:58.

46. *Esar* 582–84; *Annals of Assyrian Kings* describes Hezekiah surrounded in Jerusalem "like a bird in a cage" in *AfOB* 9, p. 58 lines 12–18; *Era Epic* 4.18–19; Hillers, *Treaty-Curses*, 69–70; Jer 5:26; 48:43–44; 50:24; Ezek 17:15–21; Hos 7:12; similar to: Josh 23:13.

47. Jer 4:24; 8:16.

48. Beckman, *Hittite Diplomatic Texts*, 139; Jer 4:5–6, 13, 29; 5:15–17; 6:23; 11:22; 15:2; 18:17, 21; 19:9; 21:4–7; 41:4–18; 46:3–5; 49:37; 50:13–15; 51:1–4; 52:4–16.

49. Jer 4:13.

50. Similar language: Isa 11:4; 30:28; 33:11; Jer 4:13; *Enuma Elish* 1.105; 2.95–105.

51. Deut 28:22–24; 29:19; Wiseman, *Vassal-Treaties*, 90, col. 7, lines 528–30 (*VTE* sect 63–64) says "there is no fertility in iron ground and no rain or dew comes from bronze skies" with reference to drought; Walton and Matthews, *Genesis-Deuteronomy*, 263; Basil the Great, *Exegetical Homilies*, 3.8; Lienhard, *Exodus, Leviticus, Numbers, Deuteronomy*, 323. Elijah claimed this drought curse when Israel rebelled (1 Kgs 17:1) and an ample rain blessing of Deut 28:12 when the prophets of Baal were killed (1 Kgs 18:44–45). Drought is also a curse under the "Laws of Hammurabi," 50.64–71 (often with famine following, 49.53–54, 66–67, 80) in Roth, *Law Collections*, 136–38; also drought curse in *VTE* sect 63–64 with famine *VTE* sect 47, 56, 62, 74, 85.

17. Vineyard ruined with thorns (Isa 27:4; compared with Isa 5:10).[52]

18. Threshed (Isa 27:12; similar language to Ethiopia and Babylon: Isa 18:5; 21:10).

19. Only unclean birds will dwell in destroyed land (Isa 34:10–12).[53]

These annihilating judgments on gentile nations continue in later Isaiah, as Lena Sofia Tiemeyer developed (Isa 59:15–20; 63:1–6; 66:12–16).[54]

Continuing this emphasis, early Judaism developed a rationale that considered that these Gentiles were sinners[55] and unclean,[56] and thus excluded from blessed afterlife.[57] For example, many of these Isaiah prophecies were extended as a *pesher* in early Judaism to identify the rising new threat of Rome will be destroyed.[58] In contrast, Israel's salvation in early Judaism was grounded upon Israel being uniquely chosen by God as God's "portion and inheritance,"[59] and thus blessed "above all the nations,"[60] with a national hope of restoration into kingdom.[61]

These judgments on the nations usher in a new exodus for Israel's righteous remnant (Isa 26:7). Righteous and faithful Judah and Jerusalem are protected (Isa 26:1–4, 15; 27:6, 13) and invited to the kingdom banquet (Isa 25:6). Meanwhile, the curse is reversed to blessing for Judah as Yahweh reigns (Isa 24:23; 25:8). Yahweh's kingdom provides peace, animals grazing,

---

52. Lev 26:26.

53. Joseph Blenkinsopp claims that Isa 34:10 *lilh* is Lilith, Adam's second wife who is being installed as a heavenly queen among unclean birds in Isa 34:12 ("Cityscape to Landscape: The 'Back to Nature' Theme in Isa 1–35," in Grabbe and Haak, "*Every City Shall be Forsaken,*" 44) but there is no evidence that the word "night" (*lilh*) should be translated as a name when it is translated in LXX as "night watch" (νυκτὸς) and combined with the word "day" (Isa 34:10; MT: *yom*, LXX: ἡμέρας). Rather, the level of devastation is described as a place dominated by unclean birds (Oswalt, *The Book of Isaiah: Chapters 1–39*, 615).

54. Tiemeyer, "Death or Conversion."

55. Ps 9:17; Tob 13.6; *Jub.* 33.23–24; *Pss. Sol.* 2.1–2.

56. B. *Šabb.* 17b; *b. AZ* 36b; *y. Šabb.* 1.3.

57. *Tosefta Sanhedrin* 13:2 where rabbi Joshua argues the point from Ps 9:17; *b. 'Avodah Zara* 2b–3a; Kaminsky, "Israel's Election."

58. Blenkinsopp, *Opening the Sealed Book*, 77 and 102 identifies Isa 34:9 as extended judgment to Rome (*Tg. Isa.* 34:2 and *Tg. Ps.-J.*), 98 extends Isa 24:7 and Isa 31:8 to Rome on the basis of Qumran (CD 4.13–14; 1QM11.11–12).

59. *Pss. Sol.* 17.15, 23; *Jub.* 23.24; *LAB* 7.3; 10.2; 12.4; 14.5; Gal 2:15; *2 Bar.* 82.5; Sir 50.25–26; *4 Ezra* 6.56; Second benediction of *birkat ha-torah* line 117; DiSante, *Jewish Prayer*, 67.

60. *Pss. Sol.* 11.9; 11.8–11; *LAB* 11.1; 19.8; 30.4; 35.2.

61. *1 En.* 90.34–38; *Jub.* 1.15–25; *Pss. Sol.* 17.21–46; *m. Sanh.* 10.1.

and the vulnerable defended (Isa 25:4; 26:6, 12; 27:10). In Yahweh's kingdom the people are forgiven and they worship Yahweh their redeemer (Isa 24:14, 16; 25:1, 3, 9; 26:13, 15; 27:9, 13).

CHAPTER 9

Redemption and Salvation

THE IDEA OF "REDEMPTION" (*g'l*) originates in family law, in recovery from indentured service or repurchase of property by the nearest kinsman so that the redeemed might live and work their land again (Lev 25:25-26, 47-55; Ruth 2:20; 3:9-12; 4:1-12).[1] Goldingay defines this familial concept of redeemer.

> A restorer (*gō'ēl*) is a member of the family who has the resources and capacity to come to the aid of another member of the family in need and is under moral obligation to do so. Yhwh agrees to be defined by that family relationship with Israel and the obligations it brings. Punishment cannot be the last word in this relationship.[2]

Isaiah strongly develops Yahweh as Israel's redeemer. The second half of Isaiah repeatedly calls Yahweh "the Redeemer" in contexts of redeeming Judah, when only one other prophet used this title only once (Isa 41:14; 43:14; 44:6, 24; 47:4; 48:17; 49:7, 26; 54:5, 8; 59:20; 60:16; 63:16; Jer 50:34). The first half of Isaiah does not use the title "redeemer" of Yahweh, but the theme is clear that God is determined to redeem his people (Isa 9:1-7; 11:1-11; 26:1-9; 35:1-10).[3] Eichrodt developed Isaiah's concept of Yahweh Redeemer.

> Yahweh is the "*go'el*," the Redeemer, who is obligated to ransom his near of kin (Isa 43:3; 49:26; 60:16); the wife who has been

---

1. Blenkinsopp, *Isaiah 40-55*, 110-11.
2. Goldingay and Payne, *Isaiah 40-55*, 1:51.
3. Oswalt, "God's Determination to Redeem His People."

visited with double the appropriate punishment needs to be appeased and encouraged to enable her to forget her misery (Isa 40:2; 54:6ff); Yahweh's love is the bestowing of a privilege which is bound to work out in the form of Israel's supremacy over other nations (Isa 43:4; 49:22ff; 52:4f; 60).[4]

When the term *g'l* is used of God it always indicates that God frees the redeemed from the power and authority of another.[5] Such a relationship is not one of equals but it certainly is a personal one with intimacy.[6] This intimacy is sourced in the covenant, which expresses divine election (Isa 14:1; 43:20; 49:7). Page Kelley explains, "To refer to the Lord as Israel's Redeemer means two things. First, it means that the covenant bonds that bind Israel to God and God to Israel are strong and intimate as family ties. Second, it means that no price is too great for God to pay for the redemption of His people (Isa 43:3-4; 54:5-8)."[7]

Yahweh initially redeemed Israel by exodus from Egypt (Isa 43:1; 63:9; Exod 15:13; Pss 77:16; 106:10). Such redemption (*g'l*) appears in parallel with the standard Deuteronomic exodus synonym "ransom" (*pdh*; Deut 7:8; 9:26; 13:6; 15:15; 21:8; 24:18; Isa 35:9-10; 51:10-11; Jer 31:11; Hos 13:14). As redeemer, Yahweh formed Israel from the womb through exodus from Egypt and will redeem them back from captivity to Babylon (Isa 44:24; 60:16). Israel belonged to Yahweh before the exile as his bondservant, but God sold them (Isa 1:14). He sold Israel without receiving any money for them, therefore he will not pay any money to redeem them (Isa 52:3, 5). Instead, Yahweh gave the nations Egypt, Ethiopia, and Seba as a ransom for the redemption of Israel (Isa 43:1, 3-7; 11:11). These nations had not been within the Babylonian empire but Cambyses, Cyrus's successor, received them in battle from Yahweh for the freeing of Israel.[8] This form of redemption is that of bringing Israel back from physical bondage and captivity (Isa 43:5-7; 45:13; 48:20; 49:11, 14; 52:2-3; 53:12).

While there is some development of "ransoming" Israel in the first half of Isaiah (Isa 35:9-10 [*pdh*]) the emphasis in Isaiah for Yahweh "redeeming" (*g'l*: Isa 44:22-23; 48:20; 52:9) Israel has to do with Yahweh orchestrating the new exodus from Babylon in the second half of Isaiah (Isa 41:14; 43:14; 47:4; 48:17; 62:12; 63:4). Yahweh, the general, prophesied his redemption of Israel (Isa 44:6; 59:20). Yahweh called Israel as a forsaken wife in rebellion

4. Eichrodt, *Theology of the Old Testament*, 1:255.
5. Köhler, *Old Testament Theology*, 234.
6. Snaith, *Distinctive Ideas of the Old Testament*, 107.
7. Kelley, *Judgment and Redemption in Isaiah*, 59.
8. North, *The Second Isaiah*, 120.

to redeem her back with his loyal love (Isa 54:5, 8; 63:4, 9). This makes Israel the redeemed of God (Isa 35:9; 51:10; 62:12; 63:4). Such a concept of holy redemption includes separating out a people, land, or whatever Yahweh touches as a distinct group experiencing the benefits of redemption. The responsibility of the redeemer was to see that the redeemed received the full rights and privileges of their redemption. Yahweh has a legal relationship with Israel where he expresses his loyal love and pity (Isa 63:9). Such redemption provides Yahweh the opportunity to declare and demonstrate that he is the king (Isa 44:6). Yahweh redeems Israel by choosing Israel and demonstrating this redemption for all to see by bringing them back in a new exodus (Isa 49:7, 26; 60:16).

A frequent parallel statement with *g'l* is that of Yahweh as "savior" (*mwšy'*; Isa 60:16).[9] Yahweh is Israel's savior (Isa 12:2; 17:10; 33:22; 35:3–4; 37:20, 35; 38:20; 43:3, 11–12; 44:26; 45:15, 21–22; 49:6; 60:16). Even Isaiah's own name (*yšyhw*) reminds Israel with the meaning that "Yahweh saves" (Isa 1:1; 2:1; 7:3; 13:1; 20:2–3; 37:2–6, 21; 38:1–4, 21; 39:3–8). Isaiah speaks often of God's salvation (Isa 45:8; 46:13; 49:6, 8; 51:5–8; 52:7, 10). Yahweh promised to send a savior to deliver Israel (Isa 19:20). Though Yahweh is himself the savior, he gives Egypt and Cush in the place of Israel to facilitate them in a new exodus (Isa 43:3; 45:15; 49:26; 63:8). Salvation is in repentance and quiet trusting of Yahweh (Isa 25:9; 30:5, 18; 59:20). In fact, there is no savior except Yahweh (Isa 43:11; 47:15). All will see that Yahweh is the savior bringing about redemption for Israel (Isa 60:16). Ultimately, "Israel is saved by Yahweh with an everlasting salvation" (Isa 45:17). This salvation is strong (Isa 59:1, 16; 63:1, 5) and provides protection from times of trouble (Isa 25:9; 33:2, 6; 45:17; 49:8; 59:11, 17; 60:18; 61:10). Salvation is described as "near" (Isa 7:3–10; 8:11–14; 27:8—28:5; 29:17–24; 31:8–9; 33:10–24; 37:6–7, 21–35; 38:4–5; 62:11), "sure" (Isa 55:10), already accomplished (Isa 43:1), free (Isa 52:3; 55:1), joyful (Isa 35; 49:13; 51:3; 60:5; 61:10), a future eschatological era (Isa 4:2–6; 9:1–7; 11:1–16; 14:1–2; 19:18–25; 24:14–16a; 25:1–8; 30:18–26; 32:1–8, 14–20; 35; 45:6; 49:6; 51:4–5; 52:10), and everlasting (Isa 45:17; 51:6, 8; 54:8–10).

The conception of redemption indicates that Israel is forgiven (Isa 40:1–2). Yahweh swept away their sins like a cloud that nothing might hinder their return to him (Isa 44:22). Eichrodt summarized the concepts of forgiveness as limited to time and particular acts.

---

9. Blenkinsopp, *Isaiah 40–55*, 112.

Whether forgiveness is described as the wiping out of a record of guilt,[10] the abolition and removal of a burden,[11] the covering or taking far away of a guilt that cries out accusingly for vengeance,[12] or the passing over of such,[13] a ransom from slavery,[14] or the healing of a mortal sickness,[15] or whether it is rendered with *slh*, without the use of concrete imagery, as a passing over, an exercise of forbearance,[16] all these are originally connected with the idea of the remission on a particular occasion of guilt that has accrued, and the restoration thereby of the earlier relationship until new guilt makes new forgiveness necessary.[17]

A new day was dawning which required a radical break with past practices and sinful ways. Huey identified that "the only person God would look upon with favor was the person of humble and contrite spirit (Isa 57:15; 66:8), the one who practiced justice toward his fellow man (Isa 56:1; 58:6–12), and was obedient to God (Isa 48:18–19)."[18] Israel was forgiven not on its own merit (Isa 43:25), but as a work of God's grace (Isa 43:4). This forgiveness is an "inward, personal and spiritual redemption" with the removal of sin from every aspect.[19] Forgiveness extends to Israel (Isa 43:25; 44:22; 54:8) and gentiles (Isa 19:20–22; 45:20–23; 49:6; 51:4–5). However, forgiveness has not finally resolved Israel's sin condition in the post-Babylonian-captivity in which Israel continues to sin, be dispersed by Greece and Rome, and need redemption unto kingdom.[20]

The fact of redemption should wipe away fear and cause people to turn to Yahweh (Isa 43:1; 44:22). Redemption causes joy (Isa 44:23). Yahweh is the one who blesses in many ways including: healing, guiding, comfort, and peace (Isa 57:18–19). This blessing extends from the temple to Jerusalem

10. [Footnote in the original:] Isa 43:25; 44:22; Jer. 18:23; Pss 51:3, 11; 109:14; Neh 3:37.

11. [Footnote in the original; bracketed verses added by Kennard:] [Isa 58:6]; Micah 7:18; Pss 32:1; 85:3.

12. [Footnote in the original:] Isa 38:17; Pss 32:1; 85:3; 103:12; Neh 3:37.

13. [Footnote in the original; bracketed verses added by Kennard:] [Isa 31:5]; Amos 7:8; 8:2; Micah 7:18.

14. [Footnote in the original:] Isa 44:22 and the description of God as *g'l* in Ps 103:4 and Isa 40–66.

15. [Footnote in the original:] Isa 1:6; Hos 14:5; Jer 8:22; 17:14; Ps 103:3; 107:17, 20.

16. [Footnote in the original:] Isa 55:7; Amos 7:2; Jer 5:1, 7; 31:34; 33:8; 36:3; Deut 29:19; 1 Kgs 8:34, 36, 50; 2 Kgs 5:18; 24; Pss 25:11; 103:3.

17. Eichrodt, *Theology of the Old Testament*, 2:457–58.

18. Huey, "Great Themes in Isaiah 40–66," 54–55; Westermann, *Isaiah 40–66*, 76.

19. Kaiser, *Toward an Old Testament Theology*, 214.

20. Labahn, "Delay of Salvation within Deutero-Isaiah."

to Israel to gentiles (Isa 2:2-3; 11:9). The redeemed will be vindicated with covenant blessing (Isa 45:8, 23; 46:13; 51:5-6). Within the covenant there will be universal peace (Isa 2:1-4; 9:5-6; 11:1-9; 53:5). This peace involves socially being at peace with others, psychologically being at peace with oneself, and spiritually being reconciled with God.[21] This salvation comes from Yahweh's righteousness (Isa 45:8) and results in Zion being filled with justice and righteousness (Isa 33:5). All shall be in the proper order. The redeemed will have a blessed future (Isa 35:9; 51:10-11; 62:12; 63:4).

MOTIFS OF SALVATION

The salvation experience in Isaiah completely revolutionizes all phases of life. That which had been polluted by sin is now made new. These are the prominent motifs that develop salvation in addition to two extra chapters on the new exodus and kingdom, which warrant sufficient space to be chapters of their own.

Oracle of Salvation

When there is a promise statement of redemption Isaiah is utilizing a genre of an oracle of salvation.[22] Often the oracle begins with a direct address of comfort or encouragement not to fear (Isa 7:4-9; 10:24-27; 37:6-7; 41:8-16; 43:1-7; 44:1-5).[23] This is followed by a substantiating clause that Yahweh will bring about a salvation that is promised. In the first half of the book of Isaiah the salvation oracle is a leitmotiv to provide encouragement and hope within a context of judgment (Isa 2:1-5; 4; 9:1-7; chs. 11-12; 16:5; 19:18-25; 25:6—27:13; 35:1-10). With the shift to the second half of Isaiah, the genre of oracle of salvation becomes a dominant emphasis (41:8-13, 14-16; 43:1-7; 44:1-5; 48:17-19; 54:4-6; 59:9-15; 61:1-9; 63:7—64:12

---

21. Alexander, *The Prophecies of Isaiah*, 205.

22. There are several ancient Near Eastern oracles of salvation (Ashurbanipal celebrates Ishtar redeeming him in *ANET*, 3:605-6). Biblical engagement of the salvation oracle occurs in: Begrich, "Das priesterliche Heilsorakel"; Westermann, "Das Heilswort bei Deutero-jesaja"; Dion, "Patriarchal Traditions" 200-201; von Waldow, "The Message of Deutero-Isaiah," 266; Williamson, "Isaiah 1 and the Covenant Lawsuit," 393-468, esp. 406; Harner, "Salvation Oracle in Second Isaiah"; Schoors, *I Am God Your Saviour*, 46-83; Melugin, *Formation of Isaiah 40-55*, 13-14; Kapelrud, "The Main Concern of Second Isaiah"; Merrill, "Literary Character of Isaiah 40-55," 153-56; Oswalt, "God's Determination to Redeem His People"; Westermann, *Oracles of Salvation*.

23. Conrad, "Royal Narratives," 67.

[MT: 64:11]), along with hymns to Yahweh. Isaiah utilizes oracles of salvation to emphasize this redemption of Israel.

Remnant Saved

Yahweh judged all Israel. Adonai identified that it was his intention to destroy Israel as a forest cut down and burned to perhaps a remnant of a holy stump of one-tenth the size (Isa 6:11–13).[24] Isaiah took his son Shearjashub (meaning "a remnant will return") and announced to Ahaz that Yahweh will preserve Judah—although with substantial devastation—if they will trust Yahweh (Isa 7:3—8:8). The remnant that remains is defined by Leupold as "made up of those who, after the nation has been visited by the judgment of God, are the believing ones left after the experience, with whom God makes a fresh start, having preserved them for this very purpose."[25]

A remnant survives for the purpose of productivity toward God (Isa 37:4, 31). In fact, the remnant theme for the nation mirrors a remnant theme of recovering a Davidic king from Jesse's branch (Isa 11:1). This remnant Davidic king will be empowered by Yahweh's spirit to craft a kingdom that reflects the character of the spirit of Yahweh (Isa 11:1–5). The Israeli remnant may have to be regathered from all nations, but Yahweh will bring them back into his kingdom (Isa 11:11, 16). So, the king and Yahweh's kingdom-program and all participants within this kingdom-program participate within the remnant theme.

The remnant-program is boldly declared by Yahweh to prompt Israel to trust Yahweh and not to trust other nations such as Assyria or Babylon.

> Now it will come about in that day that the remnant of Israel, and those of the house of Jacob who have escaped, will never again rely on the one who struck them, but will truly rely on Yahweh, the holy one of Israel. A remnant will return, the remnant of Jacob, to the mighty God. For though your people, O Israel, may be like the sand of the sea, only a remnant within them will return. (Isa 10:20–22)

Barrett develops Isaiah's remnant-program from rescue to complete reliance upon Yahweh.

> In order to establish the remnant, the wicked had to be destroyed. The judgment not only served to eliminate the ungodly, but it also purified the remnant. Yahweh's words that He tested

---

24. Hasel, *The Remnant*, 238, 401.
25. Leupold, *Exposition of Isaiah*, 34.

them in the furnace of affliction verify this concept of purification (48:10). Other portions of the prophecy describe the characteristics of the remnant. Those left in Zion and remaining in Jerusalem in that day will be called holy (4:3). The remnant will also have regard for their Maker and the Holy One of Israel. In contrast to the idolatry that existed before judgment, the remnant will practice true worship of God (27:13). Isaiah also indicates that those of the remnant will place their complete reliance upon the Lord (10:20–22).[26]

Gerhard Hasel explains that the theological concept of "remnant," developing in holiness and commitment to Yahweh, finds its full expression eschatologically.

> Isaiah speaks of a "holy" or "purified" remnant which is to emerge in the future as a result of the inbreaking of God into history. As such the remnant is an eschatological entity . . . his main concern is to call Israel back to God and to create the condition by which some are able to become members of the eschatological remnant, the purified and holy remnant of the future. It is, therefore, no mistake to consider the remnant motif as a key element of Isaiah's theology. It is evident that Isaiah has not cast his usage of the remnant motif into a stereotyped mold. At the same time it must be maintained that the remnant motif is for Isaiah from the first to the last intensely theological.[27]

When the eschatological day of Yahweh comes, the judgment is so severe that of all the nations, very few are left. The remnant nations are those who praise Yahweh for their salvation among all nations (Isa 24:6, 14–16). Gerhard Hasel identifies that this remnant theme is also found within texts across the ancient Near East in preserving these nations before their gods.[28] These nations join as part of the remnant before God.

Hardening Reversed

In the production of the remnant, Isaiah's message fell on deaf ears, blind eyes, and insensitive hearts because Yahweh was hardening his people.

---

26. Barrett, "Theology of Isaiah," 148.
27. Hasel, *The Remnant*, 401.
28. Hasel, *The Remnant*, 101–4, 110, 375–382; *Enuma Elish* 4.109, in ANET, 34; *Atrahasis Epic* 3.3.37, in ANET, 512–14; 3.4.44; *Erra Epic*, in Gössman, *Das Era Epos*; *The Song of Ullikummi*, in ANET, 125; *Plague Prayers of Mursili II*, ANET, 396; *Legend of King Krt*, ANET, 143; Müller, *Die Vorstellung von Rest im Alten Testament*, 6–8.

Salvation is a state in which this hardening is reversed. Yahweh will remove the spiritual blindness and do away with oppressors when the people repent, returning to him (Isa 29:17–24). The results of this reversal are several. They will acknowledge Yahweh's holiness in awe of his character (Isa 29:23). They will be regenerated (Isa 29:18, 24). They will have a significant receptivity to instruction (Isa 29:24). They will rejoice in their God (Isa 29:19), as the wicked will disappear (Isa 29:20–21). The wicked disappearing is also an eschatological reversal, for as the harmful enemy is diminished or destroyed it also indicates a reversal to salvation for Israel.[29]

Creation-Recreation

Yahweh is the creator and thus incomparable above all else (Isa 44:24; 45:8, 12, 18). This creation is evident in the judgment on Rahab and Leviathan (Isa 51:9). This creation is the bringing out of an order from amid the chaos.[30] The formula "he who stretches out heavens" identifies Yahweh as the unique all-powerful creator actively at work revealing himself as such in the redemption of his people before all the world (Isa 44:24; 45:12, 18).[31] *Br'* ("created") emphasizes "God's personal historical acts of love and power towards his chosen people."[32]

> Only now have they been created, and not of old,
> Before today you have heard of them . . .
> Lest you should say: "Behold! I knew them." (Isa 48:7)
>
> Let men see and know . . . that the hand of the Lord is doing this,
> And the Holy One of Israel is creating it. (Isa 41:20)

Stuhlmueller developed Isaiah's creation theme as linked with the historical redemption of Yahweh's chosen and loved people.

> Creation is considered the first of many divine attempts to surround man with happiness and with the fullness of life. Like the call of Abraham and the choice of the Hebrew people, creation was a *free* act of God, dominated by love. The founding of the universe, like the establishment of the Israelite nation, can be

---

29. Chan, "Rhetorical Reversal and Usurpation."
30. Johnson, *From Chaos to Restoration*, 85–98.
31. Häbel, "He Who Stretches Out the Heavens," 429.
32. Stuhlmueller, "Theology of Creation in Second Isaiah," 447.

traced to no other reason than this: "it was because the Lord loved you" (Deut 7:8).[33]

Harner explained that this creative redemption is often linked with the imminent activities of Yahweh.

> It is significant in this respect to recall how often II Isaiah links creation faith with the expectation of Yahweh's *imminent* action in history, rather than his deeds in the past. Sometimes creation faith serves as the basis for the assertion of Yahweh's general sovereignty over history, with the implicit assumption that he is now about to exercise this sovereignty (40:12–17, 21–24). At other times it is linked more specifically with Yahweh's imminent redemption of Israel (40:27–31; 44:24–28; 45:9–13; 50:1–3; 51:12–16; 54:4–8) or with the mission that Yahweh gives Israel to be a light to the nations (42:5–9). In passages such as these, creation faith is linked with Yahweh's actions in the imminent future rather than his deeds of salvation in the past.[34]

One good example of this is found as part of the conclusion of the Cyrus oracle which ties God's creative activity with his redemption: "I am Yahweh, and there is no other, I form light and create darkness, I bring prosperity and create disaster, I, Yahweh do all these things" (Isa 45:6–7). Yahweh is the creator of judgment and salvation. Stuhlmueller developed that the salvation he brings is as a whole new creation repeated.

> Here, then, are the important elements in the religion of Israel which influenced II Is' theology of creation: the great historical redemptive acts of God; the fulfillment of the prophetic message; and the expression of Israelite faith was rooted in the history of His people. His faith also told Him that Yahweh was a living God, whose power was not exhausted by the great deeds of His outstanding arm in the past. This past was ever being repeated, even in His own lifetime, when the word of God was recreating the Israelite commonwealth out of the chaos of the Babylonian exile. Every first moment of creation is happening all over again, for the exodus from Babylon is nothing other than a triumph over those deities whom the Babylonians venerated as gods of creation. The momentum imparted to biblical religion by God's historical intervention will continue in II Is to keep *schopfungsglaube* always subservient to *Heilspglaube*.[35]

33. Stuhlmueller, "Theology of Creation in Second Isaiah," 464.
34. Harner, "Creation Faith in Deutero-Isaiah," 445.
35. Stuhlmueller, "Theology of Creation in Second Isaiah," 445.

That is, faith in the order of things is always subservient to salvation faith.

Regaining Paradise

With Adam in the garden before the fall, there existed an idyllic state. This state is reconstructed in great detail through Yahweh's salvation. The restoration of the pre-fall state is described in Isaiah 11:6–9 and 65:25.

> The wolf will live with the lamb,
> The leopard will lie down with the goat,
> The calf and the lion and the yearling together;
> And a little child will lead them.
> The cow will feed with the bear, their young will lie down together,
> And the lion will eat straw like the ox.
> The infant will play near the hole of the cobra,
> And the young child put his hand into the viper's nest.
> They will neither harm nor destroy on all my holy mountain
> For the earth will be full of the knowledge of Yahweh
> As the waters cover the sea. (Isa 11:6–9)

> "The wolf and the lamb shall graze together, and the lion shall eat straw like the ox; and dust shall be the serpent's food. They shall do no evil or harm in all my holy mountain," says Yahweh. (Isa 65:25)

These passages identify the great lengths within which Yahweh's peace will extend to the relationship between animals. The carnivorous animals will not eat their prey (Isa 11:6–8; 65:25). In fact, human and animal peace is regained as well, undoing the curse in the fall (Gen 3:15; Isa 11:8). Such peace and glorification of nature are the result on earth of recognizing Yahweh as their sovereign.[36] Dick Odendaal observed this fulfillment, "Important features are the paradisiacal fruitfulness (41:19; 54:1ff; 60:22), the absence of all adverse conditions (63:13ff, 25), peace (53:5; 66:23; 2:4) and animal peace (11:6–9)."[37] The new order will approximate the paradise at the garden of Eden (Isa 51:3). For the most part the oracle of the curse will be reversed. Futility will be replaced by productive labor (Isa 65:23). However, the serpent remains in a posture with its face to ground, choking down dust (Gen 3:14; Isa 65:25). This new state will be created by God (Isa 65:17) and brought about by his messiah (Isa 11:1–16).

---

36. Huffmon, "Treaty Background of Hebrew *Yada*," and Huffmon and Parker, "Further Note on the Treaty Background of Hebrew *Yada*," in contrast to Isa 5:13.

37. Odendaal, *Eschatological Expectation*, 141; Van Imschoot, *Theology of the Old Testament*, 1:73; Pentecost, *Things to Come*, 487–90.

Noahic Covenant: Divine Promise of No More Judgment

After the onslaught of the flood, God promised that the earth would never again be judged by global flood (Gen 8:22; 9:11–17; Isa 54:9). This covenant was indicated through the sign of the *rainbow* put down in the clouds (*qšt*; Gen 9:11–14). However, Yahweh used his *bow* (*qšt*) again in judgment (Isa 41:2). Yahweh used the flood motif in judgment as well, but in the remedy, Yahweh dries up these floods (Isa 44:27; 50:12; 51:10). As Isaiah refers to this, Yahweh promised that he will never again break off his covenant of peace with his people (Isa 54:9). The appeal to the Noahic covenant undergirds the certainty of the removal of judgment as Yahweh brings in his kingdom.[38] He also intimates that he will never again judge the earth with the treaty curses once he restores and reestablishes Jerusalem (Isa 62:8).

Abrahamic Covenant

The Abrahamic covenant is Yahweh's foundational election of Israel's existence as a nation (Gen 12:2–3; 15).[39] The promise of blessing is fulfilled through the whole concept of their salvation by God. The promise of a multiplied people is a specific kind of blessing. By Isaiah's day, the Abrahamic covenant had already been greatly fulfilled but it shall be fulfilled even more. Yahweh had called Israel's forefathers and still stands by these descendants.

> But you, O Israel, my servant, Jacob, whom I have chosen. You descendants of Abraham, whom I love I took you from the ends of the earth, from the farthest corners I called you. I said, "You are my servant; I have chosen you and not rejected you. So do not fear, for I am with you; do not be dismayed, for I am your God. I will strengthen you and help you; I will uphold you with my righteous right hand." (Isa 41:8–10)

Claus Westermann develops, "In language reminiscent of Genesis 15:1, Yahweh promises support and deliverance for Abraham's seed; the exiles are not to fear since the convental promises to Abraham are sure—they will be fulfilled."[40] Such a fulfillment includes increase of the population and their land. Yahweh has enlarged both so far (Isa 26:15) but he will extend them further (Isa 27:12). With reference to the kingdom state, Yahweh says: "Enlarge the place of your tent, stretch your tent curtains wide, do not hold

---

38. Westermann, *Blessing in the Bible*, 275–76.
39. Kennard, *Biblical Covenantalism*, 1:66–103.
40. Westermann, *Blessing in the Bible*, 275–76.

back; lengthen your cords, strengthen your stakes" (Isa 54:2). Westermann develops this promise of increase.

> What here reappears in all its pristine freshness—the range of Deutero-Isaiah's topics and of His theology leaves us marveling—is the old promise of increase so well known from the stories told of the patriarchs. This also lets us understand the use of the tent metaphor in an age when Israel had for long had houses as her dwelling places—Deutero-Isaiah deliberately recalls the days of old when the promise of increase mattered so much . . . The promise of deliverance is supplemented by the promise of blessing in the particular form of promise of increase.[41]

Mosaic Covenant

The Mosaic covenant was developed in the chapter on "Israel in Covenant Relationship with Yahweh," with the consequences of covenant curse developed in the chapters "Sin and Judgment" and "Motifs of Judgment." Such covenant nomism or Deuteronomism means that Israel is elect of God within Yahweh's covenant with Moses and they maintain their place of covenant blessing through obedience and availing themselves to the available means of recovery within the covenant.[42] Unfortunately, Israel rebelled and obtained covenant curse from Yahweh. However, in Yahweh's redemption of Israel, he returns them to the context in which covenant blessing is possible and initiates with a new exodus. Deuteronomy 30:1–10 predictively develops this covenant renewal, exodus, and blessings after Israel would experience dispersion and covenant curse.

> When all these blessings and curses I have set before you come upon you and you take them to heart wherever Yahweh your God disperses you among the nations, and when you and your children return to Yahweh your God and obey Him with all your heart and with all your soul according to everything I command you today, then Yahweh your God will restore your fortunes and have compassion on you and gather you again for all the nations where he scattered you. Even if you have been banished to the most distant land under heavens, from there Yahweh your God will gather you and bring you back. He will bring you to the land that belonged to your fathers, and you will take possession of it. He will make you more prosperous and numerous than

---

41. Westermann, *Blessing in the Bible*, 272–73.
42. Kennard, *Biblical Covenantalism*, 1:104–243; 2:8–24.

> your fathers. Yahweh your God will circumcise your hearts and the hearts of your descendants, so that you may love Him with all your heart and with all your soul and life. Yahweh your God will put all these curses on your enemies who hate and persecute you. You will again obey Yahweh and follow all His commands I am giving you today. Then Yahweh your God will make you most prosperous in all the work of your hands and in the fruit of your womb, the young of your livestock and the crops of your land. Yahweh will again delight in you and make you prosperous, just as He delighted in your fathers, if you obey Yahweh your God and keep His commands and decrees that are written in this book of the Law and turn to Yahweh your God with all your heart and with all your soul. (Deut 30:1–10)

Fulfilling this blessing, the new exodus will occur and Israel will be brought back. The returning exiles will not be barren but fruitful in a fruitful land (Isa 48:8, 19–21). There will be a reversal from mourning to restoration of joy (Isa 55:13; 60:17; 61:3; 3:24).

> To grant those who mourn for Zion, giving them a garland instead of ashes, the oil of gladness instead of mourning, the mantle of praise instead of a fainting spirit. So they will be called oaks of righteousness, planted by Yahweh, that He may display His splendor (Isa 61:3).

These covenant blessings will be fulfilled with an obedient Israel in their land in the state of fullness.

Davidic Covenant

The Davidic covenant provides for a Davidic king in the land with a righteous reign over Israel.[43] Stephen Henderson develops this connection of Davidic king in kingdom.

> The Davidic covenant as revealed in 2 Samuel 7 and Psalm 89 promises David that his descendant will be established on an eternal throne in the land appointed for Israel. As well, Psalm 2 portrays the king as Yahweh's vessel—the recipient of the nations as his inheritance. By this covenant, Yahweh guaranteed the presence of a king on the earth from whom He would not remove His lovingkindness.[44]

---

43. Kennard, *Biblical Covenantalism*, 2:25–72.
44. Henderson, "Isaiah's Theological Use of the Old Testament."

Isaiah joins with these others in describing the messianic ruler to come. The messianic descendant of David will obtain a victory over his enemies. He will assume the throne, receiving marvelous royal names expressing the glory of his reign. He will be supernaturally gifted with wisdom, which will evidence itself in his wise rule over the environment (Isa 11:1–10). Righteousness and the protection of the vulnerable will be an outstanding characteristic of his reign (Isa 16:5). His reign will cultivate abundant loyal love and blessings, which will last forever (Isa 55:1–5; 2 Sam 23:5; Ps 89:1–4, 28–29). In this chapter the Davidic covenant has briefly been included as a motif of salvation, but Isaiah's theology of king and kingdom will be developed in separate chapters later in this book, showing that the character of the king is reflected in the character of his kingdom.

Cyrus Oracle (Isa 44:24—45:8)

Yahweh demonstrates that he is the only God by predicting and installing Cyrus as a shepherd and messiah to restore Israel and destroy gentile oppressors. Yahweh enables Cyrus to easily conquer all the pagans holding Israel captive because God will go before him overpowering the obstacles (Isa 45:1–2). Yahweh will cause an end to Israel's judgment by causing the temple, Jerusalem, and Judah to be rebuilt after the Babylonian captivity (Isa 44:26, 28; Ezra 1:1–4). Yahweh will accomplish this through Cyrus despite him not acknowledging Yahweh. North summarized this Isaianic emphasis.

> The immediate occasion of the deliverance from Babylon is to be the conquest of the city and the overthrow of the Babylonian power of Cyrus. It is Yahweh who has stirred him to activity and is prospering all his enterprises. Yahweh has summoned him by name, has grasped his right hand in confirmation of the legitimacy of his kingly authority, and is going before him, smoothing his passage through the mountains, shattering the gate-bars of the tyrant city and giving him access to its closely guarded treasures (Isa 45:1–3; 43:3). (Notwithstanding, in 45:13 Cyrus is to carry out his commission "not for anything by way of payment or a bribe.") Cyrus does not "know" Yahweh (Isa 45:4) but Yahweh's purpose is that he shall know that it is Yahweh who has summoned him, and in 41:25 . . . Cyrus is to invoke Yahweh, acknowledge that it is Yahweh who has commissioned him. He is Yahweh's "shepherd" and shall execute the divine will

by ordering Jerusalem to be rebuilt and the temple foundations relaid (Isa 44:28).[45]

Cyrus succeeded his father as king in 559 BC, conquering Babylon in 539 BC and setting out an edict facilitating the return of a remnant of Jews to the land of Israel under Ezra's leadership during the 530s to rebuild the Jerusalem temple (Ezra 1:1–4; 2 Chr 36:22–23).[46] Josephus claims that Cyrus initiated this Jewish return in response to reading Isaiah's prophecies concerning him.[47] Through such specific prophecy and reestablishing of Jerusalem, Yahweh proves himself to be the only incomparable God. He alone creates such judgment and salvation (Isa 45:5–7).

Kingdom of Light

Light and darkness are opposing systems in the world (Isa 5:20; 59:9). Darkness is both a manner of life and God's judgment which it attracts.[48] Likewise, light is both a manner of life and the salvation which Yahweh bestows. Yahweh is the "light of Israel" who in his holiness saves a remnant while consuming others as a fire in judgment (Isa 10:17). This form of kingdom salvation is often postponed in the account until Yahweh intervenes on behalf of those who turn to him (Isa 5:16–20).[49] His messianic servant also partakes of the quality of light. Yahweh's servant is the light to gentiles which enables them to spiritually see (believe) and experience kingdom blessings (Isa 42:6–7; 49:6). As a manner of life, Yahweh's Law and just dealings will reveal the right way to live (Isa 51:4). The act of walking in light becomes a life of obedience to the Law and living at peace with others (Isa 2:3–5). Yahweh creates light both physically at the creation of the universe and re-creates it through salvation (Isa 45:7). The new exodus is accompanied by the act of Yahweh which makes the route visible and easy (Isa 42:16). This salvation manifests itself among those in darkness by showing them a great light (Isa 9:2). This concept of dawning of the kingdom includes the judgment of the oppressors by the messiah as he establishes his just kingdom

---

45. North, *The Second Isaiah*, 17.

46. Cyrus Cylinder; *Nabonidus Chronicle*; Behistun Inscription; Herodotus, *Histories*, 1.46–216; Xenophon, *Cyropaedia*; Josephus, *Ant.* 10.231–32, 247–48; 11.1–20; with dates provided by Steven Schweitzer, "Cyrus the Great," in Collins and Harlow, *Eerdmans Dictionary of Early Judaism*, 504–6.

47. Josephus, *Ant.* 11.5–7.

48. See my chapter on "Motifs of Judgment."

49. Carroll, "Eschatological Delay in the Prophetic Tradition?," 56.

(Isa 9:2; 58:8-10; 60:1-3). The salvation evident in the kingdom attracts people from all nations.

> Arise, shine, for your light has come, and the glory of Yahweh rises upon you. See, darkness covers the earth and thick darkness is over the peoples, but Yahweh rises upon you and his glory appears over you. Nations will come to your light, and kings to the brightness of your dawn (Isa 60:1-3).

Physically, the light of the kingdom will be brighter (the moon will shine like the sun and the sun will be seven times brighter; Isa 30:26). This physical light is merely an outward indicator of the glory, blessing, and intimacy which will overshadow it, namely, "Yahweh will be your everlasting light and your God will be your glory" (Isa 60:19-20).[50] Yahweh as the fullness of light shall overshadow the effect of the physical light. Otto Kaiser developed Yahweh's glory from Isaiah 24:23, "The moon will be abased, the sun ashamed; for Yahweh Almighty will reign."

> The meaning is literally that the splendor of His light, manifesting His presence, His *kabod* (Ezek 43:4; 10:8ff; 1:4ff) shines so bright that not only the holy city but the whole earth is lit by it, and the light of the sun and moon grows pale and is superfluous (Isa 60:19; Zech 14:7; Rev 21:23; 22:5).[51]

Yahweh is the supreme light within his kingdom of light. The kingdom shall overcome the darkness in the progress of salvation.

Day of Yahweh's Salvation

The day of Yahweh is an all-encompassing concept including both judgment and restoration in both the contemporary scene and in the eschatological fulfillment. Essentially, the concept is that period in human history in which the covenant sovereign personally intervenes to execute the covenant blessings (and curses) upon his vassals.[52] It is often referred to by "that day" in close proximity with Yahweh Almighty. The concept includes the historical relief from the oppression of Babylon. When this occurs, Israel is to take a taunt against the king of Babylon (Isa 14:3-4). The messianic branch rules

50. Kaiser, *Isaiah 13-39*, 303.
51. Kaiser, *Isaiah 13-39*, 195.
52. "Day of Yahweh" is primarily not a metaphor of "holy war" in these passages as Gerhard von Rad proposed ("Concept of the Day of Yahweh," 97-72); it is a fuller concept of God's presence and action of blessing and judgment as Meir Weiss demonstrates ("Origin of the 'Day of the Lord'").

in his kingdom, providing forgiveness and protection (Isa 4:2–6; 11:10). The remnant will return from everywhere in a new exodus and restoration (Isa 10:20–23; 11:11; 27:13; 49:8–9). As they come they will know that Yahweh saves them (Isa 52:6). In response to this they will praise God with thanksgiving (Isa 12:1–6; 26). "In that day they will say, 'Surely this is our God; we trusted in him, and he saved us. This is Yahweh, we trusted in him; let us rejoice and be glad in his salvation'" (Isa 25:9).

The kingdom will be a kingdom of peace such that many people will come up to it to participate (Isa 2:2–5). Marvin Sweeney identifies that the "prophet's vision of eschatological peace and co-existence among the nations of the world" includes "YHWH's sovereignty recognized by all the earth."[53] For example, likely before then, five cities in Egypt will be allied with Yahweh and will speak a Canaanite dialect (Isa 19:18). There will be an altar in Egypt and a monument on their border as a testimony to Yahweh (Isa 19:19–20). These are not Jews in Egypt, so that the Jewish temples in Elephantine and in Alexandria don't fit this description as perhaps the temple in Leontopolis might.[54] Yahweh will be known to the Egyptians and Assyrians such that there will be a highway between them enabling them to worship Yahweh together (Isa 19:21–25).

IMPLICATIONS FOR ONE'S LIFESTYLE

The great and glorious salvation which Yahweh has in store for his remnant raises significant implications to their lifestyle. This section pursues this implication concerning how they should then live.

Repentance from Sin

In the first covenant lawsuit of the book there are commands that serve as conditions by which the coming covenant curses may be averted (Isa 1:16–17). Essentially what is communicated is repentance from evil. Various figures are used: washing oneself as a means of purification and removing one's sins from view both speak about a break with evil. Obedience adds the essential positive part of repentance. There must be a forsaking of that old way of life which has been continually in opposition to the ways of God. In this change righteous acts must follow. Isaiah commands them to do good

---

53. Sweeney, "Book of Isaiah as Prophetic Torah," 50.
54. Josephus, *Ant.* 13.2; Baruq, "Is 19:18 et Leontopolis."

and seek right behavior. Several specific suggestions for application of these principles are given.

Repentance is significant throughout the whole book, though with full recognition that it will not occur before Judah is judged. The other implications of lifestyle are what Israel is to do in their repentance.

Faith

In Isaiah, faith is a comprehensive concept for the whole relationship between God and humans.[55] The word "faith" (*'mn*) in the *Hiphil* means fundamentally "to acknowledge God as steadfast, to put oneself into a relationship with God which is divinely initiated"[56] (Isa 7:9; 28:16; 43:10). Salvation is divinely initiated. It is not the act of any foreign power. Such faith in alliances showed a trust in physical strength which replaced the trust one has in God. Isaiah commands Ahaz and his people to believe steadfastly in Yahweh or Israel will not be established (Isa 7:9). This form of faith is essentially a decision with existential import that covers the whole range of human existence.[57] It allows one source of strength and security; faith in political alliance (Isa 7:1–9) and human strength (Isa 30:15–17) voids one's faith in Yahweh. Such faith in Yahweh manifests itself in obedience to God as a lifestyle of righteousness (Isa 1:21, 26). The one who believes in God will not make haste from a disturbing situation (Isa 28:16). The one so believing will have a real, meaningful existence (Isa 7:9). In kingdom, Israel will be established (Isa 49:23; 55:3; 60:4), so Israel should trust Yahweh in this day (Isa 7:9; 28:16; 43:10; 53:1).

The concept of trust is expressed in several other words. The word "belief" (*bṭḥ*) is used for belief in a god, although it occurs more often for false confidence (Isa 30:12; 31:1; 32:9–11). This word is often used of a description of a state of security but "comes to be used of the relationship with God created by trusting in and building on His promise, surrendering in a renunciation of all self-assurance to the guidance of the One who alone is powerful."[58] The idea of "leaning" or "supporting oneself" (*šʿn*) is used once of putting one's trust in Yahweh (Isa 10:20), but it is generally used of unfavorable reliance on humans (Isa 10:20; 30:12; 31:1).[59] Its use in Isaiah 10:20 shows that the object of one's trust cannot be both God and human.

---

55. Eichrodt, *Theology of the Old Testament*, 2:283.
56. Rust, *Covenant and Hope*, 85; BDB 52–53.
57. Eichrodt, *Theology of the Old Testament*, 2:283; Rust, *Covenant and Hope*, 85.
58. Eichrodt, *Theology of the Old Testament*, 2:284; BDB 105.
59. BDB 1043.

Likewise, the idea of seeking refuge (*ḥsh*) is deepened to the concept of trust (Isa 14:32).[60]

Additionally, the concept of rest in waiting expressed faith. The word "wait" (*hch*) conveys waiting for another, which is something both God (Isa 30:18) and humans do (Isa 8:17).[61] The parallel word in the context "hopefully waiting" (*qwh*) is accomplished in the midst of tension (Isa 8:17).[62] Eichrodt develops this idea of waiting as alluding to the salvation of Yahweh in Isaiah 40:31.

> Because this waiting in faith is focused on the God who is "supremely mighty and rich in power," it is precisely under the heavy pressure of adversity that it can release unsuspected forces which carry men beyond the hopelessness of the moment. The metaphor of the eagles' wings enters religious language as a most beautiful symbol of the power of faith to bear men up to God, and agrees with the earlier evidence which we have considered in bringing out the fundamental difference between the confident expectation which builds on God's promise and the tension which is the produce of feverish impatience.[63]

Other words also express this idea of quietness and rest (Isa 7:4; 18:4; 28:12; 30:15). The same idea is conveyed by words of not being in haste (Isa 5:19; 28:16; 30:16).

For Israel, faith is essential. Eichrodt describes faith as "the *fighting-line for man in relationship with God*, the only place where, in the midst of the great cosmic catastrophe, when the head-on collision of God and the world erupts with annihilating force, man both in attack and defense can preserve his link with the eternal world."[64] In all the varied ways of saying it, faith is in a person and based on some substance. When faith is placed in Yahweh, his promises serve as that in which the believer trusts. Otto Kaiser develops that such trust is essential for the maintenance of a vibrant relationship under their sovereign savior.

> In Isaiah, faith refers to the particular mode of existence of the people of God, the continuance of which depends upon faith alone (Isa 28:14ff; 30:15ff). Israel is not a people like any other. It came into being through God's act of election. Only as long as it relies entirely upon its God can it endure. Without faith,

---

60. BDB 340.
61. BDB 314.
62. BDB 875–76.
63. Eichrodt, *Theology of the Old Testament*, 2:286–87.
64. Eichrodt, *Theology of the Old Testament*, 2:284.

Israel does not exist. In the first instance this verse is concerned with the continuance of those who are directly addressed, the house of David. There is no other guarantee of their survival and continued rule than that which God has given them in His promises. If they seek security in their own human intrigues, they will have departed from the covenant and fallen inexorably under the judgment of the jealous God (Exod 20:5); if they look for their future from God, then this very moment, in human eyes so perilous, could lead to a renewal of the empire of David (Isa 8:23—9:6). Faith is strictly related to the promises of God, who carried out His work in history, and reveals Himself in the word of the prophets. It does not refer to belief in general. It is related to the word which calls for decision from here and now.[65]

Israel's salvation implies that they will be believing. Yahweh will bring them back, but it is essential that they believe to maintain their position in the land. To insure this, Yahweh will change Israel through a new covenant.

Prayer

Prayer is essential to a proper concept of faith.[66] The spiritually alive righteous individual will have their prayers answered (Isa 58:8-9). This is the one who humbles himself in fasting over sin (Isa 58:3-5) and cares for the needy (Isa 58:6-7; Jer 34:8-11; Matt 25:35-36). Prayer is hindered by sin (Isa 1:15).

Four prayers in Isaiah serve to indicate valuable lessons on prayer. All of them approach Yahweh realizing his sovereign control as the one who can solve the dilemma they find themselves within. Coupled with this is the faith that God can be appealed to in his grace to solve these dilemmas based on his promises. The judgment of Assyria is in answer to prayer. Isaiah appeals to the strong one who graciously scatters the enemies such as Assyria to save Israel (Isa 33:2-4). Isaiah continues with praise to the exalted one who is the source of justice and righteousness, establishing Judah with a sure foundation (Isa 33:5-6). This petition is coupled with the realization that the fear of Yahweh is the key human responsibility in obtaining salvation, wisdom, and knowledge (Isa 33:5-6).

When Hezekiah receives the letter from Sennacherib insulting Yahweh, he lays it out before Yahweh, praying fervently for Yahweh's rescue (Isa 37:14-20). Hezekiah praises the control Yahweh brings but laments the

---

65. Kaiser, *Isaiah 1-12*, 94-95; Luther, *Luther's Works*, 31:2:58.
66. Laurin, *Contemporary Old Testament Theologians*, 110.

insult that Sennacherib has provided to Israel and ultimately to Yahweh. These laments fuel Hezekiah's petitions for deliverance. Yahweh destroyed Assyria and Sennacherib (Isa 37:21-38).

The third prayer evidences a peculiar power which prayer bestows. Hezekiah received a clear word from Yahweh through the prophet Isaiah that he would die (Isa 38:1). The fact that the prophecy was delivered to Hezekiah directly indicated that the prophecy might be conditional. Hezekiah shows evidence of repentance and humility as he boldly petitions sovereign Yahweh and reminds him of his faithful devotion to God's will (Isa 38:2-3). Perhaps an unmentioned motive was also that at that time there was no successor to the Davidic throne (Isa 39:7; 2 Kgs 21:1). Hezekiah receives his request and more: 1) fifteen more years of life, 2) deliverance from Assyria, and 3) a sign for reassurance (the sunlight going back ten steps on the stairway) (Isa 38:7-8, 22). Hezekiah humbly acknowledges with joy that Yahweh sovereignly controls everything, giving life and forgiveness (Isa 38:9-20). Hezekiah then responds with the remedy Yahweh provided for his cure (Isa 38:21).

The fourth prayer is for the restoration of Israel from the Babylonian captivity (Isa 63:7—64:12). Yahweh is approached as the merciful sovereign who brought them out before through the exodus and who will accomplish a new exodus again (Isa 63:7-14). They request sovereign Yahweh's deliverance in light of Zion's sonship and as a demonstration of his power (Isa 63:7—64:12). Their confession of sin serves as a basis for an appeal for pardon and restoration (Isa 63:11, 17, 19; 64:6-7).

A few additional notes on prayer are sprinkled in the book of Isaiah. Worship is accomplished through a multitude of means: praise, joy, thanksgiving, proclamation, singing, and shouting (Isa 12:1-6; 25:1; 26:1). The temple will be called "a house of prayer for all nations" (Isa 56:7). There will be answered prayer during the kingdom (Isa 65:24).

Fear of Yahweh

The fear (yr') of Yahweh is a reverence and awe at the overpowering presence of God which motivates people to trust and obey God, realizing that those who disobey will have negative consequences come their way. Israel feared warlike human powers. The fear of men renders them unable to fear God (Isa 51:12-13; 57:11-12). Yahweh appeals to Israel not to fear humans because God is with them to save and has redeemed them (Isa 35:4; 41:10; 43:1, 5). The fear of Yahweh should be motivated by what he will do in response to one's behavior. Because Israel fears humans and not God, he will judge them (Isa 57:11-12). In such judgment even the mountains fear Yahweh (Isa 64:3). Otto Kaiser develops this depth of godly fear.

> Yahweh Sebaoth is Lord over all possibilities and is therefore the true ruler of history, who really casts into hopeless difficulty those who do not fear Him but fear men. Whoever fears God thinks of Him as the living God, who watches over the maintenance of His will. Consequently, the real danger for the southern kingdom does not lie in the intentions of the allies, or in groups which sympathize with them, but in the failure to be aware of the constant presence of God who judges it. For those who believe he is a firm rock, to which they can flee in every danger (Isa 8:14; 17:10; Deut 32:4; Pss 18:2; 31:2f; 42:9; 62:7; 71:3), but for those who rebel a stone of offense and of ruin (Isa 8:14-15; Luke 2:34; Rom 9:33; 1 Pet 2:8).[67]

Humans cannot redefine the fear of Yahweh to prevent God's judgment (Isa 29:13). A different word (*pḥd*) is used to express the sheer terror of those who are in the midst of God's judgment (Isa 2:10, 19; 24:17-18), whereas the remnant will be given relief from the fear (*rqz*) of turmoil in their day of salvation (Isa 14:3).

The fear of Yahweh is essentially the motivation to trust and obey, as Eichrodt explained (Isa 50:10; 63:17).

> Men shrink from injustice in view of the majesty of the divine lawgiver who alone is to be feared; and that not only in Israel (Gen 39:9; Exod 1:17, 21)—a similar attitude to the holiness of the law is assumed to exist also among the pious heathen (Gen 20:8, 11; 42:18). Hence, the fear of God is an indispensable virtue of the judge (Exod 18:21), and part of the necessary equipment of the king (2 Sam 23:3; Isa 11:2). There is a very close, almost stereotyped connection, in admonitions to observe the law, between the fear of God and walking in His ways (Deut 10:12, 20; Josh 24:14; Ps 86:1); indeed, the word by which God reveals His will is seen as the best guidance to a right fear of God (Deut 4:10; 17:19; 31:13).[68]

The fear of Yahweh will provide many benefits. The sure foundation of salvation in wisdom and knowledge will be unlocked to the one who fears Yahweh (Isa 33:6). The messiah will epitomize this disposition by delighting in the fear of Yahweh through the work of the spirit of wisdom (Isa 11:2-3). When humans are gathered for the kingdom, they will all fear Yahweh (Isa 59:19).

67. Kaiser, *Isaiah 1-12*, 118.
68. Eichrodt, *Theology of the Old Testament*, 2:273.

Righteousness[69]

In the wake of Yahweh making his people holy, it was their responsibility to live ethically righteous (Isa 1:15-17; 2:5; 35:8-9). Such a righteous condition begins by God initiating the covenant relationship and by the humans following obediently within this gracious relationship. In Yahweh all Israel will be righteous (Isa 45:25) because Yahweh commands Israel to be righteousness after the pattern of covenant nomism (Isa 24:5; 28:26; 48:18; 58:2; LXX: Isa 61:8), "Maintain justice and do what is right, for my salvation is close at hand and my righteousness will soon be revealed" (Isa 56:1). Thus, covenant nomism provides motivation that Yahweh will provide salvation for those who pursue righteousness (Isa 51:1). As such, it is only possible to be righteous in maintaining a relationship with God in light of admitting any sin that broke the relationship and a wholehearted commitment to covenant obedience. As John Oswalt identifies, "Unless justice is done and righteousness is lived out there can be no shelter from the storm of God's wrath."[70] Righteousness is the ethic Yahweh prescribes, as Lindbloom described.

> Prophetic ethics are theonomic ethics. Ethics divorced from religion would be an absurdity to the Old Testament prophets. Behind all that they apprehend as right and good they set Yahweh as the Authority and Guardian . . . Ethical requirements were regarded as ultimately prescribed by Yahweh and fear of Yahweh and love to Him provided the impulse to act in accordance with His will.[71]

In Isaiah, the love for Yahweh is absent as a motivation for righteous living; the fear of Yahweh remains a sufficient motivation. God seeks to bless the righteous (LXX: Isa 5:7; 61:8). Yahweh will eventually bless righteous remnant Judah with a new exodus unto kingdom salvation (LXX: Isa 1:26; 26:2; 41:2; 45:8; 46:12; 49:12; 59:17; 58:2; 61:8).[72] Jerusalem will be established in kingdom righteousness (Isa 1:26; 62:1-2).

---

69. This orientation to righteousness as "appropriate in Mosaic Covenant," Kennard, *Biblical Covenantalism* 1:285-89: 1) continues in the synoptics (Kennard, *Messiah Jesus*, 84-86), 2) continues mystically in Second Temple Judaism as a foretaste of eschatological judgment from God (Kennard, *Messiah Jesus*, 305-7), and 3) Paul develops more extensively as mystically already for the appropriate and retains a not-yet expression of eschatological judgment (Kennard, *Messiah Jesus*, 313-21).

70. Oswalt, "Righteousness in Isaiah," 179-80.

71. Lindbloom, *Prophecy in Ancient Israel*, 346, 348.

72. Tob 12.9; 14.11; Wis 1.15; *Pss. Sol.* 2.34; 3.4-8; 15.6; *1 En.* 1.8; CD 4.8; 1QS 5.7-11; 1QH 7.12.

CONCLUSION

As the sovereign king, Yahweh redeemed his people by bringing them back into salvation. This salvation will be climactically expressed in the kingdom brought about by Yahweh. Because of this salvation, Israel is to trust and fear Yahweh, thereby living righteously.

CHAPTER 10

Prophecies of the Sign-Child

ISAIAH ENCOUNTERS AHAZ AND prophesies about a sign-child in the Isaiah 7–9 pericope.[1] The prophecy recorded occurs around 737–732 BC (dated on the basis of the kings warring in Isa 7:1–2, namely: Ahaz 741–725, Rezin 740–732, and Pekah 737–732 BC). The date for this prophecy also can be calculated by noticing when the predictions were realized and calculating back to when the prophecy must have been said to make it fit. By this means the prophecy would be within 736–735 BC on the basis of the descriptions in Isa 7:15, which would have the child maturing into adulthood when Assyria conquered the northern kingdom of Israel about 722 BC. The date of the prophecy would also be within 735–734 BC based on the descriptions in Isa 8:4, which would have the child about two years old and speaking "my father" and "my mother" when Damascus is captured by Assyria about 732 BC. Therefore, Isaiah presents this sign prophecy as likely occurring around 735 BC.

The setting for the prophecy is that the Arameans were camping in Ephraim, causing Ahaz and Judah to fear impending invasion (Isa 7:2). Yahweh prompted Isaiah (meaning "Yahweh saves") to go with his son Shearjashub (meaning "a remnant will return") to meet Ahaz (meaning "he has grasped"). Perhaps the meaning of these names "Yahweh saves" and "a remnant will return" might encourage Ahaz and Judah so that they might believe and be redeemed. However, it does not seem as though Ahaz grasped the precariousness of the situation, so his name is ironic for the situation.

---

1. Similar encounters with a king can be found in the *Oracles to Esarhaddon* 9 1.1, 4, 6, which are easily accessible in Hays, *Hidden Riches*, 245–46.

The meeting took place at the upper pool by the highway around the laundryman's field (Isa 7:3). This location around Jerusalem cannot be placed exactly today as it could in Isaiah's day, but it is outside Hezekiah's wall based on Josephus identifying that the later Assyrian camp was on the western hills; it is the same pool where Rabshekah of Assyria met Judah's representatives (Isa 36:2–22).[2] This pool could be a tower pool by the western hills, or in the Tyropoeon valley west of the temple, or near the pool of Bethesda, or near the other sheep pool north of the temple.[3]

Isaiah went and offered any sign that Ahaz would choose for purpose of reassurance that Rezin and Pekah would not ultimately threaten Judah (Isa 7:4–11). Such an offer underscores Yahweh's sovereign ability to provide anything Ahaz would request. However, Ahaz refused to ask for a sign, pretending a false spirituality. This refusal to ask for a sign was seen by Isaiah and God as further rebellion on Ahaz's part, so Yahweh provides him with a sign (Isa 7:13).

Isaiah predicts a sign for evil King Ahaz, who is troubled by Ephraim and Aram, the two kings north of Judah. Isaiah reassures Ahaz that within sixty-five years or about 669 BC, Ephraim will be no more; in fact Esarhaddon carried away Manasseh and resettled a foreign ruling class of colonists in Ephraim by then (Isa 7:8; Ezra 4:2, 10).[4] To encourage Ahaz to believe, a sign is offered for the plural "you" of Ahaz and Judah, to provide a timeline for measuring God's encouraging rescue from the momentary threat (Isa 7:14). Because the sign is offered to the plural group surrounding Ahaz, faith is not just passive, nor does it consist in making political arrangements with Assyria, but faith includes Judah's trust of Yahweh's instruction and timing that Yahweh will fight for Judah and deliver them.[5] The timing in the passage is indicated by development of the sign-child in the passage. The prophecy indicated that a *young woman of marriageable age* (*'lmh*)[6] will

---

2. Josephus, *Ant.* 5.303; Ussishkin, "Sennacherib's Campaign to Judah," 95.
3. Dalman, *Jerusalem und seine Gelände*, 38–40; Young, *The Book of Isaiah*, 1:271.
4. Young, *The Book of Isaiah*, 275–76.
5. Wong, "Faith in the Present Form of Isaiah."
6. *'lmh* indicates a young woman of marriageable age (probably thirteen to twenty years old) as indicated by Proverbs 30:19 and in contrast to *betulahi*, which would indicate a married woman as in Joel 1:8. The issue is not virginal until LXX translates *'lmh* into παρθένος. For example, BDB 761 indicates *'lmh* means "young woman (ripe sexually; maid or newly married)." The concept includes the newly married woman who is receiving lovemaking from her man in contrast to the deceptive destructive activity of an adulterous woman (Prov 30:19–20). The word is used also of those who have a falsetto voice (1 Chr 15:20; Ps 9:1). Additionally, the young women would draw water, which is a task not reserved for virgins (Gen 24:43; John 4:7). If the point was to restrict Isa 7:14 statement to virgin, then a clearer Hebrew word meaning "virgin" (*betulim*) could have

bear a son and she will call him "Immanuel" (meaning "God with us") and at points in the child's life international affairs would transpire in an encouraging direction (Isa 7:14). That is, Assyria will sweep Ahaz's enemies away as a flood (Isa 8:6–8) but will also provide a very close shave for Judah (Isa 7:17–20), including destroying many structures (Isa 8:9–15). Some connect this Isaiah 7:14 with a similar phrase in the *Ras Shamra* 3.2.22–24 where a lady births a child king for the divine, similar to Isaiah 9:6–7.[7] However, the nearer context of Isa 7–8 continues to develop temporal markers tied to Isaiah's experience of Assyrian campaign and a child he obtains to reassure Ahaz.[8] For example, Isaiah 8:1–3 explains that Isaiah approached a prophetess with a written document indicating the sign and a child will be born to Isaiah and the prophetess with a theophoric name (*swift is the booty, speedy is the prey*) indicating a *visible manifestation of deity judging* (on the basis of the mother's naming the child "Immanuel," meaning "God with us," providentially to rescue Judah, Isa 7:14) to bring about the impending destruction of Ephraim and Aram by Assyria (Isa 8:1, 3). We do not know whether Isaiah and the prophetess were previously married or if a marriage was also arranged to produce this child. Faithful witnesses (Uriah the priest and Zechariah son of Jeberechiah) testify as witnesses to the efficacy of the prediction (Isa 8:2). By the time the child knows how to cry "my father" and "my mother," or when the baby is about one year old around 732 BC, the wealth of these two nations will be no more (Isa 8:4). During 733–732, the Assyrian king Tiglath-Pileser executed a raid on Ephraim and Aram, carrying away several of Israel's leaders (2 Kgs 15:29; 1 Chr 5:6).[9] Furthermore, by the time this child knows enough to refuse evil and choose good, implying he is becoming a man of about thirteen years old, or around 722 BC, Judah will have Assyria battling Egypt on their land such that the crops and vineyards will be wasted, and the primary food will be curds (cottage cheese) because livestock could be protected within walled cities (while crops were devastated) and honey could be collected through forays into the field when the warring armies were not nearby (Isa 7:15–19). The warring armies described as the "Assyrian bee" will sweep through, dislodging the "Egyptian fly" back to its river Nile (Isa 7:18).[10] This battle took place as

---

been chosen (Lev 21:13; Deut 22:14–20; Jud 11:37–38; Ezek 23:3, 8).

7. Driver, *Canaanite Myths and Legends*, 124–25; Engnell, "Studies in Divine Kingship," 133; Ringgren, *Messiah in the Old Testament*, 25–27.

8. Gottwald, "Immanuel as the Prophet's Son."

9. *Annals of Tiglath-Pileser* 3.

10. In the wake of Egypt battling Assyria on Judah's soil an upper Egypt hieroglyphic represents Egypt as a wasp. John Watts, *Isaiah 1–33*, 144. Theodore Lewis shows the severity of the Assyrian conquest through Assyrian documents and reliefs in, "'You

Shalmaneser swept through, forcing Egypt back toward the Nile. The difficulty of the time would remind them that Judah will only be preserved by *God's providential presence with them*, implied in the expression of the theophanic name of "*Immanuel*," or "God with us" (Isa 7:14; 8:8, 10). These predictions came true by the dates indicated. Assyrians campaigning across Israel left Galilee in the darkness of Gentile domination, as did the later Greek, Syrian, and Roman conquests (Isa 9:1–2 [MT: 8:23—9:1]).

Isaiah predicts that this dark condition will change as Israel sees the light of a Davidic son, who will bring victory and a kingdom in the wake of these conquests (Isa 9:2–7 [MT: 9:1–6], notice the singular verbs in second person within Isa 9:3 [MT: 9:2] and the third person singular references to the child in Isa 9:6–7 [MT and LXX: 9:5–6]). With the concentration on the child as the singular third person, "He shall be called his name" (*wygr' šmw*) emphasizes more likely throne names for the child, rather than theophanic names for God who delivers (Isa 9:6 [MT: 9:5]; as had occurred in Isa 7:3 and 8:1, 3). The prophecy of the ultimate Davidic king in Isaiah 11 emerges in the wake of the Assyrian destruction of Judah and probably also the destruction of Assyria (Isa 11:1 compared to chapter 10).

In the second century BC, after these temporal sign indicators had become ancient history, Jews translated the Hebrew "young woman of marriageable age" (*'lmh*) into the Greek LXX as "virgin" (παρθένος), shifting the sign in the LXX to be more definitively on the woman, who as a *virgin* would bear a son called "*Immanuel*" (Isa. 7:14 LXX). With virgin as the primary sign, the later Davidic child in the pericope emerging as the replacement child (Isa 9:6–7 [MT: 9:5–6]) for the one that had providentially provided timing for the Assyrian conquest (Isa 7:14–20; 8:1–4). This later incarnate *Immanuel* child became the lens through which the NT and Christians approached the virgin prophecy.

Both Matthew and Luke identify that Jesus was born by virgin birth, through a process that can be described as the Holy Spirit *coming upon* Mary (Matt 1:18, 20, 23, 25; Luke 1:34–35). The process Luke describes is not a sexual intercourse, as in myths of pagan deities, but rather an event of Spirit *coming upon* like at Pentecost (ἐπελεύσεται ἐπὶ σὲ; Luke 1:35; 11:22; 21:26; Acts 1:8; 8:24; 13:40; 14:19) or a *covering* like God's presence on the temple or protecting his people (ἐπισκιάσει σοι; Luke 1:35; 9:34; Acts 5:15; compare LXX: Exod 40:35; Ps 91:4). Matthew describes that this birth of Jesus fulfills Isaiah 7:14 (Matt 1:22–23). Joseph as a righteous Jew almost did not go through with the wedding, until an angel appeared to him in a dream and

---

Have Heard What the Kings of Assyria Have Done': Disarmament Passages *vis-á-vis* Assyrian Rhetoric of Intimidation," In *Isaiah's Vision of Peace in Biblical and Modern International Relations*. edited by Raymond Cohen and Raymond Westbrook, 75–100.

explained what was going on (Matt 1:18–21). Instead of having Mary stoned or divorced quietly (Deut 22:23–24),[11] Joseph took Mary as his wife, presumably in Nazareth, but he kept her a virgin until the birth (Matt 1:24–25). Of course, some of Jesus' opponents slandered Jesus as being a bastard.[12] Sometimes the miraculous is a burden to bear. However, this birth account in Luke is set up in parallel with that of the birth narrative of his forerunner John the Baptist (Luke 1:5–25). The faithful priest Zacharias offering the incense on the incense altar[13] was confronted in fear by the angel Gabriel, who promised a Nazirite-like son to them in their infertility (Num 6:2–5; Luke 1:15). This promise indicated that Zacharias's son would be filled with the Holy Spirit while in the womb so that he might come before the messiah in the spirit and power of Elijah to turn the people back to obedience and righteousness. Zacharias asked how he might know this and was rendered mute, so that when he exited the holy place to give the benediction,[14] he could not speak and all knew that he had seen a vision. Mary visited her cousin Elizabeth (Zacharias's wife), who was now six months pregnant. Upon hearing Mary's greeting, John leaped in Elizabeth's womb and the Holy Spirit filled Elizabeth so that she blessed Mary as the mother of her Lord. Luke records more of a role of women parallel to men, so Mary responds in praise similar to Zacharias's. Mary praises with joy and the hopes of a poor Jewish woman's expectations for messiah's coming kingdom. These hopes include eschatological reversal, in which the proud and mighty will be destroyed in order for the hungry, poor, and humble to be lifted up and filled (Luke 1:51–55). Such eschatological mercy is rooted in the Abrahamic covenant hopes for blessing in a land that is Israel's own, not dominated by external powers. With the birth of John the Baptist, Zacharias was filled with the Holy Spirit and prophesied about the Abrahamic redemption that the Davidic king would bring about in delivering Israel from its enemies, which in this context included the Romans but is reminiscent of Isaiah's and Ahaz's context (Luke 1:68–79).[15] Zacharias was longing for a kingdom known for

---

11. 11QTemple 61; *Sanh.* 7.4a. The betrothal was the legal equivalent of marriage in that a cancellation of it was through divorce (Deut 22:23–27; 11QTemple 66.1–8; *b. Sanh.* 57b; *m. Ketub.* 1.2; 4:2; 7.6; *m. Yeb.* 2.6; *m. Git* 6.2; Josephus, *Ant.* 4.253).

12. John 8:41; *Acts Pilate* 2.3; Origen, *Cels.* 1.28, 32, 39, 133; Tertullian, *Spec.* 30; *SB* 1. Such a designation identifies social outcasts, *Yeba.* 4.13.

13. Because the number of priests, it is likely that this is the only time in his life that the lot fell to him for this service (*Yoma* 2.2–4).

14. *M. Talmud* 7.2 indicates that the priest who offers incense should lead in the benediction.

15. These hopes for a nationalistic deliverer are anticipated by *Pss. Sol.* 17–18.

holiness, righteousness, forgiveness, and peace. John was born as an initial light to prepare Israel for the messiah and his kingdom way of peace.

Jesus' birth occurs between August, 5 BC and March, 4 BC, during the reigns of: 1) Caesar Augustus, that is Octavian (27 BC–AD 14), 2) Quirinius's governorship of Syria (twice governor during the Hebrew calendar: 4–1 BC and AD 6–9, each time having a census conducted, though Luke and Tertullian record the former one in 4 BC and Josephus only records the latter one in AD 6),[16] and 3) Herod the Great (40–4 BC; Matt 2:1, 19; Luke 2:1–2).[17] The biblical Hebrew year begins with the spring (lunar month of *Nisan*) normally in March (Exod 12:2; 13:3–4; 23:15; Deut 16:1, 6), but this means of computing the new year had largely been replaced in Israel, since the captivity, by a Syrian calendar reflecting the new year celebration *Rosh Hashanah*, which occurs around October 1st in a lunar calendar (sometimes occurring in September according to the Gregorian calendar). The Roman calendar, reflective of the regnal year of Augustus, would begin in August.[18] Luke, writing for a Gentile audience, probably followed either the Syrian or Roman calendar, so that Jesus' birth would likely be between September, 5 BC and March, 4 BC. Herod died slightly before Passover 4 BC.[19] The first census during Quirinius's governorship would have taken place around August through November, 5 BC, since a census would often be done at the beginning of a new reign so that an accurate tax could be levied and provided to Rome.

The census brought Joseph and his betrothed, Mary, late in her pregnancy, to Bethlehem to be registered under the Davidic family place (Luke 2:3–6).[20] There is no mention of a donkey to ride; Mary may have walked the eighty miles to Bethlehem while eight months pregnant. They were poor as evident by a poor person's cleansing sacrifice (Luke 2:22–24; Lev 12:8; 5:11). Joseph may have carried their food and a few tools on his back. Bethlehem was flooded with people for the census, so no room was found in the

16. Tertullian identifies a census under governor Sentius Saturnus [9–4 BC] (*Marc.* 4.19); Josephus (*Ant.* 12.277; 18.89) confirms Quirinius's governorship during 4–1 BC without mentioning a census, and then identifies that Quirinius instituted a census when he was governor again in AD 6–9 (*Ant.* 18.1).

17. Agreeing with these dates: Wright, *Jesus and the Victory of God*, 147; Sanders, *Historical Figure Jesus*, 11; Meier, *A Marginal Jew*, 1:375. The initial incorrect calculation of 0 had been done by Dionysius Exiguus in AD 533; Josephus, *Ant.* 18.1.

18. In the year AD 14 the new year began between August 19 and September 30; Meyer, *Aims of Jesus*, 115.

19. Josephus, *Ant.* 14–18; there is some evidence that for political purposes the Hebrew calendar was sometimes reckoned from September (or the lunar month *Tishri*).

20. Bethlehem is also mentioned as the predicted place of Messiah birth by Mic 5:2; *Sib. Or.* 8.478.

inn. Likewise, the dishonor of pregnancy during betrothal would dishonor them to the periphery. So, they were staying where the livestock were stored, probably in a cave, but it could have been a built stable. When Jesus was born, he was wrapped in cloth and placed in a feeding trough for animals (Luke 2:7). There is no mention of animals in the stall; the animals have been assumed by commentators, who read into the account by the location and a misreading of Isaiah 1:3 and possibly connect the birth of the king with animal benefits in kingdom (Isa 11:6-9).

In the same region shepherds were watching over their flocks by night when an angel appeared to them announcing that the anointed to be king had been born that very day in Bethlehem. Shepherds were in a despised vocation.[21] Luke is sensitive to the poor working men such as these shepherds and woodworkers (such as Joseph and Jesus).[22] The angel was joined by a multitude of angels, praising God because God intended to bless humans with peace through his pleasure with them (Luke 2:13-14).[23] The shepherds could recognize the messiah because he would be the baby wrapped and with the sign of lying in the manger, which is a "feeding trough" (Luke 2:12, 16).[24] The shepherds came to see, told what had occurred, and went home praising God for all that they had heard and seen. Those who heard the shepherds' testimony were amazed; Mary treasured and pondered these memories.

Later, maybe even in 4 BC, after Joseph had moved his family into a rented house (probably about fifteen feet square),[25] wise men[26] arrived from the East, having followed a sign-star that came to rest over the place where

---

21. *Kiddushin* 4.14; *Baba Kamma* 10.9 but *Sib. Or.* 8.480 identified shepherds visiting Jesus while a baby in Bethlehem.

22. Meier (*A Marginal Jew*, 1:278-85) explores Jesus' profession of woodworker as a constructor or day-laborer who does not own land and is thus poor, getting by from day to day.

23. The phrase "people with whom God is pleased" refers to the elect of God (1QH 4.31-35; 11.7, 9).

24. *Sib. Or.* 8.479.

25. Also after they had offered the offerings of the poor in the temple five miles away (Luke 2:24). The size of house is average dimensions for a poor family in Israel at that time.

26. The wise men are largely undescribed in Matthew, though the *Gospel of the Nazarene*, fragment 28, describes their dress in great detail, evidencing wealth and dark complexion. Many consider that they are of the best wisdom from Gentiles (Ps 72:10-11; Balaam, Num 22-24; the Persian king arrived in Rome to honor Nero as prompted by Mithras and astrology: Dio Cassius 63.1-7; Pliny, *H.N.* 30.16-17; Suetonius, *Nero* 13), or parallel to Egyptian sorceress in the Mosaic account, but there are some of this category elsewhere who are Jews (Acts 8:9-24, Simon; 13:6-11, Elymas; Josephus, *Ant.* 20.142).

Jesus was born (Matt 2:11). We don't really know what the sign star was, though there are many possibilities, but it probably had been visible for at least a year, since it could take as much as two years to plan and traverse the desert from the East, and Herod killed the children two years old and under (Matt 2:16). The wise men asked Herod where the messiah child was, and Herod's priests and scribes identified that he was to be born in Bethlehem according to Micah the prophet (Mic 5:2; Matt 2:5–6). The wise men pay homage to the child and present him with gifts worthy of a king: gold, frankincense, and myrrh. This fits with the Jewish expectation that gentiles will pay tribute to the king, with gold and frankincense, as they praise the Lord (Isa 60:6). These gifts probably paid for Joseph, Mary, and Jesus' sojourn travels to Egypt and eventually to Nazareth. The wise men were warned in a dream to not tell Herod where the child was, so they departed for their country by another way. Joseph was warned by an angel in a dream to flee, so the family became exiles in Egypt until Herod died, and then they experienced a family exodus to Galilee (Matt 2:19–20).

Herod had considered that he himself was to be the messiah; he had spent years on the temple construction project to demonstrate that he was the messiah (Matt 2:12–18; 2 Sam 7:12–15; 1 Chr 17:11–14).[27] The quote in Matthew 2:18 from Jeremiah 31:15 identified the experience of Herod's hostility to be an experience of recapitulating Israel's continuing captivity and grief since Assyria and Babylon conquered Israel (Matt 2:17–18). Within a few months, God condemned Herod to death before March 29, 4 BC.[28]

Christians made a strong case based on the authoritative Greek LXX that the biblical redaction was that Messiah Jesus was virginally born.[29] The second century AD found some Jewish retranslation of LXX texts, which changed the παρθένος into τεκνια or ἥνενις (both indicating a young girl around seven to fifteen years old) as a Jewish reaction against Christian use

---

27. Josephus, *Ant.* 15.380ff. The messiah is predicted to be the builder of the temple (2 Sam 7:13; 1 Chr 17:12; Zech 4:7–10; *Sib. Or.* 5.420–33 (this *Sib. Or.* prediction is after Herod and AD 70 destruction referring to the eschatological messiah). 4QFlor. 1.1–13 identifies that in the end times (utilizing 2 Sam 7:13) the Jerusalem temple will be built but by someone other than the messiah. Elsewhere, God is portrayed to be the builder of the temple (*1 En* 90.28–29; *Jub.* 1.17; *2 Bar.* 4.3; 32.4; 11QTemple 29.8–10; 4QFlor. 1.3, 6; *Midr. Ps.* 90.17; *Mekilta* of R. Ishmael 3).

28. Josephus, *Ant.* 17.9.3; *War* 2.1.3 describes that Herod was dead before a lunar eclipse (which occurred March 29) and the Passover (which occurred April 11) of 4 BC; Hoehner, *Chronological Aspects*, 13.

29. Ignatius, *Ep. Ephesians* 19; Irenaeus, *Haer.* 19; 21; 33.11; Tertullian, *Marc.* 3.12; 4.10; *Carn. Chr.* 1–2; 20–21; 23; *Res.* 20; Hippolytus, *Haer.* 5.3; Novatian, *Trin.* 22; Gregory Thaumaturgus, *Four Homilies* 3; Lactantius, *Inst.* 4.12; *Epit.* 44; and *Constitutions of the Holy Apostles*, 5.16.

of this prophecy, making the term more generic, as *'lmh* had been. For example, Justin repeatedly takes Jewish and Ebionite traditions to task for this LXX change and the proposal that Joseph was Jesus' biological father.[30]

However, the pericope of Isaiah continues to develop the resolution from this dispersion[31] time of Assyria in Galilee (Isa 9:1-7 [MT and LXX: 8:23—9:6]). In the dark of dispersion and Gentile domination, the light of revelation and salvation dawns, with a child born to be the Davidic king and to bring peace, forever.

This child will have throne names[32] that declare his glory as king and maybe even incarnate "*Immanuel*" ("*God with us*" incarnate, more than providence). The names might represent a theophoric condition as the child in Isa 8:1, 3, had described the Assyrian conquest, but most commentators take the names to identify the character of the child, because this section is more focused on the reign of this child who will bring peace and prosperity, rather than the emphasis of Isaiah 7-8 on conditions that God will providentially bring through Assyrian conquest. These names also fit the pattern of accession titles within accession oracles,[33] which would also focus on the child. These throne names hint at the child's divinity in a manner that sets up a Jewish two-powers view.[34] He is the "Wonderful Counselor," a quality of the ideal wise statesman, which Isaiah develops as an attribute of the messianic branch and of God (Isa 9:6 [MT and LXX: 9:5]; 11:2; 28:29).[35] Young argues that this wonderful character reflects the power of the plagues in

---

30. Justin, *Dial.* 43.3-8; 66.2-4; 67.1; 68.9; 71.3; 77.3; 84.1-3; *Apol.*1.33.1, 4-6; Kamesar, "The Virgin of Isaiah"; Rösel, "Die Jungfrauengeburt des endzeitlichen Immanuel."

31. A word that indicates people living outside of their homeland.

32. Some conjecture that these are also theophoric names to describe God, and grammatically they could be as "God Almighty" refers to Yahweh (Isa 10:21; *Tanak: A New Translation of the Holy Scriptures*, 634; Snaith, "Interpretation of El Gabor," 37; Goldingay, "Compound Name in Isaiah"; Holladay, *Isaiah*, 108-9 argues for middle names as referring to Yahweh; Wegner, *Examination of Kingship*, 183-90; "What's New in Isaiah 9:1-7?," 244-45). But the focus in Isaiah 9:6-7 [MT: 5-6] is on the child and the name that the child will be called ("He shall be called his name" [*wygr' šmw*]) not the power behind him, so throne names describing the child are preferred by most exegetes. The concept of throne names identifies qualities which are describing the child king and not primarily the God behind this child king, as would be the case if they were theophanic names.

33. Especially Egyptian accession oracles are compared: Gressmann, *Der Messias*, 245; Mowinckel, *He That Cometh*, 105; Kaiser, *Isaiah 1-12*, 102-3.

34. Segal, *Two Powers in Heaven*.

35. 1QH 11.9-10 describes the birth of the hoped-for Davidic messiah who will be called "wonderful counselor."

Egypt and conquest of the land (Ps 78:12; Judg 13:19).[36] As "Mighty God," he is the champion who can carry out those plans, a title used elsewhere in Isaiah only of Yahweh (Isa 9:6 [MT and LXX: 9:5]; 10:21). Smith and Young argue that "Mighty God" identifies the Jewish monothetistic God in a manner to set up and inform the early rabbinic two-powers heresy[37]—namely, that connecting Isa 7:14 with 9:6 [MT and LXX: 9:5] indicates that *"Immanuel"* means "God incarnate among us." The title "Everlasting Father" indicates the enduring benefactor for his people, as God supremely is, further hinting at deity (Isa 9:6 [MT and LXX: 9:5]; 63:16). As "Prince of Peace," he is the provider of universal peace (Isa 9:5–7 [MT and LXX: 9:4–6]; which also could point to Yahweh, Judg 6:24). There is no end of the increase of the rule of this child when king (Isa 9:6 [MT and LXX: 9:5]). He will rule with justice and righteousness forever (Isa 9:7 [MT and LXX: 9:6]). The character of the kingdom will reflect the character of the king.

Additionally, the zeal and word of Yahweh the general ensures that the Wonderful Counselor's kingdom will realize fullness of righteousness (Isa 9:7–8 [MT and LXX: 9:6–7]).

---

36. Young, *The Book of Isaiah*, 1:334.

37. Smith, *The Book of Isaiah*, 1:137; Young, *The Book of Isaiah*, 1:335; Segal, *Two Powers in Heaven*.

CHAPTER 11

Davidic Branch

THE DAVIDIC BRANCH IMAGERY identifies an ideal king within the Davidic lineage. Some of this imagery overlaps with the sign-child and the servant of Yahweh. For example, toward the end of the chapter on the sign-child, Isaiah identified that the "Prince of Peace" was to sit on the Davidic throne (Isa 9:6–7 [MT and LXX: 9:5–6]).

The promise of a Davidic king in Isaiah extends the Davidic covenant into a post-exilic hope for a kingdom under Yahweh's Davidic co-regent. Von Rad identified that the divine activity to establish the Davidic king joins with the exodus as the two great salvation acts of God in Israel's history.

> If we reduce the comprehensive accounts of her history which Israel wrote to what is basic theologically, that is, to those actions of Jahweh which were constitutive for Israel, the result is as follows: Jahweh twice intervened in Israel's history in a special way, to lay a basis of salvation for his people. The first was in the complex of acts which are gathered together in the avowal made by the canonical saving history (that is, from Abraham to Joshua), the other was in the confirmation of David and his throne for all time... On these two saving data rested the whole of Israel's existence before Jahweh. Even the prophets in their proclamation of the new creation of Israel cannot hark back to any other than them, the covenant at Sinai and the covenant with David.[1]

---

1. Von Rad, *Old Testament Theology*, 1:355; Kennard, *Biblical Covenantalism*, 2:25–72.

This promise of a Davidic king resonates with the conditions in Judah with a Davidic king still reigning prior to the Babylonian captivity. So, the promise of a Davidic king during the threat from Assyria and Babylon identifies that Yahweh is still committed to redeem Israel. With the promise of the rise of a Davidic king after the Babylonian captivity, there is the basis of salvation hope for Israel even though they have been destroyed.

Marvin Sweeney argues that the Davidic covenant is reconceptualized from the Davidic king in Proto-Isaiah to the Persian king Cyrus in Deutero-Isaiah to King Yahweh in Trito-Isaiah.[2] Sweeney is correct to notice that most of the clear Davidic king references are from Isa 1–39 or Proto-Isaiah. However, there is no development of Cyrus under a Davidic lineage.

Cyrus as God's shepherd (r^c) and anointed ($mśyḥ$) both involve royal imagery but are not exclusively Davidic (Isa 44:28—45:1). To extend this regal imagery from a Davidic king as Sweeney has done probably would entail further development. Part of that development recognizes that most "anointed" references in the OT are anointed to be king. Sweeney furthers his identification that Cyrus is messiah by recognizing that Cyrus's shepherd role overseeing the rebuilding of Jerusalem and the temple places him within a role of temple builder accomplished by a son of David (Isa 44:28; 1 Chr 17:11–12; 2 Sam 7:12–13). This temple builder is a theme that the Chronicler identified Cyrus would accomplish in Jerusalem (2 Chr 36:22–23). In such an identification the reference to "son of David" reduces to a metaphor of an "idealized king," which may have no relationship to David. However, the emphasis in Deutero-Isaiah is the incomparability of Yahweh, and not the Davidic king. The mention of Cyrus is merely one item to support Yahweh's incomparability.

Furthermore, Yahweh is developed as king ($melek$) over Israel throughout Isaiah, reflective of their covenant relationship (Isa 6:5; 8:21; 32:17, 22; 33:22; 41:21–22; 43:15; 44:6; 63:1–6). Though this kingship of Yahweh is not a promise of the Davidic covenant, it is reflective of the suzerainty treaty of the Mosaic covenant. However, with regard to Yahweh "reigning," the verb is employed in an eschatological sense when God rules during the kingdom age (Isa 24:23; 52:7), and that is the ultimate era of reign grounded in the Davidic covenant expectation. Though this Yahweh reigning eschatologically is at least as strongly developed throughout Isaiah (Isa 24:23; 52:7; 63:1–6). So actually, Trito-Isaiah does not uniquely develop Yahweh as king, but there is more development of the glories of kingdom in this section, as will be shown in the chapter on kingdom.

---

2. Sweeney, "Reconceptualization of the Davidic Covenant," 58.

The Davidic king role in Isaiah identifies an individual from Jesse's lineage who is spiritually enabled to bring righteous characteristics to Israel's kingdom. A Davidic king reigning in righteousness emerges in Isaiah (Isa 16:5; 32:1). The character of the king is reflected in the character of his righteous kingdom. Under his reign, all will understand and have wisdom, living in the place of blessing (Isa 32:2–8).

Isaiah overlaps the concept of a Davidic messiah reigning with the possibility of Yahweh Sabaoth co-reigning in kingdom (Isa 24:23; 52:7). Furthermore, the imagery of Yahweh as warrior also develops the context of the messianic king who comes to do judgment battle (Isa 31:4; 59:16–17; 63:5). Kenneth Barker develops this fusion of Yahweh and messiah reigning in kingdom.

> All passages that speak of a future coming of God or Yahweh to His people onto the earth, or that speak of a future rule of God or Yahweh over Israel or over the entire earth, are ultimately Messianic—indirectly or by extension. For to be fully and literally true, they require a future literal Messianic Kingdom on the earth.[3]

In Isaiah 63:1–6, Yahweh is pictured as a fierce warrior, judging the wicked severely in wrath. He was appalled that no one stood with him, so he carried out vengeance on his enemies and provided salvation for his people by the power of his arm. As in the exodus, for some the battle brings death but for his own the battle brings salvation. In this eschatological conflict, even Egypt cries out to Yahweh in her oppression and Yahweh promises to send them a savior and a great one (or possibly an advocate)[4] (Isa 19:20). In a passage which speaks figuratively of the return from the Babylonian captivity and more directly of the return which initiates the kingdom, the imagery of Yahweh as king and shepherd is extended to the messiah (Isa 40:10–11). Such a picture develops the compassionate salvation and guidance which the messiah has for his people Israel.

The messianic era (Isa 2:2–4) is the context in which the branch will be revealed (Isa 4:2). The branch will be a descendent of Jesse and David (Isa 11:1). This one will be beautiful and glorious (Isa 4:2). The spirit of Yahweh will rest upon him, fully empowering him with divine abilities of knowledge, wisdom, counsel, and power (Isa 11:2). He will rejoice in submission and obedience in the fear of Yahweh (Isa 11:3). From this submission and divine wisdom, the Davidic branch will judge all in righteousness

---

3. Barker, "Categories of Messianic Prophecy."

4. *Rb* can mean "strong" or "great one" or it could be a participle from *ryb*, which would denote "an advocate." Alexander, *Prophecies of Isaiah*, 360.

(Isa 11:4-5). These judgments will be carried out in his divinely given powers with severity, for he will slay the wicked with his breath (or spirit) as was the case with Yahweh (Isa 11:4; similar to 40:7).[5] This branch from the root of Jesse will rally the people of the earth, especially scattered Israel, to his kingdom and to the glorious rest which this kingdom provides (Isa 11:10, 12). As developed before, Yahweh will join in lifting the standard to assemble Israel after a new exodus.[6] So this kingdom is brought about by a co-regency of Yahweh and the Davidic branch (Isa 11:12).

The Davidic messianic king endowed by Yahweh's spirit fosters righteousness for the vulnerable (Isa 11:4-5). One metaphor to describe this practice is that righteousness will be a belt to girdle hips or loins. Perhaps these belt allusions refer to the struggle for righteousness through the metaphor of belt wrestling, which was common in Mesopotamia and the Hellenistic world.[7] However the imagery emerges, the Davidic king will righteously reign in a manner that protects the vulnerable, such as orphans and widows.

Marvin Sweeney developed that there is another reconceptualization of the Davidic covenant by shifting from the individual recipient to "the people who accept the covenant are now the recipients of that relationship."[8] Sweeney's argument heavily builds from Isa 55:3-5.

> Incline your ear and come to me. Listen, that you may live;
> And I will make an everlasting covenant with you all,
> As the faithful mercies shown to David.
> Behold, I have made him a witness to the peoples,
> A leader and commander for the peoples.
> Behold, you will call a nation you do not know,
> And a nation which knows you not will run to you,
> Because of Yahweh your God, even the Holy One of Israel;
> For he has glorified you. (Isa 55:3-5)

It is through this reconceptualization that the Davidic covenant shifts in the book of Isaiah to primarily point to the coming kingdom, which brings substantial encouragement for Judah through the impending difficulties from Assyria and Babylon. However, Sweeney also argues for this shift by

---

5. Similar to *Enuma Elish* table 1, lines 105-110; Eichrodt, *Theology of the Old Testament*, 2:55; 1 Sam 16:14; 18:10; 19:9; Judg 9:23.

6. Groswell, "Messianic Expectation," 132-33.

7. Homer, *Iliad*, 23:710; Homer, *Odyssey*, 24:89; Gordon, "Belt-Wrestling in the Bible World"; Chiera, *Proceedings in Court*, 4:53-55; Young, *Study of Old Testament Theology Today*, 53-55; *The Book of Isaiah*, 1:386.

8. Sweeney, "Reconceptualization of the Davidic Covenant," 47.

appeals to Cyrus and Yahweh replacing the Davidic role, which I previously countered as extrapolating Isaiah beyond the evidence in the direction of Chronicles.

John Collins argues that there are four messianic paradigms in early Judaism: Davidic messiah (anointed king),[9] Son of God,[10] priest, and Danielic Son of Man.[11] Only the first model, that of the Davidic messianic king fits the Davidic covenant material. However, the Davidic king and the Danielic Son of Man are joined to develop the messianic king imagery. Combining these images, the Jewish apocalyptic writings of *1 Enoch* 37–71; *4 Ezra* 11–12; and *2 Apocalypse of Baruch* 39–40 develop a coming deliverer who will defeat the enemies of Israel. Qumran joins in with this sentiment. For example, the Qumran *Florilegium* text 4Q174 interprets 2 Samuel 7:11-14 as a promise that there will be a descendant of David who destroys the enemies of God and will reign on an everlasting throne. The text refers to a "shoot"[12] which is the Davidic messiah from Isaiah 11:1 and Jeremiah 23:5 and 33:15.

> This passage refers to the Shoot of David, who is to arise with the Interpreter of the Law, and who will [arise] in Zi[on in the La]st Days, as it is written, "And I shall raise up the branch of David that is fallen" (Amos 9:11). This passage describes the fallen booth of David, [w]hom He shall raise up to deliver Israel.[13]

Appendix B to the *Rule of the Benediction* (1QSb 5:21) expresses a blessing on "the prince of the congregation,[14] that God will raise up for him the

---

9. Davidic king references include: *Pss. Sol.* 17.32; 18.57; *Shemoneh 'Esreh* 14; Sir 47.11, 22; 1 Macc. 2.57; CD 7.20; 12.23—13.1; 14.19 (=4Q266 frag. 18, 3.12); 19.10–11; 20.1; 1QS 9.11; 1QSa 2.11–12, 14–15, 20–21; 1QSb 5.20; 1QM 5.1; 4Q161; 4Q252 frag. 1 5.3–4; 4Q381 frag. 15.7; 4Q382 frag. 16.2; 4Q458 frag. 2, 2.6; 4Q521 frag. 2 4, 2.1; 4Q521 frag. 7.3; 4QFlor 1.10–13; 4QPat 3–4.

10. Messianic Son of God references include: 1QSa (1Q28b); 4Q174 (4QFlor) 1.10–12; 4Q246 1.9; 2.1 and 4Q369; *1 En.* 105.2; *4 Ezra* 7.28–29; 13.32, 37, 52; 14.9.

11. Collins, *The Star and the Scepter*, 3–14, esp. 12; Marv Pate (*Communities of the Last Days*, 107–32) follows him in this analysis to an abbreviated fashion.

12. For branch of David texts: 4Q161 frag. 7–10.iii.22; 4Q174 frag. 1–3.i.11; 4QpIsa. frag. 7–10 iii 22; 4QCommentary on Genesis A 5.3–4; 4Q252 frag. 1 v. 3–4; 4Q285 frag. 5.3–4; *Pss. Sol.* 17.4, 21, 27–36; 18.7.

13. 4Q174 3.11–13 initially translated by WAC, 228, but corrected by VanderKam and Flint, *Meaning of the Dead Sea Scrolls*, 265 and 450, ch. 11 n. 7.

14. Additional texts speak of this messiah as the prince of the congregation (CD 7.19–20; 1QSb 5.20; 1QM 3.16; 5.1; 4Q496 frag. 10.3–4 (1QM 3.11–15); 4Q161 frags. 2–6.ii.17; 4QTestim 9:13; 1QM 11:6; 4Q285 frag. 4.2, 6; 5.4; 6.2; 4Q376 frag. 1.iii.1, 3; 4QpIsaiah 2:6.2:15; *Jub.* 31.18; *Sib. Or.* 3.469) and the Davidic "Messiah of Israel" (CD 12:23—13:1; 14:19; 19:10–11; 20.1; 1QS 9:11, 16; 10:11; 1QSa 2:11–22).

kingdom of His people," which, as Collins observes, is heavily indebted to Isaiah 11:

> To dispense justice with [equity to the oppressed] of the land (Isa 11:4a). [May you smite the peoples] with the might of your hand and ravage the earth with your scepter; may you bring death to the ungodly with the breath of your lips! (Isa 11:4b) . . . and everlasting might, the spirit of knowledge and of the fear of God (Isa 11:2); may righteousness be the girdle [of your loins] and may your reins be girded [with faithfulness] (Isa 11:5).[15]

Such a reign of messiah sometimes has him referred to as "the scepter."[16] In fact, the sectarian perspective of Qumran means that the Davidic messiah would destroy that portion of Israel that would not align themselves with the Qumran community.[17] This judgment to establish the kingdom is also presented by *1 Enoch* as occurring by Daniel's Son of Man.

> On that day all the kings and the mighty and the exalted, and those who possess the earth, will stand up; and they will see and recognize how he sits on the throne of his glory, and righteous are judged in righteousness before him, and no idle word is spoken before him. And pain will come upon them as upon a woman in labor . . . And pain will take hold of them, when they see that Son of Man sitting on the throne of his glory.[18]

This deliverance will entail a judgment and then a celebration of cleansing to prepare for the kingdom. The Qumran text known as *The War of the Messiah* (4Q285 fragment 5) comments upon Isaiah 10:34—11:1 developing the effectiveness of the shoot of Jesse to begin the kingdom.

> [This is the] Branch of David. Then [all forces of Belial] shall be judged, [and the king of the Kittim shall stand for judgment] and the Leader of the congregation—the Bra[nch of David]— will have him put to death. [Then all Israel shall come out with timbrel]s and dancers, and the [High] Priest shall order [them to cleanse their bodies from the guilty blood of the c]orpse[s of] the Kittim.[19]

15. Collins, *The Star and the Scepter*, 60-61.
16. CD 7.19-20=4Q266 frag. 3.iv.9; 1QSb 5.27-28; 4Q161 frags. 2-6.ii.17.
17. 1QM with 1QS 1:23-24; 2:14-17; 9:16.
18. *1 En.* 62.4-5; and in 52.4 this messiah is called the Anointed One; 4Q382 frag. 16 2.
19. 4Q285 fragment 5 translated by WAC, 293, but corrected VanderKam and Flint, *Meaning of the Dead Sea Scrolls*, 266, and 451, ch. 11 n. 11; cf. *Pss. Sol.* 17.4, 21-36; 18.5-7; 4QpIsa^a frags.7-10 iii 22-29 and echoed in 1QSb 5.21-26, *4 Ezra* 13.2-10;

The Qumran text 4Q252 fragment 1, 5:1-5, commenting on Genesis 49:10, develops the messiah as the branch of David who reigns forever.

> A ruler shall [no]t depart from the tribe of Judah when Israel has dominion. [And] the one who sits on the throne of David [shall never] be cut off, because the "ruler's staff" is the covenant of the kingdom, [and the thous]ands of Israel are "the feet," until the Righteous Messiah, the Branch of David, has come. For to him and to his seed the covenant of the kingdom of His people has been given for the everlasting generations, because he has kept . . . the Law with the men of the *Yahad*.[20]

The Qumran manuscript *Messianic Apocalypse* identifies these Jewish expectations for a kingly messiah to bring in a kingdom program that meets real needs.[21]

> [the hea]vens and the earth will listen to his messiah, and none therein will stray from the commandments of the holy ones.
> Seekers of the Lord, strengthen yourselves in his service!
> All you hopeful in [your] heart, will you not find the Lord in this?
> For the Lord will consider the pious, and call the righteous by name.
> Over the poor his spirit will hover and will renew the faithful with His power.
> And he will glorify the pious on the throne of the eternal kingdom,
> He who liberates the captives, restores sight to the blind, straightens the b[ent].
> And the Lord will accomplish glorious things which have never been
> . . .
> For he will heal the wounded, and revive the dead and bring good news to the poor.
> This reign of the Lord's anointed one will have heaven and earth obeying Him, benefited by him in kingdom and fellowshipping before him forever.[22]

Matt 2:23; Acts 13:23; Rom 15:12; Heb 7:14; Rev 5:5; 22:16; Clement of Alexandria, *Strom.*5.6; *Paed.* 1.7; Justin Martyr, *Apol.* 1.32; *Dial. Tryph.* 87, Irenaeus, *Haer.* 3.17.1; 4.33.1 and probably 4Q285 5.1-6 and *T. Levi* 18.7.

20. 4Q252 fragment 1, 5:1-5 translated by WAC, 277, but corrected James VanderKam and Peter Flint, *The Meaning of the Dead Sea Scrolls*, 266; a similar point is made by 4Q521 column 2, and 4Q521 frag. 7.3.

21. 4Q521 as quoted in Vermes, *Jesus the Jew*; "Qumran Forum Miscellanea I," *JJS* 43(1992): 303-4; Puech, " Une apocalypse messianique"; Similar sentiments are echoed by Maimonides, *Thirteen Principles of the Faith*, no. 12; *Yad haHazaqa* contained in Patai, *The Messiah Texts* 323-27.

22. 4Q521 frag. 2, 4.ii.1; 1QSa 2.14-15, 20-21.

This left Israel with an expectancy for a coming Davidic king. With the Maccabean failure, and especially that of Judas Maccabeus in 164 BC, another was expected. Pompey conquered Israel for Rome in 63 BC which fostered a sense that the Davidic king could come at any time, perhaps prompted by reflection on Daniel 2 and 7. For example, shortly after Pompey's capture of Jerusalem in 63 BC the *Psalms of Solomon* celebrates the expected Davidic messiah.

> Behold, O Lord, and raise up unto them their king, the son of David,
> At the time in which thou sees, O God, that he may reign over Israel thy servant.
> And gird him with strength, that he may shatter unrighteous rulers,
> And that he may purge Jerusalem from the nations that trample her down to destruction.[23]

Matthew identifies the messiah by having angels, magi, priests, Herod, and the blind acknowledge that emergent Jesus was anticipated to be a sign-child Davidic king (Matt 1:23; 2:5–6; Mic 5:2). Other NT authors also identify Jesus as the Davidic covenant king already, with a greater extent of his reign in the future (Heb 1:5, 8–13; Acts 2:25–36; 13:33–38). However, much of the Isaiah expectation of a messianic Davidic king on earth reigning in kingdom has not been realized by the time that this author writes this chapter.

---

23. *Ps. Sol.* 17.23–25.

CHAPTER 12

Servant of Yahweh

THE "SERVANT OF YAHWEH" from the servant songs is a trusted envoy and prophet who provides atonement (Isa 42:1–11; 49:1–7; 50:4–11; 52:13—53:12; and maybe 61:1–3). Often Isaiah 61:1–3 is not included because there is no mention of the word "servant" ('*bd*) in that text. The term "servant" ('*bd*) is used in several ways throughout Isaiah including for generic servants (Isa 24:2; 22:20), generic witnesses such as Isaiah (Isa 43:10; 44:26; 50:10; 54:17), the Assyrian general Rabshakeh (Isa 36:9), Hezekiah and his ambassadors Eliam, Shebna, and Joah (Isa 37:24; 36:11; 37:5), and David (Isa 37:35). However, in the four servant songs it refers to a spiritually instructed individual in the midst of sinful and blind Israel (Isa 42:1, 19; 53:9). This servant in the servant songs is an individual who trusts Yahweh throughout discouragement and suffers for other's sins, of which he is innocent (Isa 42:1; 49:3, 4, 5, 6, 7; 50:10; 52:13; 53:4–6, 9–11). This means that the servant in the servant songs is not Israel corporately because they are spiritually deaf and dumb, doubting Yahweh in discouragement and suffering for their own sins, thus needing Yahweh's redemption (Isa 14:2; 20:3; 40:27; 41:8; 42:19; 44:1–2, 21; 48:20; 45:4; 56:6; 65:8–15; 66:14). The concept of "servant" ('*bd*) in the servant songs is one who is chosen for a special ministry by God (Isa 42:1). The regal description of the servant "prohibits an understanding of 'servant' as slave or lackey, but determines its meaning as 'trusted envoy' or 'confidential representative.'"[1]

---

1. Williams, "Poems about Incomparable Yahweh's Servant," 75.

Many identifications have been attempted concerning the servant of the servant songs. Antti Laato identifies Cyrus as the servant[2] because he is named in the text of Isaiah, even though Cyrus is never called a "servant" (*'bd*) by Isaiah—instead he is called "shepherd" (*r'*, Isa 44:28) and "anointed" or "messiah" (*mšyḥw*, Isa 45:1). Bo Lim analyzed and distinguished between these two figures, clearly delineating them.[3] Klaus Baltzer developed that this servant of Yahweh might be Moses[4] because of the prominence of the exodus theme, but Moses is never mentioned in Isaiah as servant (*'bd*). By extrapolation, some consider the servant to be a new Moses figure, fostering the new exodus, but Isaiah develops the concept with categories that extend beyond any Mosaic description, especially with regard to atonement. For example, J. G. McConville identifies the servant as Ezra, who leads an exodus from Babylon.[5] John Goldingay identifies Josiah and Zerubbabel as this servant because they also lead to a new exodus from Babylon.[6] None of these named figures are presented by Isaiah as a righteous servant, who trusts Yahweh throughout discouragement, suffering and redeeming others from their sins, of which he is innocent (Isa 42:1; 49:3, 4, 5, 6, 7; 50:10; 52:13; 53:4-6, 9-11). Qumran noticed these features and even changed aspects of the servant in 1QIsa and 4Q541 from the MT to be more ultimately messianic with regard to offering himself as an atonement for humanity.[7]

The servant of Yahweh was chosen by God before he was born (Isa 42:1, 6; 49:1).[8] The LXX identifies that Yahweh's servant is an ideal "Jacob" or "Israel" by adding both of these names (LXX: Isa 42:1).[9] The LXX assumes Yahweh's initial choice and forming of Israel (the point of MT Isa 42:1, 6) and adds that God will come alongside his servant with divine help (LXX: Isa 42:1, 6). Yahweh's prediction and guarantee of the servant's effective role in bringing about kingdom salvation is grounded upon incomparable

---

2. Laato, *The Servant of YHWH and Cyrus*, 45-46.

3. Lim, *The "Way of the Lord,"* 74-88.

4. Baltzer, *Deutero-Isaiah*, 124-37 and repeatedly through the commentary as a major theme.

5. McConville, "Ezra-Nehemiah and the Fulfillment of Prophecy," 217-19.

6. Goldingay, *The Message of Isaiah 40-55*, 150.

7. 1QIsa 52:14 replaces the MT "marring" (*mšḥt*) with a Qal singular "I have anointed," indicating that God established the sacrifice role for his messiah, and 1QIsa 51:5 replaces the MT first person "My righteousness" with a third person "His arm," also indicating messianism, also 4Q541 9.1.1.2 "he will atone" (Hengel and Bailey, "The Effective History of Isaiah 53," 101, 103, 108, 146).

8. Outside the servant songs Israel is described as called from the womb (Isa 41:8; 43:10; 43:11; 44:1-2, 21, 24; 45:4; 48:12).

9. Ekblad, *Isaiah's Servant Poems*, 59. Such names further argue against viewing the servant as historically past Moses, contra Baltzer.

Yahweh (Isa 42:9). To facilitate this kingdom salvation, Yahweh placed his spirit on the servant, anointing him as a "messiah" and delighting in him (Isa 42:1; perhaps 11:2–3 and 61:1).[10] This servant will not be loud or boisterous as he faithfully works for justice (Isa 42:2–3, 6). As a humble prophet, Yahweh's servant is teachable to grow into a clear spokesman who will bring salvation and the proper order to the earth (Isa 42:1–4; 50:2). Extending this, Qumran understood that the messiah would teach the Law as the "teacher of righteousness" (Isa 42:4).[11] Furthermore, rabbinic Jews anticipated the messiah to teach the Law in an internalized new covenant form.[12] Matthew presents Jesus as teaching the Law in this prophetic new covenant fashion (Matt 5). Even contemporary and rabbinic Jews identify that Jesus taught the Law in a new covenant form.[13] However, Judaism rejected Jesus' teaching as dangerous because Jesus' healing and exorcism ministry was so effective in leading some Jews astray into Christianity (John 11:48–50).[14]

Additionally, Matthew 12:18–20 applies Isaiah 42:1–4 as fulfilled in Jesus' withdrawing from conflict with the Pharisees to facilitate kingdom ministry, even to provoke gentiles to hope. That is, the prophetic individual who is Yahweh's servant will be "a covenant to the people, as a light to the nations" (Isa 42:6; 49:6). Not that Israel, nor Moses, would have a global evangelistic role, but Yahweh's servant will include the nations within the kingdom salvation plan. Luke extends this idea at Jesus' presentation and his cleansing in the temple as a baby, and Simeon praised God that he saw Jesus as the future salvation of Israel and gentiles (Luke 2:25–33 with 2:32 quoting Isa 42:6). Isaiah's servant regularly begins each day meditating on the faithful sustaining message of Yahweh (Isa 50:4–5). The servant's speech is Yahweh's select arrow or sharp sword to hit the target of people's heart issues (Isa 49:2).[15] The servant's prophetic speech encourages the weary with hope

---

10. The spirit of Yahweh was also placed on Israel outside the servant songs (Isa 44:3), but they were sinful, so they suffered for their own sins (Isa 40:2). In the NT the Holy Spirit also came upon Jesus to equip him for divinely empowered ministry (Matt 3:16; 12:28; Mark 1:10; 9:40; Luke 3:22; 4:18; 11:20; John 1:32–33; 3:2; 9:33; 10:38; 14:10; Acts 2:22; *Gos. Hebrews* 2; *Gos. Ebionites* 4.2).

11. 4Q174 1.11–12; CD 6.7; 7:18–19; 4QFlor 1.6–11; 4QTestim 13–17; 4Q541; 4QpPs (4Q171) 3:13–16; 1QpHab 1.13; 2:2, 8–9; 5:10; 7:4–5; 11:5; CD 1.11; 20.1, 28, 32.

12. *Gen. Rab.* 98.9; *Eccl. Rab.* 11.1; *Mid. Tanh., Ki Tavo,* par. 4; Midrash fragment, *BhM* 6.151–52; *Halakbot G'dolot*, ed. Hildesheimer, 223 top; Azulai, *Hesed l'Avraham* 13c-14a; Vital, *Sefer haHezyonot*, 160; *Mid. Talpiyot* 58a; Yemenite Midrash, 349–50; Yitzhaq of Berdichev, *Imre Tzaddiqim*, ed. Tz'vi Hasid, 10 [5b].

13. Josephus, *Ant.* 18.63–64; *b. 'Abod. Zar.* 17 1/t; *Hul.* 2.24; *Qol. Rab.* 1.8[3].

14. Josephus, *Ant.* 18.63–64; *b. Sanh.* 103a; *b. Ber.* 17b; *b. Sanh.* 107b; 43a; 67b; *b. Sotah* 47a; *Sib. Or.* 8.206–7.

15. Perhaps this sharp sword imagery is utilized for Christ by Rev 1:16; 2:12, 16.

(Isa 50:4). The servant's role extends to kingdom miracles rescuing the blind and prisoners from their respective darkness (Isa 42:7, also true of 61:1).[16] Yahweh guarantees this salvation to preserve his honor and to rescue the nations from idolatry (Isa 42:8–9).

The servant epitomized Israel in being the ideal as well as summing them up as their corporate personality head (Isa 49:3 and LXX 42:1). The concept of corporate personality is essentially the idea that no human is an individual by himself; all exist within the community which provides essential dimensions of human life. Scott identifies that "the group—whether family, clan or nation—was looked upon as a corporate unity or as a person; on the other hand, the individual member of the group was considered as a representative of the whole."[17] Blocher explains this concept as applied to the servant as representing Israel.

> They instituted head communities. The head sums up or represents the whole, yet it cannot be mistaken for the body, not even in a kind of vague, fluid dialectic between the two. It is the head, not the body. And yet, at the same time, the body is nothing without the head, and the head truly expresses the body. Now the Servant seems to be the head of Israel, the head of that community which he is to redeem and restore.[18]

In this case, the servant is part of the community and stands above it as the ideal. Delitzsch developed a pyramid that Henri Blocher used to aptly illustrates this principle.

> The scope of God's redemptive dealings with man seems to grow narrower and narrower. God starts, as it were, with the whole human race, first at the time of Adam, and then again after the Flood. Then one line of the human race is chosen: God makes his covenant with Abraham and his descendants: only Isaac and his line are chosen—Isaac, not Ishmael. Even among Isaac's children, only one—Jacob, not Esau—is chosen. And then getting narrower, the prophets make it clear that not all those who descend from Israel (Jacob) are truly Israel. Only a remnant will inherit the promise. But where is this remnant when we look for

---

Outside the servant songs Israel is also identified as having a mouth of sharp sword (Isa 59:21) and being concealed and obscure (Isa 51:16).

16. Jesus healed blind in fulfillment of this prophecy (Matt 8:9:27–31; 11:5; 12:22; 15:30–31; 20:34; 21:14–15; Mark 8:22–25; 10:42; Luke 4:19; 11:14; 18:42–43; John 9:11; Pilate letter to Claudius contained in *Acts of Peter and Paul* 40–42 and Tertullian, *Apol.* 5.21; b. Sanh. 107b; 104b; 43a; 67b; b. Soṭah 47a; Sib. Or. 8.206–7).

17. Scott, "Exegetical and Theological Study of Isaiah," 65 n. 19.

18. Blocher, *Songs of the Servant*, 41.

it? When God looks for a man to intervene and establish justice in the land he finds none (Isa 59:16; Ezek 22:30). Ultimately only one person remains after the sifting process, only one truly Israel, in whom God is glorified. And he said so. He said quite clearly, "I am the true Israel." He used the Old Testament's most common symbol for Israel; the vine: "I am the true vine" (John 15:1–7; cf. Ps 80:8–16; Isa 5:1–7; Jer 2:21; 6:9; Hos 10:1; see also Matt 21:33–43 and parallels). In him the pyramid reaches its apex.[19]

The messianic servant is the ideal Israel, who fulfills all that Israel was to fulfill and who authors the salvation that Israel and the Gentiles shall experience in abundance (Isa 42:1–4; 49:1–13; Matt 12:18–20).

The servant will be given by Yahweh to himself as a new covenant to the people of Israel and as a light to the nations (Isa 42:6; 49:8, LXX 49:6). Young identifies that the servant in being the covenant provides all the blessings of the covenant.

> To say that the Servant is a covenant is to say that all the blessings of the covenant are embodied in, have their root and origin in, and are dispensed by him. At the same time he is himself at the center of all those blessings, and to receive them is to receive him, for without him there can be no blessings.[20]

The NT applies this covenant role of the servant in Jesus' Last Supper cup as it commemorates Jesus' giving himself in death and resurrection as the "blood of the covenant" that provides everlasting forgiveness and looks toward kingdom (Matt 26:28; Mark 14:24; Luke 22:20; 1 Cor 11:25). From this covenant, the servant effects for Israel the salvation of the people Israel (Isa 42:6–7; 49:8–9; Jer 31:33–40) and salvation of the land of Israel (Isa 49:8; Jer 31:33–40; Acts 3:20–25; Rom 9:4; 11:26–27; Heb 11:15). Through the new covenant, Yahweh the creator guarantees his servant's mission, providing strength to accomplish salvation (Isa 42:5–9; 49:5). This new covenant transformation empowers with internal new covenant spirit to facilitate believers to walk in Yahweh's re-creation. The servant will be protected by Yahweh to show forth God's glory and be a new covenant for regathering his people Israel to himself and will also extend salvation light to the nations (Isa 42:6; 49:3, 5–6).

Also, Paul argued for a synergism working with God for salvation and ministry by quoting Isaiah 49:8 which identified that the favorable time of

---

19. Blocher, *Songs of the Servant*, 41–42; Young, "Of Whom Speaketh the Prophet," 136.

20. Young, *The Book of Isaiah*, 3:120–21.

salvation is at hand in applying Jesus' ministry into the Corinthian Christians' lives (2 Cor 6:2). Such cooperation insured that God's grace was not in vain.

Unfortunately, Yahweh's servant was rejected by his own people, disheartening him from immediately seeing the rewards of kingdom until later when Yahweh will bring about justice for his servant (Isa 49:4; 53:10–12). This Jewish rejection of the servant will likely include the servant being beaten on his back, part of his beard being torn out, with accusers spitting on him (Isa 50:6; also 53:5, 10), which are similar abuses done to Jesus at his trials and mockings (Matt 26:67; 27:26, 30; Mark 15:19; Luke 22:63; John 19:1). That is, Yahweh's servant was despised by Israel even though Yahweh's evaluation of him is that he is Israel's redeemer and holy one (Isa 49:7;[21] 52:14; 53:3).

The righteous servant declares that by his being rejected while trusting Yahweh, he learned to comfort the weary (Isa 50:4–9). The servant was condemned by people who will wear out and was reassured that ultimately Yahweh would prevent him from being disgraced because Yahweh would vindicate him. Furthermore, Yahweh applies the lessons from his servant's experience to others by reminding believers to live by faith, while unbelievers are warned about judgment (Isa 50:10–11).

In early Judaism, eschatological atonement was expected through the messiah's priestly ministry.[22] One possibility of this eschatological atonement

---

21. Ekblad, *Isaiah's Servant Poems*, 84, 113 understands φαυλίζοντα to refer to the servant despising his own life, but the verb is active rather than middle so it is better to understand it as in agreement with the MT, namely that "others despise" the servant. Additionally, Ἁγιάσατε is taken by him to be a command to sanctify the servant, but such an aorist indicative could also describe the "holy one" of Israel, consistent with the MT construct noun.

22. 1QS text 7 1.19; 11QMelch 12.7–8; 4Q541; *1 En.* 39.4–6; 41.2; 48.1–4; 51.4–5; 61.4; 62.14; *T. Levi* 18; Kennard, *Messiah Jesus*, 302–5; Pate and Kennard discuss other possible allusions Paul may have made to Isaiah 52–53 (*Deliverance Now and Not Yet*, 173–76). Some of these claimed allusions (such as Rom 4:25 "justification" as reflecting Isaiah 53:11 "justify") only work on the level of the Vulgate or English text; neither the MT nor the LXX have any similarity in phrase or theology to that of Paul unless viewed through a lens of LXX Ps 105:31 or MT Ps 106:31 (Kennard, *Biblical Covenantalism*, 3:43–52, esp. 48–49). An important issue that emerges is whether or not pre-Christian Judaism expected a suffering messiah. Those who say yes include Cullmann, *Christology of the New Testament*, 55–56, 60; Lohse, *Märtyrer und Gottesknecht*, 104; Knohl, *Messiah before Jesus*, 90–91, 96–101; Joachim Jeremias, "παῖς θεοῦ," *TDNT* 5:677–717. Jeremias summarizes the evidence for the messianic interpretation of the Isaianic servant in Palestinian Judaism: 1) this interpretation was confined to Isaiah 42:1–9; 43:10; 49:1–2 and 6–7; and 52:13—53:12; that 2) in relation to Isaiah 42:1–9 and 52:13—53:12, the messianic understanding is "constant from pre-Christian times"; and 3) the messianic interpretation of the passion sayings of Isaiah 53 can be traced back at least

was through the concept of Isaiah's "servant of the Lord" providing an atonement through his own sacrificial death (Isa 53). Yahweh promises to exalt his servant because he voluntarily provided a "substitutionary atonement," having *died as a vicarious sacrifice on behalf of guilty people* to cleanse and save them (Isa 52:13-15). Isaiah has Israel respond in a confession of their sin and belief in the servant's atoning death (Isa 53:1-9; Zech 12:10-11). Israel's confession probably takes place as the servant is honored in kingdom, so it appears to be eschatological in kingdom. This confession fits the pattern of the servant offering himself as purification and guilt offering *on their behalf*, thus "vicarious atonement." Because of the effectiveness of the "guilt" (MT) or "sin" (LXX) offering by the servant, the servant will be blessed with a continuing inheritance (Isa 53:10-12).

The concept of a dying and rising god has antecedents in ancient Near Eastern religions. In Canaanite Tammuz myth there is a god who dies and rises, and the king is a divine substitute on behalf of the people, pictured with figures of a shepherd and a lamb (similar to Isa 53:6-7). In this ritual, the high priest struck the king on the cheek and pulled his ear as a part of the ritual distortion of his appearance (perhaps alluded to in Isa 52:14). Tammuz is stricken with suffering in lamentation, carried to the place of imprisonment like a criminal, and dies, thereafter given a dishonorable burial.[23] This myth bears some resemblance to the servant's death, but Yahweh polemicizes it and overrules those carrying it out by giving the servant a rich man's burial (Isa 53:9). Furthermore, the Babylonian *Ras Shamra* myth

---

with a high degree of probability to the pre-Christian period, though not with the same certainty. Hengel and Bailey strengthen the case with Qumran scrolls possibly present before Jesus, for 1QIsa 52:14 has "I have anointed" indicating that God established the sacrifice role for his messiah, and 1QIsa 51:5 has "his arm" also indicating messianism, also 4Q541 9.1.1.2 "he will atone" ("Effective History of Isaiah 53," 101, 103, 108, 146). Strack and Billerbeck (*Kommentar zum Neuen Testament*, 2:273-99) say that the "Old Synagogue" also knew of "a suffering Messiah, for of whom no death was determined, i.e. the messiah ben David" and a "dying Messiah, of whom no suffering was mentioned," the messiah ben Joseph (Strack and Billerbeck, *Kommentar zum Neuen Testament*, 2:273-24). Yet when it cites the passages of the suffering Messiah ben David from rabbinic literature, they are all late texts (Strack and Billerbeck, *Kommentar zum Neuen Testament*, 2:282-91) For example, later *Tg. Ps.-J.* the "servant" of Isaiah 52:13 is identified as "the messiah": "See, my servant, the messiah, shall prosper; he will be exalted, great, very mighty," and 53:10c is made to read, "They will look upon the kingdom of their messiah, many sons and daughters will be theirs." Those who do not think that this is pre-Christian Judaism giving evidence of a suffering messiah expectation include: Hooker, *Jesus and the Servant*, 56-67; Strack and Billerbeck, *Kommentar zum Neuen Testament*, 2:273-74; Menard, "*Pais Theou* as a Messianic Title," esp. 84-85; Longenecker, *Christology of Early Jewish Christianity*, 105; Fitzmyer, *Luke X-XXIV*, 156-66.

23. Engnell, "The 'Ebed Yahweh' Songs and the Suffering Messiah," 57, 78-79, 84; Ringgren, *Messiah in the Old Testament*, 45-46.

has Baal as a dying and rising god, exalted after his death. Baal is put in the grave by Anat, who later resurrects him and restores him to his throne. This, too, Yahweh polemicizes, showing this servant to be superior; for while Baal needed memorial sacrifices offered at his burial, the servant's death was the actual atonement for the sins of others.[24] Furthermore, the Isaiah servant is sinless; these other pagan gods are not (Isa 53:9). In contrast to these mythological beings resisting their suffering and death, the servant suffers voluntarily in obedience to Yahweh's will (Isa 50:5-6; 53:7; perhaps Matt 26:42, 52-53), setting his face like flint toward Jerusalem and the suffering (Isa 50:7; Luke 9:51).

Differing interpretations of the suffering servant in Isaiah 53 are reflected in the translations, however David A. Sapp and Otto Betz present convincing cases for the following development: 1) MT—the servant's afflictions and death are portrayed as vicariously atoning, 2) the LXX tones down the servant's suffering (he does not die, but is divinely rescued), almost to the point of being representative atoning, and 3) *Tg. Pseudo-Jonathan* removes the suffering from the servant messiah and identifies that Israel's enemies instead will die.[25] This reinterpretation makes Israel's enemies become the sacrifice of atonement, perhaps through the lens of Isaiah 43:3 redemption by providing Egypt or Cush in Israel's place. There is perhaps an "Isaac Typology" (based on Genesis 22:1-14) that lies behind Isaiah 53, and its influence is to be seen in early Judaism and also throughout the New Testament where the motif of suffering and death in an atoning and vicarious sense emerges.[26] Sometimes adherents of a pre-Christian origin of the suffering messiah appeal to three texts thought to be important exceptions to the rule: *4 Ezra* 7:28-30; *Targum Isaiah* 53; and the "Pierced Messiah" text (4Q285). The first mentions the death of the messiah as the climax of the temporal messianic kingdom. However, it is important to note that there the messiah does not suffer; rather, after having lived long and well for four hundred years, he simply dies with the rest of humanity. His death,

---

24. Hyatt, "Sources of the Suffering Servant Idea," 83.

25. For numbers 1 and 2 see Sapp, "The LXX, 1QIsa, and MT Versions of Isaiah 53"; while Otto Betz treats the *Targum*, "Jesus and Isaiah 53," in Bellinger and Farmer, *Jesus and the Suffering Servant*, 70-87, esp. 73. One example of this shift is evident in Isa 52:14 "many were horrified" becomes replaced in the targum by "the house of Israel waited for him many days." Chilton, *The Glory of Israel*, 35.

26. For an explanation of and an apologetic for an "Isaac Typology," see Wood, "Isaac Typology in the New Testament"; Daly, "Soteriological Significant of the Sacrifice of Isaac"; Gubler, *Die Frühesten Deutungen des Todes Jesu*, 336-75. Rosenberg, "Jesus, Isaac and the Suffering Servant"; Riesenfeld, *Jesus Transfiguré*, 86-96; Strack and Billerbeck, *Kommentar zum Neuen Testament aus Talmud und Midrash*, 3:746; Vermes, *Scripture and Tradition in Judaism*, 193-97, 217-27; Schoeps, *Paul*, 141-49.

therefore, has no apparent theological significance. Likewise, the Aramaic translation (*Targum*) of Isaiah 53 is not evidence for the concept of a suffering messiah when it transposed (probably in reaction to Christianity) the afflictions of the suffering servant of Isaiah 53 *from* the messiah *to* Israel or the surrounding Gentile nations. Moreover, both texts are dated after the birth of Christ and cannot be used as testimony for pre-Christian Jewish messianic understanding. With regard to the pierced messiah text, it cannot for grammatical reasons be invoked to support the idea of a suffering messiah.[27] Thus that text should read, "The leader of the community [the Prince of the Congregation] will kill him [the leader of the Kittim]." N. T. Wright's comments represent a fair-minded solution to the issue:

> There was not such a thing as a straightforward pre-Christian Jewish belief in an Isaianic "servant of YHWH" who, perhaps as Messiah, would suffer and die to make atonement for Israel or for the world. But there was something else, which literally dozens of texts attest: a large-scale and widespread belief, to which Isaiah 40–55 made a substantial contribution, that Israel's present state of suffering was somehow held within the ongoing divine purpose; that in due time this period of woe would come to an end, with divine wrath falling instead on the pagan nations that had oppressed Israel (and perhaps on renegades within Israel herself); that the explanation for the present state of affairs had to do with Israel's own sin, for which either she, or in some cases her righteous representatives, was or were being punished; and that this suffering and punishment would therefore, somehow, hasten the moment when Israel's tribulation would be complete, when she would finally have been purified from her sin so that her exile could be undone at last. There was, in other words, a belief, hammered out not in abstract debate but in and through poverty, exile, torture and martyrdom, that Israel's sufferings might be, not merely a state *from* which she would, in YHWH's good time, be redeemed, but paradoxically, under certain circumstances and in certain senses, part of the means *by* which that redemption would be affected.[28]

Yahweh promised to exalt his servant because he voluntarily provided a "substitutionary atonement," having *died as a vicarious sacrifice on behalf of guilty people* to cleanse and save them (Isa 52:13–15). Such substitutionary atonement is evident in that the servant will "sprinkle" many nations (Isa 52:15) after the pattern of atonement being accomplished wherever the

---

27. Schiffman, *Reclaiming the Dead Sea Scrolls*, 346.
28. Wright, *Jesus and the Victory of God*, 591.

blood is applied (Exod 24:6, 8; Ps 51:7 [MT: 51:8] "hyssop" to sprinkle).[29] Yahweh promises to exalt his servant because the servant will wisely accomplish this through his own wisdom (Isa 52:13 especially emphasized in LXX; 53:11).[30]

While the MT acknowledged that many were appalled at the servant's disfiguring, the point that the LXX emphasized was that the servant was not glorified among humans (Isa 52:14). So maybe the point is not the severity of marring (a possible way to take MT Isa 52:14) as much as the incongruity of abuse of someone Yahweh highly values (Isa 52:13) when so many humans view him in a de-honored manner (LXX Isa 52:14, and another way to take comparative *m* of the MT; repeated as the point of 53:3a and b).[31]

Israel responds in a confession of their sin and belief in the servant's atoning death (Isa 53:1-9; Zech 12:10-11). Israel's report reflects their confusion that they thought of the servant as a "sapling" barely breaking ground from its "root," or as LXX reframes to be a "child" or "little servant" (Isa 53:2). Israel admits that there was no splendor or beauty in the servant to call attention to him.[32] In fact, Isaiah has Israel confessing that they despised[33] the servant and did not really know him (Isa 53:3). Their growing perception eventually included the realization that the servant was the effective weapon-wielding arm of Yahweh (Isa 51:1). With such high regard for the servant, Israel's confession probably takes place as the servant is honored in eschatological kingdom. This public confession fits the pattern of testifying to the situation surrounding a guilt offering (Lev 5:1 with MT Isa 53:10). The servant offered himself as the agent[34] of purification and guilt offering *on their behalf*, thus "vicarious atonement." The atonement was broad as to include physical, emotional, spiritual, and covenantal sickness and pain, including a remedy for covenant violation (Isa 53:4-5). Because of the effectiveness of the "guilt" (MT) or "sin" (LXX) offering by *the servant, the servant will be blessed with a continuing inheritance* (Isa 53:10-12).

29. MT and Vulgate have "sprinkle," which the Syriac retains as meaning "purify," though LXX deviates to "wonder" and targums to "scatter"; Oswalt, *The Book of Isaiah: Chapters 40-66*, 374.

30. The causation is evident in the *Hiphil* imperative and the causal adverb (Waltke and O'Connar, *Introduction to Biblical Hebrew Syntax*, 668).

31. Oswalt, *The Book of Isaiah: Chapters 40-66*, 379; Goldingay and Payne, *Isaiah 40-55*, 2:292-93.

32. Sapp, "The LXX, 1QIsa, and MT Versions of Isaiah 53," 191, identifies that 1QIsa^a has them seeing and not desiring themselves instead of the servant.

33. The *Niphal* passive participle expresses the result of the subject's own action (Davidson, *Hebrew Syntax*, 137 sect. 100 R 7).

34. Isa 53:3-5, 11 provide examples of genitive of agency and *lamed* of agency (Waltke and O'Connor, *Introduction to Biblical Hebrew Syntax*, 210, 617).

Isaiah presents Israel understanding that the human abuse and death of the servant was ultimately because Yahweh placed Israel's iniquity and covenant curse upon the servant as a vicarious substitutionary atonement as an expression of guilt or a purification offering (Isa 53:3–6, 10). Especially in Isaiah 53:4, the people declare that God smites the servant. The basic root *nkh* usually means "striking" or "violent killing" in OT and early Jewish contexts (Exod 21:12; Num 35:11, 15; Isa 14:6; 66:3)[35] unless the object of the beating does not kill, like Balaam's staff (Num 22:23–32). Thus, the emphasis is "violent killing" but the term does not essentially mean killing. The Hophal passive participle *mkh* (smitten) in Isaiah 53:4 when used as coming from God is identified by emphasis as *smiting with covenant curse* broadly in the OT, early Judaism, and in Isaiah (Lev 26:21; Num 11:33; Deut 28:59; Isa 1:6;[36] 10:26; 27:7; 30:26; 53:4).[37] However, in Ezekiel, God claps (*nkh*) his hands together and no covenant curse is conveyed (Ezek 21:14 [MT: 21:19], 17 [MT: 21:22]; 22:13), showing that the term from God does not essentially mean death by covenant curse. However, Israel confesses their perception that God was striking the servant, which implies "penal atonement." Thus, by emphasis Israel's confession declares that the servant *receives the covenant curse from God* that would have come upon humans, resulting in the servant's death. This is a softer but compelling case for penal death here because the evidence splits as it expresses the confessed understanding of Israelites rather than a claim of reality or God's assessment.

The theological meaning of the servant's death is carried by the sacrificial terminology. The servant atones for many nations and Israel in their sin through the pattern of covenantal atonement (purification or "guilt offering" in MT, and "sin offering" in LXX). Responding to the servant's marred appearance, the divine assessment is that "he will sprinkle many nations" (Isa 52:14–15; *yzh*). Such a concept of corporate sprinkling indicates the establishment of a covenant and atonement forgiveness which accompanies this relationship (Exod 24:8; Heb 9:13; 1 Pet 1:2). To effect this atonement forgiveness, eschatological Israel confesses that they understood that the servant was cursed by God (Isa 53:4–6). The concept of divine curse might be considered if the servant is viewed as taking upon himself the cup of

---

35. J. Conrad, "נָכָה," *TDOT* 9:415–18; this term (*nkh*) if accomplished by humans does not carry the semantic field of covenant curse, merely "killing," which term in Zech 13:7 conveys that the Shepherd will be struck (*nkh*) by humans and his followers will scatter.

36. Perhaps Isa 1:6 *mkh* is self-inflicted wounds rather than covenant curse due to Israel's sins.

37. Covenant curse when from God: Cornelis Van Dam, "נָכָה," in *NIDOTT & E* 3:103–4; CD B 19.8; 4Q166 2.12; 4Q169 frag. 3–4 1.5; 11QTemple 55.6–8.

God's wrath (which is a penal imagery in the context, Isa 51:17, 22). However, if the crushing "to bear away sins" is viewed through the metaphor of the scapegoat at the Day of Atonement (Lev 16:20-22), then the servant provides vicarious but not penal sacrifice (Isa 51:17, 22; 53:4). In the Day of Atonement, the sins of the people are confessed upon the scapegoat to bear them away into the wilderness. This vicarious "bearing" of the people's sin is what the servant accomplishes (Isa 53:4, 10). *The servant's death propitiates our corporate iniquities, that is, to bring atonement and peace with God.* Such atonement and reconciliation are what one would expect as benefits from a *guilt offering* (Isa 53:10 MT identifies *'sm* as "guilt offering," though the LXX identifies it as a "sin offering," LXX: δῶτε περὶ ἁμαρτίας). In a Leviticus framework, these sacrifices would be vicarious but not penal as they avert covenant curse for Israelites.[38] There is no object taken, so no reparations are required, only Israel's conscious confession of their sin, which is in fact the voice of Isaiah 53:1, "Who has believed our message?" Isaiah presents this confession of corporate Israel as in the future kingdom era (Isa 52:7-10; 54:1-17). Presumably, individual Israelites could confess their sin earlier than that expression of kingdom and have the atonement benefits of the servant applied to them. John Oswalt describes this substitution sacrifice from Isaiah 53:4-6, 10-12.

> It is here and in vv. 10-12 that the issue of the substitutionary suffering of the servant, and thus his capacity to deliver his people, comes to the fore. He does not suffer merely as a result of the people, but in the people. He suffers *for* them, and because of that, they do not need to experience the results of their sins.[39]

As has been shown, the servant's substitutionary sacrifice is informed especially by the language of the cult, not a courtroom situation (especially Lev 5:1, 17; 10:17; 16:22; 17:16; 20:19; and Num 9:13; 14:34).

In Isaiah 53:5 the "piercing," "crushing," "chastening," and "scourging" are each metaphors of the death of the servant, along with "slaughter" and "cut off" of Isaiah 53:7-8. We should not focus on the "pierce" and "scourge" as though they were specifically descriptive of Roman scourging and spear-piercing on a cross, for neither was Rome present nor was this means of death being used in Isaiah's eighth century BC. For example, "scourging" (*bḥbrtw*) in Isaiah 53:5 simply means "stripe" or "blow" or "strike" as in Genesis 4:23. So the word has no conscious allusion to Roman scourging. Likewise, we

---

38. Kennard, *Biblical Covenantalism*, 1:293-303.

39. Oswalt, *Isaiah 40-66*, 385, and for contextual development 386-87, 401; for a discussion on a range of interpretations of Isaiah 53 see Pate and Kennard, *Deliverance Now and Not Yet*, 92-96.

should not ignore the other metaphorical terms, especially "crushing," which is repeated again when this is identified as a guilt offering (Isa 53:5 *mrk'*; 53:10 *dk'*). So, I take these terms as simply metaphors of the servant's death rather than specific predictions to be accomplished in his death.

The NT refers to Isaiah 53 directly in several places, but the amazing thing is that none of these references develop the atonement that Isaiah's servant of the Yahweh undertakes. For example, Matthew 8:17 describes the miracles accomplished by Christ the healer as he carries our infirmities (quoting Isa 53:4). John 12:38 acknowledges that no one believed the report about these miracles (quoting Isaiah 53:1). 1 Peter 2:22 indicates the silence that Jesus maintained before his accusers was a mimetic atonement pattern[40] for Christians to follow (quoting Isa 53:9). Luke 22:37 identifies (through Isaiah 53:12) that Jesus was to be classified with criminals. Acts 8:32-35 quotes some of the physical surroundings (such as Jesus being silent in his death) to recognize the servant's death as Jesus' death (quoting Isa 53:7-8). Paul makes two direct citations following the LXX and being rather dissimilar to the MT.[41] Isaiah 52:15b is quoted in Romans 15:21 and Isaiah 53:1a is quoted in Romans 10:16. Neither Pauline quote has Christological nor sacrificial value. Of these passages, only 1 Peter adds in the mimetic atonement context that Jesus "bore our sins in his body on the cross," with imagery of the Christians having strayed like sheep (1 Pet 2:24-25 probably alluding to Isa 53:4-6, 10). So at least Peter probably recognized that Isaiah 53 also describes Christ's death as vicarious substitutionary atonement, though his emphasis in the context is on instruction for servants suffering to follow Jesus in silent mimetic atonement (1 Pet 2:18-23). Additionally, with no clear statement using Isa 53 in the NT for vicarious atonement, the synoptic and Acts pattern identifies more with mimetic atonement. There is no mention of Isaianic servant atonement in Hebrews, but both Isaiah and Hebrews develop their views reflecting Mosaic covenant language.

---

40. Mimetic atonement is where an example sets a pattern to emulate. Such a view was common in early Judaism and Greco-Roman literature (Pate and Kennard, *Deliverance Now and Not Yet*, 22-71; 2 Macc 6.18-7.42; 4 Macc 10.10; 11.12, 20, 27; 16.24-25; 17.2, 11-12, 18; *Wis.* 3.5-6; 7.14; 11.19; 12.22; deaths of Socrates, Cato, Diogenes, Demonax, and Seneca: Seneca, *Epis.* 24.6-7; Epictetus, 4.1 168-72; Plutarch, *Tranq. An.* 475D-F 1.11; Tacitus, *Annals* 15.62; Seeley, *The Noble Death*).

41. Pate and Kennard discuss other possible allusions Paul may have made to Isaiah 52-53 (*Deliverance Now and Not Yet*, 173-76). Some of these claimed allusions (such as Romans 4:25 "justification" as reflecting Isa 53:11 "justify") only work on the level of Vulgate or English text; neither the MT nor the LXX have any similarity in phrase or theology to that of Paul.

In *1 Enoch* and some Qumran texts, the teaching about the Isaianiac suffering servant combine[42] with *Merkabah*[43] mysticism. *1 Enoch* joins mainstream Judaism in announcing the afflictions of the righteous are to be seen as mimetic atonement, especially at the culmination of the messianic woes.[44] In this context, the Son of Man as messiah[45] employs a representative role of suffering on behalf of the elect.[46] That is, the heavenly Son of Man appropriates to himself the afflictions of the elect so that the elect on earth may enjoy in heaven the glory of the Enochian Son of Man. This glory already exists in heaven,[47] but the public resurrection of the elect will vindicate them before the wicked.[48]

Meanwhile the teacher of righteousness viewed himself as Isaiah's suffering servant providing vicarious atonement for his community.[49] Thus, to

---

42. Pate and Kennard (*Deliverance Now and Not Yet*, 75–77) follow Nickelsburg (*Resurrection, Immortality, and Eternal Life*, 71–72) in connecting these imageries in contrast to Sjöberg's contentions (*Der Menschensohn im ältiopischen Henochbuch*, 116–39).

43. Since *merkabah* means "throne" or "chariot," in *merkabah* mysticism there is a presentation of a Jewish divine throne in a real divine temple in heaven simultaneously with that of God inhabiting the temple on earth. That is, both the heavenly and earthly temples are real and different things that may be occurring in these different realities. For example, the heavenly temple is normally thought to be where God's presence dwells (Isa 6:4), but the amazing thing is that with the cleansed tabernacle God dwells on earth, with the ark of the covenant serving as his throne (Exod 40:34–38). However, the uncleanness of the earthly temple dislodges the divine presence from the earthly temple, while it remains in the heavenly temple (Ezek 1:4–28; 11:22–25). The different conditions of the pure heavenly temple and the occasionally unclean earthly temple show that they are both real in this multidimensional Hebraic framework rather than the idealism of the earthly shadows that a Platonism would portray (*1 En.* 14; 37–71; *2 En.* 15–17; *4 Ezra* 9.26–10.59; 13.35–36; *2 Bar.* 4.2–7; 6.9; 32.4; Gal 4:26; Heb 12:22; Rev 3:12; 21:2, 10; *Asc. Isa.* 9; *Adam and Eve* 37; *Apoc. Ab.* 29; *Exod. Rab.* 43.8; *m. Hag.* 2.1; *b. Hag.* 14a; 15a; *Hek. Rab.* 20.1; *b. Sanh.* 38b; Pate and Kennard, *Deliverance Now and Not Yet*, 98–103; Sholem, *Jewish Gnosticism*; Lincoln, *Paradise Now and Not Yet*, 9–32, 169–95; Dean-Otting, *Heavenly Journeys*; Gruenwald, *Apocalyptic and Merkavah Mysticism*, 29–72; Schafer, *Kehhalot-Studien*; Chernus, "Visions of God in Merkabah Mysticism"; Isaacs, *Sacred Space*, 59–61; Koester, *Hebrews*, 97–100).

44. *1 En.* 43.4; 47.1–2; 48.6; 103.9–104.8.

45. *1 En.* 46.1–7; 48.2–10; 52.4.

46. *1 En.* 39.6; 48.1–4; 51.4–5; 61.4; 62.14.

47. *1 En.* 39.4–5; 41.2 much like Rom 8:28–30; Col 3:1–4.

48. *1 En.* 62.14–16.

49. 1QH 15.8–27 esp. 15.18 and 16.4–17.36; 11QMelch. 6–25. The teacher of righteousness probably understood himself to be on the verge of exaltation in Jerusalem (1QH 14.28–36; 15.24–28). However, the Damascus Document suggests that the teacher of righteousness died before he could deliver of his promises (CD 19.34–35; 20.13–16). Deliverance was recalculated to be forty years later (CD 20.13–16; 11QMelch.; 1QS 8.1–16).

be associated with him is to experience divine forgiveness.[50] The Qumran covenanters identified the teacher of righteousness with Melchizedek, who was expected to atone for the Qumran covenanters' sins,[51] which equated with deliverance of the righteous from the age of the messianic woes into kingdom.[52] After the teacher of righteousness died, his followers recalculated that for this deliverance to occur at the end of forty years, it would entail their mimetic suffering to fill up what was lacking from the teacher's sufferings.[53] However, after the forty years came and went with no rescue, the Qumran covenanters reinterpreted their deliverance mystically to mean that they were caught up to heaven in the worship setting with and because of the teacher of righteousness's vicarious atonement.[54]

Additionally, because of Qumran's separation they also considered that the community itself atoned for its members through a sacrifice of humility, prayer, and mystical community worship, provided the member repents of sin and submits to the community discipline (Pss 51:17; 141:2);[55] nonmembers remained unclean as sinners. 1QS identifies that God's merciful justification occurs at the eschatological judgment for those who reflect the narrow way from their heart.[56] Actually, the Babylonian Talmud considered that confessional prayer and the study of *torah* were more effective in atoning than animal sacrifice, so those practices replace burnt offerings for atonement in traditional Judaism.[57]

Furthermore, mimetic atonement is celebrated among Jews. For example, ben Sir considers that a virtuously righteous life atones.[58] Additionally, Maccabean and other Jewish martyrs were seen to propitiate the sins of

---

50. Especially 1QH 15.18.

51. 11Q Melch. 6–8.

52. 11Q Melch. 9–25.

53. The teacher of righteousness probably understood himself to be on the verge of exaltation in Jerusalem (1QH 14.28–36; 15.24–28). However, the Damascus Document suggests that the teacher of righteousness died before he could deliver on his promises (CD 19.34–35; 20.13–16).

54. 1QH 11.19–38; 15.26–36.

55. Prayer: 1QS 3.8; 5.6–7; 8.5–6, 10; 9.4–5; 1Q34 1+2; 4Q400 frg. 1 lines 15–16; 4Q508 frg. 2 2–3; 22+23; 4Q509 frg. 16 3; 5–6 ii, 7; 11Q5 27.2–11; *Jub.* 5.17–18; 34.18–19; *Festival of Prayers*; *Pss. Sol.* 3.8; 9.6; Philo, *Mos.* 2.23–24; *Spec.* 2.196 esp. within 193–203; *Legat.* 306; *LAB* 13.6; *b. Ber.* 26b; mystical worship: *1 En.* 14.8–25; *T. Levi* 3.4–5; *Songs of the Sabbath Sacrifice*; 1QH 11.19–38; 15.26–36.

56. 1QS 11.2–3, 12,13–15; also 4QMMT C.31.

57. *B. Ber.* 32b; *b. Menaḥ.* 110a.

58. Sir 3.3, 35.5–6, 9.

the people as their own mimetic deaths and suffering redeemed Israel from the domination of foreign powers.[59]

With the destruction of the Jerusalem temple in AD 70 and 135, some forms of early Judaism continued to offer purification sacrifices including those of the Day of Atonement in synagogues[60] and in alternative Jewish temples such as the Jewish Elephantine temple (near the Aswan High Dam in Egypt).[61] Several other Jewish frameworks without a functioning Jewish temple practiced modified purification sacrifices and Day of Atonement sacrifices from their synagogues.[62] While these approaches were acknowledged, Yoḥanan ben Zakkai additionally proposed (similar to Prov 16:6) that acts of mercy and loving-kindness remained as an effective atonement to cleanse and forgive on the basis of Hosea 6:6.[63] Philo identified that confession atones,[64] as does repentance,[65] affliction,[66] and prayer.[67] Pinḥas ben Yair drew all these categories together as a narrow way of salvation unto everlasting life for holiness, cleanness, and righteousness.

> Heedfulness leads to [physical] cleanness, cleanness to purity, purity to separateness, separateness to holiness, holiness to humility, humility to the shunning of sin, the shunning of sin to saintliness, saintliness to the Holy Spirit, the Holy Spirit to the resurrection of the dead.[68]

---

59. *1 En.* 43.4; 47.1–2; 48.6; 103.9—104.8; 4 Macc 6.29; 17.21–22; 4Q171 frg. 1–10 ii 8–11.

60. Philo, *Mos.* 2.23; *Seder 'Abodah*; *b. Meg.* 31a.

61. Porten, *Archives from Elephantine*, 128–33, 279–82, 311–14.

62. The Jewish practice would have sacrifice complete the reconciliation process (Lev 1–7; *Ep. Aristeas* 170–71; *Sir.* 34.18–19; 35.12; Philo, *Spec.* 1.236f). Continuing this practice, Matthew 5:23–24 and Acts 18:18; 21:23–27 supports Jewish Christian participation in Jewish sacrifices. In contrast, *Gos. Eb.* 7 as recorded by Epiphanius, *Pan.* 30.16.4–5 has Jesus condemn such practice of Jewish sacrifices. Of course, the Law prescribes the Levitical sacrifices for Israel (Lev 1–7, 16:1—17:9). Additionally, the OT describes the kingdom era under the messiah as continuing to practice these sacrifices that atone (Jer 33:18; Ezek 43:18—46:24), though Hebrews 10:1–8 ceases the sacrifices for now for any new covenant people who would be disturbed by their reminder, and *Lev. Rab.* 9.7, written four centuries after the destruction of the temple (fifth century AD), ceases the ritual sacrifices in the messianic kingdom.

63. *The Fathers according to Rabbi Nathan* cited by Neusner, *Idea of Purity in Ancient Judaism*, 68.

64. Philo, *Post.* 70–72.

65. Philo, *Spec.* 1.188.

66. Philo, *Leg.* 3.174; *Congr.* 107.

67. Philo, *Mos.* 2.24.

68. *M. Soṭah* 9.15; *y. Šeqal.* 3.3.

Obviously, Christianity takes things into a messianic sacrifice and kingdom, but that stretches the connections made by Isaiah through the lens of the claims made by the Gospels, Acts, and 1 Peter concerning Jesus.[69] That is, the Gospels and Acts populate Jesus within a range of servant of Yahweh verses that develop his prophetic and healing ministry and how one might recognize who the servant happens to be, whereas 1 Peter joins the Enochian idea of "son of man" and Qumran's "teacher of righteousness" vicariously atoning for others within a context of mimetic atonement (1 Pet 2:18–25).

THE ANOINTED ONE OF ISAIAH 61

Some see Isa 61 as a fifth servant song because the individual is "anointed by the Holy Spirit" to do a mission similar to that of Isa 42:7 and 49:9.[70] However, the designation of "servant" is not used in the passage, so it is better to refer to it as a passage concerning the "messiah" or "anointed one" (Isa 61:1 *mšḥ*). Yahweh anointed the speaker of this section (Isa 61:1). The anointed one has the spirit of Adonai Yahweh[71] rest upon him for particular roles associated with jubilee year and realized in kingdom. In Luke 4:17–21, Jesus in the Nazareth synagogue summarized his ministry as spirit-endowed to accomplish these Jubilee healings and freedoms by citing Isaiah 61:1–2. Accordingly, the messiah was sent by Yahweh to preach the good news to the poor, opening the kingdom to them (Isa 61:1; perhaps alluded to in Matt 5:3 and Luke 6:20). This messiah bound up the broken-hearted, which includes healing and encouraging. This messiah proclaimed freedom for captives, which in the Gospels especially includes releasing individuals from demonic bondage (Matt 12:28). However, release from imprisonment is promised by the speaker (Isa 61:1). This messiah proclaimed, as comfort for those who mourn, the beginning of the favorable year of the Lord, or Jubilee, and the day of judgment of Yahweh's wrath upon rebels (Isa 61:2). This message includes both sides in one encouraging message for those who grieve injustice in this life. The message entails Yahweh making a new covenant relationship with Israel (Isa 61:8). This message both externally pictures

---

69. See Kennard, *Messiah Jesus*, 107–56 for Jesus' development of Law and traditions concerning cleansing and sacrifice, 293–332 for Jesus' messianic sacrifice, and 377–414 for Jesus' messianic rule.

70. Beuken, "Servant and Herald of Good Tidings."

71. MT, Syr, and targums have *Adonai*, which doubles with Yahweh as names for God related to the spirit, whereas 1QIsa^a and mss^k, LXX, and the Vulgate simply have Yahweh as the name for God here.

encouragement (garland) as well as providing medicine to the internal new covenant healing (oil of gladness) of believers from a dim spirit of mourning to the consistent strength of righteous living planted and praised by Yahweh (Isa 61:3, 10). Israel will be blessed as new covenant priests and servants of God within the Mosaic covenant blessing (Isa 61:6, 8; Exod 19:6). Within renewed covenant blessing, ancient and destroyed cities will be rebuilt to initiate a new kingdom era (Isa 61:4). Many immigrants will join the Jewish people in working among the flocks and fields of the kingdom (Isa 61:5). The kingdom will be strengthened by the wealth that the nations will bring into kingdom (Isa 61:6). The metaphor of "double portion" instead of shame (Isa 61:7; also 40:2 MT but absent in LXX) that Israel received indicates double from Yahweh for her sins, probably meaning a full restitution after the pattern from the guilt offering (Exod 22:4, 7, 9 [MT: 22:3, 6, 8]).[72] This shame is reversed to a "double portion" of joyous covenant blessing in the land, perhaps alluding to a full inheritance of blessing as was to accrue to the firstborn son (Deut 21:17; Isa 61:7). One feature of Yahweh's blessing is to both transform Israel and to give Israel work in removing the structure and deeds of injustice, such as robbery (Isa 61:11, 8). As Israel frames the kingdom in righteousness, they will be known and recognized by the nations for their just practices (Isa 61:9). The messiah delights in Yahweh for the role of righteous savior that Yahweh has planned for him (Isa 61:10-11). The messiah's righteousness is his clothes, priest's headdress, and bridal jewels. Under the messiah's leadership, the kingdom becomes attractive in living righteousness consistently and as fertile as a garden (Isa 61:11).

Jesus Christ proclaimed the positive aspect of this kingdom ministry as applying to himself through the promise of the favorable year of Yahweh (Luke 4:18-21). In this context, Jesus underscored that his healing ministry served as a present expression of the full kingdom jubilee. However, the Jews of Nazareth would have none of this since they refused to bring those in need of healing to Jesus, thwarting Jesus' healing ministry in their hometown (Luke 4:23-27). Instead, those who heard Jesus in the synagogue tried to kill him by attempting to push him off the Nazareth cliff, but Jesus escaped out of their midst (Luke 4:28-30). Within progressive fulfillment, Isaiah has in view a messianic ministry in the fullness of kingdom, while Jesus claims sufficient evidence to warrant an earlier stage of kingdom healing and release surrounding him that shows continuity with that later stage.

---

72. Goldingay, *The Message of Isaiah 40-55*, 15; though the metaphor could also refer to multiple generations that have suffered covenant curse consequences from Exod 20:5; therefore they are forgiven. It would be harder to maintain this meaning in Isa 61:7 "double portion" of covenant blessing.

The idea of "anointed" or "messiah" is mentioned in two other places in Isaiah unrelated to this Isaiah 61 passage. Cyrus is a predicted anointed one or messiah to conquer for God and who is upheld in this conquest by God's right hand, but he does not fit the Davidic king specifics to be identified as the servant-king (Isa 45:1).[73] Yahweh will go before Cyrus to open or break the double doors[74] to facilitate a new exodus for the people of Israel to return to the land (Isa 45:1–3; Ezra 6:3–5, 15 recounts this return decree in 538 BC that is accomplished before 515 BC).[75] Additionally, Cyrus is used by God to judge Babylon, who are to "anoint" their weapons for war in their impending judgment and destruction (Isa 21:5).

SUMMARY

The servant is anointed by the spirit of Yahweh, who gives him unusual abilities of wisdom and thereby a ministry of proclaiming salvation and the kingdom. In the role of the servant, he made a covenant for the people through his atoning death. This results in his exaltation to the place of privilege with Yahweh, though he also is God. In his role as king, he shall come to judge the ungodly in the eschatological day of Yahweh and usher in the kingdom with its abundance of blessing.

---

73. Aquila softens the word in Greek from "Christ" to "the merciful" (Goldingay, *Isaiah 40–55*, 2:20). *B. Meg.* 12a increases the individuals in conversation with Yahweh speaking to the messiah about Cyrus.

74. "Double" is based on the Hebrew use of dual in Isa 45:1 "doors," *dlt'm*. Perhaps this is a divine accomplishment to leave Babylon's gates open on the night of Cyrus's attack as Xenophon describes occurred (*Cyropedia* VII, 5.28).

75. Watts, *Isaiah 34–66*, 697–98.

CHAPTER 13

Exodus unto Kingdom

ISAIAH ECHOES THE EXODUS theme in a more prominent manner than any other prophet of the Old Testament.[1] In fact, the exodus theme is so prominent in Isaiah 40–66 that Claus Westermann claims that in this portion of Isaiah, "the Exodus is so conspicuous that all the other events in Israel's history recede into the background."[2] However, the theme of the exodus in Isaiah is no longer the narrow way to enter the Promised Land under Moses and Joshua, because in Isaiah's emphasis this new exodus is about regathering into the land after the Babylonian captivity. A new highway will emerge from the East, as across the Euphrates, to facilitate a new exodus recovering Israel from captivity as they had been recovered during the original exodus (Isa 11:15–16; Exod 14–19). Furthermore, since when Israel regathers in the land under Zerubbabel, Ezra, and Nehemiah, Israel continues to need repentance and renewal, the exodus theme in Isaiah also echoes with a future eschatological call to enter into kingdom that is yet to be realized.[3] In both God's recovery

---

1. Anderson, "Exodus Typology in Second Isaiah," 181–84; "Exodus and Covenant in Second Isaiah," 347; Stuhlmueller, "The New Exodus as a Way to Creative Redemption," in *Creative Redemption in Deutero-Isaiah*, 59–98; Longman, *How to Read Exodus*, 148; Lim, *The "Way of the Lord"*; Estelle, *Echoes of Exodus*, 149; though the second exodus motif is questioned by Simian-Yofre, "Exodus in Deuteroisaias"; Watts, "Consolation or Confrontation?"

2. Westermann, *Isaiah 40–66*, 22.

3. Zillessen, "Der alte und der neue Exodus"; Fischer, "Das Problem desneuen Exodus in Isaias"; Anderson, "Exodus Typology in Second Isaiah," 181; Kiesow, *Exodustexte im Jesajabuch*; Barstad, *A Way in the Wilderness*; Watts, *Isaiah's New Exodus in Mark*; Pao, *Acts and the Isaianic New Exodus*, 55–59; Estelle, *Echoes of Exodus*, 150.

of Israel after the Babylonian captivity and also eschatologically, Yahweh responds to the plight of Israel having lost their way in need of traversing a "way-less" wilderness by a new narrow exodus "way" (*drk*).[4] Such a "way" (*drk*) can mean "walk" (Isa 11:15), "path" (Isa 9:1 [MT: 8:23]; 30:11; 35:8; 37:29, 34; 40:3; 42:16; 43:16, 19; 49:9; 51:10; 57:10, 14; 62:10), describe one's "condition" (Isa 40:27; 48:15; 53:6; 55:7; 65:2) or "moral behavior" (Isa 2:3; 8:11; 10:24; 15:5; 40:14; 42:24; 55:7; 56:11; 57:17–18; 58:13; 59:8; 66:3), and the fact that Yahweh "leads" Israel on this new exodus way that they should travel (Isa 30:21; 42:16; 45:13; 48:17; 49:11; 55:8–9; 58:2; 63:17; 64:5 [MT: 64:4]). By emphasis, *drk* includes both the journeying path and consistent moral behavior. However, Markus Zehnder considers the "eschatological miracle road" to be a unique Isaianic use of this word for future hope provided by Yahweh's leading Israel toward kingdom.[5] From this exodus perspective, any time that Israel is not in covenant faithfulness and blessing in the land, Yahweh continues to offer Israel the opportunity for an exodus of recovery unto kingdom.[6]

Ulrich Simon summarizes the continuity between Israel's exodus from Egypt and the new exodus into kingdom.

> God's providential care for Israel overrules foes and adversities in history. The first Exodus manifested the order of redemption. Then God appointed Moses to lead the oppressed people from Egypt through the Sea to the desert; the covenant of Sinai sealed the liberation. In the second Exodus YHWH raises up his conqueror, his second Moses, who represents the New Covenant; he gathers up Israel, scattered in the desert, and leads the exiles back to their land. Therefore, God banishes fear from Israel by doing again what he has done before; the new Exodus differs slightly in the sequence of events and surpasses the first in scale.[7]

Philip Harner argues that creation faith bridges from the exodus tradition out of Egypt to the expectation of the imminent restoration of Israel.[8]

---

4. Lund, *Way Metaphors*, 144; Barstad, *A Way in the Wilderness*; Hoffman, *Doctrine of the Exodus*; Zehnder, *Wegmetaphorik im Alten Testament*.

5. Zehnder, *Wegmetaphorik im Alten Testament*, 110, except perhaps maybe in Jer 31:9 and Mal 3:1. He also sees the emphasis of *mslh* as this eschatological miracle road (Isa 11:16; 19:23; 40:3; 49:11; 62:10).

6. Lund, *Way Metaphors*, 38, 145; Stock, *The Way in the Wilderness*.

7. Simon, *A Theology of Salvation: A Commentary on Isaiah 40–55*, 97.

8. Harner, "Creation Faith in Deutero-Isaiah," 304.

The exodus was announced in the Abrahamic covenant and the promises to the patriarchs, as Bernhard Anderson developed.

> Even though Israel's subsequent history was marred by the sin of Jacob, the "first father" (Isa 43:27; Hos 12:3), the blessings given to the patriarchs will be continued in his descendants. These blessings, which Israel had forfeited (Isa 48:18–19), include the gift of the land, the miraculous fertility of "barren" Israel (Isa 49:19–21; 54:1–3; Gen 28:14), and the mediation of saving benefits to other nations (Isa 42:6–7; Gen 12:2–3).[9]

The exodus theme develops Yahweh's election of Israel initially from Egypt and a new election that facilitates Israel to pass from death to a new life of salvation after the Babylonian captivity.[10] This choice encourages Israel that they belong and will be aided by Yahweh to obtain the kingdom in the wake of the new exodus.

> Now listen, O Jacob my servant; and Israel, whom I have chosen:
> Thus says Yahweh who made you and formed you from the womb, who will help you:
> Do not fear, O Jacob my servant and Jeshurun whom I have chosen.
> For I will pour out water on him who is thirsty and streams on the dry ground;
> I will pour out my spirit on your offspring, and my blessing on your descendants;
> And they will spring up among the grass like poplars by streams of water.
> This one will say, "I am Yahweh's" and that one will call on the name of Jacob;
> And another will write on his hand, "Belonging to Yahweh,"
> And I will name Israel's name with honor (Isa 44:1–5).

The grounding for this new exodus is from Yahweh the general, who will wage war for Israel (Isa 31:4–5). In the pattern of an eagle flying and diving to protect Jerusalem, Yahweh the general will *pass over* (*psḥ*) and rescue Israel (Isa 31:5 as the death angel *passed over* [*psḥ*] and protected Israel in Exod 12:11, 21, 27, 43, 48). Yahweh's deliverance of his people is "with a mighty hand and an outstretched arm" (Isa 40:10; 51:9; 52:10; Exod 3:20; 6:6; 13:14, 16; 15:16). Yahweh's promise of redemption is available.

King Yahweh announces his presence to Israel in the midst of Babylon.

---

9. Anderson, "Exodus Typology in Second Isaiah," 182–83.

10. Kennard, *Biblical Covenantalism*, 1:104–15; Stuhlmueller, *Creative Redemption in Deutero-Isaiah*, 125–26.

> Thus says Yahweh, your Redeemer, the Holy One of Israel; I am Yahweh your God, who teaches you to profit, who leads you in the way you should go. If only you had paid attention to my commandments! Then your peace would have been like a river, and your righteousness like the waves of the sea. Your descendants would have been like the sand, and the offspring of your inward parts like sand grains; their name would never be cut off or destroyed from my presence (Isa 48:17–19).

The announcement begins as the introduction to the Ten Commandments, "I am Yahweh your God" (Exod 20:2). In the surfacing covenant, profound covenant blessing implications emerge if Israel had been faithful within the covenant (Isa 55:3; 54:10). To facilitate this new exodus, Yahweh delivered his people from bondage with a mighty outstretched arm (Isa 40:10; 51:9; 52:10; Exod 3:20; 6:6; 13:14, 16; 15:16). Yahweh's presence among the people guarantees that he will bring his Law with him to set justice for the peoples (Isa 51:1, 4–7). In fact, God's presence among Israel for righteousness ensures Israel's redemption as a covenant blessing (Isa 51:5–6). These covenant blessings include a wholistic well-being of peace and being considered by God as righteous or appropriate within the covenant. Because Yahweh is in the midst of Israel for everlasting righteousness with the Law, Israel will pursue the righteousness of the Mosaic covenant within their hearts (Isa 51:1, 7–8). Such a condition would have facilitated their preservation with increasing numbers, rather than these occasional captivities that destroy Israel by cutting them off from the Mosaic covenant. They need to return to faithfulness within this covenant and then they will be returned to the covenant blessings of peace, righteousness, and increasing growth. The covenant blessings are ultimately grounded on the Abrahamic covenant, with Abraham and Sarah's pattern of faithfulness (Isa 48:19; 51:2; Gen 15:5; 22:17). From the basis of this initial proclamation, Yahweh calls Israel out from Babylon (Isa 48:20). Such an initial call to the new exodus should be repeated with joyful shouting.

Whenever Israel finds itself mired in sin outside her homeland, Yahweh calls out to her to "Come out from there" (Isa 52:11–12, *yṣ'* "come out" in Qal imperfect *ṣ'w* similar to Exod 13:8 Qal infinitive *bṣ'ty*, also Exod 11:8; 12:41; 13:3–4; 16:1). They are to remove themselves from anything unclean and to purify themselves. Such a call is to a new exodus because Yahweh will go before the national exodus as well as provide Israel with a "rear guard" as at the Red Sea (Isa 52:12 Piel participle *m'ṣpkm* of the root *'ṣp* similar to Exod 3:16 *w'ṣpt*, with the angel of Yahweh defending behind Israel, Exod 14:19–20). In contrast to the first exodus, in this new exodus Israel will not go out "in haste" (Isa 52:12; 49:9; Exod 12:11; Deut 16:3). Nor will Israel go out as fugitives, since Yahweh leads them out as a national entity unto kingdom.

When Yahweh has washed Israel of her sin and guilt of bloodshed, Yahweh will create a whole area of worship assembly on Mount Zion where there will be a cloud by day and a flaming fire by night as occurred at Mount Sinai and the Exodus (Isa 4:5, as in Exod 13:21-22; 19:16-19; Num 9:15-23). God's presence guides and defends Israel in the new exodus by going before his people and as rear guard (Isa 52:12; Exod 13:21-22; 14:19-20).

In response to the possibility of a new exodus, Israel prays to Yahweh to bring them out by means of the new exodus (Isa 51:9-11). Israel cries out for Yahweh to "awaken" with the strength of the arm of Yahweh to accomplish again what God had done generations ago in destroying Egypt and cutting to pieces the metaphorical chaos monster, Rahab, associated with Egypt. In the earlier Exodus, these were accomplished at the Red Sea, destroying Egyptian horse and chariots, and metaphorically the chaos monster, Rahab (Isa 51:3; 43:16-17; 51:9-10; 63:11-13; Exod 14).[11] The spirit of Yahweh divided the waters and enabled his people Israel not to stumble on dry ground in passing through the waters (Isa 51:10; 63:11-13). This victory also provided Israel with a dry pathway to cross over, redeeming them from the Egyptians. Yahweh protects Israel as she passes through the waters because Yahweh is with Israel (Isa 43:2). The metaphor is balanced by an opposite one from Daniel, such that Israel will be protected through the fire (Isa 29:6; 30:27-29; Dan 3:25, 27). Through the waters, Israel becomes the ransomed of Yahweh, such that Egypt is given in place of Israel in the Red Sea (Isa 43:1, 3; 51:9-11). Through the Red Sea, Israel is redeemed by Yahweh and responds with continuous joy as with a new song of Moses and Israel (Isa 41:1, 14; 42:10-13; 51:3, 11; Exod 15).

The premiere new exodus passage in Isaiah is Isaiah 40:1-11. In this passage, God speaks comfort to his people for this new exodus (Isa 40:1).[12] This exodus launches because God ends Israel's hard labor of covenant curse and her iniquity is removed.[13] The metaphor in the MT (Isa 40:2; absent

11. Stuhlmueller, *Creative Redemption in Deutero-Isaiah*, 88-94.

12. In MT God speaks, in contrast to 1QIsa identifying priests as speakers, or Targums identifying a prophet as speaking. Qumran expressed this statement as a *pesher* encouraging their distinctive community as those to be comforted while they prepared the new exodus way (Isa 40:1 cited in 4Q176 frag. 1, col. 1 4-8; 1QS 8.12-16; CD 7.10-13; 13.24-14.1; Brooke, "Isaiah 40:3 and the Wilderness Community"; Sawyer, *The Fifth Gospel*, 24). John the Baptist understands that his own role is preparing the exodus way for Messiah Jesus (Matt 3:3; Mark 1:1-4; Luke 3:4-7; John 1:22-27). Also, Israel is the people comforted rather than people comforting others as in the Vulgate and Jerome viewing "people" as in vocative address.

13. The three *ki* clauses are essentially equal in meaning, Watts, *Isaiah 34-66*, 605.

in LXX) that Israel received double from Yahweh for her sins probably means full restitution after the pattern from the guilt offering (Exod 22:4, 7, 9, [MT and LXX: 22:3, 6, 8]).[14] This "double portion" is reversed to a "double portion" of joyous covenant blessing in the land, perhaps alluding to a full inheritance of blessing as was to accrue to the firstborn son (Deut 21:17; Isa 61:7). The compound subject of "voice calling" probably indicates multiple individuals along the way announcing preparation for Yahweh's way to travel this exodus.[15] The imagery is as though people down the way call out, perhaps as the group is about to pass, "blessed is he who comes in the name of the Lord" (Ps 118:26). The construction imageries of straightening and smoothing the rough to become a plain and removing the hills to fill in valleys and removing steep grades to become level all point to Yahweh's aid in facilitating the exodus way (Isa 40:3-4; 43:19; 49:11). These hills will be winnowed and pulverized by Yahweh to make the way smooth (Isa 41:15-16). During the new exodus, the wilderness will be marvelously transformed. As the exodus transpires, the weighty glory of Yahweh will be seen by all flesh (humans and animals) along the way, for God's mouth has spoken this as real comfort (Isa 40:5). Those who watch and travel the exodus way will hear the announcement that they can count upon,[16] that as flesh they are as vulnerable as grass before the hot desert sirocco wind or the judging breath of Yahweh, while God excels in goodness as the flowers in their field (Isa 40:6-8). In contrast to human vulnerability, God's word remains binding and encouraging forever. With such profound generosity coming with God, those announcing[17] Yahweh's procession should position themselves so their voices will carry from the hilltops because they have a comforting message to remove fear by announcing the presence of God; declarations of "Here is your God" follow the exodus travelers (Isa 40:9). There is none to stop Yahweh, for Adonai Yahweh will come with power fostered by his weapon-wielding arm ruling for him, each bringing about God's work in his presence (Isa 40:10). Yahweh provides sight, light, and

---

14. Goldingay, *The Message of Isaiah 40-55*, 15; the metaphor could also refer to multiple generations that have suffered covenant curse consequences from Exod 20:5, therefore they are forgiven (Phillips, "Double for All Her Sins"). It would be harder to maintain Philips's meaning in Isa 61:7 "double portion" of covenant blessing.

15. Kautzsch and Cowley, *Gesenius' Hebrew Grammar*, 146b; *qwl* is neuter and *qwr'* is masculine, but both are singular.

16. Isa 40:7-8 perfect tenses take on a gnomic or proverbial sense, Waltke and O'Conner, *Introduction to Biblical Hebrew Syntax*, 488.

17. *Mbssrt* is feminine gender "herald," which may hint at female heralds or Mrs. Isaiah, or be a generic term like "teacher" (*qhlt*), though it is reflected in LXX by a male gendered term, ὁ εὐαγγελιζόμενος; Goldingay, *The Message of Isaiah 40-55*, 28; Goldingay and Payne, *Isaiah 40-55*, 86-87.

guidance on the new exodus way as his presence had guided Israel before through the wilderness toward the promised land (Isa 42:16). Such imagery presents visual guidance as the pillar of fire did in the exodus (Isa 42:16; Exod 13:21; 14:24; 33:9; Num 14:14). As Yahweh proceeds through the exodus, he brings Israel as his hired personnel with him. Ultimately, the exodus imagery extends beyond the regathering after the Babylonian captivity because rabbinic interpretations continue to appeal to this passage for the new exodus in the wake of Roman dispersions.[18] As Israel assembles into Jerusalem, they will be protected by a cloud-and-fire exodus canopy or a tabernacle brush arbor (Isa 4:5-6; Exod 13:21; 1 Kgs 8:10).[19] Perhaps, this indicates that entrance into kingdom begins with the feast of tabernacles (Matt 17:4; Mark 9:5; Luke 9:33)[20] or as early Judaism identified that the kingdom houses its living or resurrected occupants in tabernacles in close proximity to Yahweh's temple in Jerusalem (John 14:2-3).[21]

The new exodus becomes a highway of holiness (Isa 35:8). No fool or unclean person will travel on this exodus way. The ransomed of Yahweh will return on the exodus way with everlasting shouting and joy. In such an exodus, despondency gives way to hope (Isa 35:3). Water gushes in the wilderness, recovering it from barrenness (Isa 35:6-7; 41:17-18; 43:20; 49:10; 55:1) as water had previously gushed from the rock in the earlier exodus (Isa 43:20; 48:21). What had been a burning simmering sand of a mirage becomes a pool with abundance of water, grass, reeds, papyrus, and blooming blossoms covering the fields (Isa 35:1-2, 6-7; 4:3-5). As the flowers blossom profusely, those who travel on the exodus will rejoice and praise God as they return to the promised land (Isa 35:1-2, 7). The exhausted and impaired will be healed on the exodus way (Isa 35:3-6). Additionally, threatening animals will be excluded from this exodus way such that Israel will travel this new exodus without threat (Isa 35:9).

Yahweh comes gently as a shepherd tending his flock and gathering his lambs, even carrying Israel in the exodus (Isa 40:11). Israel in exodus is a flock guided by the divine shepherd, who provides water and good grazing, moderate temperatures, and compassionate guiding on a raised and unobstructed highway (Isa 35:6-7; 40:11; 41:17-20; 43:19-21; 48:21; 49:9-11; 55:13). The

---

18. Teugels, "Consolation and Composition."

19. Watts, *Isaiah 1-33* (rev. ed.), 76.

20. *Lev. Rab.* 27.1.

21. *1 En.* 39.5; 41.2; 45.1; 91.13 (texts B and C); the resurrected deceased receive their afterlife houses in ranks due to merit (*1 En.* 39.4; 41.2; *2 En.* 62.2; *b. B. Bat.* 75a; *Ruth Rab.* 3.4; *Pesiq. Rab.* 31.6).

lamb that the shepherd compassionately carries is usually the one that cannot keep up with the flock (Isa 40:11; Ezek 34:12-23, 31; Ps 23:1-3; Luke 15:4-6).[22]

In the wake of Isaiah developing Yahweh's incomparability, the exodus theme returns in Isaiah 40:27-31. In contrast to Israel's destructive captivity, Yahweh is generously just. Israel cries out in lament, "Why?" and, "I am lost with my way hidden from Yahweh" (Isa 40:27).[23] However, Yahweh answers as the everlasting God from creation on who does not himself get weary but gives his strength to the weary and any who lack vigor (Isa 40:28-31). Metaphors of amazing stamina describe those traveling with Yahweh in the new exodus: they will fly upon eagles' wings, they will run and not get tired, and they will walk and not become weary.

Israel will be gathered from all points of the compass (Isa 43:5-7; 48:20; 49:1). In fact, due to the transformation of Israel, other peoples will join in the benefits of Yahweh's justice and follow Israel into the kingdom (Isa 49:6; 51:5; 55:5). Israel will be regathered, for nothing can stop it. The remnant enters into Jerusalem with joy, singing to Yahweh. Israel is multiplied and enlarged (Isa 9:3; 60:22).

As soon as Moses had led Israel from the Red Sea, they grumbled due to lack of water and Yahweh temporarily healed their grumble-tested condition by transforming the bitter waters they could find to become sweet (Exod 15:22-26).[24] God also brought gushing water from the split rock (Isa 48:20-21; 49:10; Exod 17:2-7; Num 20:8). In fact, Yahweh's salvation is figured by the generosity and abundance of the water Israel is able to draw, such that Israel will worship Yahweh with gratitude (Isa 12:3). Yahweh also provides food for them along the exodus way, but it is overshadowed by the promise of sweet water in the wilderness (Isa 49:10). The new exodus does not need the grumbling test, but when the poor and needy seek water, Yahweh will answer them directly, for he is committed to their well-being

---

22. With this text, sometimes there is a common illustration of a shepherd breaking the leg of a straying sheep, probably first mentioned by Robert Munger as a surprising practice of a contemporary Syrian shepherd (*What Jesus Says: The Master Teacher and Life's Problems*), but there is no ancient evidence of this practice and there is no biblical reason to mention such a practice. The biblical emphasis is on compassion, not discipline. Jewish shepherding practice would carry a lamb as a means of bringing it back to the flock without harming it even if it had strayed (*Sem. Rab.* 2.2; Luke 15:4-6; Matt 18:12-14) and most shepherds have enough sheep in their care to avoid intentionally increasing personal care needlessly.

23. The *waw* with a second speaking word is epexegetically implying the force of an interrogative in the same manner as the LXX "καὶ τί" means "and why?" Davidson, *Hebrew Syntax*, 45R1, 53R1.

24. Buchanan, "Isaianic Midrash and the Exodus" especially compares parallel language between Exod 15 and Isa 11-12 to develop new exodus as a compelling Isaianic theme.

(Isa 41:17-20). God will bring flowing waters as he turns the wilderness into a wetland forest with ponds and ample trees and shade (Isa 41:17-20; 43:20; 44:3-4). This turning the wilderness into a garden is accomplished by the creative hand of God. The new exodus imagery has become new Eden imagery as a commemorative park (Isa 41:18-20; 51:3; Gen 2).[25] Poetically, even the trees join the joyous clapping and shouting on the exodus way unto kingdom (Isa 49:13; 55:12-13). This last exodus is so wonderful that Yahweh exhorts Israel to forget the former things (the first exodus from Egypt), for the new exodus is the gathering into kingdom (Isa 43:18).[26]

In realizing this new exodus, Jan Koole develops that those coming and those already in Jerusalem have roles to bring about kingdom.

> Yahweh's(!) way in 40:3 must mean more than remigration from Babylon and in 57:14 the removal of the obstacles in the life of the people ushers in the return of the exiles (the way of the people!), who will then be "led and comforted" (57:18) by their God, and 62:10 can be taken to mean that the people still living in destroyed Jerusalem should literally go out through the ruins of the gates to clear away the rubble from the roads to the city, so that the returning exiles can re-enter and repopulate Zion (62:12).[27]

As Israel approaches Jerusalem with joy and security, there is the call of an entrance liturgy to enter Jerusalem and to further remain faithful and trust Yahweh.

> Open the gates, that the righteous nation may enter, the one who remains faithful. Though wilt keep those of steadfast purpose in perfect peace because he trusts in God. Trust in Yahweh forever, for in Yahweh we have an everlasting rock! (Isa 26:2-4).

Yahweh's protection for Israel is especially seen in the context by his destruction of the opposition (Isa 26:5-6). Such a contrast is to provoke deep meditation and further trust and longing for Yahweh (Isa 26:4, 8-10).

The new exodus completes with Israel regathered in the land, where the land is apportioned among the tribes so that Israel might continue to dwell in such a well provided garden setting (Isa 49:8).[28] With the completion of the exodus, the kingdom begins.

---

25. Goldingay, *The Message of Isaiah 40-55*, 124.
26. North, *The Second Isaiah*, 17-18.
27. Koole, *Isaiah III*, 24.
28. Anderson, "Exodus Typology in Second Isaiah," 184.

CHAPTER 14

Kingdom

ISAIAH'S CONCEPT OF ESCHATOLOGY is a future time in history toward which history is moving. It is driven by supernatural causation to bring about the coming of Isaiah's concept of eschatological kingdom. This eschatological salvation is the climax of history in the form of the kingdom of Yahweh.

Yahweh will bring about a global era of peace (Isa 7:1; 9:6 [MT: 9:5]; 10:6; 40:2; 57:19), so that the nations willingly join in replacing their abundant weapons of war (Isa 5:28; 7:1; 10:6) with those that can facilitate their cultivation of the land (Isa 2:4; 9:4–5). Yahweh will himself reign in Jerusalem (Isa 24:23), with a Davidic king co-regency. God himself will be the protector of Jerusalem (Isa 26:4; 27:3, 5). The gates of Jerusalem will be open perpetually because in peace there will be no threat (Isa 60:11).

Out of this context of Yahweh's judgment and protection for Israel will emerge the physical and spiritual restoration of Israel, with Jerusalem as its capital (Isa 2:1–3; 32:16–20; 34:16–17). A sign or banner is raised so that the faithful remnant may be gathered from all nations around without harassment into the land to worship Yahweh (Isa 11:10–12, 15–16; 14:1–2; 27:5; 66:18–21). Idols (which were abundant in Jerusalem, Isa 2:7–8) will be removed to purify Jerusalem and the land (Isa 2:8; 4:3–4). Yahweh declares that Jerusalem and the temple will be rebuilt by Cyrus and Yahweh's kingdom plan (Isa 44:28—45:2). As Israel assembles into Jerusalem, they will be protected by a cloud-and-fire exodus canopy or a tabernacle brush arbor (Isa 4:5–6; Exod 13:21; 1 Kgs 8:10).[1] Perhaps this indicates that entrance into kingdom begins with the feast of tabernacles (Matt 17:4; Mark 9:5;

---

1. Watts, *Isaiah 1–33* (rev. ed.), 76.

Luke 9:33)[2] or as early Judaism identified that the kingdom houses its living or resurrected occupants in tabernacles with close proximity to Yahweh's temple in Jerusalem (John 14:2-3).[3] Israel will bring priests and holy objects and sacrifices along in this exodus to worship in the temple in Jerusalem (Isa 66:18-21). This great gathering occurs as the new exodus. In fact, gentiles will be instructed in these spiritual ways and join with Jews in gathering to worship Yahweh in Jerusalem (Isa 2:3-4).

A Davidic king empowered by the spirit of the Lord will establish a kingdom as a new garden of Eden (Isa 11:1-9). After a time where the family tree of Davidic kings had been cut down (sometime after Assyria being destroyed in 609 BC on the basis of Isa 9:1 relationship to Isa 8), a new branch emerges from Jesse's family tree to bring kingdom fruit again toward a Davidic kingdom (Isa 11:1). In the wake of these dark, threatening times, Isaiah predicts that this condition will change as Israel sees the light of a Davidic son, who will bring victory and a kingdom in the wake of his conquests (Isa 9:2-7 [MT and LXX: 9:1-6], notice the singular verbs in second person within Isa 9:3 [MT and LXX: 9:2] and the third person singular references to the child in Isa 9:6-7 [MT and LXX: 9:5-6]). With the concentration on the child as the singular third person, "He shall be called his name" (*wygr' šmw*) emphasizes more likely throne names for the child, rather than theophanic names for God who delivers (Isa 9:6 [MT and LXX: 9:5]). These throne names hint at the child's divinity in a manner that sets up a Jewish two-powers view[4]—that is, two persons of God within a Jewish monotheism. The divine child who will be king is the "Wonderful Counselor," a quality of the ideal wise statesman, which Isaiah develops as the messianic branch and of God (Isa 9:6 [MT and LXX: 9:5]; 11:2; 28:29).[5] Young argues that this wonderful character reflects the power of the plagues in Egypt and conquest of the land (Ps 78:12; Judg 13:19).[6] As "Mighty God," he is the champion who can carry out those plans, a title used elsewhere only of Yahweh (Isa 9:6 [MT and LXX: 9:5]; 10:21). Smith and Young argue that "Mighty God" identifies the Jewish monotheistic God.[7] Namely, that connecting Isa 7:14 with 9:6 [MT and LXX: 9:5] as read through the NT

---

2. *Lev. Rab.* 27.1.

3. *1 En.* 39.5; 41.2; 45.1; 91.13 (texts B and C); the resurrected deceased receive their afterlife houses in ranks due to merit (*1 En.* 39.4; 41.2; *2 En.* 62.2; *b. B. Bat.* 75a; *Ruth Rab.* 3.4; *Pesiq. Rab.* 31.6).

4. Segal, *Two Powers in Heaven*.

5. 1QH 11.9-10 describes the birth of the hoped-for Davidic messiah as being called "wonderful counselor."

6. Young, *The Book of Isaiah*, 1:334.

7. Smith, *The Book of Isaiah*, 1:137; Young, *The Book of Isaiah*, 1:335.

fulfillment (Matt 1:23) indicates that Jesus Christ is "*Immanuel*," meaning "God incarnate among us," going beyond the providential divine presence during the Assyrian conquests (Isa 8:8, 10). The title "Everlasting Father" indicates the enduring benefactor for his people, as God supremely is, further hinting at deity (Isa 9:6; 63:16). As "Prince of Peace," he is the provider of universal peace (Isa 9:5–7 [MT and LXX: 9:4–6], which also could point to Yahweh, Judg 6:24). There is no end of the increase of the rule of this child once he begins to reign (Isa 9:7 [MT and LXX: 9:6]). Such continuous increase provides Israel with increasing joy (Isa 9:3, 6[MT and LXX: 9:2, 5]). He will rule with justice, righteousness, and a zeal for Yahweh. The character of the king sets the tone for his kingdom.

In the second century BC, after the temporal sign indicators in Isaiah 7 and 8 had become ancient history, Jews translated the Hebrew "young woman of marriageable age" (*'lmh*) into the Greek LXX as "virgin" (παρθένος), shifting the sign in the Isa 7:14 LXX to be more definitively on the woman, who as a *virgin* would bear a son called "Immanuel." With virgin as the primary sign, the later child in the pericope emerged as the replacement incarnate divine child (Isa 9:6–7 [MT: 9:5–6]) for the one that had providentially provided timing for the Assyrian conquest (Isa 7:14–20; 8:1–4). This later incarnate Immanuel child became the lens through which the NT and Christians approached the virgin prophecy, identifying Jesus as this child who will eventually reign in kingdom (Isa 7:14 read through 9:6–7 [MT and LXX: 9:5–6]; Matt 1:18, 20, 23, 25; Luke 1:34–35).

There is no end of the increase of the rule of a new Davidic king (Isa 9:6 [MT and LXX: 9:5]). He will redeem and rule with justice and righteousness, protecting the vulnerable of society (Isa 2:3–4; 45:8, 13). The character of the kingdom reflects the character of the king. However, the character of the king is also empowered by Yahweh's spirit resting upon the Davidic king to bear virtuous fruit in the character of his reign (Isa 11:1–2). The king's character and reign will show evidence of wisdom, understanding, counsel, might, knowledge, righteousness, and the fear of Yahweh (Isa 11:2, 5). These spirit-endowed virtues will prompt him toward obedience in the fear of Yahweh and an ability to make judgments deeper than what is seen or heard, to penetrate to the level of character and true issues involved (Isa 11:3). Especially, this Davidic king will protect the poor and vulnerable as he judges the wicked (Isa 11:4). Through Yahweh the general's zeal and word, the Wonderful Counselor's kingdom will showcase righteous care for all occupants (Isa 9:7–8 [MT and LXX: 9:6–7]). The historical Davidic kingship becomes a foretaste of the character and glory of the eschatological kingdom.

The lack of righteousness in Isaiah's present (Isa 1:21; 5:7; 59:9) serves as contrast to the righteous era of the kingdom (Isa 32:16; 45:8; 61:11).[8] The character of the king shows itself guaranteeing the character of the kingdom. The Davidic king's righteous direction and judgment will protect Jerusalem in righteousness (Isa 1:26; 9:7; 11:4; 16:5). This means that the poor and vulnerable will be protected by the Davidic king (Isa 11:4). Such righteous protection will be brought to the nations as well (Isa 42:1–4).

The kingdom is centered at God's holy mountain and Jerusalem; thus all who come will know Yahweh deeply, as the waters cover the sea (Isa 11:9).

The kingdom will be a return to garden-of-Eden innocence and animal vegetarianism (Isa 11:6–9; 58:11; 65:25). For example, Isaiah emphasized predators and prey lying together in peace without the prey being eaten, namely: wolf and lamb, leopard and young goat, lion and calf, and bear and cow. In fact, all these animals are developed as vegetarians, grazing together (Isa 11:7; 56:9). Hans Wolff identified, "It is only in the Messianic End-time that the relationship of the animals to one another, as well as the relation between man and beast, will no longer be marked by dominion and conflict, but by peaceful play."[9] Neither will these animals hurt vulnerable children who are in close proximity with them (Isa 11:6). Even the hostility in the fall between humans and snakes is undone with children being unhurt while reaching into the cobra's or viper's den (Isa 11:8 undoing Gen 3:15). Though, the serpent will still bear the effects from the fall, with his head close to the ground so that it looks like he is eating dust (Isa 65:25; Gen 3:14). Peaceful relations reign.

Coming from such garden imagery, the kingdom is declared to have an abundance of harvest to provide food and provoke joy (Isa 9:3 [MT and LXX: 9:2]; 61:11). Within such agrarian abundance kingdom becomes figured as a lavish banquet (Isa 25:6). A royal invitation goes out to all the nations to join Yahweh in Jerusalem for the abundance of the banquet (Isa 25:6; 56:12). The quality of the banquet is also composed of the best foods, including aged wine and meat with marrow in its bones (Isa 25:6). This may mean that humans do not share the vegetarianism of the animals in their garden setting, but it certainly means that the kingdom banquet will have the best and thus it is something to anticipate.

With light and darkness as opposing systems in the world (Isa 5:20; 58:8; 59:9–10; 60:1–3, 19–20), the darkness fades under God's judgment.[10] Thus, light as both a manner of life and divine salvation grows under

---

8. Scobie, *The Ways of Our God*, 763–64.
9. Wolff, *Anthropology of the Old Testament*, 248; Scobie, *The Ways of Our God*, 170.
10. See my chapter on "Motifs of Judgment."

Yahweh's cultivation. Yahweh is the "light of Israel" who in his holiness saves a remnant while consuming others as a fire in judgment (Isa 10:17). His messianic servant also partakes of the quality of light. Yahweh's servant is the light to gentiles which enables them to spiritually see (believe) and experience kingdom blessings (Isa 42:6-7; 49:6; 55:5). As a manner of life, Yahweh's Law and just dealings will reveal the right way to live (Isa 51:4; 60:19-21). The act of walking in light becomes a life of obedience to the Law and a life of living at peace with others (Isa 2:3-5). Yahweh creates light both physically at the creation of the universe and re-creates it through salvation (Isa 45:7). The new exodus is accompanied by the act of Yahweh which makes the route visible and easy (Isa 42:16; 58:8; 60:1-3). This salvation manifests itself among those in darkness by showing them a great light (Isa 9:2). This concept of the dawning of the kingdom includes the judgment of the oppressors by the messiah as he establishes his just kingdom (Isa 9:2; 58:8-10; 60:1-3). The salvation evident in the kingdom attracts people from all nations.

> Arise, shine, for your light has come, and the glory of Yahweh rises upon you.
> See, darkness covers the earth and thick darkness is over the peoples,
> But Yahweh rises upon you and his glory appears over you.
> Nations will come to your light, and kings to the brightness of your dawn (Isa 60:1-3).

Physically, the light of the kingdom will be brighter (the moon will shine like the sun and the sun will be seven times brighter; Isa 30:26). This physical light is merely an outward indicator of the glory, blessing, and intimacy which will overshadow it, namely, "Yahweh will be your everlasting light and your God will be your glory" (Isa 60:19-20).[11] Yahweh as the fullness of light shall overshadow the effect of the physical light. Otto Kaiser developed Yahweh's glory from Isaiah 24:23, "The moon will be abased, the sun ashamed; for Yahweh Almighty will reign."

> The meaning is literally that the splendor of His light, manifesting His present, His *kabod* (Ezek 43:4; 10:8ff; 1:4ff) shines so bright that not only the holy city but the whole earth is lit by it, and the light of the sun and moon grows pale and is superfluous (Isa 60:19; Zech 14:7; Rev 21:23; 22:5).[12]

Yahweh is the supreme light within his kingdom of light. The kingdom shall overcome the darkness in the progress of salvation.

---

11. Kaiser, *Isaiah 13-39*, 303.
12. Kaiser, *Isaiah 13-39*, 195.

The kingdom era is also characterized by the glories of Solomonic trade with other nations from ship and caravan (Isa 60:5-9; 60:16-17; 61:6-7; 63:1). So, the best of the world's trade goods will stream into the kingdom. Such trade also further facilitates the exodus regathering of Israel into the land and worshiping God in the temple.

> Because the abundance of the sea will be turned to you,
> The wealth of the nations will come to you.
> A multitude of camels of Midian and Ephah; all those from Sheba will come;
> They will bring gold and frankincense, and will bear good news of praises for Yahweh.
> All the flocks of Kedar will be gathered together to you,
> the rams of Nabaioth will minister to you;
> They will go up with acceptance on God's altar,
> And I will glorify my glorious temple.
> Who are these who fly like a cloud and like doves to their windows?
> Surely the coastlands will wait for me; and the ships of Tarshish first,
> To bring your sons from afar, their silver and gold with them,
> For the name of Yahweh your God and the Holy One of Israel glorifies you (Isa 60:5-9).

This new kingdom era is as though the heavens and earth are made new and fresh for rejoicing (Isa 65:17-19).

> For behold I create new heavens and a new earth;
> And the former things shall not be remembered or come to mind.
> But be glad and rejoice forever in what I create;
> For behold I create Jerusalem for rejoicing, and her people gladness.
> I will rejoice in Jerusalem, and be glad among my people;
> And there will no longer be heard in her the voice and sound of crying (Isa 65:17-19).

The kingdom era is characterized by Yahweh's removal of death and mourning in the wake of death being banned (Isa 25:8; 65:19). Perhaps even a national or personal resurrection is hinted at in kingdom (Isa 26:19): "Your dead will live, their corpses will rise. You who lie in the dust, awake and shout for joy, for your dew is as the dew of the dawn, and the earth will cause to fall to the departed spirits." Early Judaism interpreted this raising of corpses as personal resurrection into kingdom.[13] Furthermore, Isaiah anticipates long life will also characterize this kingdom age (Isa 65:20).

---

13. 1QH 3.10-22; 6.34; 11.12; 1QM 12.1-4; *1 En.* 58.3; 62.14-16; 91.10; 92.2; 108.11-14; *2 Bar.*[Syriac] 30.1-5; 2 Macc 7.9-14, 22-23; 14.43-46; 4 Macc 7.19; 16.25; *4 Ezra* 7.32; *Sib. Or.* 4.180; *T. Benj.* 10.6-8; *T. Levi* 18; *T. Jud.* 24; *T. of Hos.* 6:2 interprets

THE NATIONS IN KINGDOM

The establishment of the kingdom also facilitates a new exodus and ingathering of the nations as well. Such ingathering will provide the nations with the instruction to align with peace and righteousness of the Law.[14]

In this kingdom, the nations will ultimately submit to the Davidic king (Isa 9:6-7; 11:4, 10, 14-15), bringing tribute to Jerusalem (Isa 14:1-2; 18:7; 23:15-18; 45:14 MT; 60:5-7, 11, 13, 16; 61:6; 66:12), and worship Yahweh in Jerusalem, joining in Israel's salvation (Isa 2:1-4; 19:18-25; 25:6-10a; 42:1-4; 45:22-25; 49:6; 51:4-6; 55:3-5; 56:3-8; 66:18-24).[15]

Lena Tiemeyer developed that late in Isaiah the reasoning shifts: if the gentile nations were not annihilated then they would en masse convert to Judaism (Isa 56:1-8; 66:18-21).[16] However, the theme of gentile conversion to Judaism also occurs in some earlier sections of Isaiah. In this spirit, a call is made to the ends of the earth for salvation (Isa 45:22). Such conversion would be seen by the gentiles offering prayers and sacrifices in the Jewish temple (Isa 2:3; perhaps 45:4; 56:7; 66:20-21). When the nations convert to Judaism, forgiveness extends beyond ethnic Israel (Isa 43:25; 44:22; 54:8) to include multi-ethnic gentiles (Isa 19:20-22; 45:20-23; 49:6; 51:4-5). As such, gentile peoples will be saved as proselyte Jews (Isa 45:6; 49:6; 51:4-5;

---

this text to be resurrection whereas the text speaks of the reviving of Israel on the third day; *Tg. Jon.* on Isa 27:12-13 describes salvation as being accomplished on the third day; *b. Sanh.* 90b where Gamaliel claims that God would give the resurrected patriarchs land, not merely their descendants. *Tg. Ps.-J.* Num 18:28 claims that the portion of Yahweh given to Aaron means that he will be alive again. Likewise Num 15:31 claims that the remaining guilt of the offender will be accountable in the world to come; 91b-92a; *B. Ta'an.* 2a; *B. Ket.* 111; *m. Sanh.* 10.1, 3; *T. Mos.* 10.8-10; *Gen. Rab.* 14.5; 28.3; *Lev. Rab.* 14.9; *Messianic Apocalypse* adds resurrection to a modification of Psalm 146:5-9 as a messianic expectation to be done to others; *T. Jud.* 25.4 claims this messianic resurrection would begin with Abraham, Isaac, and Jacob; *T. Benj.* claims that after these are raised the whole of Israel will be raised; *Pss. Sol.* 3.11-12; 4Q521 frag. 2, col. 2.1-13; frags. 7 and 5, col. 2.1-7; 1QH 14.29-35; 19.10-14; *Tg. Songs* 8.5; the benediction in the *Amidah*, the *Shemoneh Esre*. However, Wis 3.1; 8.19-20; 9.15 and Josephus's description of the Pharisees (*Ant.* 17.152-154; 18.1.3-5; *War* 2.151-153; 2.8.14; *Ap.* 2.217-8) follow more a Platonic immortality of the soul, but even here the soul eventually is given a body to match (Wis 9.15; Josephus, *War* 2.163). Also the biblical authors (Matt 22:23-33; Mark 12:18-27; Acts 23:6-7) and the *Eighteen Benedictions* present the Pharisees as believing the bodily resurrection of the dead; cf. Gillman, *Death of Death*, 101-142; Wright, *Resurrection*, 129-206 for the post-biblical Jewish view. The early church from the patristic through medieval eras embraced bodily resurrection instead of Platonic immortality of the soul with regard to personal eschatology (cf. Bynum, *Resurrection of the Body*; Wright, *Resurrection*, 480-552).

14. Scobie, *The Ways of Our God*, 516-17.
15. Davies, "Destiny of the Nations," 104-5.
16. Tiemeyer, "Death or Conversion"; Orlinsky, "'A Light to the Nations.'"

52:10). Thus, Isaiah's universalism is an ingathering of gentiles into Judaism; Judaism becomes an international religion beyond one ethnicity. Within Isaiah's thought-forms this means that these saved gentiles convert to Judaism and learn to practice the Mosaic Law as the basis for preparation for kingdom peace and worship (Isa 2:2-4).

> In the last days,
> The mountain of the house of Yahweh will be established as chief of mountains,
> And will be raised above the hills; and all nations will stream to it.
> And many peoples will come and say, Come let us go to the mountain of Yahweh,
> To the house of the God of Jacob;
> That he may teach us concerning his ways, and that we may walk in his paths,
> For the Law will go forth from Zion and the word of Yahweh from Jerusalem.
> And he will judge between the nations, and will reprove many peoples;
> And they will hammer their swords into plowshares and their spears into pruning hooks.
> Nation will not lift up sword against nation, and never again will they learn war (Isa 2:2-4).

Such conversion to covenant nomism is also evident in gentile commitment to celebrate Sabbath (Isa 56:4-5). In a context of kingdom, a light arises to shine on different people groups; Isaiah contemplates nations and kings coming to this light (Isa 60:1-3).

However, Isaiah describes no missionary activity among the nations to save them,[17] for mostly Isaiah has pronounced judgment upon the nations in a manner that they will not be informed, nor will the nations repent—though eventually in the kingdom context, gentiles could be included in Judaism and salvation by renouncing idolatry, converting to Judaism, men receiving circumcision, and embracing the benefits of kingdom (Ps 22:27; Isa 2:2-3; 14:1; 56:6-8; Ezek 47:22-23; Dan 11:34; Micah 4:2; Zech 2:11; 14:16; Ezra 6:21; Esth 9:27).[18] One of the kingdom benefits for the nations

17. Kaufmann, *Babylonian Captivity and Deutero-Isaiah*, 199.

18. Josephus, *Ant.* 13.257-58, 318-19; 14.285; 18.93-94; Josephus indicates circumcision caused Izates hesitation in proselytizing (*Ant.* 20.39-42); *War* 2.150; Tob 13.11; 14.6-7; *Pss. Sol.* 17.34; *T. Benj.* 9.2; *T. Jos.* 4.4-6; *T. Zeb.* 9.8; *Jos. Asen.* 12.3-5; *Mekhilta* 33.1.1; *Sipre* on Deut. 20:16-18; *b. Soṭa* 35b; *b. Sanh.* 96b; *Jdt.* 14.10; *Sipre* on Num. 15:14 [108]; *m. Ker.* 2.1; *b. Ker.* 9a; *T. Levi* 14.6; *Midrash Sipre Num.* 15:14; *b. Yebam* 46a-48b; Epictetus, *Ditr.* 2.9.19; *Sib. Or.* 4.165; *m. Tohar* 7.6; *t. Yoma* 4.20; *t. Pesaḥ* 7.13; Acts 10:28; John 18:28; Jews into Qumran: 1QS 3.3-6; Jews to John's Kingdom Judaism: Matt 3:11; Luke 3:7. Kaminsky, "Israel's Election and the Other"; Donaldson, *Judaism and the Gentiles*.

is provided by the servant of Yahweh atoning for their sins and identifying them within a covenant relationship through sprinkling with the servant's blood (Isa 52:15 after pattern of Exod 24:8).

From this post-Isaiah kingdom basis, some diaspora Jews sought conversion of gentiles to Judaism[19] and some gentile proselytes came into Judaism.[20] *Second Baruch* identified that proselytizing Gentiles must accept "the yoke of [God's] Law."[21] *Pseudo-Philo* extends Israel's election experience through the Mosaic covenant to be accomplished by divine grace within Israel, and then expands culpability for the Mosaic covenant to the whole world, much as Isaiah had done (Isa 2:2-4; 24:5-6; 25:4; 26:21).[22]

Early Jewish rationale for gentile conversion viewed Abraham as called to covenant for the nations,[23] which made Abraham the first gentile proselyte[24] and missionary to gentiles.[25] As part of the deeper back story, a few rabbinics conjectured that gentiles were offered *torah* but they rejected it and thereby were rejected by God.[26] Consequently Jewish practices were to be maintained and gentile practices (which were seen as akin to idolatry) were to be avoided, as *Jubilees* describes.

> Separate yourself from the gentiles, and do not eat with them, and do not perform deeds like theirs. And do not become associates of theirs. Because their deeds are defiled, and all of their ways are contaminated, despicable, and abominable.[27]

---

19. Tob 1.8; 13.11; Jdt 14.10; 2 Macc 3.1–3, 12, 33–39; 13.23; Theodotus, frag. 4 *P.E.* 9.22.4–6; Josephus, *Ant.* 20.34–36; *Ag. Ap.* 2.210; *m. 'Abot* 1.12; *b. Šabb.* 31a; *Sanh.* 99b; *Gen. Rab.* 39.14; 47.10; 48.8; 84.8; 98.5; *Num. Rab.* 8.4; *Eccl. Rab.* 7.8, section 1; *Pesiq. Rab Kah.* Sup. 1.6; *Pesiq. Rab.* 14.2; 43.6.

20. Jdt 14.10; Tob 1.8; 2 *Bar.* 41.4; Josephus, *Ant.* 18.82; 20.34–53; Philo, *Virt.* 102; *Spec.* 1.51–52; 4.178; 4 Ezra 3.36; *m. Bik.* 1.4; *b. Pesaḥ* 87b; *m. 'Abot* 1.12; *b. Šabb.* 31a; *Sipre Num.* 108; *Mek.* on Ex. 20:10; *b. Sanh.* 97b; petition 13 in *Shemoneh 'Esreh*; Matt 23:15; Acts 2:11; 6:5; 13:43; Justin, *Dial.* 122; Dio Cassius, *Rom. Hist.* 37.17.1; 57.18.5; 67.14.1–3; Juvenal, *Satire* 14; Horace, *Satires* 1.4.142–43; cf. Figueras, "Epigraphic Evidence for Proselytism"; Sukenik, *Jüdische Gräber Jerusalems*," esp. 13; Donaldson, *Paul and the Gentiles*, esp. 51–78.

21. 2 *Bar.* 41.3; Josephus, *Ant.* 20.44–45; *t. Demai* 2.5; *m. 'Abot* 1.12; 3.5; *b. Šabb.* 31a.

22. *LAB* 11.1–2; Philo, *Mos.* 2.36.

23. *T. Benj.* 10.9–10.

24. Philo, *Cher.* 31; *Mut.* 76; *Somn.* 161; *Spec.* 1.52.

25. *B. Ḥag.* 3a; Josephus, *Ant.* 1.161–67.

26. *Sif. Deut.* 343.4.1–2; *LAB* 11; *Mekilta* 2.

27. *Jub.* 22.16; *LAB* 9.1, 5; 12.2–10; 18.13–14; 19.7; 21.1; 25.7–13; 27; 30.1; 34.1–5; 41.3; 43.5; 44; 45.3; *Sifra* 193.1.9–11; 194.2.1, 15; *Bavli 'Abodah Zarah* 1.1.1.2/2a–b; Neusner, *Handbook of Rabbinic Theology*, 148–50, 492.

As such, God's grace and protection upon Israel contrasted with Yahweh's condemnation and destruction of the "unlawful" nations.[28] Uriel is characteristic in 4 *Ezra* claiming that there will be great joy in the salvation of the few, but no grief in the damnation of the many (Jew as well as gentile).[29] Uriel justified his response by appealing to Moses in Deuteronomist covenant nomism, "For this is the way of which Moses, while he was alive spoke to the people, 'Choose for yourself life, that you may live!' But they did not believe him, or the prophets after him, or even me who have spoken to them."[30] That is, from a Pharisaic or Rabbinic perspective, gentiles were generally viewed as perpetually outside the covenant, and thus damned.[31]

A number of early Jewish texts clarify that gentile proselytizing to Judaism joins the exclusive Jewish community including circumcision. For example, Judith describes Achior's proselytizing, after seeing "all that the God of Israel had done . . . he believed firmly in God . . . was circumcised, and joined the house of Israel."[32] The hope is as Philo describes that a proselyte is one who is "circumcised not in foreskin but in pleasures, desires, and other passions of the soul."[33] Tacitus describes this proselytizing process, "Those who are concerned to their ways follow the same practice [i.e., circumcision], and the earliest lesson they receive is to despise the gods, to disown their country, and to regard parents, children and brothers as little account."[34] The disowning may work the other way as well, as the gentile family abandons the proselyte, as occurred to Asenath—when she renounced her former gods, she was orphaned.[35] Entrance into Judaism made the gentile "righteous" or of appropriate status within the Mosaic covenant.[36] Such righteousness is substantially a living quality of choosing deeds according to *torah*.[37] Some texts include gentiles proselytizing into the eschatological kingdom (Isa 56:6).[38] While this global covenant-nominalistic culpability

28. *Pss. Sol.* 7.6-10; 8.23-34; 10.5-8; 11.1-9; 12.6; 17.1-46; *LAB* 10.4-6.
29. *4 Ezra* 7.126-31.
30. *4 Ezra* 7.129-30.
31. *Jub.* 15.26.
32. Jdt 14.10; *Sipre* on Num. 15:14 [108]; *m. Ker.* 2.1; *b. Ker.* 9a.
33. Philo, *QE* 2.2.
34. Tacitus, *Hist.* 5.5.2; Jdt 5.5-21; 7.23-28; Philo, *Virt.* 102; 181-82; 212-19; *Spec.* 1.51-52; 4.178.
35. *Jos. Asen.* 11.4-5; 12.5-15; Philo, *Spec.* 4.178.
36. *T. Sanh.* 13.2.
37. *Jub.* 7.20.
38. *Tg. Isa.*; and 1QIsa. A; *1 En.* 90.33-38; Sir 44.19-23; *Pss. Sol.* 17.31; *2 Bar.* 41.1-6; 68.1-8; 70.7-8; 72-73; *4 Ezra* 13.33-50; *Jub.* 22.20-22; *Sib. Or.* 3.719, 757-58; *T. Levi*

occasionally appears in later texts, the more common focus is on Israel's unique covenantal relationship, so there is some suspicion in early Judaism of the motive and value of proselytism.[39]

There are even some early Jewish texts that predict gentile pilgrimage into the eschatological kingdom without developing whether they have proselytized into Judaism (Isa 11:22; 66:18-20; Zech 8:23).[40] However, Isaiah does not develop a multi-ethnic Christian salvation as is developed by the NT (Matt 28:19; Mark; Luke; Acts 15; Rom 2:6—15:29; Gal 2–5).[41] Such multi-ethnic Christian salvation is a major biblical theological advance within NT theology. Isaiah serves as a bridge toward that NT theme by advancing a multi-ethnic Jewish kingdom salvation.

18.9; *T. Jud.* 24.5–6; 25.3–5; *T. Benj.* 9.2; 10.6–11; *T. Ash.* 7.2–3; *T. Naph.* 8.3–4; Philo, *Mos.* 2.44; *Ex. Rab.* 19.4; *Num. Rab.* 8.2; Evans, "From 'House of Prayer,'" 439 n. 31.

39. *B. Yeb.* 24b; 47a–b; *Mek.* on Ex. 22:20–21; *Lev. Rab.* 27.8.

40. Tob 13.11; 14.5–6; *Sib. Or.* 3.702–31, 772–75; *Pss. Sol.* 17.31; *1 En.* 90.33 and *2 Bar.* 68.5; Donaldson, "Proselytes or 'Righteous Gentiles'?"; Fredriksen, "Judaism, the Circumcision of Gentiles"; Bird, "Justification as Forensic Declaration," 125. A supercessionist approach is presented in *5 Ezra* 1.35–40 as a Christian text claiming Ezra abandoned Israel and transferred allegiance to incipient Christianity (Bergren, "Gentile Christians, Exile, and Return").

41. Kennard, *Biblical Covenantalism*, 2:214–47; 3:20–25, 66–160.

Select Bibliography

Abbott, Edwin. *Flatland: A Romance of Many Dimensions*. London: Seeley & Co., 1884.
Ackroyd, P. R. "Isaiah I–XII: Presentation of a Prophet." In *Congress Volume: Göttingen 1977*, edited by J. A. Emerton et. al., 16–48. Leiden: Brill, 1978.
———. "Isaiah 36–39: Structure and Function." In *Von Kanaan bis Kerala*, edited by W. C. Delsman et. al., 3–21. Neukirchen-Vluyn: Neukirchener, 1982.
Albright, William. *From the Stone Age to Christianity: Monotheism and Historical Process*. Garden City: Doubleday, 1975.
Alexander, Joseph A. *The Prophecies of Isaiah*. Grand Rapids: Zondervan, 1953.
Allen, Ronald Barclay. "The Leviathan-Rahab-Dragon Motif in the Old Testament." ThM thesis, Dallas Theological Seminary, 1968.
Anderson, Bernhard. *Creation Versus Chaos: The Reinterpretation of Mythical Symbolism in the Bible*. Eugene, OR: Wipf & Stock, 2005.
———. "Exodus and Covenant in Second Isaiah and Prophetic Tradition." In *Magnalia Dei: The Mighty Acts of God*, edited by Frank Moore Cross et al., 339–60. Garden City: Doubleday, 1976.
———. "Exodus Typology in Second Isaiah." In *Israel's Prophetic Heritage*, edited by Bernhard Anderson and Walter Harrelson, 177–95. New York: Harper and Brothers, 1962.
Aquinas, Thomas. *Summa Theologica*. In Great Books of the Western World 19. Chicago: Encyclopaedia Britannica, 1952.
Aristotle. *Metaphysics*. In Great Books of the Western World 8. Chicago: Encyclopaedia Britannica, 1952.
———. *Soul*. In Great Books of the Western World 8. Chicago: Encyclopaedia Britannica, 1952.
———. *Topics*. In Great Books of the Western World 8. Chicago: Encyclopaedia Britannica, 1952.
Augustine. *Christian Doctrine*. In Nicene and Post-Nicene Fathers 2. Peabody: Hendrickson, 1995.
———. *City of God*. In Great Books of the Western World 18. Chicago: Encyclopaedia Britannica, 1952.
———. *De peccatorum meritis et remissione et de baptismo parvulorum*. In *Sancti Aureli Augustini De peccatorum meritis et remissione et de baptismo parvulorum ad Marcellinum Libri Tres*, edited by Carl Franz Vrba and Joseph Zycha. Vindobonae: F. Tempsky, 1913.
———. *Enarrations on the Psalms*. In Nicene and Post-Nicene Fathers 8. Grand Rapids: Eerdmans, 1994.

Baldwin, Joyce. *Haggai, Zechariah, Malachi*. Downers Grove: InterVarsity, 1972.
Baltzer, Klaus. *Das Bundesformular. Seine Ursprung und Seine Verwendung im AT*. Wiss. Monograph. Alt Testamentum 2. New Testamentum 4. Neukirchen: Neukirchen-Vluyn, 1964.
———. *Deutero-Isaiah: A Commentary on Isaiah 40–55*. Minneapolis: Augsburg Fortress, 2001.
Barker, Kenneth. "Categories of Messianic Prophecy." Notes from ThD Theology of Isaiah class, Dallas Theological Seminary, 1980.
———. "Lord." In *Wycliffe Bible Encyclopedia*, edited by Charles Pfeiffer et al., 1048. Chicago: Moody, 1983.
———. "The Office and Functions of Ancient Kingship." Unpublished manuscript.
———. "Toward a Theology of Isaiah." Unpublished manuscript.
———. "Toward a Theology of Satan." Unpublished manuscript.
Barker, William. *Isaiah's Kingship Polemic: An Exegetical Study in Isaiah 24–27*. Tübingen: Mohr Siebeck, 2014.
Barmash, P. "Ancient Near Eastern Law." In *Oxford Encyclopedia of Bible and Law*, edited by Brent Strawn, 1:16–20. Oxford: Oxford University Press, 2015.
Barrett, Michael. "The Theology of Isaiah." *BV* 12 (1978) 144–51.
Barstad, Hans. *A Way in the Wilderness. The Second Exodus in the Message of Second Isaiah*. Manchester: University of Manchester, 1989.
Barth, Karl. *Church Dogmatics*. Edited by G. W. Bromiley and T. F. Torrance. Edinburgh: T & T Clark, 1936–69.
Baruq, A. "Is 19:18 et Leontopolis." *DBS* 5 (1952) 336–70.
Basil the Great. *Exegetical Homilies*. In Nicene and Post-Nicene Fathers Second Series 8. Peabody: Hendrickson, 1995.
Batto, Bernard. "The Covenant of Peace: A Neglected Ancient Near Eastern Motif," *CBQ* 49 (1987) 187–211.
Beckman, Gary. *Hittite Diplomatic Texts*. Atlanta: Scholars, 1995.
Begrich, J. "Das priesterliche Heilsorakel." *ZAW* 52 (1934) 81–92.
Behrens, Achin. "Gen. 15.6 und das Vorverständnis des Paulus." *ZAW* 109 (1997) 327–41.
Bellinger, William, and William Farmer. *Jesus and the Suffering Servant: Isaiah 53 and Christian Origins*. Harrisburg: Trinity International, 1998.
Bergren, Theodore A. "Gentile Christians, Exile, and Return in 5 Ezra 1:35–40." *JBL* 130 (2011) 593–612.
Berkeley. *A Treatise Concerning the Principles of Human Knowledge*. In Great Books of the Western World 35. Chicago: Encyclopaedia Britannica, 1952.
Berkouwer, Gerrit C. *Man: The Image of God*. Grand Rapids: Eerdmans, 1962.
Berman, Joshua. *Inconsistency in the Torah: Ancient Literary Convention and the Limits of Source Criticism*. Oxford: Oxford University Press, 2017.
Beuken, W. A. M. "Isa. 56:9–57:13—An Example of the Isaianic Legacy of Trito-Isaiah." In *Tradition and Reinterpretation in Jewish and Early Christian Literature*, edited by J. W. van Henten et. al., 48–64. Leiden: Lebram, 1986.
———. "The Main Theme of Trito-Isaiah 'The Servants of YHWH.'" *JSOT* 47 (1990) 67–87.
———. "*Mišpaṭ*: The First Servant Song and Its Context." *VT* 22 (1972) 1–30.
———. "Servant and Herald of Good Tidings: Isaiah 61 as an Interpretation of Isaiah 40–55." In *The Book of Isaiah: Le Livre D'Isaïe: Les Oracles et Leurs Reflectures*

Unité et Complexité de L'Ouvrage, edited by Jacqes Vermeylen, 411–42. Leuven: Uitgeverij Peeters, 1989.

Bird, Michael. "Justification as Forensic Declaration and Covenant Membership: A Via Media Between Reformed and Revisionist Readings of Paul." *TynBul* 57 (2006) 109–30.

Blanton, Thomas. "Spirit and Covenant Renewal: A Theologoumenon of Paul's Opponents in 2 Corinthians." *JBL* 129 (2010) 129–51.

Blenkinsopp, Joseph. *Isaiah 1–39*. Anchor Bible 19. New Haven: Yale University Press, 2000.

———. *Isaiah 40–55*. Anchor Bible 19A. New Haven: Yale University Press, 2002.

———. *Opening the Sealed Book: Interpretations of the Book of Isaiah in Late Antiquity*. Grand Rapids: Eerdmans, 2006.

Blocher, Henri. *Songs of the Servant*. Vancouver: Regent College Press, 2005.

Borger, Reikele, and W. G. Lambert. "Ein neuer Era-Text aus Ninive (K 9956 + 79—7—8, 18)." *Orientalia, Nova Series* 27 (1958) 137–49.

Bottéro, J. *Religion in Ancient Mesopotamia*. Chicago: University of Chicago Press, 2001.

Botterweck, G. Johannes, and Helmer Ringgren, eds. *Theological Dictionary of the Old Testament*. Grand Rapids: Eerdmans, 1977–2004.

Boutflower, Charles. *The Book of Isaiah Chapters I–XXXIX, in Light of the Assyrian Monuments*. London: SPCK, 1930.

Bovati, Petro. "Le Language Jardique du Prophete Isaïe." In *The Book of Isaiah: Le Livre D'Isaïe; Les Oracles et Leurs Reflectures Unité et Complexité de L'Ouvrage*, edited by Jacqes Vermeylen, 177–96. Leuven: Uitgeverij Peeters, 1989.

Boyle, Marjorie O'Rourke. "The Covenant Lawsuit of the Prophet Amos 3:1—4:13." *VT* 21 (1971) 338–62.

Bratcher, Robert. "Biblical Words Describing Man: Breath, Life, Spirit." *Bible Translator* 34 (1983) 201–13.

Brettler, Marc. *God is King: Understanding an Israelite Metaphor*. Sheffield: Sheffield Academic, 1989.

———. "Incompatible Metaphors for YHWH in Isaiah 40–66." *JSOT* 78 (1998) 97–120.

Bright, John. "Faith and Destiny: The Meaning of History in Deutero-Isaiah." *Int* 5 (1951) 3–26.

———. *Jeremiah*. Anchor Bible 21. New York: Doubleday, 1990.

Brooke, George. "Isaiah 40:3 and the Wilderness Community." In *New Qumran Texts and Studies: Proceedings of the First Meeting of the International Organization for Qumran Studies, Paris 1992*, edited by George Brooke, 117–32. Leiden: Brill, 1994.

Brown, Colin, ed. *The New International Dictionary of New Testament Theology*. Grand Rapids: Zondervan, 1975.

Brown, Warren, et al., eds. *Whatever Happened to the Soul?: Scientific and Theological Portraits of Human Nature*. Minneapolis: Fortress, 1998.

Brownlee, William. *The Meaning of the Qumran Scrolls for the Bible, with Special Attention to the Book of Isaiah*. New York: Oxford University Press, 1964.

Broyles, Craig, and Craig Evans. *Writing and Reading the Scroll of Isaiah: Studies of an Interpretive Tradition*. Leiden: Brill, 1997.

Brueggemann, Walter. *The Covenanted Self: Explorations in Law and Covenant*. Minneapolis: Fortress, 1999.

———. *Isaiah 1–39*. Westminster Bible Companion. Louisville: Westminster, 1998.

———. *Isaiah 40–66*. Westminster Bible Companion. Louisville: Westminster, 1998.

———. "Isaiah 55 and Deuteronomic Theology." *ZAW* 80 (1968) 191–203.
———. *A Pathway of Interpretation: The Old Testament for Pastors and Students.* Eugene, OR: Cascade, 2008.
———. *Theology of the Old Testament: Testimony, Dispute, Advocacy.* Minneapolis: Fortress, 1997.
———. "Unity and Dynamic in the Isaiah Tradition." *JSOT* 29 (1984) 89–107.
Brunner, Emil. *Man in Revolt.* Philadelphia: Westminster, 1947.
Buchanan, George. "Isaianic Midrash and the Exodus." In *The Function of Scripture in Early Jewish and Christian Tradition*, edited by Craig Evans and James Sanders, 89–109. Sheffield: Sheffield Academic, 1998.
Budge, E. A. Wallis, and L. W. King. *Annals of the Kings of Assyria.* London: British Museum, 1902.
Bultmann, Rudolf. *Theology of the New Testament.* New York: Scribner, 1951.
Buis, P. "Les formulaires d'alliance." *VT* 16 (1966) 396–411.
Bynum, Caroline Walker. *The Resurrection of the Body in Western Christianity, 200–1336.* New York: Columbia University Press, 1995.
Calvin, John. *Calvin's Commentaries.* Grand Rapids: Baker, 1979.
———. *The Institutes of the Christian Religion.* Grand Rapids: Associated Publishers and Authors, n.d.
Carroll, Robert. "Blindsight and the Vision Thing: Blindness and Insight in the Book of Isaiah." In *Writing and Reading the Scroll of Isaiah: Studies of an Interpretive Tradition*, edited by Craig Broyles and Craig Evans, 79–93. Leiden: Brill, 1997.
———. "Eschatological Delay in the Prophetic Tradition?" *ZAW* 94 (1982) 47–58.
Cassuto, Umberto, and Israel Abrahams. *The Documentary Hypothesis and the Composition of the Pentateuch.* Jerusalem: Magnes, 1961.
Cerny, Ladislav. *The Day of Yahweh and Some Relevant Problems.* Praze: Nákl Filosofické Fakulty University, 1948.
Chan, Michael. "Rhetorical Reversal and Usurpation: Isaiah 10:5–34 and the Use of Neo-Assyrian Royal Idiom in the Construction of an Anti-Assyrian Theology." *JBL* 128 (2009) 717–33.
Chernus, Ira. "Visions of God in Merkabah Mysticism." *JSJ* 13 (1982) 123–46.
Childs, Brevard. *The Book of Exodus: A Critical, Theological Commentary.* Louisville: Westminster, 1974.
———. *Introduction to the Old Testament as Scripture.* Philadelphia: Fortress, 1979.
———. *Isaiah: A Commentary.* Louisville: Westminster John Knox, 2013.
———. *Isaiah and the Assyrian Crises.* London: SCM, 1967.
Chilton, Bruce. *The Glory of Israel: The Theology and Provenience of the Isaiah Targum.* Sheffield: JSOT, 1982.
Chiera, Edward. *Proceedings in Court.* Philadelphia: Publications of the Bagdad School, 1959.
———. *Sumerian Religious Texts.* Upland: University of Pennsylvania, 1924.
Chirichigno, Gregory. *Debt-Slavery in Israel and the Ancient Near East.* JSOTSup 141. Sheffield: Sheffield Academic, 1993.
Chisholm, Robert. "A Theology of Isaiah." In *A Biblical Theology of the Old Testament*, edited by Roy Zuck et al., 305–40. Chicago: Moody, 1991.
Clements, Ronald. "Beyond Tradition History: Deutero-Isaianic Development of First Isaiah's Themes." *JSOT* 31 (1985) 95–113.
———. *Isaiah 1–39.* New Century Bible Commentary. Grand Rapids: Eerdmans, 1980.

———. *Isaiah and the Deliverance of Jerusalem: A Study of the Interpretation of Prophecy in the Old Testament*. Sheffield: JSOT, 1980
———. "The Unity of the Book of Isaiah." *Int* 36 (1982) 117–29.
Cohn-Haft, Louis. *The Ancient Near East and Greece. Source Readings in Ancient History* 1. New York: Thomas Crowell, 1965.
Collins, John. *Invention of Judaism: Torah and Jewish Identity from Deuteronomy to Paul*. Oakland: University of California Press, 2017.
———. *The Star and the Scepter: The Messiah of the DDS and Other Ancient Literature*. New York: Doubleday, 1995.
Collins, John, and Daniel Harlow, eds. *The Eerdmans Dictionary of Early Judaism*. Grand Rapids: Eerdmans, 2010.
Conrad, Edgar. "The Royal Narratives and the Structure of the Book of Isaiah." *JSOT* 41(1988) 67–81.
Constitutions of the Holy Apostles. In Ante-Nicene Fathers 7. Peabody: Hendrickson, 1995.
Conzelmann, Hans. "Der Brief an die Kolosser." In *Die Kleineren Briefe des Apostels Paulus*, edited by H. W. Beyer et al., 8:131–56. Göttingen, Vandenhoeck & Ruprecht, 1962.
Cooper, John. *Body, Soul and Life Everlasting*. Grand Rapids: Eerdmans, 1989.
Coste, J. *Righteousness in the Septuagint of Isaiah: A Contextual Study*. SCS 8. Missoula: Scholars, 1979.
Craigie, Peter, et al. *Jeremiah 1–25*. Word Biblical Commentary 26. Dallas: Word, 1991.
Cross, Frank Moore. "The Divine Warrior in Israel's Early Cult." In *Biblical Motifs*, edited by Alexander Altman, 11–30. Cambridge: Harvard University Press, 1966.
Crouch, Carly. *Israel and the Assyrians: Deuteronomy, the Succession Treaty of Esarhaddon and the Nature of Subversion*. Atlanta: Society of Biblical Literature, 2014.
Cullmann, Oscar. *Christ and Time: The Primitive Christian Conception of Time and History*. Philadelphia: Westminster, 1964.
———. *The Christology of the New Testament*. Philadelphia: Westminster, 1963.
Dalman, Gustav. *Jerusalem und seine Gelände*. New York: G. Olms, 1972.
Daly, Robert. "The Soteriological Significant of the Sacrifice of Isaac." *CBQ* 39 (1977) 45–75.
Dahl, M. E. *The Resurrection of the Body*. London: SCM, 1962.
Darr, Katheryn. "Like Warrior, Like Woman: Destruction and Deliverance in Isaiah 42:10–17." *CBQ* 49 (1987) 560–71.
Davidson, A. B. *Hebrew Syntax*. Edinburgh: T & T Clark, 1901.
Davies, Graham. "The Destiny of the Nations in the Book of Isaiah." In *The Book of Isaiah: Le Livre D'Isaïe: Les Oracles et Leurs Reflectures unite et Complexité de L'Ouvrage*, edited by Jacques Vermeylen, 93–120. Leuven: Leuven University Press, 1989.
Dean-Otting, Mary. *Heavenly Journeys: A Study of the Motif in Hellenistic Jewish Literature*. New York: Peter Lang, 1984.
Dempsey, Carol. *Isaiah: God's Poet of Light*. St. Louis: Chalice, 2010.
deRoche, Michael. "Yahweh's *rîb* against Israel: A Reassessment of the So-Called 'Prophetic Lawsuit' in the Preexilic Prophets." *JBL* 102 (1983) 563–74.
Descartes, René. *Discourse on the Method of Rightly Conducting the Reason and Seeking for Truth in the Sciences*. In Great Books of the Western World 31. Chicago: Encyclopaedia Britannica, 1952.

———. *Meditations on First Philosophy.* In Great Books of the Western World 31. Chicago: Encyclopaedia Britannica, 1952.

———. *Objections Urged by Certain Men of Learning Against the Preceding Meditations; withe the Author's Replies.* In Great Books of the Western World 31. Chicago: Encyclopaedia Britannica, 1952.

Dietrich, Manfried, et al. *Keilalphabetische Texte aus Ugarit.* Kevelaer: Butzon und Bercker, 1976.

Dijkstra, M. "Lawsuit, Debate and Wisdom Discourse." In *Studies in the Book of Isaiah*, edited by J. Van Ruiten and M. Vervenne, 251–71. Leuven: Leuven University Press, 1997.

Dillard, Raymond, and Tremper Longman. *An Introduction to the Old Testament.* Grand Rapids: Zondervan, 1994.

Dion, P. E. "The Patriarchal Traditions and the Literary Form of the 'Oracle of Salvation.'" *CBQ* 29 (1967) 198–206.

DiSante, Carmine. *Jewish Prayer: The Origins of the Christian Liturgy.* New York: Paulist, 1985.

Döderlein, Johann. *Esaias: Ex recensione textus Hebraei.* Altdorfi: Monath, 1781.

Donaldson, Terence. *Judaism and the Gentiles: Jewish Patterns of Universalism (to 135 C.E.).* Waco: Baylor University Press, 2007.

———. *Paul and the Gentiles: Remapping the Apostle's World.* Minneapolis: Fortress, 1997.

———. "Proselytes or 'Righteous Gentiles'? The Status of Gentiles in Eschatological Pilgrimage Patterns of Thought." *JSP* 7 (1990) 3–27.

Dreytza, Manfred. *Der theologische Gebrauch von RUAḤ im Alten Testament: Eine wort- und satzsemantishe Studie.* Basel: Brunnen, 1992.

Driver, Godfrey R. *Canaanite Myths and Legends.* Edinburgh: Clark, 1976.

Duggan, Michael. *The Covenant Renewal in Ezra-Nehemiah (Neh. 7:72b–10:40): An Exegetical, Literal, and Theological Study.* Atlanta: Society of Biblical Literature, 2001.

Duhm, Bernard. *Das Buch Jesaiah.* Göttingen: Vandenhoeck, 1892 and 1922.

———. *Die Theologie der Propheten als Grundlage für die innere Entwicklungsgeschichte der israelitischen Religion dargestellt.* Bonn: Marcus, 1875.

Dumbrell, William. *The Faith of Israel: Its Expression in the Books of the Old Testament.* Grand Rapids: Baker, 1988.

———. "The Purpose of the Book of Isaiah." *TB* 36 (1985) 111–28.

Dunn, James. *The Theology of Paul the Apostle.* Grand Rapids: Eerdmans, 1998.

Eichhorn, Johann. *Einleitung in das Alte Testament.* Leipzig: Weidmanns Erben u. Reich, 1783.

Eichrodt, Walter. *Theology of the Old Testament.* Philadelphia: Westminster, 1961.

Ekblad, Eugene. *Isaiah's Servant Poems according to the Septuagint: An Exegetical and Theological Study.* Leuven: Peeters, 1999.

Eliade, Mircea. *The Sacred and the Profane: The Nature of Religion.* New York: Harcourt, Brace & World, 1959.

Engnell, Ivan. *The Call of Isaiah: An Exegetical and Comparative Study.* Uppsala: Lundequotska Bokhandeln, 1949.

———. "The 'Ebed Yahweh' Songs and the Suffering Messiah in Deutero-Isaiah." *BJRL* 31 (1948) 54–96.

———. "Studies in Divine Kingship in the Ancient Near East." PhD diss., University of Uppsala, 1943.
Epistle to Diognetus. Leiden: E. J. Brill, 1964.
Erickson, Dean. Review of *The Lost World of the Torah: Law as Covenant and Wisdom in Ancient Context*, by John H. Walton and J. Harvey Walton. *JETS* 62 (2019) 612–14.
Estelle, Bryan. *Echoes of Exodus: Tracing a Biblical Motif*. Downers Grove: InterVarsity, 2018.
Evans, Craig. "Isaiah 6:9–13 in the Context of Isaiah's Theology." *JETS* 29 (1986) 139–46.
———. *The Quest for Context and Meaning*. Leiden: Brill, 1997.
———. *To See and Not Perceive: Isa 6:9–10 in Early Jewish and Christian Interpretation*. Sheffield: Sheffield Academic, 1989.
Everson, A. Joseph. "The Days of Yahweh." *JBL* 93 (1974) 329–37.
Ezra, Ibn. *The Commentary of Ibn Ezra on Isaiah*. Translated by M. Friedländer. New York: Feldheim, 1964.
Falk, Ze'ev W. *Hebrew Law in Biblical Times: An Introduction*. Winona Lake: Eisenbrauns, 2001.
Fensham, Charles. "Common Trends in Curses of the Near Eastern Treaties and *Kudurru*-Inscriptions Compared with Maledictions of Amos and Isaiah." *ZAW* 75 (1963) 155–75.
Figueras, Pau. "Epigraphic Evidence for Proselytism in Ancient Judaism." *Immanuel* 24 (1990) 194–206.
Finch, Thomas E. "The Theology of Deuteronomy with Special Emphasis on the Implications of the Hittite Suzerainty Treaties." Dallas: ThD diss., Dallas Theological Seminary, 1980.
Fischer, Johann. "Das Problem des neuen Exodus in Isaias, c. 40–55." *TQ* 110 (1929) 111–30.
Fitzmyer, Joseph. *The Aramaic Inscriptions of Sefire*. Biblica et Orientalia 19. Rome: Pontifical Biblical Institute, 1967.
———. "The Aramaic Inscriptions of Sefire I and II." *JAOS* 81 (1961) 178–222.
———. *The Gospel according to Luke X–XXIV*. Anchor Bible 28a. New York: Doubleday, 1985.
Frankel, Victor. *Man's Search for Meaning*. New York: Pocket Books, 1959.
Fredriksen, Paula. "Judaism, the Circumcision of Gentiles and Apocalyptic Hope: Another Look at Galatians 1 and 2." *JTS* 42 (1991) 544–48.
Fried, Lisbeth. "Cyrus the Messiah? The Historical Background to Isaiah 45:1." *HTR* 95 (2002) 373–93.
Fuerst, Wesley. "The Word of God in the Old Testament." *LQ* 10 (1958) 315–26.
Gammie, John. *Holiness in Israel*. Minneapolis: Fortress, 1989.
Gane, Roy. *Cult and Character: Purification Offerings, Day of Atonement, and Theodicy*. Winona Lake: Eisenbrauns, 2005.
———. "Private Preposition מן in Purification Offering Pericopes and the Changing Face of 'Dorian Gray.'" *JBL* 127 (2008) 219–22.
Gelb, Ignace. *The Assyrian Dictionary of the Oriental Institute of the University of Chicago*. Chicago: Oriental Institute of the University of Chicago Press, 1964.
Gemser, B. "The *rîb*-Controversy-Pattern in Hebrew Mentality." In *Wisdom in Israel and in the Ancient Near East: Festschrift for H. H. Rowley*, edited by M. Noth and D. W. Thomas. VTSup 3. Leiden: Brill, 1969, 120–37.

Gerstenberger, Erhard. *Wesen und Herkunft des 'Apodiktischen Rechts.'* Neukirchen-Vluyn: Neukirchener, 1965.

———. "The Woe-Oracle of the Prophets." *JBL* 81 (1962) 249–63.

Gese, Hartmut. "Der Dekalog als Ganzheit betrachtet." *ZTK* 64 (1967) 121–38.

Gevirtz, Stanley. "West Semitic Curses and the Problem of the Origins of Hebrew Law." *VT* 11 (1961) 137–58.

Gillman, Neil. *The Death of Death: Resurrection and Immortality in Jewish Thought.* Woodstock: Jewish Lights, 2000.

Glueck, Nelson. *Hesed in the Bible.* Cincinnati: Hebrew Union College, 1967.

Goetze, Albrecht. *Kleinasien.* In *Handbuch der Altertumswissenschaft*, edited by Herman Bengtson et al., 3:1–200. München: Beck, 1961.

Goldingay, John. "The Compound Name in Isaiah 9:5(6)." *CBQ* 61 (1999) 239–44.

———. *Isaiah.* Understanding the Bible Commentary Series. Grand Rapids: Baker, 2001.

———. *The Message of Isaiah 40–55: A Literary-Theological Commentary.* London: T & T Clark, 2005.

———. *Old Testament Theology.* 3 vols. Downer's Grove: InterVarsity, 2003, 2006, 2009.

———. "The Theology of Isaiah." In *Interpreting Isaiah: Issues and Approaches*, edited by David Firth and H. Williamson. Nottingham: Apollos, 2009, 168–190.

———. *The Theology of the Book of Isaiah.* Downers Grove: InterVarsity, 2014.

Goldingay, John, and David Payne. *Isaiah 40–55: A Critical and Exegetical Commentary.* London: Bloomsbury, 2014.

Gordon, Cyrus H. "Belt-Wrestling in the Bible World." *HUCA* 23 (1950–51) 131–36.

———. "Leviathan: Symbol of Evil." In *Biblical Motifs: Origins and Transformations*, edited by Alexander Altman, 1–9. Cambridge: Harvard University Press, 1966.

Gössman, Felix. *Das Era Epos.* Würzburg: Augustinus-Verlag, 1955.

Gosse, Bernard. "Sabbath, Identity and Universalism Go Together after the Return from Exile." *JSOT* 29 (2005) 359–70.

Gottwald, Norman. "Immanuel as the Prophet's Son." *VT* 8 (1958) 36–47.

Grabbe, Lester, and Robert Haak. *"Every City Shall Be Forsaken": Urbanism and Prophecy in Ancient Israel and the Near East.* Sheffield: Sheffield Academic, 2001.

Gray, John. *The Legacy of Canaan: The Ras Shamm Texts and Their Relevance to the Old Testament.* Leiden: Brill, 1957.

Greenberg, Moshe. "Some Postulates of Biblical Criminal law." In *Yehezkel Kaufmann Jubilee Volume: Studies in Bible and Jewish Religion*, edited by Menahem Haran, 5–28. Jerusalem: Magnes, 1960.

Gregory Thaumaturgus. *Four Homilies.* In Ante-Nicene Fathers 6. Peabody: Hendrickson, 1995.

Gregory the Great. *Register of the Epistles of Saint Gregory the Great.* In Nicene and Post-Nicene Fathers Second Series 15:1–111. Peabody: Hendrickson, 1995.

Gressmann, Hugo. *Der Messias.* Göttingen: Vandenhoeck & Ruprecht, 1929.

Grether, Oskar. *Name und Wort Gottes im Alten Testament.* Giessen: A Töpelmann, 1934.

Groswell, Greg. "Messianic Expectation from Isaiah 11." *WTJ* 79 (2017) 123–35.

Gruber, Mayer. "The Motherhood of God in Second Isaiah." *RB* 90 (1983) 351–59.

Gruenwald, Ithamer. *Apocalyptic and Merkavah Mysticism.* Boston: Brill, 1980.

Gubler, Marie-Louise. *Die Frühesten Deutungen des Todes Jesu*. Göttingen: Vandenhoeck & Ruprecht, 1977.
Guenter, Robert. "The Word of the Lord to the Ruling Houses in Samuel and Kings." *JETS* 62 (2019) 307–27.
Gundry, Robert. *Soma in Biblical Theology: With Emphasis on Anthropology*. Grand Rapids: Zondervan, 1987.
Gunkel, Herman, and J. Begrich. *Einleitung in die Psalmen: Die Gattungen der Religiösen Lyrik Israels*. Göttingen: Vandenhoeck & Ruprecht, 1985.
Guterbock, H. G. "Authority and Law in the Hittite Kingdom." In *Authority and Law in the Ancient Orient*, edited by John Wilson. Baltimore: American Oriental Society, 1954.
Häbel, Norman. "He Who Stretches Out the Heavens." *CBQ* 34 (1972) 417–30.
———. "'Yahweh, Maker of Heaven and Earth': A Study in Tradition Criticism." *JBL* 91 (1972) 321–37.
Hänel, Johannes. *Die Religion der Heiligkeit*. Gütersloh: Der Rufer Evang., 1931.
Hannah, Darrell. "Isaiah's Vision in the Ascension of Isaiah and the Early Church." *JTS* 50 (1999) 80–101.
Harris, R. Laird, et al., eds. *Theological Wordbook of the Old Testament*. Chicago: Moody, 1980.
Harrison, R. K. *Jeremiah and Lamentations: Introduction and Commentary*. In *Tyndale Old Testament Commentaries*, edited by D. J. Wiseman. Downers Grove: InterVarsity, 1975.
Harner, Philip. "Creation Faith in Deutero-Isaiah." *VT* 17 (1967) 298–306.
———. *Grace and Law in Second Isaiah*. Lewiston: Edwin Mellen, 1988.
———. "The Salvation Oracle in Second Isaiah." *JBL* 88 (1969) 418–34.
Harrington, Hannah. *The Impurity Systems of Qumran and the Rabbis: Biblical Foundations*. Atlanta: Scholars, 1993.
Harvey, Julien. *Le plaidoyer prophétique contre Israél après la rupture de l'alliance: Étude d'une formule littéraire de l'Ancient Testament*. Paris: Bruges, 1967.
———. "Le Riv-Pattern: Requisitoire prophetique sur las rupture de l'Alliance." *Bib* 43 (1962) 172–96.
Hasel, Gerhard. *The Remnant: The History and Theology of the Remnant Idea from Genesis to Isaiah*. Berrien Springs: Andrews University Press, 1974.
Hayes, Christine. *What's Divine About Divine Law? Early Perspectives*. Princeton: Princeton University Press, 2015.
Hays, Christopher. "The Covenant with Mut: A New Interpretation of Isaiah 28:1–22." *VT* 60 (2010) 212–40.
———. *Hidden Riches: A Sourcebook for the Comparative Study of the Hebrew Bible and Ancient Near East*. Louisville: Westminster John Knox, 2014.
Hayes, John. "The Usage of Oracles against Foreign Nations in Ancient Israel." *JBL* 87 (1968) 81–92.
Healy, Mary, and Robin Parry. *The Bible and Epistemology*. Milton Keynes: Paternoster, 2007.
Henderson, Stephen. "Isaiah's Theological Use of the Old Testament: A First Study." ThD paper, Dallas Theological Seminary, 1980.
Hengel, Martin, and Daniel Bailey. "The Effective History of Isaiah 53 in the Pre-Christian Period." In *The Suffering Servant*, edited by Bernd Janowski and Peter Stuhlmacher, 75–146. Tübingen: Mohr Siebeck, 1966.

Hillers, Delbert. *Treaty-Curses and the Old Testament Prophets*. Rome: Pontifical Biblical Institute, 1964.
Hippolytus. *The Refutation of all Heresies*. In Ante-Nicene Fathers 5. Peabody: Hendrickson, 1995.
Hirsch, Hans. "Die Incriften der Könige von Agade." *AfO* 10 (1963) 43–46.
Hobbes. *Leviathan*. In Great Books of the Western World 23. Chicago: Encyclopaedia Britannica, 1952.
Hoehner, Harold W. *Chronological Aspects of the Life of Christ*. Grand Rapids: Zondervan, 1977.
Hoffman, Yair. *The Doctrine of the Exodus in the Bible*. Tel Aviv: Tel Aviv University Press, 1983.
Holladay, John. "Assyrian Statecraft and the Prophets of Israel." *HTR* 63 (1970) 29–51.
Holladay, W. L. *Isaiah: Scroll of a Prophetic Heritage*. Grand Rapids: Eerdmans, 1978.
Holter, Knut. *Second Isaiah's Idol Fabrication Passages*. Frankfurt: Lang, 1995.
Homer. *The Iliad*. Translated by Samuel Butler. Great Books of the Western World 4. Chicago: Encyclopaedia Britannica, 1952.
———. *The Odyssey*. Translated by Samuel Butler. Great Books of the Western World 4. Chicago: Encyclopaedia Britannica, 1952.
Hooker, Morna. *Jesus and the Servant: The Influence of the Servant Concept of Deutero-Isaiah in the New Testament*. London: SPCK, 1959.
House, Paul. *Old Testament Theology*. Downers Grove: InterVarsity, 1998.
Huey, F. B. "Great Themes in Isaiah 40–66." *SWJT* 11 (1968) 45–57.
Huffmon, Herbert. "The Covenant Lawsuit in the Prophets." *JBL* 78 (1959) 285–95.
———. "The Treaty Background of Hebrew *Yada*." *BASOR* 181 (1966) 35–36.
Huffmon, Herbert, and Simon Parker. "A Further Note on the Treaty Background of Hebrew *Yada*." *BASOR* 181 (1966) 36–38.
Hurowitz, Victor. "Isaiah's Impure Lips and Their Purification in Light of Akkadian Sources." *HUCA* 60 (1989) 39–89.
Hyatt, J. Philip. "The Sources of the Suffering Servant Idea." *JNES* 3 (1944) 79–86.
Ignatius. *Epistle to the Ephesians*. In Ante-Nicene Fathers 1. Peabody: Hendrickson, 1995.
Irenaeus. *Against Heresies*. In Ante-Nicene Fathers 1. Grand Rapids: Eerdmans, 1995.
Isaacs, Marie. *Sacred Space: An Approach to the Theology of the Epistle to the Hebrews*. Sheffield: JSOT, 1992.
Jackson, Bernard. *Wisdom Laws: A Study of the Mishpatim of Exodus 21:12–2:16*. Oxford: Oxford University Press, 2006.
Jackson, Samuel. *A Comparison of Ancient Near Eastern Law Collections Prior to the First Millennium BC*. Piscataway, NJ: Georgias, 2008.
Jacob, Edmond. *Theology of the Old Testament*. Hachette: Hodder & Stoughton, 1967.
Jacobsen, Thorkild. "The Graven Image." In *Ancient Israelite Religion*, edited by Patrick Miller et al., 15–32. Minneapolis: Fortress, 2009.
Janzen, Waldemar. *Mourning Cry and Woe Oracle*. Berlin: Walter de Gruyter, 1972.
Jensen, J. *The Use of Tora by Isaiah*. Washington: Catholic Biblical Association, 1973.
Jenson, Philip P. *Graded Holiness: A Key to the Priestly Conception of the World*. Sheffield: Sheffield Academic, 1992.
Jewett, Robert. *Romans*. Hermeneia. Minneapolis: Fortress, 2007.
Johnson, Aubrey. *The One and the Many in the Israelite Conception of God*. Cardiff: University of Wales Press, 1961.

———. *The Vitality of the Individual in the Thought of Ancient Israel*. Cardif: University of Wales Press, 1964.
Johnson, Dan. *From Chaos to Restoration: An Integrative Reading of Isaiah 24–27*. Sheffield: Sheffield Academic, 1988.
Josephus. *The Life and Works of Flavius Josephus*. Chicago: John Winston, n.d.
Justin Martyr. *Saint Justin Martyr: The First Apology, The Second Apology, Dialogue with Trypho, Exhortation to the Greeks, Discourse to the Greeks, The Monarchy; or the Rule of God*. Edited by Thomas B. Falls. New York: Christian Heritage, 1949.
Kaiser, Otto. *Isaiah 1–12*. Old Testament Library. Philadelphia: Westminster, 1972.
———. *Isaiah 13–39*. Old Testament Library. Philadelphia: Westminster, 1974.
Kaiser, Walter. *Toward an Old Testament Theology*. Grand Rapids: Zondervan, 1991.
Kamesar, A. "The Virgin of Isaiah 7:14: The Philological Argument from the Second to the Fifth Century." *JTS* 49 (1990) 51–75.
Kaminsky, Joel. "Israel's Election and the Other in Biblical, Second Temple, and Rabbinic Thought." In *The "Other" in Second Temple Judaism*, edited by Daniel Harlow et al., 17–30. Grand Rapids: Eerdmans, 2011.
Kapelrud, Arvid. "The Main Concern of Second Isaiah." *VT* 32 (1982) 50–58.
Kaufmann, Yehezkel. *The Babylonian Captivity and Deutero-Isaiah*. History of the Religion of Israel 4. New York: Union of American Hebrew Congregations, 1970.
Kautzsch, E., and A. E. Cowley. *Gesenius' Hebrew Grammar*. Oxford: Clarendon, 1976.
Kazen, Thomas. "4Q274 Fragment 1 Revisited—or Who Touched Whom? Further Evidence for Ideas of Graded Impurity and Graded Purifications." *DSD* 17 (2010) 53–87.
Keener, Craig. "Miracle Reports and the Argument from Analogy." *BBR* 25 (2015) 475–95.
———. *Miracles: The Credibility of the New Testament Accounts*. Grand Rapids: Baker, 2011.
Keil, Friedrich. *The Prophecies of Jeremiah*. Commentary on the Old Testament in Ten Volumes 8. Grand Rapids: Eerdmans, 1977.
Kelley, Page. *Judgment and Redemption in Isaiah*. Nashville: Broadman, 1968.
Kendall, Daniel. "The Use of *Mišpaṭ* in Isaiah 59." *ZAW* 96 (1984) 391–405.
Kennard, Douglas. *Biblical Covenantalism: Engagement with Judaism, Law, Atonement, the New Perspective, and Kingdom Hope*. 3 vols. Eugene, OR: Wipf & Stock, 2015.
———. "A Biblical Theology of Isaiah." ThD paper for Theology of Isaiah, Dallas Theological Seminary, 1980.
———. *The Classical Christian God*. Lewiston, NY: Edwin Mellen, 2002.
———. *A Critical Realist's Theological Method: Returning the Bible and Biblical Theology to Be the Framer for Theology and Science*. Eugene, OR: Wipf & Stock, 2013.
———. *Epistemology and Logic in the New Testament: Early Jewish Context and Biblical Theology Mechanisms That Fit within Some Contemporary Ways of Knowing*. Eugene, OR: Wipf & Stock, 2016.
———. *The Gospel*. Eugene, OR: Wipf & Stock, 2017.
———. *Messiah Jesus: Christology in His Day and Ours*. New York: Peter Lang, 2008.
———. "The Reef of the O.T.: A Method for Doing Biblical Theology that Makes Sense for Wisdom Literature." *SwJT* 56 (2013) 227–57.
Keowen, B. L. *A History of the Interpretation of Isaiah 14:12–15*. PhD diss., Southern Baptist Theological Seminary, Louisville, 1979.

Kierkegaard, Sören. *Sickness unto Death.* Translated by Lowrie Walter. Princeton: Princeton University Press, 1941.
Kiesow, Klaus. *Exodustexte im Jesajabuch: Literarkritische und Motivgeshichtliche Anaylsen.* Frieberg: Universitätsverlag, 1979.
Kilian, R. "Apodiktisches und kasuistisches Recht im Licht ägyptischer Analogien." *BZ* 7 (1963) 185–202.
King, Leonard W. *Babylonian Boundary Stones and Memorial Tablets in the British Museum.* London: Longman, 1912.
Kittle, Gerhard, and Gerhard Friedrich. *Theological Dictionary of the New Testament.* Grand Rapids: Eerdmans, 1964–76.
Klawans, Jonathan. *Impurity and Sin in Ancient Judaism.* Oxford: Oxford University Press, 2000.
Kline, Meredith G. *Treaty of the Great King: The Covenant Structure of Deuteronomy.* Grand Rapids: Eerdmans, 1963.
Knohl, Israel. *The Messiah before Jesus: The Suffering Servant of the Dead Sea Scrolls.* Berkeley: University of California Press, 2000.
Knutson, F. Brent. "Literary Genres in PRU IV." In *Ras Shamra Parallels*, edited by Loren Fisher, 174–97. Rome: Pontificium Institutum Biblicum, 1975.
Koch, Robert. *Der Geist Gottes im Alten Testament.* Bern: Peter Lang, 1991.
———. *Geist und Messias.* Freiburg: Herder, 1950.
Koester, Craig. *Hebrews: A New Translation with Introduction and Commentary.* Anchor Yale Bible 36. New York: Doubleday, 2001.
Köhler, Ludwig. *Die hebräische Mensch: Eine Skizze; mit einem Anhang.* Tübingen: Mohr, 1953.
———. *Old Testament Theology.* Philadelphia: Westminster, 1967.
Koole, Jan. *Isaiah III: Volume 1; Isaiah 40–48.* Historical Commentary on the Old Testament. Kampen: Kok Pharos, 1997.
Kramer, Samuel Noah. *The Sumerians: Their History, Culture, and Character.* Chicago: University of Chicago Press, 2008.
Kraovec, Jože. *La Justice (SDQ) de Dieu dans la Bible Hebraique et l'Interpretation Juwe et Chretienne.* Frieburg: Vandenhoeck Ruprecht, 1888.
Kraus, Fritz R. "Ein zentrales Problem des altmesopotamischen Rechtes: Was ist der Codex Hammurabi?" *Geneva* 8 (1960) 283–96.
Kuhn, H. B. "God, Names of." In *Zondervan Pictorial Encyclopedia of the Bible*, 2:760–66. Grand Rapids: Zondervan, 1975.
Kuhn, Thomas. *The Structure of Scientific Revolutions.* Chicago: University of Chicago Press, 1970.
Kupper, J. R. *Correspondence de Kibri-Dagon, ARM III.* Paris: Archives Royales de Mari, 1950.
Laato, Antti. *The Servant of YHWH and Cyrus: A Reinterpretation of the Exilic Messianic Programme in Isaiah 40–55.* Coniectanea biblica: Old Testament Series 35. Stockholm: Almqvist & Wiksell International, 1992.
Labahn, Antje. "The Delay of Salvation within Deutero-Isaiah." *JSOT* 85 (1999) 71–84.
Labuschagne, Casper J. *The Incomparability of Yahweh in the Old Testament.* Leiden: Brill, 1966.
Lactantius. *The Divine Institutes.* In Ante-Nicene Fathers 7. Peabody: Hendrickson, 1995.
Lambert, W. G. *Babylonian Wisdom Literature.* Oxford: Clarendon, 1960.

Landsberger, Benno. "Die babylonischen Termini für Gesetz und Recht." In *Symbolae ad Iura Orientis Antiqul Pertinentes Paulo Koschaker Dedicatae*. Studia et Documenta ad Jura Orientis Antique Pertinentia 2. Edited by Theunis Folkers et al., 219–34. Leiden: Brill, 1939.
Lange, John P. *Commentary on the Holy Scriptures*. Grand Rapids: Zondervan, 1960.
Laurin, Robert. *Contemporary Old Testament Theologians*. Valley Forge, PA: Judson, 1970.
LeFebvre, Michael. *Collections, Codes and Torah: The Re-characterization of Israel's Written Law*. New York: T & T Clark, 2006.
Leupold, H. C. *Exposition of Isaiah*. Grand Rapids: Baker, 1971.
Lewis, Theodore. "'You Have Heard What the Kings of Assyria Have Done': Disarmament Passages *vis-á-vis* Assyrian Rhetoric of Intimidation." In *Isaiah's Vision of Peace in Biblical and Modern International Relations: Swords into Plowshares*, edited by Raymond Cohen and Raymond Westbrook, 75–100. New York: Palgrave Macmillan, 2008.
Lienhard, Joseph T. *Exodus, Leviticus, Numbers, Deuteronomy*. Downers Grove: InterVarsity, 2001.
Lim, Bo H. *The "Way of the Lord" in the Book of Isaiah*. New York: T & T Clark, 2010.
Limberg, James. "The Root רִיב and the Prophetic Lawsuit Speeches." *JBL* 88 (1969) 291–304.
Lincoln, Andrew. *Paradise Now and Not Yet: Studies in the Role of the Heavenly Dimension in Paul's Thought with Special Reference to His Eschatology*. SNTSMS 43. Cambridge: Cambridge University Press, 1981.
Lindbloom, Johannes. *Prophecy in Ancient Israel*. University of Virginia: Basil Blackwell, 1962.
Locke, John. *An Essay Concerning Human Understanding*. In Great Books of the Western World 35. Chicago: Encyclopaedia Britannica, 1977.
———. "A Discourse of Miracles." In *The Works of John Locke*, edited by G. Knaller and T. A. Dean, 9:256–65. London: C. & J. Rivington, 1824.
———. "The Reasonableness of Christianity." In *The Works of John Locke*, edited by G. Knaller and T. A. Dean, 6:1–191. London: C. & J. Rivington, 1824.
Lohfink, Norbert. *Das Hauptgebot*. Rome: Pontificio Instituto Biblico, 1963.
———. "Der Bundesschluss im Land Moab." *BZ* 6 (1962) 32–56.
Lohse, Edward. *Märtyrer und Gottesknecht: Untersuchungen zur urchristlichen Verkündigung vom sühntod Jesu Christi*. Forschungen zur Religion und Literature des Alten und Neuen Testaments 49. Göttingen: Vandenhoeck & Ruprecht, 1963.
Longenecker, Richard N. *The Christology of Early Jewish Christianity*. Studies in Biblical Theology. London: SCM, 1970.
Longman, Tremper. *How to Read Exodus*. Downers Grove: InterVarsity, 2009.
Lovejoy, Arthur. *The Great Chain of Being: A Study of the History of an Idea*. New York: Harper & Row, 1960.
Lund, Oystein. *Way Metaphors and Way Topics in Isaiah 40–66*. Tübingen: Mohr Siebeck, 2007.
Lust, Johan. "The Divine Titles הָאָדוֹן and אֲדוֹן in Proto-Isaiah and Ezekiel." In *Isaiah in Context: Studies in Honour of Arie van der Kooij on the Occasion of His Sixty-Fifth Birthday*, edited by Michaël van der Meer et al., 131–49. Leiden: Brill, 2010.
Luther, Martin. *Genesis*. In *Luther's Works*, edited by Jaroslav Pelikan. St. Louis: Concordia, 1958.

―――. *Luther's Works*. Edited by E. Theodore Bachman. Philadelphia: Fortress, 1960.
Lys, Daniel. *Rŭach: le souffle dans l'Ancient Testament*. Etudes d'histoire et de philosophie religieuses. Paris: Presses Universitaires de France, 1962.
Ma, Wonsuk. *Until the Spirit Comes: The Spirit of God in the Book of Isaiah*. JSOTSup 271. Sheffield: Sheffield Academic, 1999.
Macintosh, A. A. *Isaiah xxi: A Palimpsest*. Cambridge: Cambridge University Press, 1980.
Maimonides, Moses. *The Thirteen Principles of Faith*. Edited by Chaim Miller. Brooklyn: Kol Menachem, 2005.
Malamat, A. "Prophetic Revelations in New Documents from Mari and the Bible." In *Volume du congrès Genève 1965*, edited by Otto Eissfeldt et al., VTSup 15:206-27. Leiden: Brill, 1966.
Martin, James. "The Forensic Background to Jeremiah III 1." *VT* 19 (1969) 82-92.
Mauchline, John. *Isaiah 1-39*. Torch Bible Commentaries. London: SCM, 1962.
Mayes, A. D. H. *Deuteronomy*. New Century Bible Commentary. Grand Rapids: Eerdmans, 1979.
McCarthy, Dennis. "Covenant and Law in Chronicles-Nehemiah." *CBQ* 44 (1982) 25-44.
―――. *Treaty and Covenant: A Study in Form in the Ancient Oriental Documents and in the Old Testament*. AnBib 21. Rome: Biblical Institute, 1981.
McConville, J. Gordon. "Ezra-Nehemiah and the Fulfillment of Prophecy." *VT* 36 (1986) 205-24.
―――. "Wisdom and Torah in Deuteronomy." In *Sepher Torath Mosheh: Studies in the Composition and Interpretation of Deuteronomy*, 261-76. Peabody: Hendrickson, 2017.
McDaniel, Ferris. *Restoration to the Divine Ideal: A Biblical Theology of Isaiah*. ThD paper for Theology of Isaiah, Dallas Theological Seminary, 1976.
McDonald, H. D. *The Christian View of Man*. Westchester, IL: Crossway, 1981.
McKenzie, John. *Dictionary of the Bible*. New York: Macmillan, 1965.
―――. "A Note on Psalm 73[74]:13-15." *TS* 11 (1950) 275-82.
―――. "The Word of God in the Old Testament." *TS* 21 (1960) 183-206.
Meier, John P. *A Marginal Jew: Rethinking the Historical Jesus*. Vol. 1, *The Roots of the Problem and the Person*. New York: Doubleday, 1991.
Meisser, Bruno. "Ein altbabylonisches Fragment des Gilgamosepos." *Mitteilungen der Vorrunoderasiatische Gesellschaft* 1 (1902) 10-13.
Melugin, Roy. *The Formation of Isaiah 40-55*. New York: Walter de Gruyter, 1976.
Menard, Jacques E. "*Pais Theou* as a Messianic Title in the Book of Acts." *CBQ* 19 (1957) 83-92.
Mendenhall, G. E. "Ancient Oriental and Biblical Law." *BA* 17 (1952) 26-46.
―――. "Covenant Forms in Israelite Tradition." *BA* 17 (1954) 50-76.
―――. *Law and Covenant in Israel and the Ancient Near East*. Pittsburgh: The Biblical Colloquium, 1955.
Merrill, Eugene. "Image of God." In *Dictionary of the Old Testament: Pentateuch*, edited by T. Desmond Alexander and David Baker, 441-45. Downers Grove: InterVarsity, 2003.
―――. "Literary Character of Isaiah 40-55 Part 2 (of 2 parts): Literary Genres in Isaiah 40-55." *BSac* 144 (1987) 144-56.
Meyer, Ben. *The Aims of Jesus*. London: SCM, 1979.

Migne, J. P. *Patrologia Graeca*. Paris: Imprimerie Catholique, 1886.
Mihelic, Joseph. "The Concept of God in Deutero-Isaiah." *BR* 11 (1966) 29–41.
Miles, Jack. *God: A Biography*. New York: Random House, 1995.
Milgrom, Jacob. "Israel's Sanctuary: 'The Priestly Picture of Dorian Gray.'" *RB* 83 (1976) 390–99.
———. *Leviticus 1–16*. Anchor Bible 3. New York: Doubleday, 1991.
———. *Leviticus 17–22*. Anchor Bible 3A. New York: Doubleday, 2001.
———. *Numbers*. JPS Torah Commentary. Philadelphia: JPS, 1990.
———. "The Preposition מִן in the חַטָּאת Pericopes." *JBL* 126 (2007) 161–3.
———. "The Priestly Impurity System." In *Proceedings of the Ninth World Congress of Jewish Studies, Division A: The Period of the Bible*. Jerusalem: World Union of Jewish Studies, 1986, 115–20.
———. "The Priestly Laws of Sancta Contamination." In *"Sha'arei Talmon": Studies in the Bible, Qumran, and the Ancient Near East Presented to Shemaryahu Talmon*, edited by Michael Fishbane and Emanuel Tov, 137–46. Winona Lake: Eisenbrauns, 1992.
Millard, A. R., and P. Bordreuil. "A Statue from Syria with Assyrian and Aramaic Inscriptions." *BA* 45 (1982) 135–41.
Miller, John. "The Concept of Covenant in Deutero-Isaiah: Its Forms and Sources" PhD diss., Boston University, 1971.
Miller, Patrick. *The Divine Warrior in Early Israel*. Cambridge: Harvard University Press, 1973.
Mihinovich, Timothy. "Form Criticism and rîb in Isaiah 41, 21–42, 4." *BN* 136 (2008) 45–57.
Moberly, R. W. "Whose Justice? Which Righteousness? The Interpretation of Isaiah V 16." *VT* 51 (2001) 55–68.
Mollenkott, Virginia. *The Divine Feminine: The Biblical Imagery of God as Female*. New York: Crossroad, 1989.
Moser, Paul, ed. *Jesus and Philosophy*. New York: Cambridge University Press, 2009.
Mowinckel, Sigmund. *He That Cometh*. Nashville: Abingdon, 1956.
———. *The Psalms in Israel's Worship*. Nashville: Abingdon, 1962.
———. *The Spirit and the Word: Prophecy and Tradition in Ancient Israel*. Minneapolis: Fortress, 2002.
Muilenburg, James. "The Form and Structure of Covenant Formulations." *VT* 9 (1959) 347–65.
Müller, W. E. *Die Vorstellung von Rest im Alten Testament*. Leipzig: Bordorf-Leipzig, 1939.
Munger, Robert. *What Jesus Says: The Master Teacher and Life's Problems*. Westwood: Revell, 1955.
Murphy, Nancey. *Bodies and Souls, or Spiritual Bodies?* Cambridge: Cambridge University Press, 2006.
Murphy, Nancey, and William Stoeger, eds. *Evolution and Emergence: Systems, Organisms, Persons*. Oxford: ISSR, 2010.
Nagelsbach, C. W. E. "The Prophet Isaiah." In *Lange's Commentary on the Holy Scriptures*, edited by Philip Schaff, 6:1–715. Grand Rapids: Zondervan, 1960.
Neufeld, Thomas. *God and Saints at War: The Transformation of the Divine Warrior in Isaiah 59, Wisdom of Solomon 5, 1 Thessalonians 5, and Ephesians 6*. ThD diss., Harvard University, 1989.

———. "Put on the Armour of God": The Divine Warrior from Isaiah to Ephesians. Sheffield: Sheffield Academic, 1997.

Neusner, Jacob. Handbook of Rabbinic Theology: Language, System, Structure. Boston: Brill Academic, 2002.

———. A History of the Mishnaic Law of Holy Things. Leiden: Brill, 1978-80.

———. The Idea of Purity in Ancient Judaism. Leiden: Brill, 1973.

Neusner, Jacob, and Bruce Chilton. "Sanders's Misunderstanding of Purity: Uncleanness as an Ontological, Not Moral-Eschatological Category." In *Judaic Law from Jesus to the Mishnah*, edited by Jacob Neusner, 205-30. Atlanta: Scholars, 1993.

Nickelsburg, George. *Resurrection, Immortality, and Eternal Life in Intertestamental Judaism*. Cambridge: Harvard University Press, 1972.

Nielsen, Eduard. *The Ten Commandments in New Perspective: A Traditio-Historical Approach*. London: SCM, 1968.

Nielsen, Kirsten. *Yahweh as Prosecutor and Judge: An Investigation of the Prophetic Lawsuit (Rib-Pattern)*. Sheffield: University of Sheffield Press, 1978.

Niskanen, Paul. "Yhwh as Father, Redeemer, and Potter in Isaiah 63:7-64:11." *CBQ* 68 (2006) 397-407.

North, Christopher R. *The Second Isaiah: Introduction, Translation and Commentary to Chapters XL-LV*. Oxford: Clarendon, 1964.

Novatian. *Treatise Concerning the Trinity*. In Ante-Nicene Fathers 5. Peabody: Hendrickson, 1995.

Odendaal, Dick. *The Eschatological Expectation of Isaiah 40-66 with Special Reference to Israel and the Nations*. ThD diss., Westminster Seminary, 1966. Ann Arbor: University Microfilms, 1986.

Oehler, Gustav. *Theology of the Old Testament*. Minneapolis: Klock & Klock, 1978.

Oeming, Manfred. "Ist Gen. 15.6 ein Beleg für die Anrechnung des Glaubens zur Gerechtigkeit?" *ZAW* 95 (1983) 185-96.

Olyan, Saul. *Rites and Rank: Hierarchy in Biblical Representations of Cult*. Princeton: Princeton University Press, 2000.

Oosting, Reinoud. "The Counselor of the Lord in Isaiah 40-55." *JSOT* 32 (2008) 353-82.

Openheim, A. L. "'Siege-Documents' from Nippur." *Iraq* 17 (1955) 69-89.

Origen. *On First Principles*. In Ante-Nicene Fathers 4, 237-384. Grand Rapids: Eerdmans, 1976.

———. *Origen against Celsus*. In Ante-Nicene Fathers 4, 395-669. Grand Rapids: Eerdmans, 1976.

Orlinsky, H. "'A Light to the Nations': A Problem in Biblical Theology." *JQR* 75 (1965) 409-28.

Oswalt, John. *The Book of Isaiah: Chapters 1-39*. New International Commentary on the Old Testament. Grand Rapids: Eerdmans, 1986.

———. *The Book of Isaiah: Chapters 40-66*. New International Commentary on the Old Testament. Grand Rapids: Eerdmans, 1998.

———. "God's Determination to Redeem His People (Isaiah 9:1-7; 11:1-11; 26:1-9; 35:1-10)." *RevExp* 88 (1991) 153-65.

———. "The Myth of the Dragon and Old Testament Faith." *EvQ* 49 (1977) 163-72.

———. "Righteousness in Isaiah: A Study of the Function of Chapters 55-66 in the Present Structure of the Book." In *Writing and Reading the Scroll of Isaiah: Studies of an Interpretive Tradition*, edited by Craig Broyles and Craig Evans, 177-91. Leiden: Brill, 1997.

Otto, Rudolf. *The Idea of the Holy: An Inquiry into the Non-Rational Factor in the Idea of the Divine and Its Relation to the Rational.* Hamondsworth: Penguin, 1959.

Owens, J. J. "Jeremiah, Prophet of True Religion." *RevExp* 78 (1981) 365–79.

Pannenberg, Wolfhart. *Anthropology in Theological Perspective.* Philadelphia: Westminster, 1985.

———. *Systematic Theology.* Grand Rapids: Eerdmanns, 1988.

Pao, David. *Acts and the Isaianic New Exodus.* Grand Rapids: Baker, 2002.

Parke-Taylor, Geoffrey H. *Yahweh: The Divine Name in the Bible.* Waterloo: Wilfred Laurier, 1975.

Parpola, Simo, and Kazuko Watanabe. *Neo-Assyrian Treaties and Loyalty Oaths.* State Archives of Assyria 2. Helsinki: Helsinki University, 1988.

Patai, Raphael. *The Messiah Texts: Jewish Legends of Three Thousand Years.* Detroit: Wayne State University Press, 1979.

Pate, Marvin. *Communities of the Last Days: The Dead Sea Scrolls, the New Testament & the Story of Israel.* Downers Grove: InterVarsity, 2000.

Pate, Marvin, and Douglas Kennard. *Deliverance Now and Not Yet.* New York: Peter Lang, 2003.

Pentecost, J. Dwight. *Things to Come: A Study in Biblical Eschatology.* Grand Rapids: Zondervan, 1964.

Pettinato, Giovanni. *The Archives of Ebla: An Empire Inscribed in Clay.* Garden City: Doubleday, 1981.

Phillips, Anthony. "Double for All Her Sins." *ZAW* 94 (1982) 130–32.

Philo. *The Works of Philo: Complete and Unabridged.* New updated ed., translated by C. D. Yonge. Peabody: Hendrickson, 1993.

Pirot, L., and A. Robert, eds. *Dictionnaire de la Bible: Supplement.* Paris: Letouzey et Ane, 1957.

Plato. *Cratylus.* In Great Books of the Western World 7. Chicago: Encyclopaedia Britannica, 1952.

———. *Laws.* In Great Books of the Western World 7. Chicago: Encyclopaedia Britannica, 1952.

———. *Phaedo.* In Great Books of the Western World 7. Chicago: Encyclopaedia Britannica, 1952.

———. *Phaedrus.* In Great Books of the Western World 7. Chicago: Encyclopaedia Britannica, 1952.

———. *Timaeus.* In Great Books of the Western World 7. Chicago: Encyclopaedia Britannica, 1952.

Polak, F. K. "The Covenant at Mount Sinai in the Light of Texts from Mari." In *Sepher Moshe,* edited by C. Cohen et al., 119–34. Winona Lake: Eisenbrauns, 2004.

Polaski, Donald C. "Reflections on a Mosaic Covenant: The Eternal Covenant (Isaiah 24:5) and Intertextuality." *JSOT* 7 (1998) 55–73.

Porten, Bezalel. *Archives from Elephantine: The Life of an Ancient Jewish Colony.* Berkeley: University of California, 1968.

Porter, Stanley, and Jacqueline C. R. de Roo. *The Concept of the Covenant in the Second Temple Period.* Leiden: Brill, 2003.

Preuss, Horst. *Old Testament Theology.* Louisville: Westminster John Knox, 1991.

Prinsloo, Willem. "Isaiah 14:12–15: Humiliation, Hubris, Humiliation." *ZAW* 93 (1981) 432–38.

Pritchard, James, ed. *Ancient Near Eastern Pictures Relating to the Old Testament*. Princeton: Princeton University Press, 1974.

———. *Ancient Near Eastern Texts Relating to the Old Testament*. Princeton: Princeton University Press, 1969.

Puech, E. "Une apocalypse messianique (4Q521)." *RQ* 15 (1992) 475–522.

Raabe, P. R. "Why Oracles against Nations?" In *Fortunate the Eyes that See: Essays in Honor of D. N. Freedman*, edited by A. B. Beck et al., 236–57. Grand Rapids: Eerdmans, 1995.

Rabinowitz, Isaac. *Toward a Valid Theory of Biblical Hebrew Literature*. Ithaca: Cornell University Press, 1966.

Rahner, Karl, and Herbert Vorgrimler. *Theological Dictionary*. New York: Herder and Herder, 1965.

Ramsey, G. W. "Speech Forms in Hebrew Law and Prophetic Oracles." *JBL* 96 (1977) 45–58.

Reid, Thomas. *An Inquiry into the Human Mind on the Principles of Common Mind*. Edited by Derek Brookes. Edinburgh: Edinburgh University Press, 1997.

Reisman, Daniel. *Two Neo-Sumerian Hymns*. PhD diss., University of Pennsylvania, 1970.

Rendtorff, Rolf. "The Book of Isaiah: A Complex Unity; Synchronic and Diachronic Reading." In *New Visions of Isaiah*, JSOT Sup 214, 32–49. Sheffield: Sheffield Academic, 1996

———. *Canon and Theology Overtures to an Old Testament Theology*. Minneapolis, Fortress, 1993.

———. "The Composition of the Book of Isaiah." In *Canon and Theology*, edited by M. Kohl, 146–69. Minneapolis: Fortress, 1993.

———. *The Covenant Formula: An Exegetical and Theological Investigation*. Translated by Margaret Kohl. Edinburgh: T & T Clark, 1998.

———. "Isaiah 6 in the Framework of the Composition of the Book." In *Canon and Theology*, edited by M. Kohl, 170–80. Minneapolis: Fortress, 1993.

———. "Isaiah 56.1 as a Key in the Formation of the Book of Isaiah." In *Canon and Theology*, edited by M. Kohl, 181–89. Minneapolis: Fortress, 1993.

———. *The Old Testament: An Introduction*. Philadelphia: Fortress, 1991.

———. "Zur Komposition des Buches Jesaja." *VT* 34 (1984) 295–320.

Riesenfeld, Ernst Harold. *Jesus Transfiguré: L'arrière-plan du récit evangélique de la Transfiguration de Notre-Seigneur*. Kobenhaven: Munksgaard, 1947.

Ringgren, Helmer. *The Messiah in the Old Testament*. London: SCM, 1967.

———. "Some Observations on Style and Structure in the Isaiah Apocalypse." *ASTI* 9 (1973) 107–15.

Roberts, J. J. *First Isaiah: A Commentary*. Hermeneia. Minneapolis: Fortress, 2015.

———. "Isaiah in Old Testament Theology." *Int* 36 (1982) 130–43.

Robinson, John A. T. *The Body: A Study in Pauline Theology*. London: SCM, 1952.

Roehrs, Walter. "The Theology of the Word of God in the Old Testament." *CTM* 32 (1961) 261–73.

Rösel, M. "Die Jungfrauengeburt des endzeitlichen Immanuel: Jesaja 7 in der Übersetzung der Septuaginta." *JBTh* 6 (1991) 135–51.

Rosenberg, Roy. "Jesus, Isaac and the Suffering Servant." *JBL* 84 (1965) 381–88.

Ross, James. "The Prophet as Yahweh's Messenger." In *Israel's Prophetic Heritage*, edited by Bernard Anderson and Walter Harrelson, 98–107. Eugene, OR: Wipf & Stock, 2010.
Ross, John P. "Jahweh Seba'ot in Samuel and Psalms." *VT* 17 (1967) 76–92.
Roth, Martha. *Law Collections from Mesopotamia and Asia Minor*. Atlanta: Scholars, 1997.
———. "The Law Collection of King Hammurabi: Toward an Understanding of Codification and Text." In *La Codification des lois dans l'antiquité: Actes du Colloque de Strasbourg, 27-29 Novembre 1997*. Travaux du Centre de Recherche sur le Proche-Orient et la Grèce antiques 16, edited by Edmond Lévy, 9–31. Strasbourg: l'Université Strasbourg, 2000.
Rubin, Nissan. "Body and Soul in Talmudic and Mishnaic Sources." *Koroth* 9, "Third International Symposium on Medicine in Bible and Talmud, Dec. 7–9, 1987" (1988) 151–64.
Rust, Eric. *Covenant and Hope*. Waco: Word, 1962.
Sapp, David. "The LXX, 1QIsa, and MT Versions of Isaiah 53 and the Christian Doctrine of Atonement." In *Jesus and the Suffering Servant: Isaiah 53 and Christian Origins*, edited by William Bellinger and William Farmer, 170–92. Harrisburg: Trinity International, 1995.
Sanders, E. P. *The Historical Figure Jesus*. London: Penguin Books, 1993.
———. *Paul and Palestinian Judaism: A Comparison of Patterns of Religion*. Philadelphia: Fortress, 1977.
Sawyer, John. *The Fifth Gospel: Isaiah in the History of Christianity*. Cambridge: Cambridge University Press, 2000.
———. *Isaiah*. Daily Study Bible Series 1. Louisville: Westminster John Knox, 1984.
Schafer, Peter. *Kehhalot-Studien*. Tübingen: Mohr Siebeck, 1988.
Schaudig, Hanspeter. "Bēl Bows, Nabu Stoops! The Prophecy of Isaiah xlvi 1–2 as a Reflection of Babylonian 'Procession Omens.'" *VT* 58 (2008) 557–72.
Schiffman, Lawrence. *Reclaiming the Dead Sea Scrolls: Their True Meaning for Judaism and Christianity*. Philadelphia: JPS, 1994.
Schmitt, John. "The Motherhood of God and Zion as Mother." *RB* 92 (1985) 557–69.
Schoeps, Hans-Joachim. *Paul: The Theology of the Apostle in the Light of Jewish Religious History*. Philadelphia: Westminster, 1961.
Schoors, Anton. *I Am God Your Saviour: A Form-Critical Study of the Main Genres in Is XL–LV*. Leiden: Brill, 1973.
———. "The *Rîb*-Pattern in Isaiah XL–LV." *Bijdr* 30 (1969) 25–38.
Schulz, H. *Das Todesrecht im Alten Testament: Studien Zur Rechtsreform der Mot-Jumat-Sätze*. Berlin: Walter de Gruyter, 2019.
Schunck, K. D. "Jes. 30, 6–8 und die Deutung der Rahab im AT." *ZAW* 78 (1966) 48–56.
Scobie, Charles. *The Ways of Our God: An Approach to Biblical Theology*. Grand Rapids: Eerdmans, 2003.
Scott, Rae. "An Exegetical and Theological Study of Isaiah 49:1–13." ThM thesis, Dallas Theological Seminary, 1981.
Seeley, David. *The Noble Death: Graeco-Roman Martyrology and Paul's Concept of Salvation*. Sheffield: JSOT, 1990.
Segal, Alan. *Life After Death: A History of the Afterlife in the Religions of the West*. New York: Doubleday, 2004.

———. *Two Powers in Heaven: Early Rabbinic Reports About Christianity and Gnosticism*. Leiden: Brill, 1977.
Shakespeare, William. *Macbeth*. In Great Books of the Western World 27. Chicago: Encyclopaedia Britannica, 1952.
Sholem, Gershom. *Jewish Gnosticism, Merkabah Mysticism, and Talmudic Tradition*. New York: Jewish Theological Seminary of America, 1965.
Simian-Yofre, Horacio. "Exodus in Deuteroisaias." *Bib* 61 (1980) 530–53.
Simon, Ulrich. *A Theology of Salvation: A Commentary on Isaiah 40–55*. London: SPCK, 1953.
Sjöberg, E. *Der Menschensohn im ältiopischen Henochbuch*. Lund: C. W. K. Gleerup, 1946.
Smith, Gary. "The Concept of God/the Gods as King in the Ancient Near East and the Bible." *TrinJ* 3 (1982) 18–38.
———. *Isaiah 1–39*. The New American Commentary 15A. Nashville: B & H, 2007.
———. *Isaiah 40–66*. The New American Commentary 15B. Nashville: B & H, 2009.
Smith, George. *The Book of Isaiah*. New York: Armstrong, 1903.
Smith, M. "II Isaiah and the Persians." *JAOS* 83 (1963) 415–21.
Snaith, Norman. *The Distinctive Ideas of the Old Testament*. Philadelphia: Westminster, 1946.
———. "The Interpretation of El Gabor in Isaiah ix.5[EVV,6]." *ExpTim* 52 (1940–41) 36–37.
Sommer, Benjamin. "Allusions and Illusion: The Unity of the Book of Isaiah in Light of Deutero-Isaiah's Use of Prophetic Tradition." In *New Visions of Isaiah*, edited by Roy Melugin and Marvin Sweeney, 156–87. Sheffield: Sheffield Academic, 1996.
Sommer, F. "Ein hethitisches Gebet." *ZA* 33 (1921) 85–102.
Stamm, J. J. "Dreissig Jahre Dekalogforscung." *TRu* 27:3 (1961) 189–239.
———. "Dreissig Jahre Dekalogforscung." *TRu* 27:4 (1961) 282–305.
Stock, Augustine. *The Way in the Wilderness: Exodus, Wilderness and Moses Themes in Old Testament and New*. Collegeville: Liturgical, 1969.
Strack, H., and P. Billerbeck, eds. *Kommentar zum Neuen Testament aus Talmud und Midrash*. München: C. H. Beck, 1922–61.
Stromberg, Jacob. *An Introduction to the Study of Isaiah*. London: T & T Clark, 2011.
Stuhlmueller, Carroll. *Creative Redemption in Deutero-Isaiah*. Rome: Biblical Institute, 1970.
———. "'First and Last' and 'Yahweh-Creator' in Deutero-Isaiah." *CBQ* 29 (1967) 189–205.
———. "The Theology of Creation in Second Isaiah." *CBQ* 21 (1959) 429–67.
———. "Yahweh-King and Deutero-Isaiah." *BR* 15 (1970) 32–45.
Suganuma, E. "The Covenant Rib Form in Jeremiah 2: A Form Critical Study." *Journal of the College of Dairy Agriculture* 4 (Hokkaido, Japan: Nopporo, 1972) 121–54.
Sukenik, E. L. *Jüdische Gräber Jerusalems um Christi Geburt*. Jerusalem: n.p., 1931.
Sweeney, Marvin. "The Book of Isaiah as Prophetic Torah." In *New Visions of Isaiah*, edited by Roy Melugin and Marvin Sweeney, 50–67. Sheffield: Sheffield Academic, 1996.
———. *Isaiah 1–4 and the Post-Exilic Understanding of the Isaianic Tradition*. Berlin: Walter de Gruyter, 1988.
———. *Isaiah 1–39*. The Forms of Old Testament Literature 16. Grand Rapids: Eerdmans, 1996.

———. "The Reconceptualization of the Davidic Covenant in Isaiah." In *Studies in the Book of Isaiah: Festchrift Willem A. M. Beuken*, edited by J. Van Ruiten and M. Vervenne, 41–61. Leuven: Leuven University, 1997.

Taggar-Cohen, Ada. "Biblical *Covenant* and Hittite *išhiul* reexamined." *VT* 61 (2011) 484–86.

Tanak: A New Translation of the Holy Scriptures According to the Traditional Hebrew Text. Philadelphia: JPS, 1985.

Tertullian. *Against Praxeas*. In *The Writings of Quintus Sept. Flor. Tertullianus*, edited by Richard Ellmann. Kila: Kessinger, 1870.

———. *The Five Books against Marcion*. In Ante-Nicene Fathers 3. Edinburgh: T & T Clark, 1989.

———. *On the Flesh of Christ*. In Ante-Nicene Fathers 3. Edinburgh: T & T Clark, 1989.

———. *On the Resurrection of the Flesh*. In Ante-Nicene Fathers 3. Edinburgh: T & T Clark, 1989.

———. *The Shows or de Spectaculis*. In Ante-Nicene Fathers 3. Edinburgh: T & T Clark, 1989.

———. *A Treatise on the Soul*. In Ante-Nicene Fathers 3. Edinburgh: T & T Clark, 1989.

Teugels, L. "Consolation and Composition in a Rabbinic Homily on Isaiah 40: *Pesiqta' de Rav Kahana'* 16." In *Studies in the Book of Isaiah*, edited by J. Van Ruiten and M. Vervenne, 433–46. Leuven: Leuven University Press, 1997.

Thiselton, Anthony. "The Supposed Power of Words in the Biblical Writings." *JTS* 25 (1974) 283–99.

Thompson, J. A. *The Book of Jeremiah*. Grand Rapids: Eerdmans, 1980.

Tiemeyer, Lena-Sofia. "Death or Conversion: The Gentiles in the Concluding Chapters of the Book of Isaiah and the Book of the Twelve." *JTS* 68 (2017) 1–22.

Tillich, Paul. *Systematic Theology*. Chicago: University of Chicago Press, 1963.

Toombs, Laurence. "Love and Justice in Deuteronomy." *Int* 19 (1965) 399–411.

Torrance, Thomas. *Divine and Contingent Order*. Oxford: Oxford University Press, 1981.

Torrey, Charles Cutler. *Isaiah 40–55*. New York: Doubleday, 2002.

Tromp, N. J. *Primitive Conceptions of Death and Nether World in the Old Testament*. Biblica ete Orientalia 21. Rome: Pontifical Biblical Institute, 1969.

Ulrich, Eugene. "An Index to the Contents of the Isaiah Manuscripts from the Judean Desert." In *Writing and Reading the Scroll of Isaiah: Studies of an Interpretive Tradition*, edited by Craig Broyles and Craig Evans, 477–80. Leiden: Brill, 1997.

———. "Isaiah, Book of." In *Encyclopedia of the Dead Sea Scrolls*, edited by Lawrence Schiffman and James VanderKam, 384–86. Oxford: Oxford University Press, 2000.

Ussishkin, David. "Sennacherib's Campaign to Judah: The Archeological Perspective with an Emphasis on Lachish and Jerusalem." In *Sennacherib at the Gates of Jerusalem: Story, History and Historiography*, edited by Isaac Kalim and Seth Richardson, 75–103. Leiden: Brill, 2014.

van de Mieroop, Marc. *Philosophy Before the Greeks*. Princeton: Princeton University Press, 2016.

VanderKam, James. "Covenant." In *Encyclopedia of the Dead Sea Scrolls*, edited by Lawrence Schiffman and James VanderKam, 1:151–55. New York: Oxford University Press, 2000.

VanderKam, James, and Peter Flint. *The Meaning of the Dead Sea Scrolls: Their Significance for Understanding the Bible, Judaism, Jesus, and Christianity*. San Francisco: Harper San Francisco, 2002.

Van Gemeren, Willem. *New International Dictionary of Old Testament Theology & Exegesis*. Grand Rapids: Zondervan, 1997.

Van Goudoever, Jan. "The Celebration of the Torah in the Second Isaiah." In *The Book of Isaiah: Le Livre D'Isaïe: Les Oracles et Leurs Reflectures Unité et Complexité de L'Ouvrage*, edited by Jacqes Vermeylen, 313–17. Leuven: Uitgeverij Peeters, 1989.

Van Imschoot, Paul. *Theology of the Old Testament*. New York: Desclee, 1954.

van Kooten, George. *Paul's Anthropology in Context: The Image of God, and Tripartite Man in Ancient Judaism, Ancient Philosophy and Early Christianity*. Tübingen: Mohr Siebeck, 2008.

van Leeuwen, R. "Isa 14:12 *holeš 'al gwym* and Gilgamesh XI,6." *JBL* 99 (1980) 173–84.

Van Ruiten, J., and M. Vervenne. *Studies in the Book of Isaiah: Festschrift Willem A. M. Beuken*. Leuven: Leuven University Press, 1997.

Vawter, Bruce. *On Genesis: A New Reading*. Garden City, NY: Doubleday, 1977.

Vermes, Géza. *Jesus the Jew: A Historian's Reading of the Gospels*. Philadelphia: Fortress, 1981.

———. "Qumran Forum Miscellanea I." *JJS* 43(1992) 303–4.

———. *Scripture and Tradition in Judaism: Haggadic Studies*. Leiden: Brill, 1983.

von Rad, Gerhard. "Faith Reckoned as Righteousness." In *The Problem of the Hexateuch and Other Essays*, 125–30. Edinburgh: Oliver & Boyd, 1966.

———. *Old Testament Theology*. New York: Harper & Row, 1975.

———. "The Origin of the Concept of the Day of Yahweh." *JSS* 4 (1959) 97–108.

———. "The Theological Problem of the Old Testament Doctrine of Creation." In *The Problem of the Hexateuch and Other Essays*, 131–43. Edinburgh: Oliver & Boyd, 1966.

von Waldow, H. Eberhard. "The Message of Deutero-Isaiah." *Int* 22 (1968) 259–87.

Vos, Geerhardus. *Biblical Theology: Old and New Testaments*. Grand Rapids: Eerdmans, 1948.

Volz, Paul. *Der Geist Gottes und die Verwandten Erscheinungen im Alten Testament und im Anschliessenden Judentum*. Tübingen: Mohr [Siebeck], 1910.

Vriezen, Theodorus C. "Essentials of the Theology of Isaiah." In *Israel's Prophetic Heritage*, edited by Bernhard Anderson and Walter Harrelson, 128–46. New York: Harper & Brothers, 1962.

———. "Ruach Yahweh (Elohim) in the Old Testament." In *Biblical Essays: Proceedings of the Ninth Meeting of "Die Outestamentiese Werkemeenskap in Said-Africa, Stellenbosch July 1966,"* 50–61. Pretoria: OTWSA, 1966.

Wakeman, Mary. *God's Battle with the Monster: A Study in Biblical Imagery*. Leiden: Brill, 1973.

Waltke, Bruce. *Creation and Chaos*. Portland, OR: Western Conservative Baptist Seminary, 1974.

Waltke, Bruce, and M. O'Connor. *An Introduction to Biblical Hebrew Syntax*. Winona Lake, IN: Eisenbrauns, 1990.

Walton, John. "Understanding Torah: Ancient Legal Text, Covenant Stipulation, and Christian Scripture." *BBR* 29 (2019) 1–18.

Walton, John, and J. Harvey Walton. *The Lost World of the Israelite Conquest*. Downers Grove InterVarsity, 2017.

———. *The Lost World of Torah: Law as Covenant and Wisdom in Ancient Context.* Downers Grove: InterVarsity, 2019.

Walton, John, and Victor Matthews. *Genesis-Deuteronomy.* IVP Background Commentary. Downers Grove: InterVarsity, 1997.

Watts, John. *Isaiah 1-33.* Word Biblical Commentary. Waco: Word, 1985.

———. *Isaiah 1-33.* Word Biblical Commentary 24, rev. ed. Nashville: Thomas Nelson, 2005.

———. *Isaiah 34-66.* Word Biblical Commentary 25, rev. ed. Nashville: Thomas Nelson, 2000.

Watts, Rikki. "Consolation or Confrontation? Isaiah 40-55 and the Delay of the New Exodus." *TynBul* 41 (1990) 31-59.

———. *Isaiah's New Exodus in Mark.* Grand Rapids: Baker, 1997.

Wegner, Paul. *An Examination of Kingship and Messianic Expectation in Isaiah 1-35.* Lewiston: Mellen, 1992.

———. "What's New in Isaiah 9:1-7?" In *Interpreting Isaiah: Issues and Approaches*, edited by David Firth and H. G. M. Williamson, 237-49. Downers Grove: InterVarsity, 2009.

Weinfeld, Moshe. *Deuteronomy and the Deuteronomic School.* Oxford: Clarendon, 1972.

Weiss, Meir. "The Origin of the 'Day of the Lord'—Reconsidered." *HUCA* 37 (1966) 29-71.

Wells, Bruce. "What is Biblical Law? A Look at Pentateuchal Rules and Near Eastern Practice." *CBQ* 70 (2008) 223-43.

Wells, Roy. "'Isaiah' as an Exponent of Torah: Isaiah 56.18." In *New Visions of Isaiah*, edited by Roy Melugin and Marvin Sweeney, 140-55. Sheffield: Sheffield Academic, 1996.

Wenham, G. J. *The Book of Leviticus.* New International Commentary on the Old Testament. Grand Rapids: Eerdmans, 1979.

———. *Numbers.* Tyndale Old Testament Commentaries 4. Leicester: InterVarsity, 1982.

Westbrook, Raymond. *History of Ancient Near Eastern Law.* Leiden: Brill, 2003.

Westermann, Claus. *Blessing in the Bible and the Life of the Church.* Philadelphia: Fortress, 1978.

———. "Das Heilswort bei Deutero-jesaja." *EvT* 7 (1964) 355-75.

———. *Isaiah 40-66.* Old Testament Library. Philadelphia: Westminster, 1969.

———. *Prophetic Oracles of Salvation in the Old Testament.* Louisville: Westminster John Knox, 1991.

Wheeler, Dale. "The Covenant Lawsuit in Isaiah 1: Entrance into Isaianic Theology?" Paper for PhD course OT 180, Dallas Theological Seminary, 1980.

Whitley, Charles F. "Deutero-Isaiah's Interpretation of *sedeq*." *VT* 22 (1972) 469-75.

Whybray, R. N. *The Heavenly Counsellor xl 13-14.* Cambridge: Cambridge University Press, 1971.

Wildberger, Hans. *Isaiah 1-12.* A Continental Commentary. Minneapolis: Fortress, 1991.

———. *Isaiah 28-39.* A Continental Commentary. Minneapolis: Fortress, 2002.

Wilde, Oscar Fingal O'Flahertie Wills. *The Picture of Dorian Gray.* Philadelphia: M. J. Ivers, James Sullivan, 1890.

Williams, Prescott. "The Poems about Incomparable Yahweh's Servant in Isaiah 40-55." *SwJT* 11 (1968) 73-87.

Williams, Ronald. *Hebrew Syntax: An Outline*. Toronto: University of Toronto, 1976.
Williamson, H. G. M. *The Book Called Isaiah: Deutero-Isaiah's Role in Composition and Redaction*. Oxford: Clarendon, 1994.
———. "Isaiah 1 and the Covenant Lawsuit." In *Covenant as Context: Essays in Honour of E. W. Nicholson*, edited by A. D. H. Mayes & R. B. Salters, 392–406. Oxford: Oxford University Press, 2008.
Willis, Timothy. *The Elders of the City: A Study of the Elders-Laws in Deuteronomy*. SBLMS 55. Atlanta: Society of Biblical Literature, 2001.
Wilson, Jan. *Mesopotamia*. Herstellung: Verlag Butzon & Bercker Kevelaer, 1994.
Wiseman, D. J. *The Alalakh Tablets*. London: British Institute of Archeology Ankara, 1953.
———. *The Vassal-Treaties of Esarhaddon*. London: British School of Archeology in Iraq, 1958.
Wittgenstein, Ludwig. *Philosophical Investigations*. New York: Macmillan, 1953.
Wolff, Hans. *Anthropology of the Old Testament*. Philadelphia: Fortress, 1974.
Wong, Gordon. "Faith in the Present Form of Isaiah VII 1–17." *VT* 51 (2001) 535–47.
Wood, J. Edwin. "Isaac Typology in the New Testament." *NTS* 14 (July 1968) 583–89.
Wood, Leon. *The Holy Spirit in the Old Testament*. Grand Rapids: Zondervan, 1976.
Wright, David. *Inventing God's Law: How the Covenant Code of the Bible Used and Revised the Laws of Hammurabi*. Oxford: Oxford University Press, 2009.
Wright, Ernest. "The Lawsuit of God: A Form Critical Study of Deuteronomy 32." In *Israel's Prophetic Heritage*, edited by Bernard Anderson and Walter Harrelson, 26–67. New York: Harper and Brothers, 1962.
———. "The Terminology of Old Testament Religion and Its Significance." *JNES* 1 (1942) 404–14.
Wright, N. T. *Jesus and the Victory of God*. Minneapolis: Fortress, 1996.
———. *The Resurrection of the Son of God*. Minneapolis: Fortress, 2003.
Yadin, Yigael. *The Temple Scroll*. Jerusalem: Israel Exploration Society, 1977–83.
Young, Edward. *The Book of Isaiah: The English Text, with Introduction, Exposition, and Notes*. 3 vols. Grand Rapids: Eerdmans, 1969–72.
———. "Of Whom Speaketh the Prophet This?" *WTJ* 11 (1949) 133–55.
———. *The Study of Old Testament Theology Today*. Cambridge: Lutterworth, 2004.
Zehnder, Markus. "Building on Stone? Deuteronomy and Esarhaddon's Loyalty Oaths (Part 2): Some Additional Observations." *BBR* 19 (2009) 511–35.
———. *Wegmetaphorik im Alten Testament*. BZAW 268. Berlin: de Gruyter, 1999.
Zillessen, Alfred. "Der alte und der neue Exodus." *ARW* 6 (1903) 289–304.

Author Index

Abbott, E., 47, 70
Abraham, W., 6
Abrahams, I., 13
Ackroyd, P., 2
Agum, 14
Albright, W., 12
Alexander, J., 11, 115, 156, 188
Allen, R., 130
Anderson, B., 87, 131, 213, 215, 221
Anderson, E., 74–75
Anderson, R., 66
Aquila, 212
Aquinas, T., 63, 67, 69, 71, 74
Aristotle, 67
Augustine, 67–68, 71, 74, 138
Averbeck, R., 99
Azulai, A., 196

Bailey, D., 195
Baldwin, J., 58
Baltzer, K., 18, 48, 51, 82, 195
Barker, K., 11–12, 15, 51, 130, 188
Barmash, P., 79
Barrett, M., 157–58
Barstad, H., 213–14
Barth, K., 64, 67
Baruq, A., 146, 168
Basil the Great, 125, 149
Batto, B., 88
Baumgärtel, F., 68–69, 71–72
Beckman, G., 17, 20–22, 52, 81–86, 120, 124, 126–28, 132, 134, 142–43, 145, 148–49
Begrich, J., 121, 156
Behm, J., 72

Behrens, A., 90
Bellinger, W., 201
Bergren, T., 232
Berkeley, G., 74
Berkouwer, G., 64
Betz, O., 201
Beuken, W., 2, 10, 89, 210
Bieder, W., 68–69
Billerbeck, P., 100, 200
Bird, M., 232
Blanton, T., 87
Blenkinsopp, J., 32–33, 48, 120, 125, 130, 152, 154
Blocher, H., 197–98
Block, D., 68–69
Bordreuil, P., 64
Borger, R., 125, 149
Bottéro, J., 79
Boutflower, C., 109, 111
Bovati, P., 121
Bowling, A., 72
Boyle, M., 121
Bratcher, R., 62–63
Bratsiotis, N., 71–72
Brettler, M., 14, 24, 28, 30
Bright, J., 109, 121, 140
Brooke, G., 217
Brown, C., 66, 68, 70–71, 76
Brown, W., 74–75
Brownlee, W., 3
Brueggemann, W., 1–2, 6, 37–38, 86, 93, 123
Brunner, E., 63–64
Buchanan, G., 220
Buis, P., 82

AUTHOR INDEX

Bultmann, R., 71
Bynum, C., 228

Calvin, J., 63, 73
Carroll, R., 5, 42, 129, 166
Cassuto, U., 13
Cerny, L., 136
Chan, M., 159
Chernus, I., 207
Chiera, E., 13, 189
Childs, B., 2, 12, 43–44, 96, 111, 130, 141
Chilton, B., 5, 39, 78, 81, 86, 89, 93, 201
Chirichigno, G., 80
Chisholm, R., 71–72, 78
Cicero, 144
Clement of Alexandria, 192
Clements, R., 2, 112, 141
Cohn-Haft, L., 22, 86
Collins, J., 79, 190–91
Conrad, E., 156
Conrad, J., 204
Conzelmann, H., 71
Cooper, J., 66, 72
Coppes, L., 76
Coste, J., 56, 89
Cowley, A., 218
Cross, F., 25, 136
Crouch, C., 143, 148
Craigie, P., 122
Cullmann, O., 47
Cyrus, 51, 166

Dahl, M., 71
Dalman, G., 109, 177
Daly, R., 201
Darr, K., 30
Davidson, A., 203, 220
Davies, G. , 9, 140–41, 228
Dean-Otting, M., 207
Delitzsch, F., 197
Dempsey, C., 1, 144
deRoche, M., 121
Descartes, R., 67, 69, 71, 74
Dihle, A., 66
Dijkstra, M., 121
Dillard, R., 3
Dio Cassius, 230

Dion, P., 156
DiSante, C., 150
Döderlein, J., 2
Dommershausen, W., 40
Donaldson, T., 230, 232
Dreytza, M., 22
Driver, G., 178
Duggan, M., 18, 82
Duhm, B., 3, 147
Dumbrell, W., 78
Dunn, J., 63, 66, 68, 70–73, 75

Eichhorn, J., 2
Eichrodt, W., 23, 28, 32, 34–35, 38, 46, 53, 57–60, 73, 113, 128, 131, 152–53, 155, 169–70, 173, 189
Eissfeldt, O., 14
Ekblad, J., 195, 199
Eliade, M., 40, 93
Engnell, I., 121, 178, 200
Enns, P., 89
Epictetus, 206
Epiphanius, 208
Estelle, B., 213
Evans, C., 42, 88, 128, 232
Everson, A., 136
Ezra, I., 2–3

Falk, Z., 80
Farmer, W., 201
Fensham, C., 125
Finch, T., 18, 82
Fischer, J., 213
Fitzmyer, J., 125, 132, 144, 200
Flender, O., 65
Flint, P., 190–92
Frankel, V., 77
Fredericks, D., 66
Fredriksen, P., 232
Freedman, D., 88
Fried, L., 51
Fuchs, A., 111
Fuerst, W., 53

Gammie, J., 39, 44, 92, 96
Gane, R., 108
Gelb, I., 127
Gemser, B., 121

AUTHOR INDEX

Gerstenberger, E., 80, 123
Gese, H., 80
Gevirtz, S., 80
Gilchrist, P., 75
Gillman, N., 228
Glueck, N., 60
Goetze, A., 15
Goetzmann, J., 75
Goldingay, J., 2–3, 7–8, 10, 12–13,
    28–30, 32, 38–39, 45–48, 54,
    117–18, 133, 140, 144, 184, 195,
    203, 211–12, 218, 221
Gordon, C., 130, 189
Gosse, B., 89
Gottwald, N., 145, 178
Gray, J., 131
Greenberg, M., 80
Gregory Nyssa, 138
Gregory the Great, 138, 144
Gressmann, H., 184
Grether, O., 53
Groswell, G., 189
Gruber, M., 30
Gubler, M., 201
Guenter, R., 5
Gruenwald, I., 207
Gundry, R., 71
Gunkel, H., 121
Guterbock, H., 15

Häbel, N., 47, 159
Hamilton, V., 64
Hänel, J., 58
Hannah, D., 41
Harner, P., 121, 156, 160, 214
Harrington, H., 107
Hartley, J., 65
Harvey J., 121
Hasel, G., 157–58
Hayes, J., 79, 141
Hays, C., 38, 53, 86, 140, 144, 148, 176
Healy, M., 5
Henderson, S., 164
Hengel, M., 195
Herodotus, 51, 112, 144, 166
Hillel, 64
Hillers, D., 124–28, 132, 134, 142–45,
    148–49

Hippolytus, 7, 183
Hirsch, H., 126
Hobbes, T., 74, 130
Hoehner, H., 183
Hoffman, Y., 214
Holladay, J, 52, 184
Holter, K., 44
Homer, 189
Hooker, M., 200
Horace, 144, 230
House, P., 78
Huey, F., 155
Huffmon, H., 121, 161
Hurowitz, V., 42
Hyatt, J., 201

Ignatius, 183
Irenaeus, 63, 183, 192
Isaacs, M., 207

Jackson, B., 79–80
Jacob, E., 53, 66, 72
Jacobsen, T., 14
Janzen, W., 123
Jenson, P., 97
Jeremias, J., 199
Jerome, 217
Jewett, R., 90
Johnson, A., 23, 138
Johnson, D., 147, 159
Josephus, 3–4, 51–52, 101, 105, 108–
    10, 146, 166, 168, 177, 181–83,
    196, 228–30
Joshua, rabbi, 150
Justin Martyr, 7, 63, 184, 192, 230
Juvenal, 230

Kaiser, W., 12, 16, 38, 41, 68–69, 155
Kaiser, O., 115–16, 167, 170–71, 173,
    184, 226
Kalim, I., 111
Kamesar, A., 184
Kaminsky, J, 150, 229
Kamlah, E., 69
Kapelrud, A., 156
Kaufmann, Y., 229
Kautzsch, E., 218
Kazen, T., 105, 107–8

Kelley, P., 153
Keener, C., 6
Keil, F., 29
Kelly, P., 32
Kendall, D., 89
Kennard, D., 1, 5–6, 15, 18, 20, 40, 47, 55, 60, 62–63, 65, 78–80, 82–83, 89, 91, 93, 97, 105, 121, 147, 162–64, 174, 186, 199, 205–7, 210, 215, 232
Keowen, B., 144
Kierkegaard, S., 67
Kiesow, K., 213
Kilian, R., 80
King, L., 126–27
Klawans, J., 102
Kleinknecht, H., 69
Kline, M., 18, 82
Knohl, I., 199
Knutson, F., 18, 82
Koch, R., 23–24
Koester, C., 207
Köhler, L., 121, 153
Konkel, A., 64
Kookel, A., 65
Koole, J., 221
Kornfeld, W., 39, 43, 93, 95
Kramer, S., 141
Kraovec, J., 56
Kraus, F., 79–80
Kuhn, H., 13, 47

Laato, A., 195
Labahn, A., 155
Labuschagne, C., 44, 50–51
Lac, A., 72
Lactantius, 6
Lambert, W., 48, 125, 149
Landsberger, B., 80
Lange, J., 13
Laurin, R., 171
LeFebvre, M., 79
Leupold, H., 16, 41, 136, 157
Lewis, T., 110, 178
Lienhard, J., 125
Lim, B., 195, 213
Limberg, J., 121
Lincoln, A., 207

Lindbloom, J., 174
Locke, J., 6
Lohfink, N., 18, 82
Lohse, E., 199
Longenecker, R., 200
Longman, T., 3, 213
Lovejoy, A., 93
Lund, O., 214
Luther, M., 63, 171
Lys, D., 70

Ma, W., 7, 23
Macintosh, A., 146
Maimonides, 192
Malamat, A., 141
Martin, J., 121
Matthews, V., 125, 149
Mauchline, J., 50
Mayes, A., 18, 82
McCarthy, D., 18, 82
McComiskey, T., 39, 43, 93, 95
McConville, J., 79, 195
McDonald, H., 72, 75
McKenzie, J., 53, 66, 130
Meier, J., 181–82
Meissner, B., 13
Melugin, R., 156
Menard, J., 200
Mendenhall, G., 18–20, 82–84, 121
Merrill, E., 64–65, 156
Meyer, B., 181
Meyer, R., 71–72
Miano, D., 88
Mihelic, J., 15, 44
Mihinovich, T., 121
Miles, J., 11
Milgrom, J., 43, 91–92, 95, 97, 103–4, 108
Millard, A., 64
Miller, P., 27, 84–85, 121
Moberly, R., 56, 93
Mollenkott, V., 30
Motyer, J., 71
Mowinckel, S., 53, 121, 184
Muilenberg, J., 18, 82
Müller, W., 158
Munger, R., 28, 220
Murphy, N., 66, 71, 74–75

Nabonidus, 14
Nagelsbach, C., 115
Naudé, J., 39, 43, 93, 95
Neufeld, T., 25-26
Neusner, J., 39, 93, 98-99, 102, 209, 230
Nickelsburg, G., 207
Nielsen, K., 17, 24-25, 80, 120-21
Niskanen, P., 30
North, C., 12, 23, 47, 60, 153, 165-66, 221
Novation, 183

O'Conner, M., 38, 203, 218
Odendaal, D., 161
Oehler, G., 27
Oeming, M., 90
O'Kennedy, D., 40
Olyan, S., 40, 94, 99
Oosting, R., 47
Openheim, A., 125, 148
Origen, 41, 67-68, 71, 138, 144, 180
Orlinsky, H., 228
Oswalt, J., 2, 8, 39, 45, 47, 49, 71, 75, 90-91, 93, 98, 111-12, 116, 130, 139, 150, 152, 156, 174, 203, 205
Otto, R., 15, 40, 93
Owen, J., 121

Pao, D., 213
Pannenberg W., 66, 69
Parker, S., 161
Parker-Taylor, G., 11, 27
Parpola, S., 126-27
Patai, R., 192
Pate, C., 190, 199, 205-7
Payne, B., 68-70
Payne, D., 3, 30, 32, 45, 152, 203, 218
Pentecost, D., 161
Pettinato, G., 80
Phillips, A., 218
Philo, 99, 208-9, 230-32
Pilate, 197
Plato, 62, 67-68, 70, 74, 228
Plutarch, 206
Polak, F., 19, 83
Polaski, D., 78, 147
Porten, B., 209

Procksch, O., 53
Puech, E., 192

Rabinowitz, I., 53
Rahner, K, 66
Reid, T., 6
Reisman, D., 13
Reiter, E., 58
Rendtorff, R., 2, 18, 56
Richardson, S., 111
Riesenfeld, E., 201
Ringgren, H., 2, 99, 178, 200
Roberts, J., 83, 110-12
Robinson, J., 71
Roehrs, W., 35, 53
Rösel, M., 184
Rosenberg, R., 201
Ross, J., 5, 26-27
Roth, M., 79-80, 127, 145, 148-49
Rubin, N., 64
Rust, E., 169

Sanders, E., 89, 181
Sapp, D., 203
Sawyer, J., 130, 217
Schafer, P., 207
Schaudig, H., 48
Schiffman, L., 202
Schmitt, J., 30
Schoeps, H., 201
Schoors, A., 121
Schrenk, G., 76
Schulz, H., 80
Schunck, K., 130
Schweitzer, S., 51, 166
Schweizer, E., 68-69, 71
Scobie, C., 225, 228
Scott, R., 197
Seebass, H., 66
Seeley D., 206
Segal, A., 139, 184-85, 223
Seneca, 205
Shakespeare, W., 122
Sholem, G., 207
Simian-Yofre, H., 213
Simon, U., 1, 214
Sjöberg, E., 68-69, 207
Smith, G., 3, 14, 136-37, 141-42, 185, 223

Smith, M., 48
Snaith, N., 12, 22, 32, 60, 113, 153, 184
Sommer, B., 2, 127
Song, T., 72-73
Stamm, J., 80
Strack, H., 100, 200-1
Stromberg, J., 2
Stuhlmueller, C., 15, 27, 46-47, 53, 55, 159-60, 213, 215, 217
Suganuma, E., 121
Sukenik, E., 230
Sweeney, M., 14, 81, 89, 141, 168, 187, 189

Tacitus, 206
Taggar-Cohen, A., 18, 82
Tertullian, 7, 67-68, 144, 180-81, 183, 197
Teugels, L., 219
Thaumaturgus, G., 183
Theodotus, 230
Thiselton, A., 53
Thompson, J., 17, 52, 120
Tiemeyer, L., 150, 228
Tillich, P., 69-70, 75
Toombs, L., 56
Torrance, T., 64
Torrey, C., 3
Tromp, N., 138

Ulrich, E., 3-4
Ussishkin, D., 109-10, 177

Van Dam, C., 204
Van de Mieroop, M., 79
VanderKam, 87, 190-92
Van Goudoever, J., 78
Van Gulick, R., 74-75
Van Imschoot, P., 161
Van Kooten, G., 63
Van Leeuwen, R., 144
VanPelt, M., 69
Vawter, B., 65
Vermes, G., 192, 201
Vital, C., 196
Volz, P., 23
Von Rad, G., 46, 56, 65, 90, 136, 167, 186
Von Waldow, H., 121, 156

Vorgrimler, H., 66
Vos, G., 45, 56, 116
Vriezen, T., 2, 14, 24, 36, 39, 119, 122

Wakeman, M., 130-31
Waltke, B., 38, 66, 130-31, 203
Walton, J., 79-80, 86, 125, 149
Walton, J. H., 79-80, 86
Watanabe, K., 126-27
Watts, J., 3, 25, 29, 56, 114, 136, 145, 178, 212, 217, 219, 222
Watts, R., 213
Wegner, P., 184
Weinfeld, M., 18, 82
Weiss, M., 136, 167
Wells, R., 80-81, 89
Wenham, G., 97
Westermann, C., 46, 155-56, 162-63, 213
Wheeler, D., 136
Whitley, C., 55
Whybray, R., 46
Wildberger, H., 56
Wilde, O., 91-92, 102
Williams, P., 194
Williams, R., 38
Williamson, H., 2, 121, 156
Willis, T., 81
Wilson, J., 39, 93, 99
Wilson, M., 75
Wiseman, D., 40, 125-27, 148-49
Wolff, H., 62-66, 68-69, 71-72, 225
Wong, G., 110, 177
Wood, J., 201
Wood, L., 23
Wright, E., 11, 16-17, 79, 121-22
Wright, N., 181, 202, 228

Xenophon, 51, 166, 212

Yamauchi, E., 99
Yitzhaq of Berdichev, 196
Yohanan, rabbi, 102
Young, E., 3-5, 37, 74, 109-10, 143-44, 177, 185, 189, 198, 223

Zehnder, M., 127, 214
Zillessen, A., 213

Subject Index

Abrahamic Covenant, 162–63
Adonai, 14
Arm, 27–28, 37
Atonement, 199–210

Biblical theology, 1–2
Body, 70–72
Bowels, 74

Chaos monster, 130–31
Clean and unclean, 98–108
Cleansing, 41–42, 103–6, 199–210
Cloud Rider, 27, 54–55
Conditional prophecy, 52–53
Co-temporal, 47
Covenant, 8, 16–21, 78–112
Covenant lawsuit, 16–17, 21–22, 120–23
Creator, 13–14, 37–38, 46–49, 55
Creation-Reversal, 132, 159–61, 225
Curse, 123–28, 204
Cyrus, 51–52, 187
Cyrus Oracle, 165–66

Davidic Branch, 186–93
Davidic Covenant, 87, 164–65, 186–89, 193, 222–32
Davidic King, 186–93, 222–32
Day of Yahweh, 136–37, 167–68
Deuteronomic History, 9, 109–12
Divine Divorce, 132–33

Earthquake, 127, 135–36, 149
Elohim, 13–14
Epistemology, 4–8
Eschatological Judge, 137

Evil, 38, 49
Exodus, 213–221

Faith, 169–71
Fall-Curse, 132
Farming, 35
Father God, 29–30
Fear of Yahweh, 172–73
Fire Destruction, 134–35, 149
First and Last, 46
Flood Destruction, 127, 134
Forgiveness, 41–42
Futility Curses, 132

Gentiles, 140–51, 228–32
Gratitude, 19

Hardening, 129
Hardening Reversed, 158–59
Heart, 72–74
History, 47
Holy, 39–44, 58, 92–98
Humanity, 62–77

Idolatry, 44–45, 50, 107, 115–17
Image of God, 63–65
Incomparable, 44–55
Isaiah critical division, 2
Isaiah importance, 1, 11
Isaiah Message, 7
Isaiah unity, 2–4

Jealous, 57–58
Judge, 24–25
Judgment, 8, 123–151

SUBJECT INDEX

Kingship of God, 11–61, 222–23
Kingdom, 222–32
Kingdom of Darkness, 133
Kingdom of Light, 166–67, 225–26

Living God, 55
Love, 56, 60–61

Materialism, 118–19
Merkabah Mysticism, 207
Mind, 73–77
Monotheism, 44–55
Mosaic Covenant, 78–112, 163–64
Mother God, 30–31

Nations, 140–51, 228–32
New Covenant, 87–88
Noahic Covenant, 162

Omnipotence, 36–37
Oracle of Salvation, 156–57

Paradise Regained, 161
Potter, 37–38
Prayer, 171–72
Pride, 8, 117–19

Ransom, 33, 153–54
Rebellion, 113–15, 118–19
Redeemer, 32–33
Redemption, 152–75
Remnant saved, 157–58
Repentance, 168–69
Revelation, 4–6, 52

Righteous, 55–57, 89–92, 174
Rock or Stone, 37

Sabaoth, 25–26, 54
Salvation, 8, 56, 152–75, 213–32
Sanctification, 103–6
Savior, 33
Seraphim, 16, 41–42, 46
Servant of Yahweh, 194–212
Sheol, 138–39
Shepherd, 28–29
Signs, 6–7
Sign Child, 176–85, 223–24
Sin, 113–23
Sin Offering, 103–6
Soul, 66–68
Spirit, 22–24, 38, 68–70, 196, 223–24
Spiritual, 15
Suzerainty treaty, 16–21

Transcendence, 15

Unbelief, 117
Uncleanness, 41

Vision, 4–6

Warrior, 25–28, 54
Will, 76–77
Wind judgment, 22
Word of God, 4–6, 35–36, 53–54
Wrathful, 59–60

Yahweh, 11–13

Scripture Index

Gen
1:1–2:3	64, 132
1:20–30	55, 64–66
1:21	130
2	221
2:3–19	38, 43, 55, 96
2:7	66
2:17	132
2:23–24	65
3:14–15	161, 225
3:14–19	132
4:7–24	132
4:23	205
5:1–3	65
6:5–7	132
6:12–17	72, 134
7:11	134, 138
7:15	69
8:2	138
8:13–14	134
8:22	162
9:4–10	66
9:6	65
9:11	134, 162
9:12–16	147, 162
9:17	162
12:2–3	162, 215
13:15	147
15	162
15:5	216
15:6	90–91
17:7–19	147
18:5	73
20:12–20	173
22:1–14	201
22:17	216
24:43	177
25:8–17	138
25:22–23	67
28:14	215
29:14	72
32:11	60
34:3	73
35:29	138
37:27	138
37:35	138
38:21–22	39, 43, 93, 95
39:9	173
41:45–50	145
42:18	173
42:28	74
42:38	138
44:29–31	138
45:27	69
46:20	145
48:4	147
48:15	28
49:24	28
49:25	138
49:29–33	138

Exod
1:17–21	173
3:12–14	12
3:16	216
3:20	215–16
6:6	215–16
9:4	73
10:21–29	37

Exod (continued)

11:8–12	216
11:41	216
12:2	181
12:11–48	215
12:14	147
13:2	97
13:3–4	181, 216
13:14–16	215–16
13:21–22	217, 219, 222
14	217
14–19	213
14:5	54
14:19–20	216
14:21–31	37, 54, 69
14:24	219
15	217, 220
15:1	54
15:13	28, 32, 153
15:16	215–16
15:22–26	220
16:1	216
17:2–7	220
18:13–26	80
18:21	173
19–24	16, 40–43
19:6	211
19:10–14	94
19:16–20	217
19:22	96
20	80
20:2	216
20:5	58, 171, 211
20:8–11	96
20:13	148
20-Lev 26	18–20, 82
21–23	79
21:12	204
22:4–9	211, 218
22:22	148
23:12	66
23:15	181
24:6–8	203–4, 230
25:11–39	99
26:33–34	97
27:21	147
28:3	95
28:14–35	99
28:29	73
28:41	96
28:43	147
29	96
29:37	97
30:3	99
30:29	97
30:35	99
30:36	97
31:8	99
31:12–17	43–44, 80, 95–96, 147
33:9	219
34:21	80
35	44, 74, 96, 107
37:2–29	99
39:15–37	99
40:34–38	207
40:35	179

Lev

4:1–35	104
4:3	51
4:12	105
4:20–5:13	107
4:25–30	103
5:1	203, 205
5:2–3	100–1
5:11	181
5:17	205
6:11	105
6:17	97
6:18–27	96–97
6:22	147
6:29	97
7:1–6	97
7:18	90
7:19–21	101, 106
8:30	96
9:9	103
10–11	40, 42, 71
10:9–17	97–98, 106, 147, 205
11–16	105
11:4–39	101
11:44–47	94, 98, 101, 106
12:2	100
12:4	104

12:8	181	11:18	42, 94
13:3–46	100	11:33	204
14:8–20	108	14:14	219
14:13	97	14:34	205
14:57	98	15:27–36	80, 103–4
15:2–33	100–1, 103–4, 106, 108	16:30–33	138
16:10–22	104, 205	17:12–18:32	97
16:16–19	103, 106	18:9	97
16:29–34	147	18:11–13	106
16:30	103, 107	18:24–30	105
17:15	101	19:1	102
17:16	205	19:1–10	105
18:19	101	19:11–22	101, 103–6
18:24–30	105	20:8	220
19:2–37	40, 42–43, 90, 94–96	20:12–13	40
20:1–4	104	20:24–26	138
20:7–26	42, 94, 98, 101	22–24	140
20:19	205	22:23–32	204
21:1–15	97	23:15	104
21:8–23	96	25	96
21:16–24	97	27:4–7	81
22:4–8	101	27:13	138
22:32	42, 95	27:14	40
24:4–7	99	31:2	138
24:9	97	33:52	65
25	32	35:11–15	204
25:24–28	81	35:34	105
26:16	134	36:2	81
26:21	204		
27	20, 96	**Deut**	
27:26	97	1:16	90
27:28	97	1:17	118
		1:31	29
Num		4:10	173
3:13	97	4:19	26
4:4	97	4:24	58
4:19	97	4:37	60
5:2–4	100	5:8–10	115
5:28	98, 107	5:9	58
6:2–5	180	5:17	148
6:11	43, 95–96	6:15	58
8:7	71	7:8–9	33, 60, 153, 159–60
8:14–19	97	8:5	29
8:17	97	9:26	33, 153
9:13	205	10:12–20	173
9:15–23	217	12:12	66
11:16–17	80	12:15–22	98

Deut (continued)

13:6	33, 153
15:10	73
15:15	33, 153
15:19	97
15:22	98
16:1–6	181
16:3	216
16:18–20	90, 118
17:3	26
17:16–17	118
17:19	173
18:9–13	117
18:17–22	50
19:15	148
20:3–4	13
21:8	33, 153
21:17	211, 218
21:23	71, 105
22:23–24	180
23:6	60
23:10	100
23:17	39, 43, 93, 95
24:1	58
24:1–4	133
24:17	148
24:18	33, 153
25:1	90
25:7–10	81
26:14	106
28	124
28:1–6	123
28:3–5	120
28:15	54
28:15–29:29	106
28:16	123
28:17–18	124
28:19	124
28:21–63	119
28:23–24	145
28:31–33	134
28:47	74
28:53–57	118
28:59	204
29:16–18	116
29:18–19	58, 155
29:26	116
29:29	145
30:1–10	163–64
30:6	87
31:8	13
31:13	173
32:4	173
32:18	30
32:16	58
32:21	58
32:50	138
32:51	42, 94–95
33:19	91
33:26	27, 54

Joshua

3:5	42, 94
17:4–6	81
22:17	107
24	16, 18–20, 58, 82–83
24:14	173

Judg

2:10	138
6:24	185, 224
13:2–7	67
13:19	185, 223
19:5–8	73

Ruth

4:2–15	81

1 Sam

1:8	73
2:1–8	74
2:6	138
3:1	4
4:13	74
12	18, 60, 82
15:2–3	140–41
16:5	42, 94–95
17:32	74
20:26	100
21:4–5	40, 98
25:37	73
28:11–19	139

2 Sam

7	164, 183
7:12–13	183, 187
11:1–4	27, 43, 95
12:23	139
15:6	74
19:19	90
22:6	139
23:2	36
23:3	173

1 Kgs

2:6–9	138
6:16	97
7:50	97
8:6	97
8:10	219, 222
8:32	90
8:34–50	155
8:54	45
19:18	45
21:7	73
22:24	36

2 Kgs

5:18–24	155
6:16–17	69
10:20	43, 95
11:18	65
15:29	178
16:4	115
17:16	26
18:3–6	83, 111
18:17–37	110
19:36–37	9
20:8–10	9, 112
20:12–18	112
21:1	172
21:3	26
22:9–22	18, 20, 82
22:20	138
23:8–16	107, 117
24:17–20	146

1 Chr

5:6	178
5:26	146
6:49	97
15:12	43, 95
15:20	177
17:11–14	183, 187
17:15	4
18:14	96
23:13	97
28:17	99

2 Chr

3:4	99
3:8–12	97
3:28	138
5:11	96
6:23	90
23:17	65
23:19	92, 100, 107
26:1	96
26:16	74
29:3–21	111
29:5	96
29:6–31:21	18–20, 82–83
29:16	107
29:34	96
30:15	96
30:17–19	43, 95, 106
30:24	96
31:18	43, 95
32:21	9
32:31	112
34:13–35:19	18, 82
35:1–19	20
35:6	96
36:14	92, 107
36:22–23	51, 166, 187
44:19	96

Ezra

1:1–4	51, 165–66
2:20–21	106
4:2–10	110, 177
6:3–15	212
6:21	107, 229
9:2–10:44	18, 20, 82

Neh

2:2	73
3:37	155
7:18	155
7:65	97
9:5–10:34	18–20, 36, 82
12:30	107
12:47	96
13:30	107

Esth

9:27	229

Job

4:15	71
6:4	67
7:9	138
11:8	138
13:4	45, 116
14:4	106
14:21	139
14:45	98
15:30–32	116
17:1	69
17:13–16	138–39
18:16	116
22:14	36
24:19	139
27:3	69
28:19	99
28:24	35
30:25	67
41:1	130

Pss

1:3	116
3:2	66
4:6	91
6:3	66–67
8:5–9	62
9:1	177
11:7	60
12:6–7	106
18:2	173
18:4	139
18:10	27, 54
19:7–14	92
22:26	73
22:27	229
25:10	60
25:11	155
26:3	60
27:10	29
27:14	74
31:4	28
31:24	60
32:1	155
32:2	90, 173
33:5	60
34:18	73
35:9	67
37:28	60
38:18–19	139
40:12	74
42:5	67
42:9	173
44:12	28
45:8	60
48:15	28
50	18–20, 82
50:7–15	117
51:2–10	107
51:7	203
51:11	40, 94
51:16	117
51:17	208
52:8	116
55:15	138
62:7	173
68:5	29
68:33	27, 54
69:16	138
71:20	138
73:26	73
74:1	28
74:8	59
74:14	130
77:16	32
77:21	28
78:8	74
78:12	185, 223
79:1	92, 107
79:13	28
80:1	29

80:8–16	198	146:8	60
81	18–20, 82		
84:2	73	**Prov**	
85:3	155		
86:1	173	3:3	60
87:2	60	3:12	60
87:4	131	10:3	74
88:3	138	14:22	60
88:5	138	15:9	60
88:13	139	15:11	138
89	164	15:26	106
89:1–4	165	20:9	106
89:10	130	23:17	74
89:28–29	165	27:20	138
89:48	139	29:18	4
90:5–7	116	30:12	106
91:4	179	30:19–20	177
92:12–13	116	31:6	67
95:6–7	28, 45		
98:1	40, 94	**Eccl**	
99:4	60	3:21	69
100:3	28–29	5:14	139
103:3	155	9:2	98
103:4	155	9:5	139
103:12	155	12:7	69
103:13	29		
104:2–3	27, 47, 54	**Song**	
104:7	134	8:6	139
104:26	130		
105:42	40, 94	**Isa**	
106:10	32	1	5, 7, 84
106:38–39	92	1–5	16
106:31	90	1–12	7–8
107:17–20	155	1–39	2–3, 7–9, 187
109:14	155	1:1	2–6, 42
115:17	139	1:1–15	117
118:12	37	1:2	29–30, 75, 85, 94, 113, 115, 121–22
118:26	218		
119:9–16	92	1:3	29–30, 75, 94, 113, 114–15, 121, 166
119:32	73		
119:106	90	1:4	29–30, 75, 94, 113, 115, 121, 166
132:2–5	36		
135:5–6	49	1:5	114, 126, 166
139:7	22	1:6	114, 126, 155, 204
139:8	138		
141:2	208		
141:7	139		
145:21	72		

Isa (continued)

1:7	17, 114, 120, 124, 127, 134–35, 142–43, 145, 148–49
1:8	17, 114, 120, 124, 142–43, 145, 148–49
1:9	4, 17, 26, 114, 120, 122, 124, 142–43, 145, 148–49
1:10	14, 17, 81, 120
1:10–15	117, 122
1:14	40, 55, 66–67
1:15	171, 174
1:16	100, 107, 114–15, 122–23, 168, 174
1:17	56, 122–23, 168, 174
1:18–20	54, 76, 84, 114, 115, 122
1:21	126, 169, 225
1:23	118
1:24	36, 123
1:25	37, 115
1:26	91, 169, 174, 225
1:28	114, 115, 122
1:29	115, 123
1:30	115, 123, 149
2–4	7
2:1	2, 5–6, 141, 156, 222, 228
2:2	86–87, 121, 141, 156, 168, 188, 222, 228–30
2:3	78, 86–87, 121–22, 141, 156, 168, 188, 214, 222–24, 226, 228–30
2:4	86–87, 121, 141, 156, 168, 188, 222–24, 226, 228–30
2:5	122, 141, 156, 168, 174, 226
2:6	122, 137
2:6–22	8, 45, 113, 117, 141
2:7	118, 123, 137, 222
2:8	115–16, 123, 222
2:10	173
2:10–22	123
2:11	118, 137
2:12	118, 137
2:15	137
2:17	118
2:18	116
2:19	136, 173
2:20	116, 137
2:21	136
3:1	14, 114, 137
3:2	5
3:6	29
3:7	137
3:8	114, 118
3:9	66, 115, 118, 123
3:10	122
3:11	115, 123
3:13	16, 57, 118
3:14	16, 57, 118, 123–24, 142–43, 148–49
3:15	14, 118, 123–24, 137, 142–43, 148–49
3:16	122
3:16–4:6	117, 119, 141
3:17	126
3:18	132, 137
3:18–24	127, 143, 148
3:19	132
3:20	66, 132
3:24	124, 164
3:25	142–43, 148–49
3:26	127, 142–43, 148–49
4	156
4:1	119, 137
4:2	137, 154, 168, 188
4:3	154, 158, 168, 219
4:4	22, 154, 168, 219
4:5	135, 154, 168, 217, 219, 222
4:6	126, 142, 149, 154, 168, 219, 222
5	7
5:1–2	122, 198
5:3–7	122, 198
5:4	122
5:5	114
5:7	91, 174, 225
5:8	118, 123
5:9	36, 128, 132

SCRIPTURE INDEX

5:10	123, 128, 131–32, 150	6:12	4–5, 53, 94, 117, 127, 129, 132, 157
5:11	123	6:13	4–5, 53, 94, 117, 127, 129, 157
5:12	113, 119, 123	7–8	52, 178, 184, 224
5:13	123	7–9	176–85
5:14	66, 123, 139	7:1	138, 169, 222
5:15	118, 123, 139	7:1–25	5–6
5:16	40, 56–57, 94, 123, 166	7:2	22, 70, 74, 109, 169, 176
5:17	123, 166	7:3	2, 6–7, 109–10, 154, 169, 177, 179
5:18	115, 119, 166	7:3–8:8	157
5:19	122, 166, 170	7:4	154, 156, 169–70, 177
5:20	119, 166, 225	7:4–17	6–7, 14, 109–10
5:21	113, 117, 119	7:5	123, 154, 156, 169, 177
5:22	113, 117, 119	7:6	154, 156, 169, 177
5:23	113, 115, 117–19	7:7	154, 156, 169, 177
5:24	40, 81, 94, 113, 115, 119, 123, 134	7:8	154, 156, 169, 177
5:24	59, 127, 135, 149	7:9	128, 154, 156, 169, 177
5:25	59, 123, 127, 135	7:10	154, 177
5:26	36, 59, 123–24, 148	7:11	36, 177
5:27	124, 148	7:12	117–18, 123
5:28	124, 148	7:13	177
5:29	59, 123, 143, 148	7:14	6, 135, 177–79, 185, 223–24
5:30	59, 123, 133, 143, 148	7:15	176, 179, 224
6	7–8, 16, 39–43	7:16	179, 224
6:1	4, 6–7, 15, 39, 40–1, 57	7:17	140, 179, 224
6:2	15, 39, 40–1, 57	7:18	124, 128, 132, 140, 142–43, 148–49, 179, 224
6:3	15, 39, 40–1, 57, 94	7:19	140, 179, 224
6:4	15, 39, 40–1, 57, 207	7:20	140, 179, 224
6:5	6, 14, 15, 39, 40–2, 57, 84, 96, 98, 100, 102, 106, 119, 123, 187	8	223
6:6	6, 14, 42, 57, 84, 96, 135	8:1	6, 29, 109, 178–79, 184, 224
6:7	6, 14, 42, 57, 84, 96, 107, 115, 135	8:2	6, 29, 109, 178–79, 224
6:8	6, 14, 42, 57, 84, 96	8:3	6, 29, 109, 178–79, 184, 224
6:9	4–5, 53, 84, 94, 117, 127–29	8:4	6, 29, 109, 124, 142–43, 148–49, 176, 178–79, 224
6:10	4–5, 38, 53, 73, 94, 117, 127–29, 133	8:6	178
6:11	4–5, 53, 94, 117, 127, 129, 132, 157		

Isa (continued)

8:7	127, 134, 178
8:8	134, 178–79, 224
8:9	178
8:10	178–79, 224
8:11	36, 154, 178, 214
8:12	15, 26, 41–42, 94, 128, 154, 178
8:13	15, 26, 41–42, 94, 128, 154, 178
8:14	37, 117, 127–28, 154, 173, 178
8:15	117, 128, 173, 178
8:16	81, 178
8:17	57, 170, 178
8:18	6, 178
8:19	14, 117, 139, 178
8:20	81
8:21	13–14, 149, 187
8:21–28	117
8:22	149
9:1	4, 152, 154, 156, 179, 184, 214, 223
9:2	7–8, 152, 154, 156, 166–67, 179, 184, 223, 226
9:3	7–8, 117, 126, 152, 154, 156, 179, 184, 220, 223–25
9:4	7–8, 126, 152, 154, 156, 179, 184, 222–23
9:5	7–8, 29, 126–27, 134–35, 149, 152, 154, 156, 179, 184–85, 222–24
9:6	7–8, 35, 57, 91, 141, 152, 154, 156, 178–79, 184–86, 222–24, 228
9:7	7–8, 141, 152, 154, 156, 178–79, 184–86, 223–25, 228
9:8	54, 113, 141, 185, 224
9:9	75
9:12–21	26, 37, 59
9:15	5, 119, 123
9:17	119, 123
9:18	127, 134–35, 149
9:19	118, 123, 127, 132, 134–35, 149
9:20	118, 123, 132
9:21	118, 123
10	45
10:1	56, 118, 123
10:2	56, 118, 123
10:3	56, 118, 123
10:4	37, 45, 56, 59, 118, 123 139
10:5	36, 117, 123, 141
10:6	36, 117, 222, 141
10:7	36, 75, 117, 141
10:8	36, 117, 141
10:9	36, 117, 141
10:10	36, 116–17, 141, 149
10:11	36, 117, 141
10:12	75–76, 116–17, 141
10:13–15	117, 141
10:16	127, 134–35, 149
10:17	127, 134–35, 149, 166
10:18	66, 135
10:19	135
10:20	40, 94, 157–58, 168–69
10:21	157–58, 168, 185, 223
10:22	4, 57, 157–58, 168
10:23	26, 156, 168
10:24	26, 156, 214
10:25	26, 156
10:26	17, 26, 120, 156, 204
10:27	156
10:34	36, 191
11–12	7, 156, 220
11–35	141
11:1	15, 23–24, 157, 179, 188, 190–91, 223–24
11:1–11	152, 154, 156, 161, 165
11:2	15, 23–24, 157, 173, 184, 188, 196, 223–24

11:3	15, 23–24, 57, 157, 173, 188, 196, 223–24	13:11–22	8, 14, 36, 117
		13:12	59, 115
		13:13	59, 115, 135, 137, 143
11:4	54, 57, 91, 115, 141, 157, 188–89, 191, 223–24, 228	13:14	137
		13:15	137, 143
11:4–15	8, 22, 70	13:16	127, 137, 143–44, 148
11:5	57, 91, 157, 188–89, 191, 223–24	13:17	143
		13:18	143, 148
11:6	161, 182, 223	13:19	141, 143
11:7	161, 182, 223	13:22	143
11:8	161, 182, 223	14:1	141, 153–54, 222, 228, 229
11:9	41, 94, 115, 156, 161, 182, 223	14:1–23	8
11:10	141, 168, 189, 222, 228	14:2	141, 154, 194, 222, 228
11:11	141, 153, 157, 168, 222	14:3	167, 173
11:12	141, 154, 161, 189, 222	14:4	144, 167, 225
		14:4–21	144
11:13	141, 154, 161	14:5	115, 126, 141–42, 144
11:14	141, 154, 161, 228		
11:15	141, 154, 161, 213–14, 222, 228	14:6	141–42, 144, 204, 225
11:16	17, 120, 141, 154, 157, 213–14, 222	14:7	144, 225
		14:8	144, 225
11:22	232	14:9	138–39, 225
12:1	168, 172	14:11	139
12:2	59, 154, 168, 172	14:12	144
12:3	168, 172, 220	14:12–21	131
12:4	168, 172	14:13	144
12:5	168, 172	14:14	144
12:6	40, 94, 168, 172	14:15	144
13–35	8, 16, 140	14:16	135, 144
13:1	2, 5, 27, 54, 141	14:19	145
13:1–8	27, 36, 55, 59	14:20	141–42, 145
13:2	141	14:21	145, 148
13:3	94, 98, 140–41	14:22	143
13:4	65, 141	14:24	35–36, 140
13:6	137, 142–43	14:25	35–36, 126, 140
13:7	137, 143	14:26	35–36
13:8	127, 137, 143, 149	14:27	26, 35–36
13:9	59, 115, 132, 137, 142–43	14:28	54
		14:29	126, 146
13:10	13, 59, 115, 137, 142, 147	14:30	29, 146
		14:31	146
13:11	59, 115, 123, 141, 142	14:32	170

Isa (continued)

15:1	54, 141, 146
15:1–16:14	8
15:2	146
15:3	124, 146
15:4	66, 146
15:5	141, 146, 214
15:6	146
15:7	146
15:8	146
15:9	126, 149
16:1–4	146
16:4	123, 146
16:5	56, 72, 91, 141, 156, 165, 188, 225
16:6	8, 117, 141
16:7	146
16:8	146
16:9	146
16:10	146
16:11	74, 146
16:12	146
16:13–14	36
17:1	141
17:1–11	8, 28, 40, 54
17:2	142
17:4–6	142
17:7	49, 94, 143, 145
17:8	49, 94, 143, 145
17:10	37, 154, 173
17:11	37, 142
17:12	37, 123, 131
17:13	22, 37, 70, 131, 134, 142, 149
17:14	37, 142
18:1	123
18:1–7	8
18:2	141–42
18:4	170
18:5	146, 150
18:7	141, 228
19:1	27, 45, 54–55, 116, 142, 145
19:2	27, 45, 54–55
19:3	27, 45, 54–55, 68, 116
19:4	27, 45, 54–55, 145
19:6	145
19:7	145
19:10	66
19:10–15	145
19:14	38
19:16	127, 145
19:17	145
19:17–25	9, 26, 36, 141–42, 145, 156
19:18	145, 168, 228
19:19	145, 168, 228
19:20	6, 33, 145, 168, 188, 228
19:21	76, 146, 168, 228
19:22	146, 168, 228
19:23	146, 168, 228
19:24	146, 168, 214, 228
19:25	228
20:1	110
20:2	2, 110
20:3	2, 110, 124, 126, 145, 194
20:4	110, 124, 126, 145
20:5	110, 145
20:6	110, 141–42, 145
20:28	134
21:1	141
21:2	143
21:3	143, 149
21:4	143
21:5	147, 212
21:9	142–43
21:10	8, 14, 150
21:11	8, 14, 146
21:12	8, 14, 146
21:13	8, 14, 146
21:14	8, 14, 146
21:15	8, 14, 141, 146
21:16	8, 14, 141, 146
21:17	8, 14, 146
22	147
22:1	54, 141, 147
22:1–13	54
22:2	112, 147
22:3–11	147
22:4	59, 117
22:9	147
22:10	127, 135, 143, 147

SCRIPTURE INDEX

22:11	59, 117, 140, 147
22:12	59, 117, 124
22:13	59, 117
22:14	36, 59, 117, 147
22:15	147
22:15–25	117–18, 123, 147
22:16–17	54, 147
22:18	147
22:21	29
22:24	29
22:25	141
23:1	54, 141
23:1–18	8, 146
23:8	140
23:9	8, 36, 117, 140–41
23:11	135
23:13	94
23:15	126, 141, 228
23:16	126, 141, 228
23:17	126, 141, 228
23:18	93, 126, 141, 228
24	59
24:1	147–48
24:2	148
24:3	54, 147–48
24:4	149
24:5	9, 78, 81, 86, 90, 92, 109, 137, 147, 174, 230
24:6	137, 147, 158, 230
24:7	73, 149
24:7–13	148
24:8	148
24:10	127, 132
24:11	149
24:14	151, 154, 158
24:15	12, 154, 158
24:16	56, 151, 154, 158, 222
24:17	137, 149, 173, 222
24:18	134, 136–37, 173, 222
24:19	94, 136–37, 222
24:20	113, 136–37, 222
24:21	8, 26, 94, 117, 141, 147
24:22	8, 26, 94, 117
24:23	8, 26, 94, 117, 150, 167, 187–88, 222, 226
25:1	12–13, 137, 151, 154, 172
25:2	59, 70, 137, 148, 154
25:3	59, 70, 137, 151, 154
25:4	59, 70, 127, 141–42, 148–49, 151, 154, 230
25:5	59, 70, 137, 149, 154
25:6	59, 70, 154, 225, 228
25:6–27:13	8, 141, 156
25:7	59, 70, 131, 137, 154, 228
25:8	8, 14, 54, 131, 139, 150, 154, 227–28
25:9	8, 14, 54, 151, 154, 168, 228
25:10	137, 146–47, 228
25:11	8, 117, 137, 141, 148
25:12	137, 148
26	168
26:1	150, 152, 172
26:2	91, 150, 152, 174, 221
26:3	150, 152, 221
26:4	37, 46, 150, 152, 221, 222
26:5	148, 152, 221
26:6	9, 56–57, 151–52, 221
26:7	9, 56–57, 150, 152
26:8	9, 56–57, 66–67, 152, 221
26:9	9, 22, 45, 56–57, 66–67, 91, 115, 152, 221
26:10	9, 22, 45, 56–57, 66–67, 91, 115, 221
26:11	22, 45, 58, 127, 134, 135, 149
26:12	22, 45, 151
26:13	14, 22, 45, 139, 151
26:14	22, 45, 147–49
26:15	22, 45, 150, 162
26:17	22, 45, 149
26:18	22, 45, 116, 149

Isa (continued)

26:19	8, 131, 138–39
26:20	59
26:21	59, 141–42, 230
27:1	130–31
27:3	222
27:4	149
27:5	149, 222
27:6	150
27:7	149, 204
27:8	22–23, 69
27:8–28	154
27:9	115, 137, 150
27:10	137, 150
27:11	137, 149
27:12	145, 147, 162
27:13	145, 147, 150–51, 158, 168
28:1	8, 113, 117, 119, 123, 141
28:2	117, 119, 127, 134, 142, 149
28:3	117, 119
28:4	117, 119
28:6	23, 69
28:7	5, 119
28:8	119
28:9	78, 113, 117, 119
28:10	78, 113, 117, 119, 127
28:11	117, 128
28:12	76, 117, 128, 170
28:13	86, 117, 127
28:14	113, 170
28:15	123–24, 142–43, 145, 148, 170
28:16	37, 90, 169, 170
28:17	37, 90
28:17–22	127, 134
28:18	86
28:19	142–43
28:22	113
28:24	35
28:25	35
28:26	13, 35, 90, 174
28:27	35
28:28	35
28:29	33, 184, 223
29:1	117
29:1–4	127, 134, 139, 149
29:5	48
29:6	127, 134, 142, 149, 217
29:7	4–5, 42
29:8	67
29:9	117, 127–28, 135
29:10	5, 38, 117, 127–28
29:11	12, 117
29:12	75, 117
29:13	4, 73, 73, 76, 117, 173
29:15	117
29:16	38, 73, 117
29:17	49, 117, 154, 159
29:18	133, 154, 159
29:19	40, 154, 159
29:20	154, 159
29:21	132, 154, 159
29:22	154, 159
29:23	42, 154, 159
29:24	75, 154, 159
30:1	15, 22–23, 29, 69, 110, 115, 117, 123
30:2	110, 117
30:3	110, 117, 127
30:4	110, 117
30:5	110, 117, 154
30:6	117
30:7	117, 131, 145
30:9	76, 81
30:11	40, 76, 94, 214
30:12	40, 76, 94, 117–18, 123, 154, 169
30:13	40, 76, 94, 117–18, 133, 143
30:14	40, 76, 94, 117–18, 127, 134–35, 143, 149
30:15	40, 76, 94, 117–18, 169–70
30:16	117–18, 169–70
30:17	117–18, 169–70
30:18	57, 127
30:18–26	154
30:19	167

SCRIPTURE INDEX

30:20	167	32:19	14, 24, 70, 154, 222
30:21	214	32:20	14, 24, 70, 154, 222
30:22	98, 100, 102, 107, 116	32:21	14, 24, 70
		32:22	14, 24, 70, 187
30:26	38, 167, 204, 226	33:2	28, 154, 171
30:27	11, 22–23, 127, 134, 149, 217	33:3	37, 171
		33:4	171
30:28	11, 22–23, 217	33:5	156, 171
30:29	37, 217	33:6	34, 154, 171
30:30	28, 59, 127, 134, 149	33:8	9, 81, 86, 109
30:31	59	33:10–24	154
30:32	59	33:11	22, 127, 134–35, 149
30:33	54, 127, 134–35	33:12	127, 134–35, 149
31:1	40, 94, 110, 117, 123, 169	33:13	127–28, 134, 142–43, 149
31:2	15, 33, 69, 71, 110, 117, 123	33:14	115–16, 127–28, 134–35, 142–43, 149
31:3	15, 33, 69, 71, 110, 117	33:15	123
		33:18	72–73
31:4	117, 188, 215	33:21	14, 24, 36
31:5	117, 155, 215	33:22	14, 24, 36, 154, 187
31:6	114	34:1	3
31:7	45, 116	34:2	59, 137
31:8	154	34:3	137
31:9	154	34:4	147
31:13	115	34:5	137
32:1	154, 188	34:6	29, 137
32:2	22, 154, 188	34:7	137
32:3	154, 188	34:8–15	137
32:4	154, 188	34:10	150
32:5	119, 123, 154, 188	34:11	127, 132, 150
32:6	67, 72, 119, 123, 154, 188	34:12	150
		34:16	15, 22–23, 69, 222
32:7	119, 123, 154, 188	34:17	222
32:8	154, 188	35	154
32:9	119, 169	35:1	152, 156, 219
32:10	119, 132, 169	35:2	152, 156
32:11	119, 127, 148, 169	35:3	152, 154, 156
32:12	127, 132, 143, 148	35:4	137, 152, 154, 156, 172
32:13	127, 132, 143, 148–49	35:4–20	14, 73
32:14	132	35:5	152, 156, 219
32:15	14, 24, 70, 154	35:6	152, 156, 219
32:16	14, 24, 70, 154, 222, 225	35:7	152, 156, 219
		35:8	94, 98, 100, 108, 152, 156, 174, 214, 219
32:17	14, 24, 70, 154, 187, 222		
32:18	14, 24, 70, 154, 222		

Isa (continued)

35:9	33, 128, 132, 143, 152–54, 156, 174, 219
35:10	33, 152–53, 156
36–39	9–10, 110
36:1–6	110–111
36:2–22	109–11, 177
36:6	145
36:7	115
36:9	194
36:10	115
36:11	194
37:1–4	2, 5–6, 13, 44, 55, 111
37:4	157
37:5	2, 6–7, 22, 194
37:6	2, 6–7, 22, 154, 156
37:6–20	7, 13–14, 16
37:7	2, 6–7, 22, 154, 156
37:10–12	111, 115
37:14–20	111, 171
37:16	41, 44, 49, 55, 66, 103
37:17	41, 44, 49, 55, 66
37:19	127, 134, 149
37:20	154
37:21–36	2, 5, 6–7, 40, 111, 154, 172
37:23	94
37:24	194
37:28	75
37:29	214
37:30	58
37:31	58, 157
37:32	58
37:34	214
37:35	154, 194
37:37	172
37:38	172
38:1	2, 5–6, 52, 112, 172
38:2	2, 5–6, 52, 112, 172
38:3	2, 5–6, 52, 112, 172
38:4	2, 5–6, 13, 30, 52, 112, 154
38:5	5–6, 13, 30, 52, 112, 154
38:6	5–6, 13, 30, 52, 112
38:7	5–6, 13, 30, 52, 112, 172
38:8	5–6, 13, 30, 52, 112, 172
38:9	172
38:10	138
38:10–20	112, 172
38:15	67, 115
38:16	67, 115
38:17	67, 115, 155
38:19	91
38:20	154
38:21	2, 5, 172
38:22	2, 5, 172
39:1–8	2, 5–6, 10, 112
39:6	140
39:7	140, 172
40	84
40–66	2–3, 155, 213
40–48	10, 44, 49, 83, 85
40:1	61, 115, 154, 217
40:1–9	14
40:2	32, 37, 55, 61, 72, 115, 153–54, 217–18, 222
40:3	4, 214, 218, 221
40:4	218
40:5	15, 54, 72, 218
40:6	54, 72, 116, 218
40:7	22, 38, 54, 189, 218
40:8	54, 218
40:10	28, 188, 215–16
40:11	28–29, 188, 219–20
40:12	48, 160
40:13	46, 48, 160
40:14	48, 78, 160, 214
40:15	48, 160
40:16	160
40:17	132, 160
40:18–20	44, 45, 49, 65, 116
40:21	160
40:22	36, 48, 160
40:23	132, 160
40:24	160
40:25	40, 48–49, 94
40:26	13, 26, 35–36, 40, 46, 48–49, 55, 94

40:27	13, 26, 35–36, 46, 48–49, 55, 160, 195, 214, 220	42:2	9–10, 81, 141, 194, 196, 198, 225, 228
40:28	13, 26, 35–36, 46, 48–49, 55, 75, 160, 220	42:3	9–10, 81, 141, 194, 196, 198, 225, 228
		42:4	9–10, 81, 141, 194, 196, 198, 225, 228
40:29	49, 55, 160, 220, 220	42:5	22, 47–48, 160, 194, 198
40:30	49, 55, 160, 220		
40:31	49, 55, 160, 170, 220	42:6	57; 87, 160, 194–96, 198, 215, 226
41–42	16		
41:1	121, 217	42:7	133, 160, 194, 197–98, 210, 215, 226
41:2	57, 91, 122, 174		
41:3	122	42:8	11–12, 49, 54, 160, 194, 197–98
41:4	46–47, 51		
41:6–7	45, 116	42:9	11–12, 49, 54, 160, 194, 196–98
41:8	195		
41:8–9	51, 156, 162	42:10	194, 217
41:10	14, 57, 156, 162, 172	42:11	194, 217
41:11	14, 57, 156	42:12	217
41:12	156	42:13	26, 54, 58, 217
41:13	156	42:14	30, 75–76, 122
41:14	32, 152–53, 156, 217	42:15	30, 75–76, 122
41:14–20	40, 94	42:16	30, 75–76, 122, 214, 219, 226
41:15	156, 218		
41:16	156, 218	42:17	116
41:16–29	22, 51, 54, 65	42:18	55, 121–22, 124, 127, 142–43, 148
41:17	219, 221		
41:18	219, 221	42:19	55, 121–22, 124, 127, 142–43, 148–49
41:19	161, 219, 221		
41:20	37, 159, 219, 221	42:20	55, 121–22, 124, 127, 142–43, 148
41:21	14, 45, 49, 58, 72, 187		
		42:21	55, 57, 81, 121–22, 124, 127, 142–43, 148
41:22	14, 35–36, 45, 49, 51, 58, 72, 187		
		42:22	55, 121–22, 124, 127, 142–43, 148
41:23	35–36, 45, 49–51, 58		
41:24	35–36, 45, 49, 51, 58, 116	42:23	124, 142–43, 148
		42:24	76, 81, 115, 122, 124, 142–43, 148, 214
41:25	13, 35–36, 45, 49, 51, 58		
		42:25	72, 75, 123–24, 142–43, 148
41:26	13, 35–36, 41, 49, 51, 58, 165		
		43:1	32, 49, 153, 155–56, 172, 217
41:27	58		
41:28	58, 116	43:2	12–13, 32–33, 40, 55, 134–35, 156, 217
41:29	45, 51, 58, 116, 132		
42:1	4, 9–10, 24, 55, 66–67, 81, 141, 194–98, 225, 228	43:3	12–13, 32–33, 40, 55, 94, 152–54, 156, 165, 201, 217

Isa (continued)

43:4	12–13, 32–33, 40, 55, 60, 66, 153, 155–56
43:5	12–13, 32–33, 40, 55, 153, 156, 172, 220
43:6	40, 55, 153, 156, 220
43:7	40, 49, 55, 153, 156, 220
43:8	40, 49, 127
43:9	13, 36, 40, 49, 51
43:10	13, 35–37, 40, 46, 49, 51, 58, 169, 194
43:11	33, 35, 37, 40, 46, 58, 154
43:12	35, 37, 40, 46, 54, 58, 154
43:13	35, 37, 40, 46, 58, 165
43:14	32, 40, 46, 94, 133, 152–53
43:15	14, 40, 46, 49, 94, 187
43:16	46, 94, 214, 217
43:17	217
43:18	221
43:19	214, 218–19
43:20	32, 153, 219, 221
43:21	219
43:24	115
43:25	113–14, 155
43:27	126, 132, 215
43:28	95–96, 126, 132
44:1	33, 156, 194, 215
44:2	156, 194, 215
44:3	24, 70, 156, 215, 221
44:4	24, 70, 156, 215, 221
44:5	24, 70, 156, 215
44:6	10, 13–14, 26, 32, 35, 37, 44, 46, 49–51, 54, 130, 152, 154, 187
44:7	35, 37, 44, 49, 51, 54
44:8	35, 37, 44, 49, 51, 54, 75, 85
44:9	132
44:9–20	44, 58, 65, 116
44:13	116
44:16	127, 134, 149
44:17	149
44:18	75, 127
44:19	72, 127, 134
44:20	115, 154
44:21	194
44:22	33, 113–14, 154
44:23	33, 113–14, 122
44:24	32–33, 47–48, 54, 113–14, 152, 159–60
44:24–45:8	165, 222
44:25	32, 47–48, 54, 160
44:26	32–33, 47–48, 54, 113–14, 160, 165, 194
44:27	32, 47–48, 54, 160, 162
44:28	32, 47–48, 54, 160, 162, 166, 187
45:1	3, 13, 40, 49, 51, 54, 165, 187, 212
45:2	3, 13, 40, 49, 51, 54, 165, 212
45:3	3, 13, 40, 49, 51, 54, 133, 165, 212
45:4	3, 13, 40, 49, 51, 54, 76, 165, 194, 228
45:5	3, 13, 40, 49, 51, 54, 76, 166
45:6	3, 13, 40, 49, 51, 54, 76, 130, 140, 160, 166, 228
45:7	38, 48–49, 51, 76, 123, 130, 133, 140, 160, 166, 226
45:8	33, 57, 76, 91, 122, 156, 159, 174, 224–25
45:9	38, 123, 160
45:10	123, 160
45:11	94, 160
45:12	26, 47–49, 57, 62, 159–60
45:13	26, 47–49, 57, 62, 153, 160, 214, 224
45:14	8, 13–14, 33–34, 36, 116, 141, 228
45:15	13–14, 33–34, 36, 116, 154

SCRIPTURE INDEX

45:16	13–14, 33–34, 36, 116, 127
45:17	13–14, 33–34, 36, 116, 154, 156
45:18	13–14, 33–34, 36, 48–49, 116, 132, 156, 159
45:19	13–14, 33–34, 36, 91, 116, 132, 133, 156
45:20	13–14, 33–34, 36, 73, 76, 116, 228
45:21	9, 13–14, 33–34, 36, 49, 56–57, 116, 141, 154, 228
45:22	9, 36, 49, 51, 56–57, 141, 154, 228
45:23	9, 36, 49, 51, 56–57, 141, 156, 228
45:24	9, 36, 49, 51, 56–57, 141, 228
45:25	9, 36, 49, 51, 56–57, 141, 174, 228
46:1–2	50, 116
46:3–4	30, 50, 57
46:5–9	13–14, 44, 50, 116
46:8	73, 114
46:9–11	49, 50–51
46:11	47
46:12	56, 73, 91, 174
46:13	33, 57, 156
46:24	76
47:2	126
47:3	126
47:4	26, 32–33, 40, 94, 152–53
47:5	133
47:6	59
47:7	72
47:10	73
47:11	123
47:14	127, 134, 149
47:15	33, 154
48	16
48:2	26, 94
48:3–5	117
48:6	49, 75, 114, 117
48:7	49, 75, 114, 117, 159
48:8	75, 114, 117, 164
48:9–21	164
48:10	158
48:12	46, 48–49, 121–22
48:13	46, 48–49, 121–22
48:14	28, 60, 121–22
48:15	122, 214
48:16	23, 32–33, 40, 47, 94, 122
48:17	23, 32–33, 40, 47, 94, 123, 152–53, 214, 216
48:18	90, 123, 155, 174, 215–16
48:19	74, 123, 155, 215–16
48:20	33, 153, 194, 216, 220
48:21	219–20
48:22	115, 126
49–55	10
49:1	10, 13, 67, 74, 194–95, 198, 220
49:2	10, 13, 67, 194, 196, 198
49:3	10, 13, 67, 194–95, 197–98
49:4	10, 13, 57, 67, 194–95, 198–99
49:5	10, 13, 67, 194–95, 198
49:6	9–10, 13, 33, 67, 141, 154, 194–96, 198, 220, 226, 228
49:7	10, 13, 40, 61, 67, 94, 152–54, 194–95, 198–99
49:7–26	32, 33
49:8	87, 154, 168, 198, 221
49:9	13, 28–29, 45, 50, 133, 168, 198, 210, 214, 219
49:10	13, 28–29, 45, 198, 219–20
49:11	153, 198, 214, 218–19
49:12	91, 174, 198
49:13	61, 122, 154, 198, 221

Isa (continued)

49:14	61, 153
49:15	30, 61
49:16	61
49:18	45, 55
49:19	45, 55, 215
49:20	45, 55, 215
49:21	215
49:22	28, 32, 72, 76, 153
49:23	28, 32, 72, 76, 153, 169
49:24	28, 32, 72, 76, 153
49:25	28, 32, 72, 76
49:26	132, 148, 152, 154
50:1	122, 126, 132, 160
50:1–11	10, 58, 113
50:2	37, 132, 160, 196
50:3	37, 133
50:4	194, 196, 199
50:5	194, 196, 199, 201
50:6	194, 199, 201
50:7	194, 199, 201
50:8	57, 194, 199
50:9	194, 199
50:10	173, 194–95, 199
50:11	139, 194, 199
50:12	12, 162
51:1	61, 120, 174, 216, 219
51:1–15	108
51:2	61, 216
51:3	61, 154, 217, 221
51:4	9, 24, 37, 57, 81, 141, 154, 166, 216, 226, 228
51:5	9, 24, 37, 56–7, 141, 154, 156, 216, 220, 228
51:6	9, 24, 37, 56–7, 141, 154, 156, 216, 228
51:7	56, 73, 81, 154, 216
51:8	56, 128, 132, 143, 154, 216
51:9	26, 33, 37, 54, 130–31, 159, 215–17
51:10	26, 33, 37, 54, 131, 153–54, 156, 162, 214, 217
51:11	26, 33, 37, 54, 73, 153, 156, 217
51:12	47–49, 160, 172
51:13	47–49, 160, 172
51:14	47–49, 160
51:15	26, 47–49, 160
51:16	47–49, 160, 197
51:17	137, 205
51:17–23	60, 66, 127
51:22	205
52:1	40, 49, 94, 98, 100
52:2	49, 153
52:3	49, 153–54
52:4	49, 153
52:5	49, 153
52:6	49, 168
52:7	14, 154, 187–88
52:8	14
52:9	14, 33, 153
52:10	14, 37, 54, 94, 154, 215–16
52:11	14, 98, 100, 216
52:12	14, 216–17
52:13	195, 202–3
52:13–53:12	10, 194
52:14	199, 202–4
52:15	4, 103, 108, 202, 204, 206, 230
53	201–2, 206
53:1	4, 169, 200, 203, 205–6
53:2	116, 200, 203
53:3	67, 199–200, 203–4
53:4	67, 194, 200, 203–6
53:5	67, 113–14, 156, 161, 194, 200, 203–6
53:6	67, 119, 194, 200, 203–6, 214
53:7	4, 67, 113–14, 200–1, 203, 205–6
53:8	4, 67, 113–14, 200, 203, 205–6
53:9	67, 115, 194, 200–1, 203, 206

53:10	67, 103, 107, 194, 199–200, 203–6	56:3	9–10, 56, 81, 141, 228
53:11	67, 91, 194, 199–200, 203, 205	56:4	9–10, 56, 81, 86, 109, 141, 228–29
53:12	66–14, 153, 199–200, 203, 205	56:5	9–10, 56, 81, 86, 109, 141, 228–29
54:1	57, 161, 215	56:6	9–10, 56, 81, 86, 109, 141, 194, 228–29, 231
54:2	161, 215		
54:3	161, 215		
54:4	32–33, 156, 160, 195	56:7	9–10, 56, 81, 94, 141, 172, 228–29
54:5	13, 26, 32–33, 40, 94, 133, 152–54, 156, 160, 195	56:8	9–10, 56, 81, 141, 228–29
54:6	14, 32–33, 153, 156, 160, 195	56:9	118, 128, 132, 143
		56:9–59:8	10
54:7	32–33, 60–61, 153, 160	56:10	75, 118
		56:11	66, 75, 118, 123, 173, 214
54:8	32–33, 60–61, 133, 152–55, 160	56:12	118, 123, 173, 225
54:9	60–61, 154, 162, 195	57–58	16
54:10	60–61, 86, 154, 195	57:1–2	118, 123
54:11	195	57:3	117, 121–22
54:14	57	57:4	113–14, 117, 122
54:16	115	57:5	117, 122–23
54:17	57, 194	57:6	117, 122
55:1	123, 154, 165, 219	57:7	117, 122
55:2	165	57:8	117, 122
55:3	9, 60, 66, 87, 141, 165, 169, 189, 228	57:9	117, 122
		57:10	117, 122, 214
55:4	9, 60, 66, 141, 165, 189, 228	57:11	116, 172
		57:12	91, 116, 123, 172
55:5	9, 13, 60, 66, 141, 165, 189, 220, 226, 228	57:13	22, 40, 116, 123
		57:14	214, 221
		57:15	40, 44, 73, 94, 155
55:6	122	57:16	127
55:7	115, 122, 155, 214	57:17	59, 73, 214
55:8	36, 214	57:18	126, 155, 214, 221
55:9	36, 134, 214	57:19	155, 222
55:10	53	57:20	115, 139
55:11	53	57:21	14, 115, 126
55:12	221	58:1	113–14, 121–22
55:13	6, 164, 219, 221	58:2	13, 57, 90–91, 117, 122, 174, 214
56–66	3–4, 10, 187		
56:1	9–10, 56, 81, 91, 141, 155, 174, 228	58:3	117–18, 122–23, 171
		58:4	115, 117, 171
56:2	9–10, 56, 81, 96, 141, 228	58:5	117, 171
		58:6	115, 126, 155, 171
		58:7	155, 171

Isa (continued)

58:8	155, 167, 171, 225–26
58:9	84, 118, 155, 167, 171, 226
58:10	84, 133, 155, 167, 226
58:11	84, 114, 155, 225
58:12	84, 155
58:13	36, 41, 43, 54, 81, 84, 94, 96, 214
58:14	36, 41, 43, 54, 81, 84, 94, 96
59:1	154
59:1–15	118
59:2	13, 115
59:3	118–19, 123
59:4	119, 123, 132
59:6	123
59:7	123
59:8	76, 118, 214
59:9	10, 13, 24, 56, 118, 127, 133–34, 156, 166, 225
59:10	10, 13, 24, 56, 127, 133, 156, 225
59:11	10, 13, 24, 56, 133, 154, 156
59:12	10, 13, 24, 56, 76, 113–15, 133, 156
59:13	10, 13, 24, 56, 73, 114, 119, 123, 156
59:14	10, 13, 24, 56, 118, 156
59:15	10, 13, 23–24, 26, 28, 32, 56, 119–20, 123, 150, 156
59:16	37, 54, 57, 58, 91, 118, 154, 188
59:17	10, 13, 23–24, 26, 28, 32, 37, 54, 57, 58, 91, 118, 150, 154, 174, 188
59:18	10, 13, 23–24, 26, 28, 32, 126, 150
59:19	10, 13, 23–24, 26, 28, 32, 150, 173
59:20	10, 13, 23–24, 26, 28, 32–33, 78, 113–14, 150, 152–54
59:21	10, 13, 23–24, 26, 28, 32, 87, 150, 197
60	153
60:1	167, 225–26, 229
60:2	133, 167, 225–26, 229
60:3	167, 225–26, 229
60:4	169
60:5	141, 154, 227–28
60:5–20	8, 13–14, 32
60:6	141, 227–28
60:7	141, 227–28
60:8	227
60:9	40, 94, 227
60:11	141, 222, 228
60:13	141, 228
60:14	40, 94
60:16	33, 76, 141, 152–54, 227–28
60:17	164, 227
60:18	154, 227
60:19	46, 167, 225–27
60:20	225–26
60:21	37
60:22	161, 220
61	210–12
61:1	4, 10, 24, 36, 56, 73, 156, 194, 196–97, 210
61:2	10, 24, 56, 137, 156, 194, 210
61:3	10, 24, 56, 156, 164, 194, 204, 211
61:4	10, 156
61:5	10, 156, 211
61:6	9–10, 13, 141, 156, 211, 227–28
61:7	10, 156, 211, 218, 227
61:8	10, 56, 60–61, 87, 91, 156, 174, 211
61:9	10, 75, 156, 211
61:10	56, 66–67, 154, 211
61:11	211, 225
62:1–2	56, 174

SCRIPTURE INDEX 287

62:3-5	21, 61	64:5	59, 115, 214
62:8	28, 30, 41, 94, 134, 163	64:6	22, 91, 98, 100, 102, 119, 126, 172
62:9	28, 30, 41, 94	64:7	30, 172
62:10	214	64:8	29, 38, 61
62:11	154	64:10	94
62:12	33, 41, 94, 153-54, 156	64:11	94, 135, 149
		64:11	41, 127, 134
63:1	154, 227	65:1-66:17	10
63:1-6	10, 13, 27, 55, 57, 137, 150, 187-88	65:1	4
		65:2	29, 117, 214
63:4	133, 153-54, 156	65:3	115-16
63:5	26, 28, 33, 54, 154, 188	65:4	71, 117
		65:5	94, 115-17, 127, 134-35, 149
63:6	26, 28, 33, 54, 137		
63:7	26, 28, 33, 54, 61, 172	65:6	116
		65:7	116
63:7-64:12	10, 156, 172	65:8	115, 117, 149
63:8	26, 28, 31, 33, 54, 61, 154, 172	65:8-15	194
		65:11	94, 117, 149
63:9	32, 61, 133, 153-54, 172	65:12	45, 117, 123, 149
		65:15	117, 149
63:10	23-24, 26, 28, 33, 37, 40, 54, 75, 94, 114, 172	65:16	14
		65:17	73, 161
		65:20	227
63:11	23-24, 26, 28, 33, 37, 40, 54, 75, 87, 94, 114, 172, 217	65:23	161
		65:24	172
		65:25	94, 115, 161, 225
63:12	23-24, 26, 28, 33, 37, 40, 54, 75, 94, 114, 161, 172, 217	66	16
		66:1	121-22
		66:2	122
63:13	23-24, 37, 40, 54, 75, 94, 114, 161, 172, 217	66:3	66, 123, 214
		66:4	123
63:14	23-24, 37, 40, 54, 75, 94, 114, 161, 172	66:7-13	31
		66:9	14
63:15	41, 58, 61, 74, 94, 161	66:12	9, 141, 150, 228
		66:13	150
63:16	29-30, 32, 58, 61, 75, 94, 152, 185, 224	66:14	73, 150, 194
		66:15	127, 134, 137, 149-50
63:17	38, 61, 73, 94, 127, 172-73, 214	66:16	122, 127, 134-35, 137, 149-50
63:18	61, 94		
63:19	61, 94, 172	66:17	71, 92, 94, 98, 102, 106-7, 115-16, 137
63:25	161		
64:1	135	66:18	6, 9-10, 141, 222-23, 228, 232
64:2	134-35		
64:3	134, 173	66:19	6, 9-10, 141, 222-23, 228, 232
64:4	13		

Isa (continued)

66:20	6, 9–10, 94, 108, 141, 222–23, 228, 232
66:21	6, 9–10, 141, 222–23, 228
66:22	6, 9–10, 141, 228
66:23	6, 9–10, 81, 141, 161, 228
66:24	6, 9–10, 127–28, 134–35, 138, 141, 149, 228

Jer

1:4–5	67
2:7	92
2:20	115
2:21	198
3:1	132–33
3:6–13	115
3:8	58, 132–33
3:9	92
5:1–7	155
6:4	43, 95, 98
6:9	198
7:30	92, 107
10:5	36
12:7	67
15:9	66
17:2	115
18:3–6	38
18:23	155
19:5	117
19:13	107
22:7	43, 95, 98
23:5	190
25:15–28	60
25:30	36
27:3	146
31:10–11	28, 33, 153
31:15	139
31:31–34	87, 155
31:33	81, 87
31:33–40	198
32:34	92, 107
33:8	155
33:15	190
33:18	108
34:8–11	171
36:3	155
40:11–12	146
43:13	145
46–51	140
48:4–34	146
50:34	32, 152
51:7	60
51:27–29	36, 43, 95, 98

Lam

2:11	75
4:21	60

Ezek

1:4–6	167, 226
1:4–28	207
1:5–22	41
3:12–13	36, 41
5:11	92, 104, 107
6:3	115
7:20	65
7:26	4
8:6	104
9:7	92, 107
10:1–22	41
10:8–10	167, 226
11:16	104
11:19	72
11:22	41
11:22–25	207
12:22–23	4
18	90
18:5–18	90
20:7–31	92, 107
21:14–17	204
22:3–24	92, 107
22:10	100
22:13	204
22:26	40, 98, 106
23:7–38	92
23:31–33	60
23:38–39	104
24:13–14	107
24:21	104
25–31	140

28:22	41, 94
28:25	94
31:15–17	138
31:27	138
34:12–13	28
36:18	92, 107
36:24–37:28	87
36:25–33	108
36:26	72
37:23	92, 107
37:24	28
37:26–28	104
38	131
39:18	29
42:20	41, 94
43:4	167, 226
43:6–9	91–92, 106–7
43:12	97
43:18–44:31	108
44:23	40, 98, 108
45:3	97
45:4–5	108
47:22–23	229
48:8–21	104
48:11–15	40, 97

Dan

2	193
3:1–15	65
3:24–27	135, 217
7	193
7:15	68
9:24	91
9:25	51
10:20–21	69
11:34	229
12:2	139

Hos

2:19–20	21
4:13	115
4:16	28
5:3	92
6:10	92
10:1	198
11:1	30
12:10	4
13:14	33, 153
14:5	155

Joel

1:8	177
2:16–18	42, 58, 94
2:28–32	24, 36, 70, 87–88
3:9	98

Amos

1:1	135
1–2	140
3:7–8	36
7:2	155
9:2	138

Jonah

2:3	138
3:4–10	53

Mic

2:10	107
2:12	28
3:5	98
4:2	229
4:6–8	28
5:2	181, 183, 193
7:18	155

Nah

1	131
1:2	58

Hab

2:2	4
2:16	60
2:18	75

Zeph

3:19	28

Hag

2:11–14	101, 106

Zech

1:5–6	54
1:9	69
2:11	229
3:3–5	108
4:10	35
7	117
7:12	36
8:23	232
11:17	45, 116
12:1	68
12:10–11	200, 203
14:5	135
14:7	167, 226

Mal

1:11–12	92, 107–8
2:4–5	96
3:3	99, 108

Matt

1:18–25	179–80, 193, 224
2:1–20	181, 183, 193
3:3	4, 217
4:14	4
5:3	210
5:29	71
8:17	4, 206
12:17–21	4, 196, 198
12:28	210
13:13–17	4, 42, 129
15:7	4
15:8	117
17:4	219, 222
18:12–14	28–29
21:33–43	198
24:29	147
25:35–36	171
26:28	198
26:42	201
26:52–53	201
26:67	199
27:26–30	199

Mark

1:1–4	217
4:11–13	42, 129
7:6	4
9:5	219, 222
13:24–25	147
14:24	198
15:19	199

Luke

1:5–25	180
1:15	180
1:34–35	179, 224
1:51–55	180
2:1–2	181
2:3–6	181
2:7	182
2:12–16	182
2:22–23	100–1, 181
2:24	181
2:25–33	196
2:34	173
2:35	66
3:4–7	217
3:38	65
4:17–21	4, 210–11
4:23–27	211
4:28–30	211
8:10	42, 129
9:33	219, 223
9:34	179
9:51	201
10:18	144
11:22	179
11:37–41	108
15:4–6	28
21:26	179
21:34	73
22:20	198
22:37	206
22:63	199

John

1:22–27	217
2:16	71
3:8	70

4:7	177	**1 Cor**	
4:24	69	2:14	70
8:41	180	3:10–15	138
11:48–50	196		
12:38–41	42, 129, 206	**2 Cor**	
14:1	74	6:2	199
14:2–3	219, 223	7:3	74
14:27	74		
15:1–7	198	**Gal**	
16:6	73–74	1:15	67
19:1	199	2–5	232
		6:18	70

Acts

1:8	179	**Eph**	
2:23	76	2:15	71
2:25–36	193	4:9–10	138
2:26	74	6:14–17	26
3:20–25	198		
5:15	179	**Phil**	
6:9	4	4:23	70
8:24	179		
8:28–30	4	**1 Thess**	
8:32–35	206	5:8	26
10:28	108		
11:3	108	**2 Tim**	
13:33–38	193	4:22	70
13:40	179		
14:19	179	**Phlm**	
15	232	25	70
28:24–28	42, 129		
		Heb	
Rom		1:5	193
1:3	72	1:8–13	193
1:23	116	6:10	58
2:6–15:29	232	9:13	204
8:16	70	11:15	198
9:4	198	11:37	7
9:27–29	4, 38		
9:33	173	**Jas**	
10:16	4, 206	3:9	65
10:20	4		
11:26–27	198		
13:20	72		
15:12	4		
15:21	206		

1 Pe

1:2	204
1:11	36
2:6–8	37, 173
2:18–23	206
2:24–25	206
3:19	138

Jude

5–7	135

Rev

4:6–9	41
5:6	41
6:1–6	41
7:11	41
14:3	41
15:7	41
17–18	27
18:13	71
19:4	41
21:23	167, 226
22:5	167, 226

www.ingramcontent.com/pod-product-compliance
Lightning Source LLC
Chambersburg PA
CBHW071234230426
43668CB00011B/1435